MW01252755

The Age of Productivity

The Age of Productivity

Transforming Economies from the Bottom Up

Carmen Pagés, Editor

Inter-American Development Bank

palgrave
macmillan

First published in 2010 by
PALGRAVE MACMILLAN® in the United States – a division of
St. Martin's Press LLC, 175 Fifth Avenue, New York, NY 10010.

Where this book is distributed in the UK, Europe and the rest of the world,
this is by Palgrave Macmillan, a division of Macmillan Publishers Limited,
registered in England, company number 785998, of Houndmills, Basingstoke,
Hampshire RG21 6XS.

PALGRAVE MACMILLAN is the global academic imprint of the above
companies and has companies and representatives throughout the world.

PALGRAVE® and MACMILLAN® are registered trademarks in the
United States, the United Kingdom, Europe and other countries.

ISBN: 978–0–230–62352–1   (paperback)
ISBN: 978–0–230–62350–7   (hardback)

Library of Congress Cataloging-in-Publication Data

The age of productivity : transforming economies from the bottom up / edited by
Carmen Pagés.
    p. cm.
  Includes bibliographical references and index.
  ISBN 978–0–230–62352–1
  1. Labor productivity—Latin America.   2. Labor productivity—Caribbean
Area.   3. Manpower policy—Latin America.   4. Manpower policy—Caribbean
Area.   I. Pagés, Carmen.
  HD57.A33 2009
  331.11'8098—dc22

                2009049087

A catalogue record of the book is available from the British Library.

Design by MPS Limited, A Macmillan Company

First edition: April 2010

10 9 8 7 6 5 4 3 2 1

Printed in the United States of America.

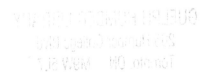

Contents

About the Contributors

Manuel Agosin is a professor in the Department of Economics at the Universidad de Chile.

Juan Pablo Atal is a research assistant in the Research Department of the Inter-American Development Bank.

Juan Blyde is an integration and trade economist in the Integration and Trade Department of the Inter-American Development Bank.

Matías Busso is a research economist in the Research Department of the Inter-American Development Bank.

Eduardo Cavallo is a research economist in the Research Department of the Inter-American Development Bank.

Alberto Chong is a principal research economist in the Research Department of the Inter-American Development Bank.

Christian Daude is an economist and coordinator of the Latin American Economic Outlook at the Organisation for Economic Co-operation and Development.

Eduardo Fernández-Arias is a principal research economist in the Research Department of the Inter-American Development Bank.

Arturo Galindo is a senior research economist in the Research Department of the Inter-American Development Bank.

Pablo Ibarrarán is a senior social development specialist in the Strategic Development Division of the Office of Strategic Planning and Development Effectiveness at the Inter-American Development Bank and a research fellow at the Institute for the Study of Labor.

Alejandro Izquierdo is a senior research economist in the Research Department of the Inter-American Development Bank.

Juan José Llisterri is a principal science and technology specialist in the Science and Technology Division of the Social Sectors Department at the Inter-American Development Bank.

Eduardo Lora is the general manager and chief economist, a.i., of the Research Department at the Inter-American Development Bank.

Carlos Ludena is an economist in the IDB Young Professionals Program assigned to the Research Department at the Inter-American Development Bank.

Lucía Madrigal is a consultant in the Poverty Reduction Group at the World Bank.

Alessandro Maffioli is a senior social development specialist in the Strategic Development Division of the Office of Strategic Planning and Development Effectiveness at the Inter-American Development Bank.

Mauricio Mesquita Moreira is a principal integration and trade economist in the Integration and Trade Department of the Inter-American Development Bank.

Juan Carlos Navarro is a principal science and technology specialist in the Science and Technology Division in the Social Sectors Department at the Inter-American Development Bank.

Hugo Ñopo is a senior education economist in the Education Division of the Social Sectors Department at the Inter-American Development Bank.

Carmen Pagés is a principal research economist in the Research Department of the Inter-American Development Bank.

Charles Sabel is the Maurice T. Moore Professor of Law at Columbia Law School.

Carlos Scartascini is a senior research economist in the Research Department of the Inter-American Development Bank.

Rodolfo Stucchi is a research fellow in the Office of Evaluation and Oversight at the Inter-American Development Bank.

Mariano Tommasi is a professor in the Department of Economics at the Universidad de San Andres.

Pluvia Zúñiga is a consultant in the Science and Technology Division of the Social Sectors Department at the Inter-American Development Bank.

Preface

Over the last 15 years, countries in Latin America and the Caribbean have shown progress in economic and social indicators. Between 1994 and 2008, the region grew at an average rate of 3.3 percent per annum. With an annual population growth of 1.4 percent, per capita income increased by 1.9 percent. Nevertheless, from a long-term perspective, growth in Latin America and the Caribbean has lagged behind other emerging economies. Contrary to popular belief, low investment is not necessarily to blame for this performance. Low and slow productivity, rather than impediments to factor accumulation, provide a better explanation for Latin America's low income compared to developed economies and its stagnation relative to other up-and-coming developing countries.

According to research estimates, Latin America's productivity is about half its potential and it is not catching up with the frontier. Closing the productivity gap with the frontier would actually close most of the income per capita gap with developed countries. Viewed in a comparative global context, slow productivity growth is responsible for slower growth in Latin America. For a region starved for growth, diagnosing the causes of this poor productivity and attacking their roots is a high development priority.

For this reason, the Inter-American Development Bank dedicated this year's issue of its flagship publication—*Development in the Americas*—to the study of the low productivity that is weighing down the region. The picture that emerges is of a region populated by a few very productive firms and many other firms of extremely low productivity; the region's challenge is to raise the proportion of medium-level productivity firms. Simply increasing the ranks of such firms—without actually changing the productivity of individual firms in the region—could double aggregate productivity, a boost large enough to close the gap with the productivity frontier. This is but one of the findings in this volume that challenges us to rethink current policy in the region.

On another front, this book points to the service sector—particularly the extensive retail subsector—as the major culprit in the region's productivity problems. Agricultural productivity has actually grown at a healthy rate but a relatively small percentage of the labor force is still engaged in farming. And while productivity in industry has languished, the number of workers in this sector has declined as well. That leaves services, the most unproductive sector where the lion's share of the workforce is employed, with devastating consequences for aggregate productivity. The implication is that a growth strategy focused on boosting exports may be at best incomplete, and at worst misguided; a better approach with higher returns might be to prime the large, nontradable services sector.

The causes of the low productivity that plagues the region are many and varied. High rates of informality screen small, inefficient firms from the competition of better, more productive businesses. Some social policies conceived with the best intentions end up having unintended results on productivity because they actually push more and more people into low-productivity activities. High transport costs, lack of credit, macroeconomic volatility, discriminatory tax regimes, a lack of innovation, and insufficient or poorly designed productive development policies have all played a role in retarding productivity growth throughout the region.

Identifying the shackles on productivity growth is relatively easy. Designing and implementing a coherent set of policies to unleash a country's productive potential is far more difficult. This book takes a major step in this direction, offering suggestions based on a sound and at times eye-opening diagnosis that dares to break with convention.

It is with great pleasure that I present this book to policymakers, entrepreneurs, workers, and all those anxious to see Latin America and the Caribbean realize its growth potential. It is my sincere hope that, armed with the information and ideas contained in this volume, together we can usher in the Age of Productivity in our region.

Luis Alberto Moreno
President, Inter-American Development Bank

Boxes

Figures

Tables

Acknowledgments

Development in the Americas (DIA) is the flagship publication of the Inter-American Development Bank. This issue was produced under the direction of Carmen Pagés, principal research economist of the Research Department. Rita Funaro, publications coordinator of the Research Department, was the general editor of the volume. Carlos Andrés Gómez-Peña, technical and research assistant, was the technical editor of this volume. Hugo Hopenhayn, Andrés Neumeyer, Chang Tai-Hsieh, and Pete Klenow were external technical advisors. Santiago Levy, vice president for Sectors and Knowledge, proposed the topic for this study and provided constant guidance and technical advice throughout the life of this project.

The principal authors of each individual chapter are presented below:

Chapter 1	Eduardo Lora and Carmen Pagés
Chapter 2	Christian Daude and Eduardo Fernández-Arias
Chapter 3	Carmen Pagés in collaboration with Carlos Ludeña
Chapter 4	Matías Busso, Lucía Madrigal, and Carmen Pagés
Chapter 5	Juan Blyde and Mauricio Mesquita Moreira
Chapter 6	Eduardo Cavallo, Arturo Galindo, and Alejandro Izquierdo
Chapter 7	Alberto Chong and Carmen Pagés
Chapter 8	Juan Pablo Atal and Hugo Ñopo
Chapter 9	Pablo Ibarrarán, Alessandro Maffioli, and Rodolfo Stucchi
Chapter 10	Juan Carlos Navarro, Juan José Llisterri, and Pluvia Zúñiga
Chapter 11	Eduardo Fernández-Arias in collaboration with Manuel Agosin and Charles Sabel
Chapter 12	Carlos Scartascini and Mariano Tommasi

Francisco Arizala, Juan Pablo Atal, Oscar Becerra, Gonzalo Iberti, Carolina Izaguirre, Melisa Ioranni, Mikael Larsson, John Jairo León, Fabiana Machado, Lucía Madrigal, Pedro Martínez, Ariel Mecikovsky, Karina Otero, Mauricio Pinzón, Vanessa Ríos, Paola Vargas, and Gonzalo Vázquez Baré all provided excellent research assistance.

Many other people contributed their technical input and valuable suggestions to this report, including Manuel Agosin, Luis Alberto Arias, Pedro Auger, Alberto Barreix, Jere Behrman, Camilo Bohórquez, Matías Busso, Adriana Camacho, Gabriel Casaburi, Martin Chrisney, Gustavo Crespi, Julián Cristia, José Cuesta, Carl Dahlman, Rick Doner, Kurt Focke, Jeff Frieden, Annabelle Fowler, Stephen

Haggard, Jordi Jaumandreu, Julia Johannsen, Ravi Kanbur, David Kang, Homi Kharas, Phil Keefer, Florencia López Bóo, Ernesto López-Córdova, Eduardo Lora, Lucía Madrigal, Mario Marcel, Victoria Murillo, Flora Painter, Nina Pavcnik, Christina Pombo, Adam Przeworski, Jerónimo Roca, Diego Restuccia, Laura Ripani, Andrés Rodríguez-Clare, Fabio Schiantarelli, Ben Ross Schneider, Charles Sabel, Sebastian Saiegh, Anna Serrichio, Chad Syverson, Ernesto Stein, Claudia Suaznabar, Luis Tejerina, Jim Tybout, Christian Volpe, and Luisa Zanforlin. This book would not have been possible without the outstanding and patient editing work of Rita Funaro and Carlos Andrés Gómez-Peña.

The opinions expressed in this publication are those of the authors and do not necessarily reflect the views of the Inter-American Development Bank, its board of directors, or the technical advisors.

1

The Age of Productivity

Productivity isn't everything, but in the long run it is almost everything.

Paul Krugman

The economies of Latin America and the Caribbean suffer from a chronic low-growth disease. Unfortunately, the region has become so accustomed to this economic ailment, that it no longer considers growth its most pressing problem. And yet, the countries of the region are paying dearly for not assigning economic growth the highest priority.

How costly has the lack of growth been for the region? Some counterfactuals provide a vivid illustration. Take, for example, Argentina, which in 2006 had an income per capita of US$12,258 (purchasing power parity [or PPP] adjusted).[1] If from 1960 onwards, it had grown at the same rate as the rest of the world, excluding Latin America and the Caribbean, in 2006 it would have had an income per capita similar to that of the United Kingdom (US$27,800). By the same calculation, Venezuela and Uruguay would have had in 2006 the income per capita of Israel and Spain, respectively; that is almost three times Venezuela's current income and twice that of Uruguay's. Similarly, the income per capita of Bolivia, Honduras, Jamaica, Peru, and El Salvador would have been more than double what they reported in 2006, and in Nicaragua, more than triple. Even Chile, a country heralded for its superior economic performance over the past 25 years, underperformed the rest of the world when assessed from a long-term perspective. Had Chile grown on par with the rest of the world since 1960, its income per capita in 2006 would have been the same as that of Portugal and Greece. Brazil, which has suffered relatively less when measured with this yardstick, would nonetheless be relishing an income per capita almost 25 percent higher than what it is enjoying today. Only two countries, Panama and the Dominican Republic, have grown at levels comparable to the world average (excluding the region). Given these figures, it is not surprising that in 1960, the average income per capita in Latin America and the Caribbean was almost one-quarter that of the United States while today it is only one-sixth. In contrast, several East Asian countries, which in 1960 had income levels much below Latin America and the Caribbean, are fast approaching or have joined the ranks of high-income nations.

This book argues that low productivity growth is the root cause of Latin America's poor economic growth and that achieving higher productivity must be at the epicenter of the current economic debate. Escaping relatively unscathed from the worst international financial crisis since the Great Depression, the region should avoid basking in complacency or proceeding down the road of diminished expectations; instead, it should seize the opportunity to pursue a determined, ambitious productivity agenda. Why productivity? Because income gaps opened up, not due to a lack of investment in physical and human capital or to the slow growth of the labor force, but rather, due to a chronic productivity growth deficit. If productivity in Latin America and the Caribbean (referred to in this book as the region) had grown at the same rate as that in the United States, the income per capita of the region relative to the United States would have remained unchanged at one-quarter, even with the reported investments in human and physical capital. If, on the other hand, productivity had converged to the U.S. level—that is, if the physical and human resources that Latin American and Caribbean countries currently enjoy were used with the productive efficiency of those in the United States—per capita income would have doubled and the income of the region relative to that of the United States would have been one-third. However, with higher productivity, investment and education would certainly have increased as well, narrowing the gap even further and over time converging on the income levels of developed countries (see Figure 1.1).

The good news is that while increasing the stock of physical or human capital may require resources that are unavailable in low-income countries and may even be wasteful if productivity is low, boosting productivity may "simply" require the willingness to transform policies and institutions in light of successful experiences elsewhere. The objective of this study is not only to investigate the causes of the region's poor productivity performance, but also, crucially, to identify and propose policy options to unleash an age of productivity in Latin America and the Caribbean.

The productivity challenge cannot wait. Millions of people in Latin America and the Caribbean are suffering from limitations that could be solved if existing resources were better utilized. Millions of workers are condemned to low productivity jobs that do not pay enough to lift themselves and their families out of poverty. Over a decade ago, the region pioneered a

Figure 1.1   Latin American GDP Per Capita Relative to U.S. GDP Per Capita, 2005: Typical Latin American Country under Different Scenarios

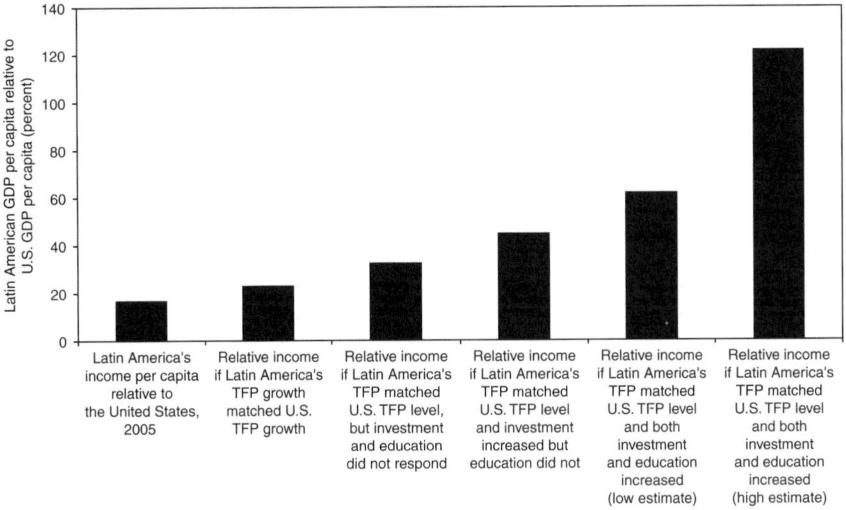

Source: Authors' calculations based on World Bank (2008), Barro and Lee (2000), Heston, Summers, and Aten (2006). For details see Chapter 2.

new generation of programs to combat poverty by means of income transfers linked to investment in the human capital of poor families. On balance, these programs have had a positive impact but by themselves cannot achieve a central objective: to provide poor workers with higher incomes thanks to higher productivity rather than transfers from the national budget. Unless productivity increases, poor children and young people who are now benefiting from these programs will eventually be healthier and more educated than their parents when they join the labor force, but will still be poor.

Doing More with the Same

Raising productivity implies finding better ways to more efficiently use the existing labor, physical capital, and human capital of the region. One standard way to measure gains in efficiency is to compute increases in total factor productivity (TFP), that is, the efficiency with which the economy transforms its accumulated factors of production into output. Reporting that TFP grew 1 percent is equivalent to saying that 1 percent more output was obtained from the same productive resources. This is the preferred measure of productivity in this book, yet it is computationally demanding because it requires measuring all inputs used in production, something that is not always feasible. Other partial measures of productivity are also commonly used. Distinguishing between TFP and these other indicators is important because they capture different things. For example, one often-used measure of productivity is output per worker, which is calculated on the basis of the size of the labor force. This measure does not consider education or capital as factors of production, and therefore, the increase in production due to higher average education or more physical capital would be measured as an increase in productivity. Output per worker then is a reflection of factor accumulation—more physical capital and more human capital—and pure efficiency gains. As stated, a key result presented in this book is that the GDP growth gap of the region is mostly associated with efficiency growth gaps rather than accumulation gaps. Consequently, the focus of this study is on the drivers of the level and growth of TFP rather than on the determinants of human or physical capital accumulation.

Beyond Technological Progress

Typically, efficiency gains are calculated as a residual, that is, as the portion of growth that cannot be accounted for by the accumulation of factors. In that way productivity becomes—as Robert Solow, Nobel laureate and creator of the modern theory of economic growth, famously said—"a measure of our ignorance." Since Solow's seminal work in 1957, this residual has often been treated as a measure of technology, with technological progress credited as the main determinant of productivity growth.

This book, however, argues that attaining aggregate efficiency gains is a very complex problem that goes well beyond technological growth. It requires incentives to be aligned, fair competition for resources, and the opportunity for firms with good ideas to thrive and grow. Low productivity is often the unintended result of a myriad of market failures and poor economic policies that distort incentives for innovation, prevent efficient companies from expanding, and promote the survival and growth of inefficient firms. These market and policy failures are more prominent in developing economies—Latin America is no exception—and are an important factor explaining their relatively lower levels of productivity. Thus, economic development requires shedding layers of bad policies and correcting for key market failures that conspire against productivity growth. The upshot is that while high-income economies must rely to a larger extent on promoting innovation to grow, the region can explore additional avenues for growth. This does not imply that innovation and technology adoption are not important sources of productivity growth in developing countries;

quite the opposite. It simply means that in addition to increasing the productivity of each firm by promoting innovation and technology adoption, other potential sources of growth are available to developing countries and should be considered and tried, if appropriate. While such advances would provide only temporary sources of growth, they could provide a huge leap forward similar to the gains enjoyed during the rapid urbanization and structural transformation of the 1950s and 1960s.

Beyond Manufacturing

The diagnoses and policy proposals on the productivity problems of Latin American and Caribbean economies concentrate almost exclusively on the industrial sectors, and sometimes on manufacturing alone. However, in order to boost growth and per capita income, the region must boost productivity of the nontradable sector.

Industrialization and prosperity are usually considered synonymous, and with good reason: developed countries became rich when, thanks to the industrial revolution, the labor force that was concentrated in the agricultural and traditional craft sectors shifted to industrial manufacturing, which has much higher productivity.

Latin American countries tried to follow this route to prosperity during the second half of the twentieth century, but their attempts at industrialization were only partially successful. Quite remarkably, the share of industrial employment is now lower in Latin America than in both East Asia and the developed world. Combined with the declining share of employment in agriculture, this situation has swelled the ranks of the service sector and contributed to its meager productivity growth compared to either developed or fast-growing East Asian economies. Unlike developed countries, which first prospered with industry and then transformed themselves into service economies, the region's economies became tertiary (or service-based) halfway along the road from poverty to prosperity.

Since industrial sectors in Latin America and the Caribbean account for barely 20 percent of the labor force, solving the problems of competitiveness or technological backwardness in this sector will do little to overcome underdevelopment. It is estimated that raising the growth of productivity of the manufacturing sector to the rate of that in East Asia would hardly change aggregate productivity growth. In contrast, aggregate productivity could double if productive growth in the very laggard service sectors rose to match the productivity growth of these sectors in East Asia.

Raising the productivity of services is a must to improve the standard of living of all Latin American and Caribbean people: most workers are employed in the service sector, and the competitiveness of the primary and industrial sectors depends on having good transport and communications, efficient storage and distribution systems, and many other services.

The Many Faces of Low Productivity

Low productivity is not universal; it is concentrated in some firms. This study uncovers dramatic differences in productivity, even within narrowly defined sectors. Across countries, the least productive companies tend to be the smallest ones, and, throughout the region, size and productivity are related. Small companies (particularly those with fewer than ten employees) account for the bulk of the economy in Latin America, more so than in higher income economies, while there is a dearth of medium-level—and in some cases high-level—productivity firms.[2] But the problem goes beyond the large number of small firms with low productivity. Much of the labor force in Latin America and the Caribbean is self-employed, often selling their products in the streets of the region's cities. If these workers are considered one-person enterprises, as in fact they are, the phenomenon of pulverization of economic activity into millions of tiny enterprises with low productivity is even more significant.

Reducing the share of small manufacturing firms and increasing the share of medium-sized manufacturing firms so as to match the size distribution of manufacturing firms in the United States—leaving productivity levels of individual firms unchanged—would almost double manufacturing productivity in the countries for which this computation can be performed. This boost would be large enough to close the manufacturing productivity gap with the United States. This means that, unlike other regions of the world, the overwhelming presence of small companies and self-employed workers is a sign of failure, not of success. In some countries, highly productive small firms face growth constraints, such as limited access to credit, in becoming medium or large firms. In others, the excess of small firms appears to be associated with a plethora of implicit subsidies to small firms; they can more easily evade taxes, social security mandates, and other regulations than medium and large firms. These subsidies help low productivity firms gain market share and prevent high productivity firms from gaining the same.

The large proportion of very small firms also manifests the failure of many small companies to innovate and become medium-level productivity firms and of medium productivity firms to enter the market and attract labor from small, less-productive firms. While all firms spend few resources on research and development relative to developed economies, small firms are even less likely than larger firms to innovate. Large businesses can distribute the high fixed costs of innovation across a larger volume of sales, and have better access to financial services, technology, consulting, and specialized human-capital markets.

The proliferation of many small firms of very low productivity is particularly acute in the service sectors where millions of Latin American and Caribbean workers have taken refuge and the problems of low earnings and high levels of poverty are more extreme.

Clearly, the region is making poor use of its available resources. Much capital and many workers could be much more productive if employed more efficiently, even if they performed similar activities within the same economic sector. In Latin America, reallocating resources could increase aggregate productivity by approximately 50–60 percent. In some countries, such as Mexico, these gains could be around 100 percent. Yet, the greatest room for improvement lies outside the manufacturing sectors. The commercial retail sector, is a potential reserve of enormous gains: in Mexico and Brazil the productivity of this sector could be catapulted to around 260 percent, and similar gains could be achieved in other services. Extensive resource misallocation is a symptom of the lack of fair competition for resources, as policies, market failures, or location advantages favor some firms over others for reasons other than their relative efficiency.

In sum, productivity levels in a given economy are the result of forces and incentives guiding the decisions of existing and prospective firms that determine the mix of firms in an economy, the productivity of each firm, and the firm's size, given its productivity. Each of these factors can be altered by market and policy failures in ways that reduce productivity. The question then becomes, which policies or market failures are associated with Latin America's poor productivity performance and how can they be transformed to unleash an age of productivity?

Policies for Productivity

With the right economic policies, Latin American governments can go a long way toward solving the productivity problem. Many of the problems arise from market failures that have yet to be properly addressed, and others from failed economic policies that, often unintentionally, have taken a toll on productivity. In particular, this book explores whether policies on trade, credit, taxes, social protection, aid to small firms, innovation, and industrial promotion are at the root of the problem, or instead part of the cure for the low productivity growth disease of the region. This list is not exhaustive and some of the omissions, such as education or regulatory policies, may surprise readers. However, this book focuses on the less-studied dimensions of productivity that may be vitally important for the design of public policy in Latin America and the Caribbean. One of the major conclusions of this study is that many policies—often in areas not commonly associated with productivity—may have intended, or even unintended, effects on efficiency. These often-overlooked policy areas are the focus of this book while many of the absent topics have been left to the ongoing research agenda of the IDB.

Trade and the High Productivity Toll of Transport Costs

Free trade has often been touted as a boon to productivity. Opening the door to imports should expose producers to greater competition, forcing them to cut costs and increase their efficiency while providing greater access to more and better inputs, particularly capital goods. But there are other very important channels through which international trade affects productivity that have been less studied. Even without changing the productivity levels of firms, international trade can boost aggregate productivity by helping to reallocate resources in favor of more productive uses.

Unfortunately, transport costs have in large part prevented the region from capitalizing on the productivity potential of international trade. For most countries, transport costs represent the highest percentage of the cost of trade, especially exports, and distance or geography are not the only reasons why. Cargo transport costs of Central American countries, as a proportion of the value of their exports to the United States, are higher than China's. Why? Their ports and airports are grossly inefficient. And the situation in Latin America is not much different. Inadequate physical infrastructure is to blame in some countries, but more important are the support activities for the movement of cargo and the inefficiencies caused by inadequate regulation, lack of competition in services, and deficient operating procedures and information systems. Inefficiencies in domestic cargo transport are even greater than those of international transport; crumbling infrastructure and traffic congestion seriously affect the productivity of firms operating in Latin American cities.

Too Little Credit

Despite the financial deregulation of the 1990s, the depth of Latin American credit systems remains very low by international standards. Consequently, lack of credit is one reason why there is so much dispersion in the productivity of firms. Without credit, productive firms cannot expand and less-productive firms cannot make the technological changes and investments needed to raise their productivity. The credit drought has another damaging effect on productivity: it weakens the incentives for informal firms to comply with tax, legal, and social security provisions. This hurts productivity by allowing unproductive firms to survive because they have lower costs than their formal counterparts. Expansion of credit would make a strong contribution to formalizing employment.

However, increasing the supply of credit is not enough to improve productivity; it must be sustainable. Continued episodes of credit boom and bust, typical of Latin America in the past, tend to be harmful for productivity in the long term. If credit crises are frequent, small, but potentially efficient, firms have no more chance of surviving than inefficient ones. Moreover, firms have a greater incentive to invest in more malleable but less-productive technologies, better suited to a volatile economic environment.

Latin America and the Caribbean have made notable financial progress in the last decade, helping the region weather with relative success the financial earthquake of 2008–2009. Still, it is too early to shout victory. The region is far behind in its capacity to create, identify, and execute property rights over the assets and obligations of firms. This is perhaps the most difficult and crucial step if financial systems are to support the growth of productivity. Moreover, more credit for enterprises is not always synonymous with higher productivity; loans must be channeled to enterprises with higher productive potential. When credit is granted to unproductive enterprises, it perpetuates the misallocation of effort, work, and capital that reduces a country's productivity. National development banks or public credit subsidies are classic cases in point. Certainly, these banks and programs can contribute much to productivity growth, but targeted mechanisms must ensure that credit flows to the most productive—or potentially productive—firms. This distinction is not easy, but is indispensable to avoid wasting the country's productive resources.

Taxes: Simplify, Simplify, Simplify

Although the worst aberrations have already been corrected, tax systems in the region remain extremely complex, segmented, and ineffective. It takes an average of 320 hours per year for Latin American and Caribbean firms to file taxes compared to an average of 177 hours in high-income countries. In some countries tax-related transactions can take as many as 2,000 hours a year. Almost all countries have multiple tax regimes for firms of different sizes, and tax collection is decidedly low (17 percent of gross domestic product [GDP] in 2005 compared to 36 percent in industrial countries). Taxes on profits are high by international standards, yet collection is very inefficient due to high evasion, particularly among small and microfirms. Evasion is not only a problem of collection but also of productivity. Tax systems distort the allocation of productive resources: the sectors and firms that expand are not necessarily the most productive but rather those that enjoy higher tax breaks or can evade their tax obligations more easily.

Since tax systems are so complex and smaller enterprises contribute minimally to tax collection, tax administrations in 13 of the 17 Latin American countries studied have established simplified regimes for them, and two other countries simply exempt them from taxes. Since the simplified regimes benefit small enterprises with sales and employee levels below certain limits, firms try to stay within these limits to avoid a sharp drop in their profitability; this maneuvering contributes to the low number of intermediate-sized enterprises in Latin America. Simplified tax regimes for small enterprises are a collection of all the defects of a bad tax system: discrimination by size, easier evasion, less cross-control between firms, and limited information for tax control.

Latin American tax regimes bear much of the responsibility for the region's productivity problems because they encourage the survival of unproductive firms, obstruct the growth of small and large enterprises alike, and foster a deeply unequal and segmented business universe. Tax regimes differentiated by sector, size of enterprise, or for other reasons distort the allocation of resources, divert the scarce managerial resources of enterprises, and are an extra burden for the public administration, while paradoxically decreasing collection. A well-designed tax system should create incentives to pay taxes and prevent evasion. Simplifying, unifying, and enforcing the tax provisions that apply to enterprises could contribute greatly to productivity; in turn, higher productivity would boost both GDP and tax receipts.

Redrafting Social Policy

Only one out of three Latin American workers is covered by social security systems and other compulsory benefits for legal wage earners, such as health insurance, pensions, unemployment and disability insurance, and home finance. This limited coverage is not surprising given the cost for both employers and workers and the low value many workers appear to assign to these benefits. Often, workers prefer to work independently or for a company that evades contributions to these programs, in exchange for a slightly higher net wage than they would receive in a formal enterprise. These behaviors help explain the pulverization of economic activity and the tragedy of low productivity in the region.

Given the limited coverage of social security programs and other labor benefits, governments have implemented various social protection programs for workers without coverage.

Social security and protection systems are justifiable for many reasons, and a vigorous social policy is clearly essential in a region characterized by so many deficiencies and inequities. However, well-intended but poorly conceived remedial solutions to low coverage reinforce the incentives for informal employment and aggravate their negative impact on productivity. Over time, the coexistence of parallel social security and protection regimes can trap the region in a vicious circle that is harmful to productivity. Since lower productivity results in lower real wages, governments understandably try to buoy workers' standards of living with more social programs, particularly for those in the informal sector. This further widens the gap between the cost of formal and informal work and leads to more self-employment and microenterprises that do not offer their workers social security coverage. This trend generates more low productivity jobs, decreases the labor supply for more productive formal enterprises, and prevents increases in real wages, closing the circle.

The answer is not to eliminate social protection mechanisms but to cut the linkage of benefits and funding with employment. Universal coverage services, such as health insurance, or even retirement pensions, can be funded with fewer distortions by general taxation and supplemental payments. Services such as universal education funded from general state budgets do not generate strategic behavior toward informality, or impact negatively on productivity. Services that depend on preferences, savings options, and household income levels, such as home finance, can be offered more efficiently by the financial market, with direct subsidies for the poorest families. Only insurance against risks inherent in the employment relationship, such as unemployment or industrial accidents, should be tied to it.

SME Programs: Can One Size Fit All?

Large companies are, in general, more productive than small ones but it is important to understand why. One possibility is that productivity causes size, that is, firms with better projects, ideas, or management find it more profitable to be bigger. Another reason might be economies of scale: having several automobile production plants is inefficient when a single plant could produce the same number of automobiles with fewer resources. Finally, larger companies may be more productive because they have better access to credit or can train their workers more easily. In light of this, firms in a sector do not need to consolidate—which could lead to unproductive monopolies—but they do need expanded financial services and training programs. This has been the logic behind the numerous support programs for small- and medium-sized enterprises (SMEs) in Latin America, most of which are aimed at improving access to credit, offering training, fostering product innovation, and achieving standardized quality certifications (ISO).

For micro- and SME-support programs to make a significant contribution to productivity, they need to raise the productivity of enterprises far above the cost of the programs, or the additional capital and labor used by these enterprises can be more productively used by other enterprises. However, on average, small firms—particularly the smallest ones—do not necessarily use additional resources more productively than medium and large firms. If anything, most of the evidence suggests the opposite: many of the smallest firms are actually too large relative to what they should be because they benefit from implicit subsidies in the form of unpaid taxes and social security contributions. Thus, they may not be able to employ additional labor or capital very productively, particularly relative to larger firms.

Do SME programs increase firms' productivity? Unfortunately, evaluations of these programs have been few and far between and when done, the variable of focus has been employment rather than productivity. Yet, the objective should not be to create jobs but to create productive jobs, which can occur in an enterprise of any size, including but not limited to SMEs. Estimates in this volume suggest that SME programs may indeed boost the productivity of beneficiary firms; however, in the aggregate, the effects would be greater if support was not restricted to SMEs but, rather, was open to all firms. Focusing attention on SMEs is to target an instrument rather than an objective, with the risk of developing a large mass of very small enterprises that survive thanks to public subsidies and creating many low productivity jobs that could have been high productivity jobs if created elsewhere. To minimize this risk, in addition to opening up support programs to firms of all sizes, they should be targeted to formal firms. This has the double advantage of selecting firms that are more likely to benefit from these programs—the evidence, for example, indicates that small formal firms are more likely to benefit from such programs than small informal firms—and in addition, provides incentives for the formalization of firms.

New Ideas for Innovation

Although many Latin American firms invest in innovation, their financial commitment amounts to a mere 0.5 percent of gross revenue compared to 2 percent, or four times higher, in countries associated with the Organization for Economic Cooperation and Development (OECD). Latin American enterprises spend most of their innovation dollars on assimilating the technology in new equipment and machinery, while developed countries invest primarily in research and development. Unfortunately, the long-term return on this investment in innovation is reduced by firms' limited technological ability to assimilate imported technology.

Who invests the most in innovation? It is not the largest firms, or the biggest exporters, or even those that receive the most foreign investment. Investment in innovation as a percentage of sales is the highest in enterprises with good access to finance, effective intellectual property protection, and technological cooperation with their clients, suppliers, or entities involved in the transmission of applied knowledge. In some countries, the market creates incentives for enterprises to invest more in innovation. The main obstacles to innovation are lack of finance, long return periods, small domestic markets, and a shortage of trained personnel. Consequently, deepening credit markets, lowering transportation costs, and improving education and worker training can boost the incentives for firms to innovate.

Enterprises are not the only agent of innovation. In fact, the public sector is the biggest spender on research and development, but its focus is on basic research rather than productive activity. Activity is concentrated in universities and public research centers, which, with valuable exceptions, have little influence on productive innovation and have a low scientific performance by international standards.

Today's deficiencies in innovation are the legacy of a first generation of policies that emphasized the supply of human capital and scientific infrastructure, ignoring demand and evaluation and neglecting connections with productive sectors. A second generation of policies in fashion during the last two decades attempted to fill this vacuum by creating incentives for innovation in firms, especially by means of innovation funds awarded by competition or through tax breaks. Now, a third generation of policies is focusing on solving failures in communication among the various actors in innovation systems and overcoming previously identified problems.

Working Together

Innovation is not the only productivity policy plagued by coordination failures. The success of a large hotel project depends on, among other factors, adequate water and electrical services, a nearby airport, good access routes to sites of interest, and tourist safety. From the extraction of natural resources to the provision of health services, everything depends on the coordinated efforts of individuals, enterprises, and institutions in the private and public sectors.

"Leveling the playing field" so that all sectors have access to all resources under equal conditions was the slogan during the heyday of the Washington Consensus. Although valid in some respects, this slogan is not useful for sectoral policy, because sectors are unique and may require inputs and support institutions specific to them.

Industrial policies are back in vogue but styled differently than in the past. Today they are understood as a set of instruments and institutions that facilitate coordination and generate specific public inputs required by specific sectors. Although the final product may be exports or goods tradable internationally, that is not the objective of these new industrial policies. Rather, the goal is to resolve coordination problems and provide inputs for sectors handpicked for their potential comparative advantages or externalities over other sectors. In fact, a better name for these policies is productive development policies to emphasize that they are not limited to the industrial sector and to link them directly to productivity rather than to promoting an economic activity as an end in itself.

Some successful new productive development policies have been in traditional sectors, such as agriculture, in which public-private partnerships have achieved groundbreaking technical developments. Outstanding examples are genetically improved rice varieties or soy seeds adapted to the Brazilian *savannas*. Other successes have been in completely different sectors such as information or nanotechnology.

Since the new productive development policies identify sectors ("doomed to choose")[3] with no guarantee of success and must promote exploration of new activities and forms of production, they must be proactive but restricted in their scope. This requires institutions that promote public-private cooperation, exploit the information advantages of the private sector, create incentives for risk-taking, and above all discourage rent-seeking behavior—a major challenge indeed.

Why So Difficult?

Since productivity is the art of achieving more with the same, policies aimed at increasing productivity should be the sweethearts of any political system. Unfortunately, raising productivity is a complex task that requires identifying appropriate policies, understanding the conflicts between different objectives, securing the resources to implement the policies, dealing with those who would prefer the status quo or other policies, and maintaining sustained efforts in complementary areas until they bear fruit. It is such an uncertain task, which requires so much coordination, effort and patience, that it is rarely the priority of political systems. Distributing subsidies to unproductive enterprises or increasing social programs for the unemployed, low-income families, small firms, or informal workers is easier and reaps greater and more immediate political returns.

If enterprises are champions of productivity their interests tend to coincide with the general well-being of society. This is a rarity for individual firms operating in isolation but is more likely when businesses join forces in high-level associations to spawn policies. When firms must interact before presenting their demands, they are more likely to take into account the indirect effects on the rest of the economy. In an economy with a centralized government, a stable political system, and a small number of parties, a highly structured business influence that may be driven by a concentrated economic structure will likely favor the adoption of policies that promote productivity not only for the individuals in the main sector but also for those in others. However, in many countries, productive structures have become diversified, the powers of national governments have been decentralized, and in some cases weakened, and political systems are now more participative and porous, which has led to a Balkanization of the effort to derive benefits from public policies.

With terrifying frequency, productivity is the innocent victim of that effort resulting in enterprises that are highly profitable not because they are productive but because they extract income through special concessions or special regulations; labor unions that create barriers to entry and carve out special benefits for their members and higher costs for everyone else; small private enterprises that despite being unproductive manage to stay in business because they evade taxes and social security contributions; sectors—agriculture, mining, manufacturing, transport or commerce— that extract benefits from special tax treatment or some subsidy hidden in a corner of the national budget; informal workers who receive social benefits for which they would have to pay if they were formal; and public enterprises whose monopoly position allows them to drag down the productivity of everyone with their bad service and high costs. In short, countless behaviors add up to benefits for particular enterprises or workers that are not based on higher productivity and that, taken together, are part of the explanation of the tragedy of low productivity in the region.

Putting policies that raise productivity into practice depends on how private interests are organized. But more crucially, it depends on the capacity of the state and the political system to (a) maintain stable and credible policies that enable the private sector to invest and innovate with a long-term horizon; (b) adapt policies to changes in economic circumstances; and (c) coordinate the policies of different areas—economic, social and institutional—taking into account their effects on each other. If the government lacks these capabilities, business organizations or influential economic groups will advocate policies that offer immediate benefits, even at the cost of aggregate productivity and, ultimately, the welfare of society as a whole.

The productivity of a country is the composite of the actions of millions of individual enterprises and workers. With few exceptions, no isolated action of a company or worker can be sufficiently important to have a measurable impact on aggregate productivity. But the sum of all actions is decisive. An understanding of the tragedy of productivity in the region requires not only an understanding of how individual policies (tax, social, commercial, credit) impact productivity, but how the political economy of a country impacts these policies as well.

Productivity as a national objective faces problems of "collective action": everyone would benefit individually if others paid taxes, were more productive, faced more competition, and worked harder, as long as the burden of responsibility does not lie with them personally. As in a football stadium, if everyone is seated, the one person standing sees the game better. But when many are standing, no one can enjoy the game. How can everyone be made to sit down simultaneously, when the person who sits down first loses out if the others fail to follow suit? How can every enterprise and worker—in the public and private sectors—be convinced to act in a manner conducive to greater individual productivity? How can a country's political system be forced to internalize the objective of productivity as an integral part of its normal actions?

What to Do

To have even a possibility of success, policy recommendations for raising productivity must take into account the way private interests are organized and the capacity of the state and the political system to articulate and implement policies. Although these circumstances are difficult to change radically, the possibilities of success can improve by concentrating on just a few points.

Make productivity a central theme of the public discourse, as growth, inflation, or unemployment currently are, and as on occasion even something as diffuse as "competitiveness" can be. Raising productivity depends on citizens and opinion leaders demanding adequate policies from the political system. In some cases, setting up national councils can be a valuable tool, provided they are institutionalized by law and endure over time. This requires an institutional framework that separates strategy from policy design and evaluation, has great credibility, and is protected from particular rent-seeking conducts.

Disseminate the effects of policies on long-term productivity. This applies to both direct policies to improve productivity and others with indirect effects such as social or tax policies. Explain how these policies affect the productivity of the benefited sectors—such as microenterprises or informal workers—as well as the aggregate productivity of all productive sectors. This implies creating independent and transparent institutions to monitor and evaluate the impact.

Incorporate business and labor into the policy debate through organizations at the highest level that represent national interests, rather than through more specific sectoral or interest groups. It is also useful to promote the formation of groupings with the broadest possible coverage and strengthen their capacities.

Invest in developing the capacity of the state to adopt long-term policies. When they have long-term career prospects, lawmakers, public officials, and judges can invest more in their capacities and in developing effective forms of cooperation with other actors. A judicial branch with stability and political independence are crucial for credible policies.

Involve entities that guarantee credibility thanks to their political independence, technical seriousness, and permanence on the national scene. Certain academic bodies, nongovernmental organizations, or multilateral organizations that can facilitate political transactions and oversee compliance with commitments could all fit this bill.

Anticipate the indirect consequences of reforms on political actions. Decentralization of the state and the emergence of new political parties can be desirable for increasing citizen participation and opening channels of representation to excluded social groups, but they can also have negative effects on the capacity of the political system to adopt policies to raise productivity. The instruments of economic and social policy that most affect productivity must be isolated from these trends toward fragmentation.

It would be risky to propose a policy recipe to improve productivity since each country's specific economic, social, institutional, and political circumstances determine the advisability, viability, effectiveness, and stability of policies. However, the following is a tentative list of "what to do" and "what not to do" in each of the major areas analyzed in this report. It is

Table 1.1 How to Improve Productivity

	What to do	*What not to do*
General strategy	Make productivity an objective of the state.	Identify productivity with international competitiveness or, even less, with exports.
	Facilitate access to productive resources for all types of enterprises.	Concentrate on industry or some "fashionable" sector.
	Look for productivity gains within enterprises as well as between them, facilitating the movement of resources from less productive to more productive firms.	Confuse social policies with productivity policies.
	Support success, not failure; support what has growth potential, not what is stagnant with no prospects.	Support the weakest, most unproductive or smallest enterprises simply because they are small.
	Evaluate the impact of public policies on productivity and disseminate the results widely.	
	Design mechanisms against the regulatory capture of programs and institutions that allocate credit, subsidies, authorizations, concessions, or support of any type.	
Trade and transport infrastructure policy	Generate conditions to promote port and airport efficiency. Create competition when possible (open markets, seas and skies to all).	Defend route monopolies.
	Promote consultation and coordination of service suppliers to exploit economies of scale and complementarities.	Postpone or save on maintenance costs of transport infrastructure.
	Eliminate customs inefficiencies.	Protect inefficient enterprises, rejecting the use of mechanisms such as safeguards and antidumping tariffs.
Financial policy	Facilitate the use of a good credit-and-guarantee reputation to access credit.	Intervene in credit markets through specific allocations or controls on interest rates.
	Make property and company registries more flexible and cheaper.	Allocate credit using first-tier public banks.
	Strengthen systems to protect creditor rights.	Be complacent about macroeconomic achievements and weaken fiscal strengthening processes.
	Strengthen credit information systems.	

(continued on next page)

Table 1.1   Continued

	What to do	What not to do
	Expand supervision and financial regulation to include macroeconomic risks.	
	Make explicit and public all public subsidies for credit, including guarantees	
Tax policy	Simplify the tax regime on production and profits for all firms.	Create special tax regimes based on sector or size of enterprises.
	Create positive incentives for formalization (i.e. credit, aid restricted to formal firms).	Give aid to informal firms
	Penalize tax evasion with increased effectiveness and credibility.	Tax financial transactions.
	Use self-control mechanisms to avoid evasion (such as VAT).	Tolerate tax evasion.
	Broaden the tax base to include microenterprises and the self-employed.	
Social protection policy	Cut the link between social security funding and employment.	Use the labor market to execute social policy.
	Guarantee that all workers are covered against common risks, irrespective of their labor situation.	Finance social protection programs for informal workers from payroll taxes.
	Finance universal social programs from general taxation.	Convert programs to combat poverty into a parallel social security system for informal workers.
	Guarantee an effective and broad-based social security network that protects workers in transition.	Confuse programs to invest in the human capital of the poor with programs to insure against risks.
	Promote mechanisms such as unemployment insurance that offer effective protection against dismissal.	
	Unify the pension and health systems.	
SME-support policies	Evaluate the impact of existing programs on productivity.	Grant tax breaks or relax compliance with social security regulations for SMEs over larger enterprises.
	Concentrate on the SMEs with the greatest possibility of success.	Give permanent or long-term support.
	Make any support conditional on achieving measurable targets and on formality status.	Include social objectives in SME policies.

(continued on next page)

Table 1.1 Continued

	What to do	*What not to do*
Innovation policies	Link research to business activity.	Allocate resources to supply without evaluating the results.
	Grant financial stimulus or tax breaks to technology programs and services offered to enterprises.	Ignore demand from business and interactions with the rest of the innovation system.
	Strengthen intellectual property rights.	
	Correct the failures of coordination between the actors in innovation systems.	
	Promote competitive mechanisms as instruments for allocating resources to the supply side (professional and technical education, universities and technology centers) and evaluate results.	
Productive development policies	Stimulate development of sectors with positive externalities and the capacity to pull other sectors up.	Give preference to sectors simply because they are industrial or receive foreign investment.
	Identify failures of coordination and information and help solve them with persuasion, incentives, etc.	Support failed projects or enterprises.
	Promote joint exploration of opportunities between public and private sectors.	
	Let the losers go.	
Political reforms and strategies	Make productivity a central theme of public attention.	Fragment the design and discussion of productivity policies among multiple groups of agents and debate arenas.
	Disseminate the effects of policies on productivity.	Use subsidies and other harmful concessions for productivity as an instrument of political negotiation.
	Bring the business and labor sectors into the debate.	
	Invest in developing the capacity of the state.	
	Involve entities that guarantee credibility.	
	Anticipate the indirect consequences of the reforms on political actions.	

a tentative list because knowledge is limited, and because the conclusions must often be qualified in ways that are discussed in the rest of this volume. The list that follows is, therefore, an invitation to delve more deeply into the themes of greatest interest to each reader.

This chapter ends where it began: income per capita in the region has lagged behind the rest of the world not because the Latin American and Caribbean people invest less than others or work less, but because, in relative terms, the region's productivity has plummeted.

It is crucial to reverse this phenomenon. A country's standard of living can be raised by exploiting the fact that—for reasons of nature—some crop or mineral or energy source can be produced or extracted at very low cost in relation to the international price; it can also be raised for a time by borrowing. But the lag that Latin America and the Caribbean have suffered for decades in relation to the rest of the world shows prima facie that in the medium term, these strategies are not viable. In the end, there is no substitute for producing more effectively, innovating, training, adapting, changing, experimenting, reallocating, and using work, capital, and land with greater efficiency; in short, there is no substitute for higher productivity.

In the past 15 years, after many setbacks, Latin American societies have succeeded in building a social consensus in favor of macroeconomic stability. Thanks to this, the region has come through the worst international financial crisis since the Great Depression in relatively good shape. This is no minor achievement, and reflects the capacity of these societies to build consensus around fundamental issues. The challenge now is to build a politically feasible social consensus in favor of productivity so that this macroeconomic stability can lead to a development process stimulated by the growth of productivity, which is the real foundation of shared and lasting prosperity.

Notes

1. This figure and the rest of the figures in this paragraph are detrended with a Hodrick-Prescott filter to eliminate the effect of short-term fluctuations. See Chapter 2 for further details.
2. The term "small firms" in this book refers to the low end of the size distribution, and often, when data is available, it also encompasses microenterprises.
3. This term was coined by Hausmann and Rodrik (2006).

2

Aggregate Productivity: The Key to Unlocking Latin America's Development Potential

Measuring Aggregate Productivity

Most countries in Latin America and the Caribbean have been growing slowly for a long time and consider themselves increasingly poor relative to the rest of the world, including both advanced countries and peer countries in other regions. Actual declines in income per capita for substantial periods of time have been common. However, it would be misleading to blame low investment for this failure. Low and slow productivity, as opposed to impediments to factor accumulation, is the key to understanding Latin America's low income relative to developed economies and its stagnation relative to other developing countries that are catching up. A fortiori, the main development policy challenge in the region is to diagnose the causes of poor productivity and attack their roots. This chapter documents the key dimensions of weak productivity at the aggregate level in an analytical framework that helps this diagnosis, and in that way provides a basis for the rest of the book. It draws heavily from Daude and Fernández-Arias (2009), where the statistical and technical details are spelled out.

The first question is how to measure aggregate productivity. Standard economic analysis estimates aggregate productivity, or total factor productivity (TFP), by looking at the annual output Y (measured by the gross domestic product [GDP]) that is produced on the basis of the accumulated factors of production, or capital, that are available as inputs. For any given stock of capital, the higher the output, the more productive the economy. Capital is composed of physical capital, K, and human

Box 2.1   Production Functions

Standard economic analysis posits mapping accumulated factors of production or physical and human capital, K and H, respectively, to output Y. This mapping is assumed to have constant returns to scale (i.e., if factor inputs K and H increase by x percent, output Y would also increase by x percent, as if the same economy "expanded" by x percent). Consider the mapping $Y = AF(K,H)$, where the constant-returns-to-scale function $F(.)$ describes how the combinations of accumulated factors can be transformed into output and the scaling parameter A converts it into observed output Y. Output per worker Y/L can be similarly decomposed expressing factors of production in per-worker terms ($k = K/L$ and $h = H/L$) to obtain $Y/L = AF(k,h)$.

In these formulations, the parameter A represents the level of aggregate efficiency or TFP: a higher A means that more output is produced with the same factors of production input, either total or per-worker. TFP is estimated as a residual to reconcile observed output with what is not accounted for by $F(K,H)$, or $F(k,h)$ in the case of output per worker. The key to estimating TFP is how to model the function $F(.)$.

Except when noted, this chapter uses a standard Cobb-Douglas production function:

$$Y = AK^a H^{1-a} = AK^a (hL)^{1-a} \tag{1}$$

where a is the output elasticity to (physical) capital.[a] A standard value of $a = 1/3$ is used.[b]

(continued on next page)

capital H. Physical capital takes the form of means of production, such as machines and buildings. Human capital is the productive capacity of the labor force. It amounts to the headcount of the labor force (or raw, unskilled labor), L, magnified by a multiple h, reflecting the average qualification of the labor force as measured by its education, so that $H = hL$. TFP measures the effectiveness with which accumulated factors of production, or capital, are used to produce output.

Therefore, output Y results from the combination of factors of production K and H at a certain degree of TFP. Likewise, output growth over time results from an accumulation of factors of production and productivity growth. The attribution of output level and growth to factors and productivity is made by using production functions that map factors into output: what is not accounted for by factors of production as estimated by the production function is attributed to productivity.

(*continued*)

The decomposition of income per capita $y = Y/N$, where N is the size of the population as opposed to the labor force, gives rise to an extra term reflecting the share of the population in the labor force (L/N, denoted by f), which in turn results from the share of the working-age population (a demographic factor) and the rate of its participation in the labor force:

$$y = \frac{Y}{N} = A \left(\frac{K}{L} \right)^a h^{1-a} \frac{L}{N} = A k^a h^{1-a} f \tag{2}$$

[a] Output Y is computed as PPP adjusted to real gross domestic product (GDP) from Heston, Summers, and Aten (2006); labor input and population from the World Bank (2008); education input from the Barro and Lee (2000) database following Psacharopoulos (1994), and capital input from Penn World Tables (PWT) following Easterly and Levine (2001). Given data availability, the sample consists of 76 countries, of which 18 are in Latin America and the Caribbean, for the period of 1960–2005. Small countries with less than one million inhabitants are excluded from the analysis. Annual series are filtered with the Hodrick-Prescott filter to retain the trend using a smoothing parameter of 7. TFP is obtained as a residual.

[b] See Klenow and Rodríguez-Clare (2005). Although there is some debate regarding the validity of this assumption, Gollin (2002) shows that once informal labor and household entrepreneurship are taken into account, there is no systematic difference in this parameter across countries associated with the level of development (GDP per capita) or any time trend. Hence its uniformity across countries and time appears to be a reasonable assumption.

TFP is a comprehensive measure of the efficiency with which the economy is able to transform its accumulated factors of production K and H into output Y. (Unless noted, this chapter uses a standard Cobb-Douglas production function with a capital share of $a = 1/3$; see Box 2.1 for details).

There are, however, other partial measures of productivity that are commonly used. One is a variant of this TFP measure calculated on the basis of the size of the labor force L rather than total human capital H, so that education is not considered a factor of production and, therefore, the increase in production due to higher average education h would be reflected in higher productivity. Another partial measure of productivity is so-called labor productivity, or Y/L. In this case, physical capital K is also neglected as a factor of production, and therefore an economy whose labor

Figure 2.1 Productivity Indexes

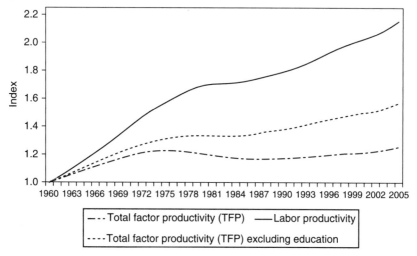

Source: Authors' calculations based on Heston, Summers, and Aten (2006), World Bank (2008), and Barro and Lee (2000).

Note: The indexes include 76 countries, and 1960 is the base year for all calculations.

force enjoys more capital at its disposal would tend to exhibit higher productivity. Figure 2.1 shows that the trends of these alternative productivity measures differ substantially; thus, the conclusions may vary depending on the productivity measure selected.

The inadequate use of the alternative productivity measures may produce misleading conclusions. For example, an increase in the labor productivity measure does not indicate whether such improvement was produced by more education of the labor force (better quality of the labor input), the accumulation of physical capital (unrelated to the labor input), or something else (unrelated to all factor inputs). (In the case of the alternative TFP measure based on raw labor *L*, the effect of education becomes unnecessarily confounded with the measure of TFP.) Arguably, the discrimination of these three different sources is relevant for diagnosis and policy action. Thus, the preferred measure of TFP is a productivity measure that is not contaminated by the evolution of factor inputs.

TFP measures the efficiency with which available factors of production are transformed into final output.[1] This measure of productivity includes a technological component and tends to increase as the technological frontier expands and new technology or ideas become available and are adopted, but it is also affected by the efficiency with which markets work and are served by public services. An economy populated by technologically advanced firms may still produce inefficient aggregate results and this will therefore translate into low aggregate productivity. In particular, market and policy failures may distort the efficiency with which factors are allocated across sectors, and across firms within sectors, thus depressing aggregate efficiency (see Chapter 4 for further analysis of this topic). The upshot is that, while increasing the stock of accumulated factors may require resources that are unavailable in low-income countries and may even be wasteful if productivity is low, boosting productivity directly may "simply" require the willingness to reform policies and institutions by taking advantage of successful experiences elsewhere.

It is important to understand what TFP includes and does not include. Because the estimations herein do not consider the effectively employed labor force and physical capital but the entire stocks available for production, partially utilized factors (e.g., unemployment or underemployment) would reflect in low productivity. In order to avoid the fluctuations this accounting would induce on productivity due to the business cycle, the annual series of output and factors are filtered to retain only their trends, thus obtaining trend productivity. Therefore, in the calculations, only structural underutilization of resources would be reflected in low productivity.[2] At the same time, because labor input is measured as the size of the labor force, variations in the share of the population in the labor force (be it for demographic reasons or the choice of working-age population to participate in the labor force) do not directly affect TFP. In other words, a smaller labor force as a share of the population is not reflected in lower productivity. On the other hand, the quality of education, which may differ significantly across countries, is reflected in the productivity measure inasmuch as it impinges on the working capacity of the labor force.[3] Similarly, the age profile of the labor force also entails differences in experience akin to the quality of education.

The above framework can be directly applied to account for output per worker Y/L (or "labor productivity") in terms of TFP and per-worker factor intensities: $k = K/L$ ("capital intensity") and $h = H/L$ (education of the labor force) (see Box 2.1 for details). It is useful to relate this production function framework to a welfare framework, such as the traditional measure of GDP per capita ($y = Y/N$), where N is the size of the population. This is an income measure commonly used to gauge welfare across countries. In this case, differences in income per capita, or in its growth, can be attributed to TFP and per-worker factor intensities, as before, and an extra term reflecting the share of the population in the labor force (L/N, denoted by f).[4] TFP is central to understanding income-per-capita diversity across countries and to acting on the root causes of underdevelopment. The enormous diversity of income per capita that exists across

Figure 2.2 Income Per Capita and Productivity across Countries, 2005

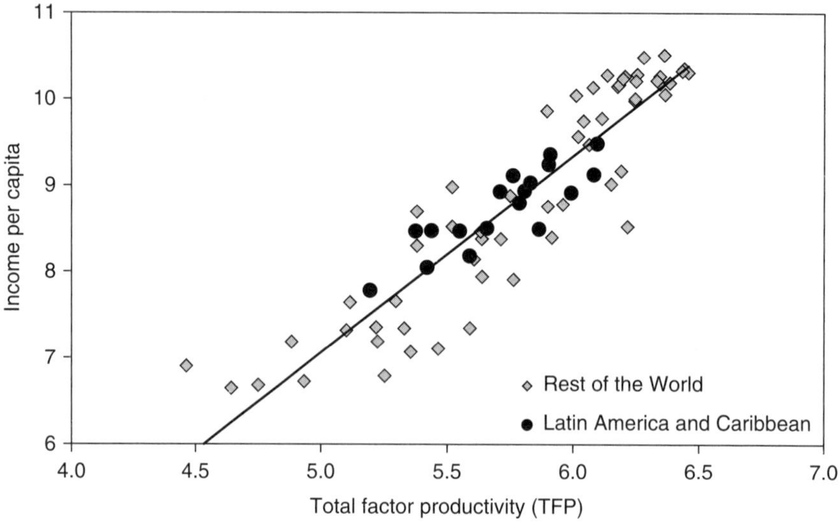

Source: Authors' calculations based on Heston, Summers, and Aten (2006), World Bank (2008), and Barro and Lee (2000).

Note: Income per capita and TFP measured in logarithmic scale.

countries coincides to a large extent with their aggregate productivity levels as measured by TFP. In effect, TFP and income per capita move in tandem (see Figure 2.2). In this sample, a simple statistical exercise measuring their association indicates that, if TFP were the same across countries in the world, the country income variation today would be 84 percent less than it actually is: countries differ mainly in their TFP. (This is an established observation [Hall and Jones 1999]; this chapter will show the mechanisms behind such a strong relationship.)

Most analyses in this chapter consider the productivity of the "typical" country in Latin America and the Caribbean, represented by a simple average of country productivities irrespective of whether the country is large or small. Similarly, it considers the simple average of income per capita (*y*), and the corresponding per-worker factor of production intensities (*k,h,f*), to represent typical characteristics. However, to represent the region as a whole, where the productivity of larger countries is more influential because it applies to larger stocks of productive factors, it considers a synthetic country by summing up inputs and outputs of countries in the region. (More generally, various country groupings are represented following similar methods.)

In what follows, TFP is the measure of aggregate productivity and represents the productivity of the typical Latin American country (TFP_{lac})

Figure 2.3   Productivity Diversity within Latin America and the Caribbean, 2005

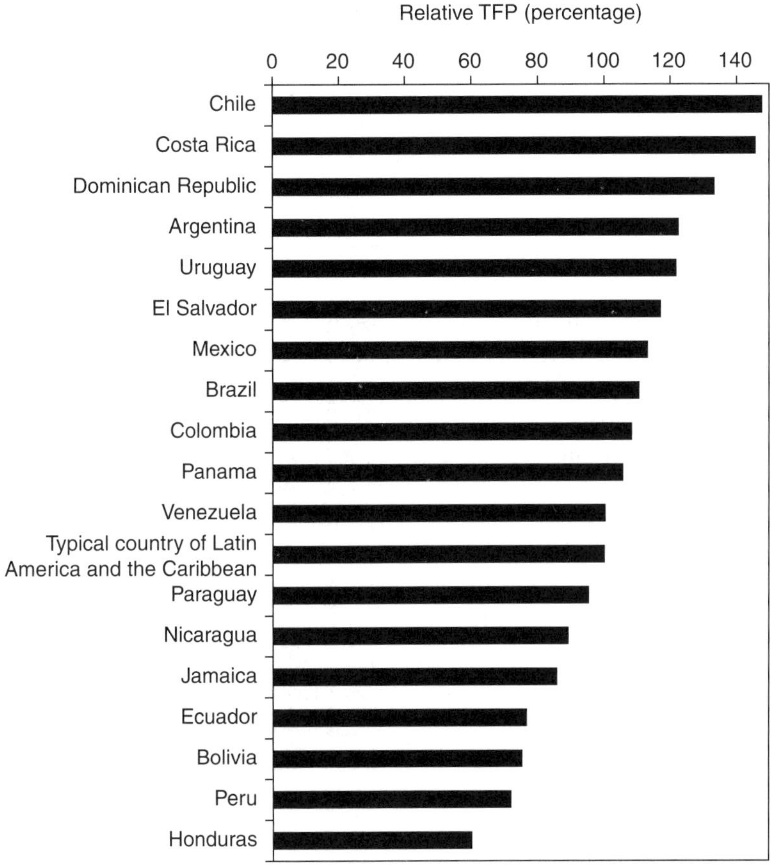

Relative TFP (percentage)

Source: Authors' calculations based on Heston, Summers, and Aten (2006), World Bank (2008), and Barro and Lee (2000).

Note: Country TFP relative to typical country of Latin America and the Caribbean.

and of the region (TFP_{LAC}). However, before analyzing regional aggregates, it may be useful to note the substantial diversity in productivity levels across countries in the region. Figure 2.3 shows an estimation of current productivity levels in each country relative to the typical country in Latin America (as of 2005).[5]

Stylized Facts of Aggregate Productivity in Latin America

This section reviews the evolution of aggregate productivity in the economic development of Latin America, both in levels and in growth,[6] using traditional tools of growth and development accounting (see Box 2.2

Box 2.2   Growth and Development Accounting

Traditional growth accounting decomposes the growth rate of GDP per capita using a transformation of equation 2 (Box 2.1) to obtain equation 3. The growth rate of TFP is obtained as a residual after accounting for the growth rates of factor inputs (the growth rate of a variable x is denoted by $\hat{x}$).

$$\hat{y} = \hat{A} + a\hat{k} + (1-a)\hat{h} + \hat{f} \tag{3}$$

The above equation can also be used to account for the growth gaps between two countries or groups of countries, so that the growth gap in income per capita can be decomposed into the sum of the growth gap in TFP, the (weighted) factors' growth gaps, and the gap in the growth of labor-force intensity:

$$Gap(\hat{y}) = Gap(\hat{A}) + aGap(\hat{k}) + (1-a)Gap(\hat{h}) + Gap(\hat{f})$$

Development accounting looks at levels rather than growth rates. It utilizes equation 2 (from Box 2.1) to compare the components behind income per capita between an economy of interest and a benchmark economy taken as a development yardstick, denoted by "*" in equation 4:

$$\frac{y}{y^*} = \frac{A}{A^*}\left(\frac{k}{k^*}\right)^a \left(\frac{h}{h^*}\right)^{1-a} \frac{f}{f^*} \tag{4}$$

A logarithmic transformation of the above equation can then be used to account for the contribution of the TFP gap and that of factor intensities to the overall income per capita gap:

$$Log\left(\frac{y}{y^*}\right) = Log\left(\frac{A}{A^*}\right) + aLog\left(\frac{k}{k^*}\right) + (1-a)Log\left(\frac{h}{h^*}\right) + Log\left(\frac{f}{f^*}\right)$$

for details). In order to highlight the region's weaknesses and anomalies, the patterns are benchmarked against the rest of the world (ROW) and selected groups of countries, such as the East Asian tigers (EA), (currently) Developed countries (DEV), and "Twin" countries (TWIN, countries whose income was initially, in 1960, comparable to that of Latin American countries).[7] Unless noted, comparisons are made between the typical countries of each region. Following convention, the U.S. economy

Figure 2.4   Productivity Growth and GDP Per Capita Growth Gaps, Latin America and the Caribbean vs. the Rest of the World

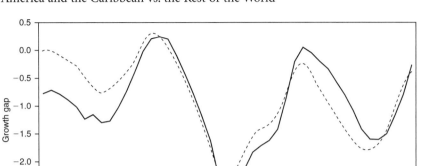

Source: Authors' calculations based on Heston, Summers, and Aten (2006), World Bank (2008), and Barro and Lee (2000).

is the technological frontier against which total gaps in productivity are estimated.

Three stylized facts of TFP in Latin America are central to the diagnosis of some main weaknesses in the region's economic development.

Fact 1. Slower growth in Latin America is due to slower productivity growth.

It is well known that Latin American income per capita grows systematically more slowly than that of the rest of the world (there is a negative gap in income-per-capita growth, $\hat{y}$).[8] The first stylized fact is that this gap can be largely attributed to a negative gap in TFP growth, rather than to differences in the pace of factor accumulation (see Box 2.2 for details on the accounting framework): the per capita income growth gap is essentially due to a gap in TFP growth. In fact, since 1960, the annual growth gaps in GDP and in TFP relative to the rest of the world appear equally large and systematic (Figure 2.4).[9] Factor accumulation in Latin America was in line with the rest of the world and, in particular, progress in education held its own; what sets apart Latin American growth is TFP stagnation.[10]

Systematically slower growth has meant an ever-increasing income-per-capita gap relative to most countries. Table 2.1 shows the increase in

Table 2.1   Potential Increase in Income Per Capita if Latin America Performed Like Other Regions over 1960–2005 (percent)

	Rest of the World	East Asia	Twin Countries	Developed Countries	United States
Equal income-per-capita growth	54.0	376.4	90.4	91.9	55.9
Equal TFP growth	47.3	141.3	50.0	67.2	39.2

Source: Authors' calculations based on Heston, Summers, and Aten (2006); World Bank (2008); and Barro and Lee (2000).

this gap since 1960 relative to benchmarks. For example, had the typical country in Latin America grown at the same pace as its counterpart in the rest of the world since 1960, by now its income per capita would be some 54 percent higher. The claim is that the growth gap is mostly due to slower productivity growth: had TFP grown as it did in the rest of the world since 1960, the same factor accumulation would have allowed typical income per capita in Latin America to be some 47 percent higher, virtually offsetting the overall deterioration of relative income. The responsibility of slower productivity growth for slower income growth of the typical Latin American country holds true in comparisons with all benchmarks (see Table 2.1, where the relative income deteriorations are shown to virtually disappear had TFP grown at par).[11]

Fact 2. Latin America's productivity is not catching up with the frontier, in contrast to theory and evidence elsewhere.

Traditional theory suggests that less productive countries should be able to increase their productivity faster because they can adopt technologies from more advanced economies, benefiting from advances at the frontier without incurring the costs of exploration. It is true that TFP is not just technology—it can be argued that it mostly reflects inefficiencies in how markets work—but the catching-up argument works just as well for policies and institutions: backward countries have the benefit of being able to improve by learning, rather than inventing.

The rest of the world tends to follow this expected convergent pattern, but Latin America deviates substantially. Figure 2.5 shows the evolution of productivity in Latin America and the typical countries of benchmark regions relative to the frontier, customarily taken as the United States (normalizing the indexes to 1 by 1960). Until the debt crisis of the 1980s, the typical country in Latin America was slower in catching up and has actually distanced itself further since then. This divergent pattern in recent decades holds true not only for the typical Latin American country but

Figure 2.5   Productivity Catch-Up: Contrast with Selected Regions

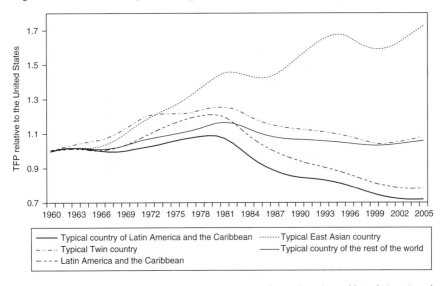

Source: Authors' calculations based on Heston, Summers, and Aten (2006), World Bank (2008), and Barro and Lee (2000).

Note: Productivity index relative to the United States. The reference year is 1960.

for the region as a whole (as Brazil's early dynamism slowed down). Other benchmarks further highlight Latin America's anomalous productivity.

The failure to catch up on productivity is widespread across Latin American countries. Figure 2.6 shows all countries in the sample ranked by the proportional increase in their TFP over the entire period (relative to the corresponding increase in the United States): there is a substantial concentration of Latin American countries in the fourth quartile. The United States (at 0 by definition) is about the median, like Brazil, and only Chile shows some degree of convergence to it; the productivity gap relative to the United States actually grew in the rest of the Latin American and Caribbean countries in the sample over the period of 1960–2005.

Fact 3. Latin America and the Caribbean's productivity is about half its potential.

Current levels of estimated TFP for Latin American countries relative to the productivity frontier, taken as that of the United States, are uniformly subpar (see Figure 2.7).[12] In particular, the aggregate productivity of the typical Latin American country (which, being an average, is subject to less statistical error than that of individual countries) is about half (52 percent). For the region as a whole, TFP is about 55 percent.

Figure 2.6   Cumulative Productivity Catching Up around the World, 1960–2005

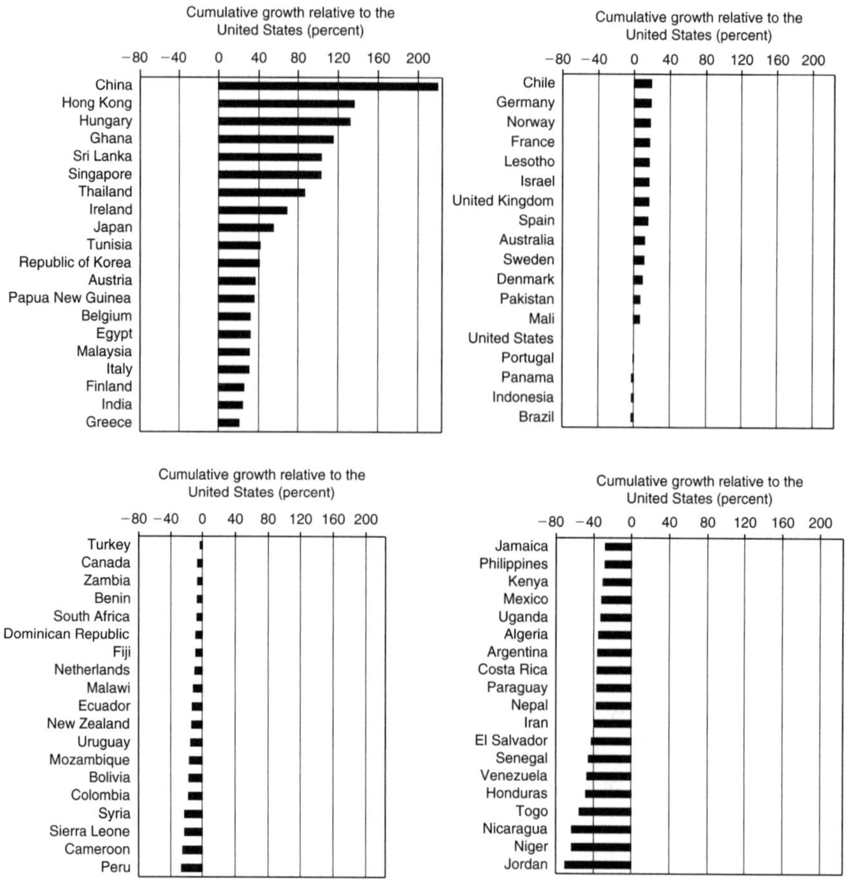

Source: Authors' calculations based on Heston, Summers, and Aten (2006), World Bank (2008), and Barro and Lee (2000).

If factor inputs are kept constant, income per capita would move pari passu with TFP. Therefore, if TFP increased to its potential, the income per capita of the typical Latin American country would double (to about a third of the U.S. level). In this thought experiment, a better combination of the same inputs emulating what is feasible in another economy, using existing technologies, would render a substantially larger output. This is an artificial scenario because productivity and factor accumulation are interlinked and changes in productivity are bound to have indirect effects on factor accumulation (and vice versa). However, this direct income effect of closing the productivity gap provides a measure of the relevance of this gap: relative to the United States, the income per capita of the typical Latin

Figure 2.7   Relative Productivity in Latin America, 2005

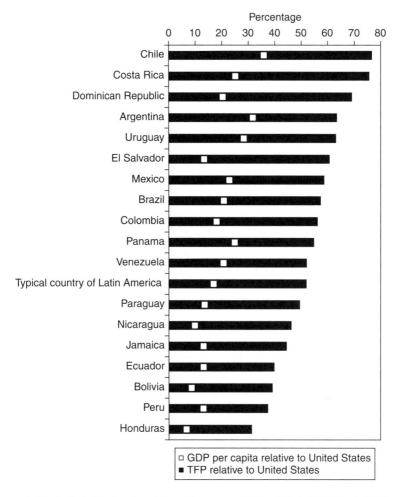

Source: Authors' calculations based on Heston, Summers, and Aten (2006), World Bank (2008), and Barro and Lee (2000).

American country would increase from 16.8 percent to 32.4 percent (and from 20.6 percent to 37.2 percent for the region as a whole).

The sizable room for improvement associated with productivity catching up is in some sense good news for Latin America to the extent that economic policy reform, even without greater investment, can unlock rapid progress in income per capita (i.e., high growth). This potential to improve productivity in the typical Latin American country by 93 percent, which would result in almost doubling its income, is much less in the typical East Asian country (35 percent), twin country (43 percent), or developed country (only 16 percent).

These key stylized facts are robust to relevant changes in the methodologies used to estimate productivity, as tested in Daude and Fernández-Arias (2009). For example, estimating the physical capital series K with alternative methods commonly used in the technical literature (Caselli 2005) makes negligible difference. Defining the labor input L as working-age population instead of labor force, with the effect that TFP becomes more sensitive to changes in the desired participation rate in the labor force (everything else being equal, less participation would translate into lower aggregate productivity), makes little difference and in fact would further lower productivity relative to the United States.[13]

The findings are also robust to the production function model utilized. The Cobb-Douglas production function used is the conventional approach for a number of good reasons, but has the empirical drawback of collapsing all productivity concerns into a single parameter, the factor-neutral productivity parameter A or TFP. To test the robustness of the model, Daude and Fernández-Arias (2009) consider a model-free method of estimation in which the degree of aggregate efficiency with which a country produces is only based on the possibilities revealed by the production achievements of the rest of the countries.[14] Once the production frontier theoretically attainable with the country's factor inputs using "best practices" is estimated, a relative efficiency or TFP index E can be estimated reflecting actual output relative to the frontier (so E is an index between 0 and 1). It turns out that this index of aggregate relative efficiency E is very highly correlated to estimated relative TFP across countries and its value for the typical Latin American country is similar to the estimated relative TFP, which buttresses the previous findings.

Productivity and Factor Accumulation

To appreciate the relevance of productivity for the overall economic development process, the interplay between productivity and factor accumulation must be explored: the indirect effects of productivity gaps on the incentives to accumulate production factors may account for a substantial portion of the observed development gaps. In fact, the traditional tools previously utilized underestimate the importance that closing the productivity gap would have on welfare. After a full measure is obtained, it becomes clear that the central development question is how to close the productivity gap.

In an accounting sense, a gap in income per capita can be attributed to a gap in productivity (A), physical-capital intensity (k), human capital intensity (h), or labor-force intensity (f) (see Box 2.2, especially equation 4). For example, a development accounting exercise that benchmarks the typical Latin American country with the United States would indicate that if the productivity gap is closed, then relative income would roughly double (TFP in the typical Latin American country would increase by $A^*/A = 1.93$ times or roughly twice, and so would income). An accounting decomposition of the contributions of each underlying gap to the current income gap with the United States would indicate that the productivity gap accounts for about 37 percent, and accumulated factors for the remaining 63 percent.[15]

While the income boost produced by closing the productivity gap in this simple accounting calculation is sizable, it would apparently leave most of the observed income gap intact. This metric would suggest that productivity is an important but not predominant variable behind income gaps; but then how is it possible that income is so closely associated with productivity across countries (as shown in Figure 2.2)? In what follows, this question is addressed to show that this accounting attribution severely underestimates the effect that closing the productivity gap would have in closing the income gap because it does not consider that factor accumulation would in turn react to the higher returns generated by an increase in productivity. In particular, what follows in Fact 4 will be shown.

Fact 4. The income-per-capita gap with respect to the United States would largely disappear if the productivity gap is closed.

In market economies, private investment in physical capital is such that the marginal return to investing equals the cost of capital as perceived by individual investors, within the financing conditions available to them. The private return appropriated by an individual investor may very well be a fraction of the social return to investing if, for example, it provides positive externalities to other firms (i.e., non-patentable innovations, etc.) or if the firm's returns are heavily taxed away. As shown in Klenow and Rodríguez-Clare (1997), these price-like wedges are fully reflected in the capital-output ratio $\kappa = K/Y$: impediments to physical-capital investment leading to a wedge between net marginal returns (net of cost of capital) across countries correspond to lower capital-output ratios. Productivity differences across countries, however, would be irrelevant for the capital-output ratio. Nevertheless, for any given impediments to physical-capital accumulation, as measured by the capital-output ratio, an increase in TFP would boost private returns relative to the status quo and lead to a higher stock of accumulated physical capital.[16] In fact, closing the TFP gap would alter incentives, boosting not only physical-capital investment but also investment in education. These are indirect effects of closing the productivity gap that ought to be attributed to it.

How much is the overall effect of closing the TFP gap, inclusive of these indirect effects? The following provides some estimations based on the methodology developed in Daude and Fernández-Arias (2009).

Taking into account the boost to physical-capital investment that closing the productivity gap would imply, the overall contribution of the TFP gap to the per-capita-income gap would include not only the direct, or accounting, effect mentioned above, but also an indirect effect via the promotion of higher intensity physical capital. If education is conservatively taken to be exogenous, meaning that investment in education does not increase with higher TFP, then the total TFP contribution for the typical Latin American country (as of 2005) would amount to 55 percent of the income gap, of which 37 percent is the direct effect mentioned above and 18 percent is the additional indirect effect via induced physical-capital accumulation. This is a conservative estimate of the overall relevance of the productivity gap.

In this scenario of physical-capital intensity endogenously reacting to changes in productivity and exogenously given education, the remaining 45 percent that makes up the entire income gap is divided into the contribution of impediments to physical investment, which, as explained, are reflected in the capital-output ratio κ (12 percent), human capital intensity or education h (25 percent), and labor-force intensity f (8 percent) (see Figure 2.8).[17] According to these results, a development agenda exclusively focused on physical-capital investment that eases impediments such as undue spreads in the financial system, high taxation, and uncertain property rights would be circumscribed to a margin of 12 percent (unless the investment also fosters productivity, an issue explored at the end of this section). There is some variation across countries, but the conclusions hold broadly.[18]

If, alternatively, investment in human capital (education), which is dominant among the remaining factor-related gaps, is also recognized as an endogenous variable that would likely react to an increase in productivity, the case for a predominant effect of the productivity gap becomes stronger.[19] In this context, its consideration will add an additional indirect effect of closing the productivity gap.[20]

This more complete decomposition in which both types of capital react to productivity changes crucially depends on how elastic education demand is to increased productivity.[21] A high elasticity like the one suggested in Erosa, Koreshkova, and Restuccia (2007) implies that closing the productivity gap would allow Latin America to surpass the United States in income per capita (by some 11 percent)! This is so despite the gap in labor-force intensity and the impediments to physical-capital investment, because with such elasticity the workforce in Latin America would be

Figure 2.8   Overall Contribution of Closing the Productivity Gap (endogenous capital [K])

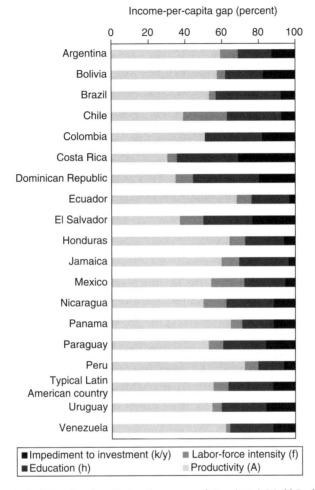

Income-per-capita gap (percent)

Legend:
- ■ Impediment to investment (k/y)
- ■ Labor-force intensity (f)
- ■ Education (h)
- ▨ Productivity (A)

Source: Authors' calculations based on Heston, Summers, and Aten (2006), World Bank (2008), and Barro and Lee (2000).

more educated than that in the United States for a given income level. A more conservative elasticity consistent with the typical Latin American country and the United States having the same propensity to education (the same education for a given level of income) implies that closing the TFP gap would reduce the income-per-capita gap by 73 percent, up from the conservative estimate of 55 percent, half of which are indirect effects through both physical capital and education. This reinforces the conclusion that Latin America's income-per-capita gap would largely disappear if the productivity gap is closed.[22]

Once the productivity gap is established as the key, the main policy question is then how to close the productivity gap. As mentioned, the aggregate productivity gap reflects a variety of shortcomings in the workings of the overall economy and should not be narrowly interpreted as a technological gap. However, in answering this question it is important to recognize that factor accumulation, both physical and human capital, may be important to reduce the productivity gap. For example, physical-capital investment may embody new technologies to help catch up with the frontier and human capital investment may facilitate innovation and the adoption of more advanced technologies. This amounts to studying the effects of capital accumulation on productivity, a direction of causation that is opposite to tracing the indirect effects of closing the productivity gap through factor accumulation. This analysis would answer the question of how far addressing distortions in capital accumulation would go in increasing income via its indirect effects on increased productivity (on top of the direct effects noted above). (These indirect effects would, of course, also take into account that increased productivity further boosts capital accumulation and so on.)

In the conservative scenario in which education is totally inelastic to increased returns, then policies successfully closing the education gap and eliminating the impediments to physical-capital accumulation (closing the capital-output gap) would reduce the 55 percent contribution of the productivity gap depicted in Figure 2.8 by only a third (of which only a third, or about 6 percent of income per capita, would be imputable to impediments to physical-capital investment). Therefore, two thirds of the productivity gap problem, what might be called the core productivity gap, would remain. The previous estimations are based on the calibrated model in Córdoba and Ripoll (2008). Extending this model to cover the alternative scenario in which education is elastic to income (see Daude and Fernández-Arias 2009) yields a revised decomposition in which the contribution of the productivity gap of 73 percent is marginally reduced to a core productivity gap of 58 percent. These results confirm that policies focused on shortcomings of factor accumulation are relevant but not decisive for addressing the productivity gap: the productivity gap is not the result of insufficient investment but, largely, of other, more specific productivity shortcomings.

Conclusions

Low and slow productivity as measured by TFP, rather than failures in factor accumulation, is the key to understanding Latin America's low income relative to developed economies and its stagnation relative to other developing countries that are catching up. Specific aspects of the problem are:

a) Slower growth in Latin America is due to slower productivity growth;
b) Latin America's productivity is not catching up with the frontier, in contrast to theory and evidence elsewhere; and
c) Latin America's productivity is about half its potential.

Higher productivity would entail not only a more efficient use of accumulated capital stocks, both physical and human, but also faster accumulation of these production factors in reaction to the increased returns prompted by the productivity boost. All things considered, closing the productivity gap with the frontier would actually close most of the income-per-capita gap with developed countries.

Therefore, the key to the economic development question in the region is how to close the productivity gap. The main development policy challenge in the region is to diagnose the causes of poor productivity and act on its roots. The analysis suggests that policies easing physical and human capital accumulation would help improve productivity but would leave untouched most of the productivity problem. Resolving the aggregate productivity issue will require specific productivity policies that address core defects. While impediments to technological improvement at the firm level is part of the problem, aggregate productivity depends on the efficiency with which private markets and public inputs support individual producers. Furthermore, firms' productivity is heterogeneous, meaning aggregate productivity also depends on the extent to which the workings of the economy allocate productive factors to the most productive firms. These considerations open up a rich agenda for productive development policies.

Notes

1. In this formulation, TFP would also reflect the natural resource base (natural capital) of each country. Resource-rich countries would tend to exhibit larger (but possibly less dynamic) measured TFP. Since Latin America is a resource-rich region, this observation implies that a symptom of low productivity would signal an even more serious ailment. (On the other hand, it could be argued that natural resources give rise to backward development and ultimately lower productivity [the "natural resource curse hypothesis"]; see Lederman and Maloney [2008] for a critical view of this hypothesis.) In any event, the weight of natural resources–based production in GDP is only significant in a few countries and should not distort the overall picture shown in this chapter.

2. The choice of measurement implies that an economy with higher structural unemployment is less productive because it wastes available resources.

3. To the extent that quality differences affect the education spectrum uniformly, the aggregative measure h would not be distorted and they would only be reflected in TFP differences.

4. The parameter f depends on the share of working-age population (a demographic factor) and the rate of its participation in the labor force.

5. Country TFP estimations may be subject to errors in measuring the underlying economic variables that would tend to be cancelled out in regional TFP estimations, for example, that of the typical country, which we regard as substantially more reliable.

6. The 18 Latin American and Caribbean countries included in the sample are Argentina, Bolivia, Brazil, Chile, Colombia, Costa Rica, the Dominican Republic, Ecuador, El Salvador, Honduras, Jamaica, Mexico, Nicaragua, Panama, Paraguay, Peru, Uruguay, and Venezuela.

7. The latter group of "twin" countries was constructed by selecting all countries in the sample whose 1960 income per capita fell in the interquartile range of Latin American countries (incomes within the second and third quartile).
The East Asian tigers are Hong Kong, Korea, Malaysia, Singapore, and Thailand; developed countries are Australia, Austria, Belgium, Canada, Denmark, Finland, France, Germany, Greece, Hungary, Ireland, Italy, Japan, Korea, Netherlands, New Zealand, Norway, Portugal, Spain, Sweden, the United Kingdom and the United States; twin countries are Algeria, Fiji, Greece, Hong Kong, Hungary, Iran, Japan, Jordan, Portugal, and Singapore; countries of the rest of the world include Benin, Cameroon, China, Egypt, Ghana, India, Indonesia, Israel, Kenya, Lesotho, Malawi, Mali, Mozambique, Nepal, Niger, Pakistan, Papua New Guinea, the Philippines, Senegal, Sierra Leone, South Africa, Sri Lanka, Syria, Thailand, Togo, Tunisia, Turkey, Uganda, and Zambia.

8. The growth rate of a variable x is denoted as $\hat{x}$.

9. In the sample, most of the variability in growth gaps in individual Latin American countries can be explained by their TFP growth gaps.

10. Not only stagnation but actual decline in some periods after 1980, possibly associated with the impact of the debt crisis (see Blyde, Daude, and Fernández-Arias 2009). Since technology only improves, it is noted in passing that a declining TFP over some periods reinforces the notion that it is only partially technologically determined.

11. It is true that a gap in the rate of factor accumulation with respect to the typical East Asian country was very important until about a decade ago, but this pattern is a peculiarity of East Asian development that need not suggest a Latin American weakness.

12. Estimations are as of 2005. Trend aggregate productivity, as measured here, is slow moving, and therefore 2005 estimates are applicable to the present.

13. Blyde and Fernández-Arias (2005) show that the use of employed labor instead of labor force to measure factor input makes little difference in Latin America. While the use of actual hours worked would be a more accurate measure of

labor input, data are not available for a large number of countries over a long period of time, limiting the possibility of a broad and structural comparison across countries. However, it is well known that such refinement does not substantially alter measured TFP (see Restuccia 2008).

14. In particular, they estimate a production possibility frontier using a Data Envelope Analysis (DEA) following Jermanowski (2007).
15. The decomposition method is explained in Box 2.2.
16. This process would, of course, take time; this analysis abstracts from transitional issues.
17. The attribution to the education gap also becomes relatively more important because its closing would have an additional indirect effect through increased physical capital accumulation.
18. Nevertheless, note that the subpar investment margin has been increasing since the 1980s.
19. Economic returns are clearly not the only motivation behind individual education decisions.
20. Both indirect effects would actually reinforce each other because of the complement between physical and human capital in the production function.
21. A complete decomposition would further recognize that labor force participation is also endogenous.
22. At the same time, the contribution of impediments to physical capital investment would amount to 14 percent.

3

Productivity in Latin America: The Challenge of the Service Sector

Since at least the 1950s, scholars have viewed development as a process of progressive transformation: economies based predominantly on traditional sectors, with "tradition" equated with agriculture, evolve toward economies dominated by modern sectors, often associated with industry.[1] This process of transformation is prompted by gains in agricultural productivity, which in turn encourages increasing numbers of agricultural workers to migrate to industries with higher productivity. Understanding shifting patterns across sectors, as well as the evolution of productivity within sectors, can yield important clues about the determinants of aggregate productivity.

Given this realization, it is unfortunate that the majority of productivity studies either work with aggregate macrodata, which by definition cannot assess productivity differences across different parts of the economy, or explore in great detail firm-level data for the industrial sector—a small and in many ways dwindling part of the economy.[2] This implies that most productivity studies miss something quite obvious but very important: aggregate productivity is the weighted average of the productivity of different parts of the economy (Lewis 2004). If a large part of the economy underperforms, so will aggregate productivity.

This chapter explores the productivity performance of different sectors of the economy in Latin America, both relative to each other and relative to the same sectors in the productivity frontier (taken to be the United States). Following the idea that productivity in the aggregate depends not only on the relative performance of some sectors but also on their size, this chapter explores how the changing size of different sectors has an increasing or decreasing weight on the performance of the whole. The good news is that labor productivity in agriculture is growing at a healthy rate. The bad news is that the dismal performance of the service sector—and within

---

Box 3.1   Sector-Level Data

Data on labor productivity at the sector level is obtained from a database recently produced by the Groningen Growth and Development Centre (GGDC) of the University of Groningen 10-Sector Database (Timmer and de Vries 2007). Ideally, TFP would be the measure of productivity, following the overall direction of this book. However, given the difficulty in finding data on human and physical capital at the sector level, the measure of productivity used throughout this chapter refers to labor productivity.

The data gathers information on gross domestic product (GDP) at constant national prices and total employment in ten economic sectors of nine Latin American economies for the 1950–2005 period. The countries covered by the data are Argentina, Bolivia, Brazil, Chile, Colombia, Costa Rica, Mexico, Peru, and Venezuela. The sectors are agriculture, hunting, forestry, and fishing; mining and quarrying; manufacturing; electricity, gas, and water; construction; wholesale and retail trade, restaurants, and hotels; transport, storage, and communication; finance, insurance, real estate, and business services; community and social and personal services; and government services. Sectors are often grouped in three larger categories: agriculture, hunting, forestry, and fishing; industry (grouping mining and quarrying; manufacturing; electricity, gas and water; and construction); and services (composed of the remaining sectors).

(continued on next page)

---

it, of large subsectors such as retail trade—are increasingly dragging down aggregate productivity. The implication is that while it is becoming commonplace to focus on upgrading the quantity and quality of exports as a growth strategy, improving the productivity of the large, nontradable service sectors could yield higher returns.

Good and Bad Performers at the Sector Level

The poor performance of aggregate productivity in Latin America described in Chapter 2 needs to be assessed at the sector level. Understanding the behavior of each of the parts helps identify which sectors of the economy are increasingly becoming roadblocks—and therefore where to focus policies aimed at improving productivity growth, which may differ at the industry level. Because of a lack of data about human and physical capital in sectors other than agriculture, this chapter will mainly focus on labor productivity instead of total factor productivity (TFP), the preferred measure of productivity used throughout this volume (see Box 3.1). As

(continued)

Data from the GDGC dataset are also available for a number of countries in East Asia (Indonesia, Japan, Malaysia, Singapore, South Korea, Taiwan, and Thailand) and Hong Kong, as well as for nine high-income economies (Denmark, France, Italy, Japan, the Netherlands, Spain, Sweden, the United Kingdom, and the United States). Data for East Asian and high-income countries cover the 1970–2005 period. The database is available at http://www.ggdc.net/databases/10_sector. htm.

Data to construct TFP measures in agriculture presented in Box 3.2 were collected principally from the Food and Agricultural Organization Corporate Statistical Database, FAOSTAT (http://faostat.fao.org), and cover a 40-year period from 1961 to 2001. The data includes 116 countries and covers three outputs (crops, ruminants, and nonruminants) and nine inputs (feed, animal stock, pasture, land under crops, fertilizer, tractors, milking machines, harvesters and threshers, and labor in agriculture). Crops include cereals, pulses, roots and tubers, and primary oil crops. Ruminants include bovine cattle, sheep, goats, and camelids (considering both meat and milk production). Nonruminants include pigs, poultry (chickens, ducks, geese, and turkeys), eggs, rabbits, rodents, honey, and cocoons. For further information, see Ludena et al. (2007).

mentioned in Chapter 2, the evolution of both variables differs in that TFP subtracts from labor productivity the contribution to growth that is due to an increasing accumulation of human and physical capital. This implies that some differences in productivity performance across sectors could be due to differences in capital accumulation—differences that, unfortunately, this chapter cannot distinguish from differences in sector efficiency.

Since the measure of productivity used in this chapter differs from that used in the rest of the volume, it is important first to assess how labor productivity has fared in the aggregate over the years. Just as with TFP, the performance of labor productivity has been disappointing in Latin America. After a period of relatively high growth from 1950 through 1975, labor productivity took a huge downturn during the lost decade of the 1980s and fell, in a period in which labor productivity in developed, high-income, and East Asian economies was expanding at 2.7 and 4.6 percent, respectively (Figure 3.1).

Labor productivity growth—hereafter referred to simply as *productivity growth*—returned to positive territory from the 1990s onward, with

Figure 3.1   Average Annual Labor Productivity Growth by Region and Period, 1950–2005 (percent)

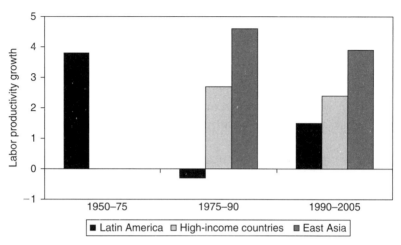

Source: Authors' calculations based on Timmer and de Vries (2007).

average growth rates of 1.5 percent. However, compared with other regions, productivity gains during the last 15 years have been below those of East Asia and high-income economies, which grew at almost 4 percent and 2.4 percent, respectively.

Are these patterns the same for the entire economy or do they differ by economic sector? The answer certainly is that they differ by sector. Some sectors in Latin America have done relatively well in terms of productivity growth, and have even outperformed similar sectors in other regions in some periods. This is the case for agricultural productivity, which has grown faster than other sectors in the economy (see Box 3.2). Moreover, in the most recent period—1990 to 2005—productivity growth in agriculture in Latin America exceeded that of East Asia and almost matched agricultural productivity growth in industrial countries (Figure 3.2).

While agriculture has been a relatively good performer, industry and services have been the great laggards. Latin America's productivity growth in these sectors grossly underperformed compared to East Asian and industrial countries. This was true during the 1980s, when productivity in industry and services in Latin America actually declined at a time when productivity in these sectors was growing fast in the rest of the world. It was true again during the 1990s and early years of the twenty-first century, when productivity growth rates were positive but below those of the other two comparator regions. The case of the service sectors is the

Figure 3.2   Average Annual Labor Productivity Growth in Agriculture, Industry, and Services, 1951–2005 (percent)

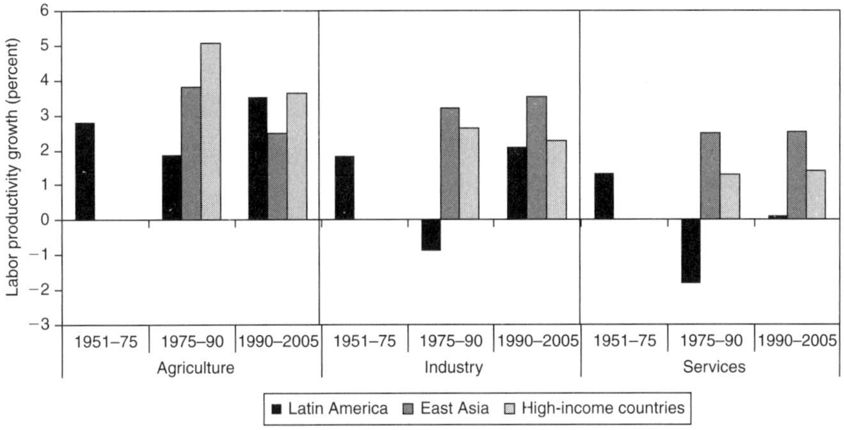

Source: Authors' calculations based on Timmer and de Vries (2007).

most dramatic. In this large part of the economy, productivity fell sharply during the 1980s and has remained stagnant for the last 15 years. The gap is large relative to East Asia, where productivity in services has grown by about 2.5 percent a year in the last 15 years, and also relative to high-income countries, where productivity in services has increased by about 1.4 percent a year.

A look into more disaggregated sector categories reveals similar patterns. Throughout the period, productivity has grown more in sectors where Latin America has a comparative advantage, such as agriculture and other primary activities as well as mining—all intensive in the use of natural resources, which Latin America has in abundance. Productivity in these sectors has expanded at around 3.5 percent per year in the most recent period (Figure 3.3).

Yet, the picture is grimmer in most categories of services, particularly for retail and wholesale trade; finance; community, personal, and government services; and transportation. Productivity growth is also low in construction, another important sector in all economies. The worst performers have been retail and wholesale trade and financial services. Productivity has declined even in the latter period of generally positive productivity growth in the rest of the economy. This implies that labor productivity in these sectors has deteriorated both during the 1980s and in the most recent years, illustrating how poorly services have performed in Latin America.

Figure 3.3   Average Labor Productivity Growth by Sector, Latin America, 1950–2005 (percent)

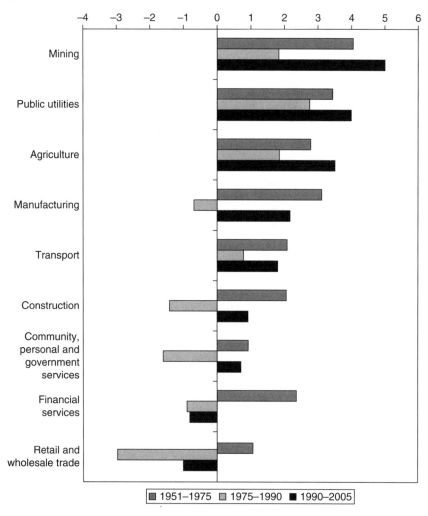

Source: Authors' calculations based on Timmer and de Vries (2007).

Patterns are similar across individual countries in Latin America (Figure 3.4). To a larger or smaller degree, all show positive productivity growth in agriculture in the most recent years. In addition, many of the mining-intensive countries show important gains in the mining sector. In keeping with the regional average, most countries—with the exception of Peru—show productivity losses in services, particularly in retail and wholesale trade and in the finance services sector.

The picture is extremely heterogeneous across sectors in a few countries. Bolivia, for example, experienced large productivity gains in mining

Figure 3.4   Average Annual Labor Productivity Growth by Sector, 1990–2005 (percent)

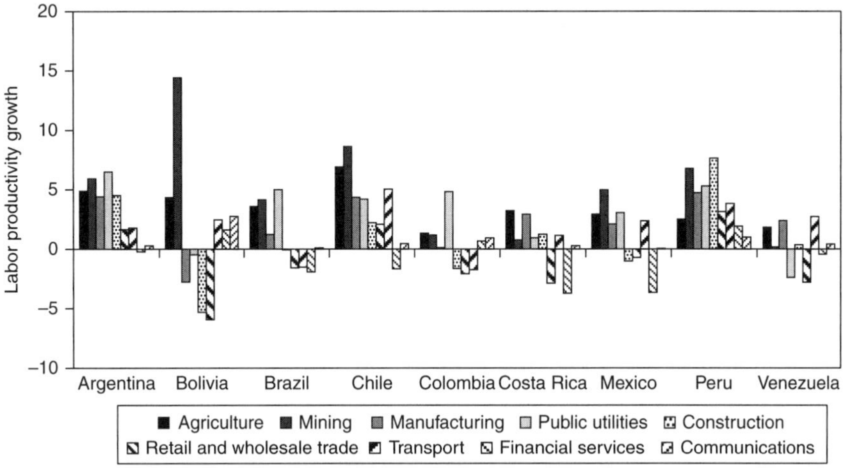

Source: Authors' calculations based on Timmer and de Vries (2007).

and agriculture from 1990 to 2005, but experienced large productivity losses in manufacturing, construction, and the trade sector.

Given this heterogeneous but overall disappointing performance, it is no surprise that across many sectors, labor productivity did not converge to the world frontier but rather declined in relative terms. Yet, comparing labor productivity in a sector across countries is notoriously difficult because of the lack of comparable (Power Purchase Parity [PPP] adjusted) sectoral output data across a large set of countries. Duarte and Restuccia (forthcoming) calibrate a model to measure sectoral productivity differences between each country and the United States. Their generated data is used here to show whether the productivity in different economic sectors in Latin America, as well as in East Asia and high-income countries, is converging to the productivity of those sectors in the United States. The good news is that in the last 30 years, agricultural productivity in the region has advanced considerably, from 25 percent of the productivity of the United States in 1973 to about 50 percent of U.S. levels in 2005 (Figure 3.5). Yet there is a long way to go to close the remaining gap.

The calculations in Duarte and Restuccia (forthcoming) indicate that, with the exception of Argentina, Colombia and Mexico, all countries have made advances to close the productivity gap in agriculture since 1973. Yet, the fact that these figures have been estimated based on a model, rather than on actual productivity yields across countries, may account for some of the variations in the evolution of productivity in this sector relative to those presented in Figure C (Box 3.2), based on yields across different

Figure 3.5   Evolution of Labor Productivity in Each Sector Relative to the United States, 1973–2004

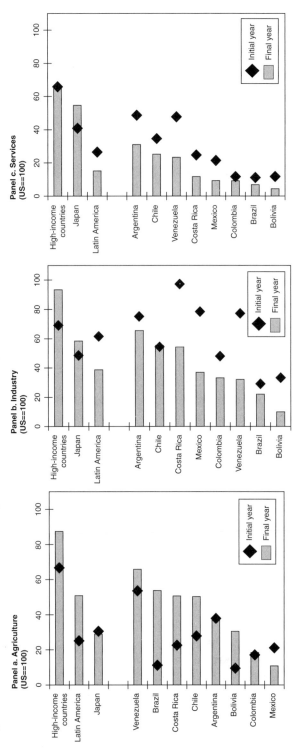

Source: Authors' calculations based on Duarte and Restuccia (forthcoming).

Box 3.2   Agriculture: The Productivity Star of Latin America?

Agricultural productivity is historically important, as it plays a key role in the process of industrialization and development. Countries whose trade and pricing policies create a strong bias against agriculture were unsuccessful in industrialization (Stern 1989; Krueger, Valdes, and Schiff 1991). Agricultural productivity improves broader economic growth through several transmission mechanisms, including the generation of additional demand for goods and services produced outside of agriculture, as income from agriculture increases; savings through increased farm incomes, which can then be invested in both agriculture and other sectors; release of labor to the industrial sector; provision of cheap food for urban areas, enabling them to maintain wage rates at competitive levels; and provision of raw materials to support industry (Timmer 2002; DFID 2005).

World TFP growth in agriculture averaged close to 1 percent a year during the 1961–2001 period (Figure A). Unlike in other sectors, measures of capital and other inputs used in the production of crops

Figure A   Annual Growth in TFP in Agriculture, 1961–2001 (percent)

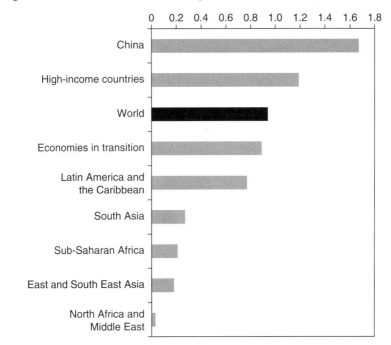

Source: Based on Ludena et al. (2007).

(continued on next page)

(continued)

and livestock are available for agriculture, and therefore (TFP) can be computed (see Ludena et al. 2007 for a description of how these TFP figures are computed).[a] Relative to other regions, Latin America and the Caribbean has experienced the highest growth rate in agricultural productivity among developing regions (except for China and economies in transition), at almost 0.8 percent a year. Growth rates in productivity in other regions such as Asia or Africa have been lower: almost four times less than the rate in Latin America and the Caribbean.

Despite the relatively good performance of agriculture relative to other sectors in Latin America and to other developing economies, there are important reasons not to be complacent. First, while labor productivity has grown faster in agriculture than in other sectors in Latin America, Duarte and Restuccia (forthcoming) find this pattern to hold across the large number of countries they examine. Thus, what matters for convergence to the frontier is not so much that agricultural productivity grows faster than in other sectors but the extent to which this happens in Latin America relative to the United States and other developed economies (see Martin and Mitra 2001 for a comparison of TFP growth in agriculture and manufacturing). Figures computed by Ludena et al. (2007) and Ludena (2009) and summarized in Figure A indicate that growth in agricultural TFP in Latin America was less than that of the world or the industrialized countries, which suggests that part of the labor productivity catch-up, documented in Figure 3.5, may be attributed to faster capital accumulation rates in this sector relative to the frontier.

Figure B Annual Growth in TFP, Technical Change, and Efficiency in Agriculture, Latin America, 1961–2007 (percent)

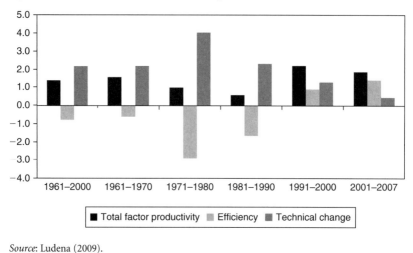

Source: Ludena (2009).

(continued on next page)

(continued)

Latin America's gains in agricultural productivity are associated mostly with powerful inventions like genetically modified crops (GMCs) that are resistant to herbicides or the use of global positioning systems (GPS) for fertilization and harvesting. These inventions were for the most part developed in high-income countries, but with important spillover effects in developing economies (Ludena et al. 2007). In contrast, efficiency changes—that is, whether the existing technology is used more efficiently irrespective of whether that technology is itself improving—have been negative from the 1960s through the 1980s although they have become positive in the last two decades (Figure B).

While total productivity growth has been highly heterogeneous across countries (Figure C), certain patterns are evident: countries

Figure C TFP Growth in Agriculture by Country, Latin America, 1961–2007 (percent)

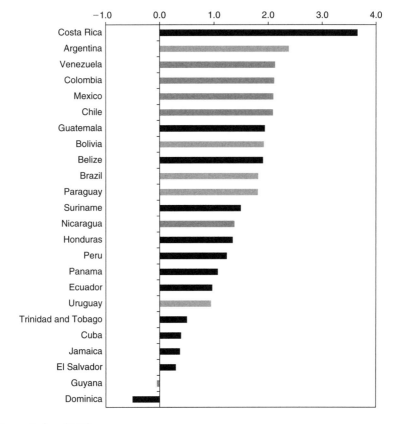

Source: Ludena (2009).

Note: Countries in gray are land-abundant countries (more than 12 hectares per laborer). Countries in black are land-constrained countries.

(continued on next page)

(continued)

with higher land availability have performed better than those with land limitations. Land-abundant countries (defined as those with 12 or more hectares per laborer) have grown at an annual average rate of 1.5 percent. With the exception of Costa Rica, countries with land constraints experienced lower average productivity growth rates, which suggests the importance of land availability and scale factors in agricultural productivity.

[a] Using a measure of TFP, Ludena et al. (2007) estimate productivity growth for agriculture from 1961 to 2001 for 116 countries around the world—including most Latin American and Caribbean countries—using a nonparametric Malmquist index (Färe et al. 1994) with data from FAO (2009). This is the most recent and complete analysis of agricultural productivity in the region. It not only analyzes sector-wide agricultural productivity, but also explores productivity growth at the sectoral level for both crops and livestock.

types of crops. In relative terms, Venezuela, Brazil, Costa Rica, and Chile show the highest levels of labor productivity in agriculture when compared to the United States. In contrast, Argentina, Bolivia, Colombia, and Mexico have the highest productivity gap in this sector; in addition, with the exception of Bolivia, they also have achieved the smallest gains during the last 30 years. For Argentina, low productivity growth was to blame during the 1980s, but this trend has been reversed during the most recent years (Figure 3.4).

Again, unsurprisingly, the bad news relates to the grim situation in the industrial and service sectors, although for different reasons. In the industrial sector, the picture is one of large relative decline (Figure 3.5, Panel b). Industrial labor productivity, which by 1973 was around 60 percent of that of the United States, had fallen to only 40 percent by 2004. In terms of individual countries, all lost ground relative to the industrial sector in the United States, with the exception of Chile. For some, losses have been huge. For example, while by 1973, Costa Rican industrial productivity was on a par with U.S. levels of efficiency, by 2004, labor productivity in this sector was only 54 percent that of the United States. Venezuela and Mexico suffered a similarly large decline during the same period, from around 80 percent to approximately 35 percent of the frontier efficiency.

In the service sector, the relative decline was lower, but given the low initial levels of productivity in that sector, the gap with the frontier is now huge. In 2004, services attained productivity levels of less than 15 percent of those of the United States (Figure 3.5, Panel c) This trend is shared by all Latin American countries since all experienced a relative decline in the service sector. Even in the countries with the highest relative efficiency, labor productivity in services is only 30 percent of that attained in the United States. In some countries (Mexico, Colombia, Brazil, and Bolivia), this figure is dismally low, standing at less than 10 percent of the frontier level.

Back to the Big Picture

As stated, aggregate (labor) productivity in the economy is just an average of the productivity in all sectors weighted by the share of employment in each sector. If some sectors perform poorly and they account for an important share of economic activity, their poor performance is bound to be reflected in the aggregate figures. The question then is one of magnitude. To what extent is the poor aggregate performance of the economy the consequence of the performance of specific sectors?

A very simple decomposition provides the first answer to the question of how sector productivity explains aggregate productivity. This decomposition makes use of the fact that the change in aggregate productivity in a given period can be decomposed into three terms. The first, known as the *within term*, captures how much of the change in aggregate productivity can be explained by the change in productivity within each sector (multiplied by the share of employment in each sector at the beginning of the period). The second term, known as the *between term*, captures the change in productivity associated with the reallocation of employment from low productivity to high productivity sectors (measured as the sum of the changes in the employment share multiplied by the initial level of productivity in each sector). The last term, known as the *cross term*, is an accounting term that reconciles growth in the aggregate with the *within* and *between* terms; it captures whether labor is reallocated to sectors that are growing in productivity.

The contribution of the different components of productivity growth has been uneven over the different periods. During the high-growth period of the 1950s and 1960s, growth was fueled by large within-sector gains but also, quite importantly, by large gains driven by the reallocation of workers from less to more productive sectors (*between* sectors) (Figure 3.6). The *cross term* was also positive, although minor compared to the other sources of productivity growth.

In contrast, during the lost decade of the 1980s, negative aggregate labor productivity gains were driven mostly by negative gains in productivity

Figure 3.6   Productivity Decomposition across Periods in Latin America, 1950–2005 (annual growth rates)

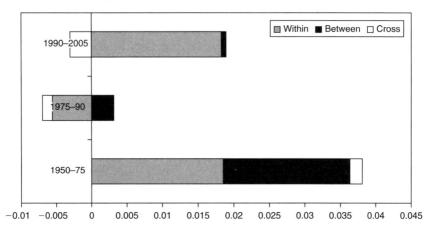

Source: Authors' calculations based on Timmer and de Vries (2007).

within most sectors, although this dismal picture was partly compensated by positive gains associated with reallocation across sectors. Fortunately, aggregate labor productivity growth resumed in the 1990s and early years of the twenty-first century, again fuelled by *within*-sector productivity growth. An important difference relative to the earlier period was the insignificant role played by reallocation across sectors in the latest period, a contribution that accounted for half the productivity growth during the period of higher growth.

These trends suggest that an important engine of growth during the early years of the sample has ceased to operate. This engine, known in the economic literature as *structural transformation,* is a well-known phenomenon in development economics. It refers to a situation observed in most countries in which labor is first reallocated, away from agriculture and toward the industrial sector, and later from the industrial sector to services. This process is triggered by the combination of faster productivity gains in agriculture than in other sectors with a tendency of people to spend less on food, relative to manufactured goods and services, as income rises. Gains in agricultural productivity make it possible to feed the population with a progressively smaller share of the labor force. Labor then reallocates to the industrial sector (and to cities) to meet the burgeoning demand for products other than foodstuffs. Finally, when productivity rises enough in the industrial sector (or if imports meet the internal demand for industrial goods), labor moves away from the industrial sector toward the service sector (Duarte and Restuccia forthcoming).

The reallocation of resources across sectors can have important consequences for aggregate productivity. As labor productivity tends to be higher in the industrial sector than in agriculture, shifts that favor the industrial sector can yield important productivity gains in the aggregate—which appear, in the former decomposition as reallocation gains. At later stages of the structural transformation, when labor moves from industry to services, productivity gains depend considerably on the productivity of the service sector relative to industrial sectors. Depending on the relative performance of the service and industrial sectors, the engine slows down and can even reverse if resources are shifted toward less productive sectors.

There are important differences in productivity levels across sectors. While labor productivity in the agricultural sector is slowly converging to the productivity in the industrial sector, the difference in labor productivity across the two sectors is still quite large (Figure 3.7). In contrast, average productivity of the service sector has been declining relative to productivity in industry. By 1962, average productivity in the service sector became roughly equal to productivity in the industrial sector (that is, productivity in services was 100 percent that of industry), only to start a long relative decline. By 2005, labor productivity in the service sector was only 60 percent of that in the industrial sector. While in principle, the productivity of workers who switch sectors may not be the same as the productivity of the average worker in each sector, calculations seeking to account for such

Figure 3.7   Evolution of Labor Productivity Relative to Industry, Latin America, 1950–2005 (industrial productivity 1950 = 100)

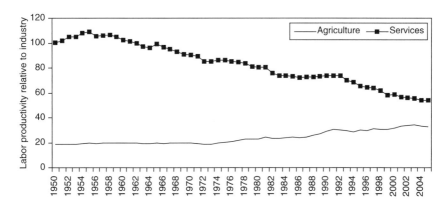

Source: Authors' calculations based on Timmer and de Vries (2007).

Notes: Unweighted average of Argentina, Bolivia, Brazil, Chile, Colombia, Costa Rica, Mexico, Peru, and Venezuela.

  Services comprise wholesale and retail trade, transport, finance, community services, and government services.

Figure 3.8   Productivity Growth Decomposition by Region, 1990–2005 (annual growth rates)

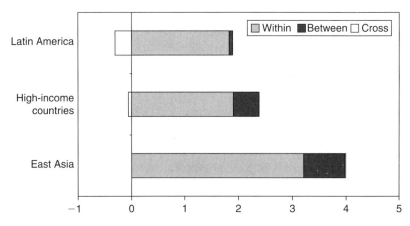

Source: Authors' calculations based on Timmer and de Vries (2007).

differences also indicate that the relevant productivities converged in the 1960s and have been diverging ever since.[3] This implies that until the 1960s, workers exiting agriculture and finding jobs in other sectors produced more on average than the workers left behind. Workers moving from industry to the service sector also produced more in their destination sectors. In this environment, reallocation was always productivity-enhancing.

Yet from the early 1960s onward, shifts from industry to services detracted from overall productivity. This sheds light on the causes of the declining power of reallocation as an engine of growth in the region, as well as on the increasing drag that services may be exerting on overall productivity growth.

These transformations have also been occurring in countries outside the region, but they seem to be faster and more productivity-detracting in Latin America than in East Asia or developed economies. Comparisons with these other regions confirm that Latin America gets less of a productivity boost from reallocation (Figure 3.8). In East Asia, reallocation brought as much as 0.8 percentage points of productivity growth per year during the 1990–2005 period. In developed countries, this contribution was lower, but still amounted to about 0.5 percentage points a year. In Latin America, this contribution was less than 0.1 percent.

Where Is Everyone?

Mapping out the share of workers employed in each sector in the region is the first step toward understanding how the process of productive transformation is operating in Latin America. The last 35 years have witnessed important changes in the allocation of employment. The share of employment in agriculture in Latin America has declined substantially from approximately 40 percent to about half that in the latest count (Figure 3.9). Such figures are still above those typical of the developed world, but below those observed in East Asia. This decline in agriculture's share of employment, plus the fact that Latin America has fewer workers in industry and more in services than East Asian countries, suggests that the region is further advanced in its structural transformation, a fact that has an enormous bearing on productivity trends. Quite remarkably, the share of industrial employment is lower in Latin America than in both East Asia and the developed world, a fact also noted in Pagés, Pierre, and Scarpetta (2009). In that study, the authors estimate whether employment in the manufacturing sector is statistically lower in Latin America than in the rest of the world at comparable levels of income and find evidence that this is the case, particularly for the 1970–1989 period. In contrast, East Asia now has a larger share of employment in industry than it had in the early 1970s. All this indicates that Latin America has passed through the middle stage of development, in which labor moves from agriculture to industry, faster than other economies. As a result, it now has a much higher share of resources allocated to services than East Asia. Thus, the performance of the service sector is of utmost importance for Latin America's aggregate productivity.

Within countries, there are important differences in the speed at which they have undergone the structural transformation and the extent of the productivity boost or knock they have received from this process. Countries such as Peru, Bolivia, and Colombia still have important stocks of workers in agriculture, with shares above 20 percent of the labor force. Therefore, they could still reap some dividends by shifting more resources toward other sectors. In terms of employment, the industrial sector in Latin America, with the exception of Mexico, Bolivia, and Costa Rica, now employs fewer people than it did in the early 1970s. In contrast, during the same period, employment in industry in East Asia has increased. At the other extreme, countries like Argentina, Chile, and Venezuela have very low shares of employment in agriculture and have already converged to a share of services that is close to the level in high-income economies, yet productivity in services relative to industry is quite low when compared to both developed and East Asian economies (Figure 3.9).

In sum, Latin American economies have shifted resources away from industry faster than other economies, even relative to countries with higher levels of development. At the same time, and perhaps for this reason, services are showing minimal gains in productivity. This suggests that, more and more, aggregate productivity trends depend on the performance of the service sector.

Figure 3.9 Share of Employment by Economic Sector, 1970–2005

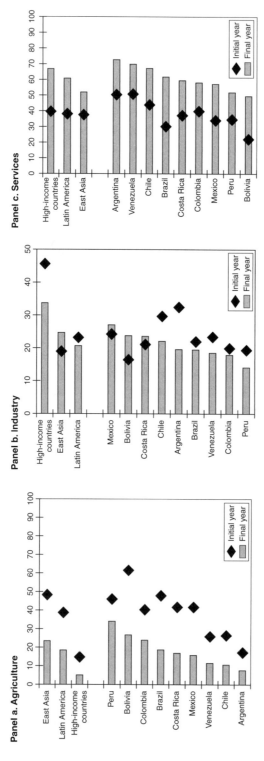

Source: Authors' calculations based on Timmer and de Vries (2007).

Note: High-income countries are Denmark, France, Italy, Japan, the Netherlands, Spain, Sweden, the United Kingdom, and the United States. East Asia is Hong Kong, Indonesia, Korea, Malaysia (1972), the Philippines, Singapore, Taiwan, and Thailand. Bolivia's data are from 2003.

Place the Blame on Services

Contrary to common belief, today the performance of the service sector matters more than the performance of the industrial sector for aggregate productivity. If industrial productivity in Latin America had grown at the rate it did in East Asia during the 1990–2005 period, annual aggregate labor productivity growth in Latin America would have increased from 1.5 percent to 1.8 percent a year, hardly a pathbreaking change. Instead, if labor productivity growth in services had matched the rate in East Asian countries, productivity growth would have risen to 3.1 percent a year, or approximately twice as much.[4]

The calculations discussed above do not take into account the possible reallocation effects that changes in productivity in the industry or service sector might bring about, or their further implications for productivity. In terms of the decompositions presented above, the counterfactual calculations are made under the simplifying assumption that changes in sector productivity change *within* effects only; they do not induce additional changes in *between* effects caused by further adjustments in employment allocation resulting from the assumed changes in productivity. To account for all these additional effects, estimates based on a general equilibrium model are required. Duarte and Restuccia (forthcoming) do so, and their results are similar to the ones presented herein, suggesting that in this particular case the reallocation effects induced by differences in productivity growth would be quite small.[5]

Duarte and Restuccia also present some additional and powerful insights. They find that in a large sample of countries spanning the 1973–2004 period, rapid productivity growth in the industrial sector explains all episodes of aggregate catch-up with the United States. This is particularly true during the earlier years of the sample, when industrial employment had a higher weight. On the other hand, low labor productivity in services explains all the experiences of slowdown, stagnation, and decline in relative aggregate productivity between individual countries and the United States.

The importance of the service sector resides in its sheer volume. In comparison, rapid productivity growth in agriculture, while important, delivers smaller effects in the aggregate due to the relatively smaller size of the agricultural sector. Duarte and Restuccia also find that the effects of productivity growth in agriculture are dampened by the increased reallocation of labor away from agriculture that tends to accompany such increases in productivity. Nonetheless, faster growth in agricultural productivity could bring sizeable effects for some countries, such as Colombia and Peru, due to their relatively large agricultural sectors with relatively low productivity.

Services are also key elements for productivity growth in developed countries. Farrell (2006) summarizes a series of studies produced by the McKinsey Global Institute on productivity and states that the primary source of the productivity acceleration of the 1990s was not due to information technology, as has often been affirmed. Instead, she traces productivity growth to the performance of six sectors of the economy (wholesale trade, retail trade, securities, semiconductors, computer manufacturing, and telecommunications), of which four are in the service sector. Moreover, the recent stagnation in labor productivity of many European countries relative to the United States is associated with the failure of the service sector to catch up with productivity in the United States (see Duarte and Restuccia forthcoming).

Latin America has a lower share of employment in the industrial sector than either East Asia or developed countries. While it may be argued that East Asia has a comparative advantage in industry or that it is less advanced in the process of structural transformation, it is more difficult to explain why Latin America has less industrial employment than the high-income countries, which arguably are more advanced in structural transformation and have higher costs of labor.

A number of possible explanations may account for this more rapid decline in the share of industrial employment in Latin America. An obvious reason is that as productivity growth in the service sector has been low, more service-sector workers are needed to produce a given bundle of goods and services in Latin America relative to other regions.

Government policies that increase capital costs may also induce a faster reallocation of employment toward services, which are more intensive in labor and less intensive in capital. This is the answer proposed by Neumeyer and Hopenhayn (2004) to explain the rapid reallocation of employment toward services in Argentina during the 1975–1990 period. The authors build a theoretical model in which the increase in the cost of capital accounts for this reallocation of employment. They argue that a number of factors contributed to increasing capital costs in that period. First, a default on international debt led to higher interest rates. Second, higher tariffs and import quotas also played a role in making capital imports more costly. Finally, uncertainty over the continuation of protection led to investment uncertainty, as firms were weary of sinking resources into capital-intensive sectors that could become less profitable if protection was lifted.

Trade liberalization during the 1990s is another factor frequently blamed for the reduction of industrial employment in Latin America. In a relatively short span of time governments substantially lifted restrictions on international trade. Reforms were deep and encompassed all countries.

Not only were trade tariffs substantially reduced but the dispersion across products and sectors was practically eliminated. This far-reaching process of reform hit the industrial sector particularly hard, as protection had led many firms to continue comfortably with the status quo and undertake few productivity upgrades. As competition increased with openness, many firms restructured and improved their productivity, but many also had to downsize or close. There is some evidence that the reduction in tariffs led to a decline in industrial employment (Revenga 1997; Haltiwanger et al. 2004). Overall, however, the effects directly attributable to trade do not seem to be that large, although small open economies may be an exception, given the relatively larger effects found on industrial employment in Uruguay (Casacuberta, Fachola, and Gandelman 2004).

Shortcomings in the business environment and costly regulations and taxes may also hit the industrial sector harder than other sectors. In particular, economies of scale in the production of certain goods may indicate that the optimal scale of production is larger in industry; this implies that it is more difficult for the industrial than the service sector to operate below the radar of authorities, avoiding taxes and regulations. This factor could explain the much larger share of informal activities or the smaller size of establishments in services (Chapter 4). All these factors would bias firm creation and employment allocation toward the service sector.

A large migration of workers from industry to services may in turn explain why labor productivity in the service sector has increased by so little. If better opportunities are lacking, and workers are forced to create their own jobs in service activities that have low entry costs and low productivity, aggregate productivity will decline. The evidence indicates that firms created due to necessity rather than as a result of an entrepreneurial drive tend to be of lower productivity and invest less in productivity upgrades or worker training (Carpio and Pagés 2009). In part, this lower investment rate may be associated with lower access to credit, as firms that operate informally (that is, those that are not officially registered and do not pay taxes) tend to have lower access to formal credit markets.

Yet, quite importantly, a large share of firms operating below the government's radar may also deter the entry of high productivity firms in the service sector. Even when high-productivity firms can produce goods at a lower cost and sell them at a lower price than informal firms, the latter can enjoy a cost advantage due to tax and regulatory evasion. The cost advantage gained in this fashion can amount to a quite significant share of costs and profits and can prevent more productive, formal firms from entering the market and/or gaining market share. This in turn results in low productivity, low-paid jobs, and poorer work conditions in the service sector. A large share of informality may not only be a consequence of low productivity growth, but it may also, to a large extent, be a driver of the low growth of productivity in Latin America's service sector.

Last but not least, it is important to consider the potential externalities that the service sector generates in the rest of the economy. A more efficient distribution of goods and services due to more efficient transportation, communication, and retail and wholesale trade activities improves the productivity of agricultural and industrial activities (Chapter 5). The fact that Latin America suffers from low and stagnant productivity in these key sectors has much to do with the low productivity growth of industrial activities. In fact, high transportation costs have effects similar to tariffs in reducing a firm's productivity (see Chapter 5).

Could the region reindustrialize itself again? The rising number of middle class citizens with deeper pockets and increasingly more sophisticated consumption habits in countries like India and China offer valuable opportunities for growth of the industrial sector. Finding these opportunities will require much ingenuity on the part of entrepreneurs; but it will also require well-designed public policies that help coordinate actors, promote the search for potentially successful niches, breach coordination failures, and provide essential public goods in the areas of opportunity (see Chapter 11). It will also require reducing domestic and international transportation costs, so that the geographic location of the region far from emerging markets in Asia does not reduce this opportunity. This will entail more investments in infrastructure, but also, very importantly, greater efficiency of the service sector. At the end of the day, much of the success of the industrial sector will boil down to better logistics, ports, airports, communications, and transportation.

Conclusion

It has become commonplace to focus on boosting exports and improving the quality of tradable goods as a strategy to improve competitiveness and income levels. However, the analysis presented in this chapter suggests that increasing productivity in the service sector is key to increasing aggregate productivity in economies with large tertiary sectors.[6] Latin America has already joined this group, and unless it manages to propel productivity in vast sectors of the economy, productivity levels relative to the United States and other developed countries will continue to decline. The outlook is brighter in the agricultural sector, but its declining weight as a share of overall economic activity implies that its importance as a source of aggregate productivity gains is fast declining. While much more work is required to understand the poor performance of services in the region, this volume advances some hypotheses that will be explored in the chapters that follow. Chief among them is that high rates of informality are shielding small firms—the vast majority of which are very inefficient—from the competition of better, more productive business models. In addition, insufficient competition and lack of appropriate regulations in ports and airports, and traffic congestion in large cities, make transportation inefficient and costly, with effects reverberating across the entire economy.

Notes

1. See, for example, Lewis (1954).
2. A notable exception is the series of studies by the McKinsey Global Institute on a number of different economic sectors for quite a large set of countries. The series is summarized in Lewis (2004) and Farrell (2006).
3. In the jargon of economists, marginal products may be different than average products. Assuming a Cobb-Douglas production function and constant returns to scale, computing labor shares from national accounts for each sector allows marginal products to be computed in manufacturing and services. Such calculations indicate that marginal products became equal around 1970. From then on, marginal products in services have consistently declined relative to marginal products in manufacturing.
4. The authors' calculations were estimated using the decompositions mentioned above—in which aggregate productivity growth is decomposed into *within*, *between,* and *cross* terms—and, in the *within* term, substituting the growth in manufacturing or services in Latin America with growth in these sectors in East Asia, while keeping the *between* and *cross* terms unchanged.
5. Duarte and Restuccia (forthcoming) find these induced reallocation effects to be quite important in some of their contrafactual exercises—particularly when simulating different rates of growth in agriculture—thus showing the importance of building and employing a general equilibrium model in order to correctly account for these effects.
6. The tertiary sector is the service sector.

4

Productivity from the Bottom Up: Firms and Resource Allocation in Latin America

Consider a leading sports team. To succeed, it must be staffed with good players and they must be placed in the right positions. Just like a successful sports team, the productivity of an economy depends on two basic factors: the productivity of its firms (the players) and the allocation of its available resources (labor and capital) among its firms (the positions). And just as a team full of stars can play poorly if players are assigned to the wrong positions, aggregate productivity depends on much more than the productivity of individual firms. Of course, it would be difficult to put together a successful team—or economy—with weak or inexperienced players.

The findings presented in this chapter suggest that, first, the quality of players in Latin America varies widely, with a few very productive firms and many firms of extremely low productivity. If anything, the region suffers from a deficit of firms with medium levels of productivity. There is also a strong relationship between productivity and size: the more productive firms tend to be larger. This implies that many resources are locked up in very small—often one-person—firms, of very low productivity. If Latin American countries had the same share of medium and high productivity firms as the United States, the region's productivity and gross domestic product (GDP) would nearly double. In contrast, attempting to increase aggregate productivity by increasing the productivity of the weakest and smallest firms would seemingly yield very low returns in terms of aggregate productivity unless somehow, enormous increases in the productivity of the weakest firms could be attained.

Second, not only is Latin America a region of mostly weak players, but it also makes poor use of existing resources (labor and capital). With existing technologies, productivity and GDP in the region could grow at a rate of 40–60 percent depending on the country, simply by reassigning labor and capital more efficiently across existing firms.

The great dispersion in firms' productivity and the inefficient use of available resources prompts a number of questions. What explains the low proportion of firms with medium levels of productivity? How can highly efficient firms coexist with firms that are much less efficient at producing similar goods? How could the region make better use of existing resources? What is the role of market and government failures in explaining productivity and resource allocation across Latin American firms?

Productivity beyond Technology

Typically, economists estimate aggregate productivity growth as the portion of GDP growth that cannot be explained by either the accumulation of physical and human capital or the growth of employment. This unexplained portion reflects how well countries are able to extract more output out of a given set of inputs. However, since this method calculates productivity as a residual, productivity becomes—in Robert Solow's words, "a measure of our ignorance." Since Solow's seminal work fifty years ago, this residual has often been treated as a measure of technology, with technological change considered the main determinant of productivity growth.

In recent years, however, a number of new studies, mostly for developed economies, are beginning to look beyond aggregated figures to better understand what drives this residual. Using microdata from individual establishments, this research has shown that behind the aggregate figures of productivity lies a wide dispersion in productivity levels across firms, even within narrowly defined industries producing rather homogenous goods (Eslava et al. 2004; Foster, Haltiwanger, and Syverson 2008; and Syverson 2004, 2008). This implies that low productivity countries may have firms that manage to achieve levels of efficiency comparable or close to those of the world frontier in that industry. Indeed, the heterogeneity of productivity within each country is much greater than the dispersion in productivity across poor and rich countries (Banerjee and Duflo 2005).

The wide dispersion in firms' productivity prompts a number of new insights. The most obvious one is that since aggregate productivity is given by the average productivity of all firms weighted by firms' size, low productivity economies are those in which there are either a large number of low productivity firms, or for some reason, high productivity firms are small, and thus they have little weight in the aggregate. This in turn raises the question of what determines the mix of firms that operate in an economy, the productivity of each firm, and the firm's size, given its productivity.

Each of these factors can be altered by market and policy failures in ways that reduce productivity. Thus, how to explain that highly efficient firms can coexist with much less efficient firms producing a similar good? What allows low productivity firms to survive? If policies distort which firms operate in the market, and either promote the survival of poorly performing firms or the exit of more efficient ones, then the performance of the economy will suffer due to the poor quality of existing firms.

Policy or market failures can also affect aggregate productivity by altering the relative size of firms within a sector: for example, by helping low productivity firms gain market share, or preventing productive firms from gaining it. If say, directed credit policies allocate credit to firms in which additional capital yields low revenues, and deny credit to firms in which additional capital could yield very high revenues, aggregate productivity suffers because productive firms are too small, and unproductive firms are too large. In this environment, two types of policy actions increase productivity: those that help expand the size of firms in which resources yield high returns; and those that take resources away from firms in which resources yield low returns. Both these strategies increase the aggregate production that can be attained with exactly the same technologies and the same amount of capital and labor.

Therefore, quite importantly, when the allocation of resources is distorted, potentially large gains in productivity can be achieved simply by making the appropriate policy changes and without having to invest in more resources or improve the technologies of firms. As discussed below, resource misallocation (the poor use of existing resources) is much more pervasive in developing countries. Thus, while developed countries need to rely mostly on innovation and technology improvements to achieve productivity gains, developing countries can boost productivity enormously by enacting policies that improve the use of existing resources and promote greater competition among firms. Of course, such a process of economic transformation is not free of cost. Labor and capital reallocation is costly in that it may be accompanied by important social friction and welfare costs. Finding ways to compensate those who stand to lose from such policies can bring important overall gains.

All this is not to imply that innovation and technology adoption are not important sources of productivity growth in developing countries (see Chapter 10 for more on this subject). It simply means that low-income economies are low-income in part precisely because of the presence of a large number of distortions that prevent the optimal use of existing resources. Therefore, in addition to increasing the productivity of each firm by promoting innovation and technology adoption policies, other potential sources of growth are available to developing countries and should be considered and tried, if appropriate. More importantly, part of the disparity in income between richer and poorer countries can be explained by the presence of these distortions and the accompanying misallocation of resources. Therefore, enacting the right policies and correcting for important market failures can help bridge the productivity gap between Latin America and the frontier.

The Productivity of Latin American Firms

The Region: More Unequal in Productivity

As is well known, Latin America suffers the greatest income inequality in the world. The region also displays a great deal of inequality in productivity, even within narrowly defined economic sectors (Figure 4.1). Productivity is measured as total factor productivity (TFP), as computed in Hsieh and Klenow (forthcoming) (see Box 4.1).[1]

While all countries experience some degree of productivity inequality, the dispersion appears to be greater in Latin America than in the United States or China. In Colombia and Venezuela, firms in the 90th percentile of productivity are more than 500 percent more productive than firms in the 10th percentile, while in the rest of the countries this difference is on the order of 300 percent, and in the United States it is of 200 percent.[2] However, caution should be applied in making country comparisons, as data coverage varies across countries and dispersion measures are sensitive to the sample used. In the United States, data cover all establishments of one or more employees; in China, establishments with sales above US$600,000 per year; and in Latin America, establishments with ten employees or more. Figures for all Latin American manufacturing establishments, for those countries where such figures are available (Mexico and El Salvador), also suggest more dispersion in productivity in Latin America than in the United States.[3]

Against these large differences, productivity differentials across countries pale in comparison. For example, TFP in the United States is double that of Latin America, a much smaller differential than what is observed across firms within a given country and economic sector.

This large dispersion implies that, within fairly narrowly defined industries, certain firms are able to squeeze much more output out of the same amount of inputs than others. This disparity may be due to extreme variations in the processes and technologies used by firms to produce and compete in the same industry, or could be related to differences in

Figure 4.1   Productivity Dispersion in Manufacturing Firms, Selected Countries

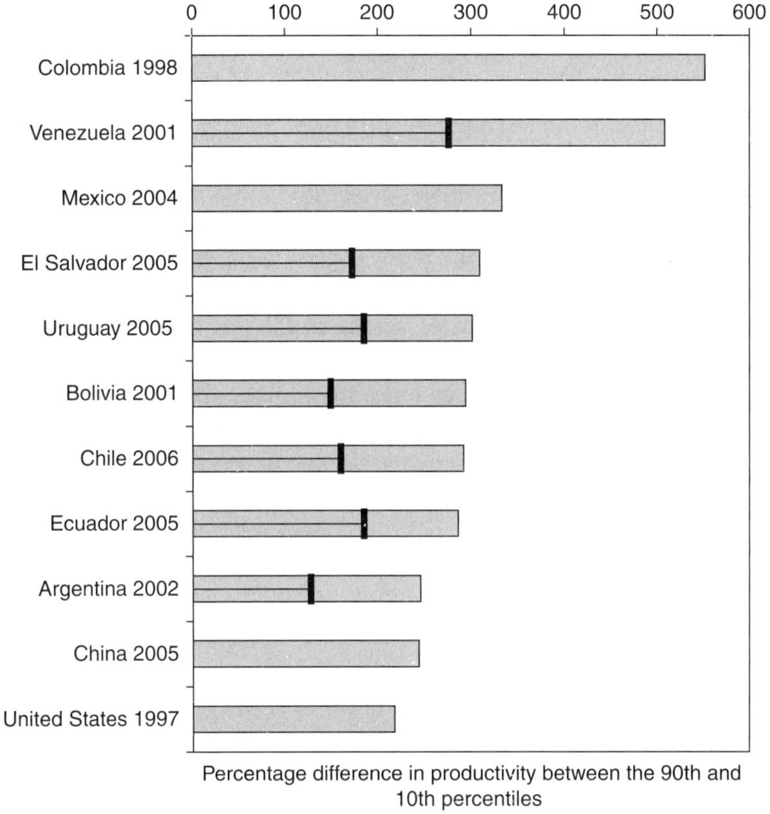

Percentage difference in productivity between the 90th and
10th percentiles

Sources: Argentina, Neumeyer and Sandleris (2009); Bolivia, Machicado and Birbuet (2009); Chile, Busso, Madrigal, and Pagés (2009a,b); Colombia, Camacho and Conover (2009); Ecuador, Arellano (2009); El Salvador, Atal, Busso, and Cisneros (2009); Mexico, authors' calculations based on 2004 Census data; Uruguay, Casacuberta and Gandelman (2009), Venezuela, authors' calculations based on Venezuelan Annual Industrial Survey, INE (2001); China and the United States, Hsieh and Klenow (forthcoming).

Note: Figures are for establishments with ten or more employees, except in China, which covers plants with sales above US$600,000 and the United States, where all establishments of one or more employees are covered.

The lines inside the bars represent the percentage difference in productivity between the 50th and the 10th percentiles of the productivity distribution.

the human capital or managerial skill of the managers/owners of firms.[4] Carpio and Pagés (2009) find some evidence for the latter in a sample of microenterprises in Brazil, since they find a strong relation between the education of the owner and the TFP of a firm. Also, this extreme heterogeneity is driven by the distance between the best and the median firms, and more importantly, by the difference between the firms with median productivity and the lowest productivity firms (see lines within the bars in

---

Box 4.1   Data Matters

Results presented in this chapter are based on a series of country studies analyzing establishment-level data produced by individual country statistical offices. Unfortunately, only a subsample of countries in the region collects these data, and of those, even a smaller number make these data available to researchers. Despite such constraints, data for ten Latin American countries has been assembled, and the authors of this chapter are grateful to the many individual researchers who participated in this endeavor.

The coverage of data varies across countries, but in general, they constitute censuses of the largest, formally established firms, with a random sample of the smaller ones. In all cases, the data have a longitudinal component, allowing individual establishments to be followed over time (at least in the census part of the data). The datasets are representative at the national level and span a period of nearly ten years. In most cases, coverage is restricted to the manufacturing sector, although in Mexico and Uruguay, data coverage extends beyond manufacturing to other economic sectors.

The data have been processed with the objective of insuring cross-country comparability. Notably, the analysis was restricted to firms with ten or more employees, since in many countries, the sample frame covers only this subset of firms. When available, information on how indicators change when the smallest firms are added is also provided. In all countries, industries were defined at the four-digit level of disaggregation in the International Standard Industrial Classification (ISIC). Productivity measures are defined as TFP at the establishment level, as computed in Hsieh and Klenow (forthcoming).

Figure 4.1 presenting the percentage difference in productivity difference between the median and the 10th lowest percentile of productivity). This indicates that heterogeneity is greater at the lower end of the distribution due to the presence of very unproductive firms (this is shown by the fact that the distance between the productivity at the 10th lowest percentile and at the median—marked with a line inside the bar in Figure 4.1—is higher than the distance between the 50th and the 90th—which is given by the rest of the bar not marked with a line).

Differences in productivity within narrowly defined industries appear to be much higher in nonmanufacturing sectors. While such data are available only for Mexico and Uruguay, in both countries, differences in productivity across firms are much higher in the service sector, particularly in communication and transportation in Uruguay, and in retail in Mexico.[5]

The relevant question—to be addressed at the end of the chapter—is what drives such extensive heterogeneity and, more importantly, the predominance of very unproductive firms, particularly in the service sector.

Small in Productivity and Size

Firms that are more productive than their competitors should win market share over time, hiring more labor and capital and expanding their production. This implies, that in a well-functioning economy, firm size (measured either by value added, employment, or assets) should be positively correlated with firm productivity.[6] The evidence strongly indicates the presence of a positive relationship between productivity and size. Compared to manufacturing firms employing 10–19 workers, manufacturing firms in the 20–49 range are about 50 percent more productive. Productivity more than doubles in firms of more than 100 workers. In Bolivia, Venezuela, and El Salvador, productivity in the largest firms is about 150 percent higher than for firms in the 10–19 worker category (Figure 4.2). Productivity indicators for the smallest firms are difficult to come by, as few establishment-level datasets cover the whole spectrum of firms (see Box 4.1).

Notwithstanding the strong relationship between firm size and productivity, there is much heterogeneity, even among manufacturing firms of roughly the same size, as highlighted in Figure 4.3 for Mexico (Panel a)

Figure 4.2   Productivity by Firm Size Relative to Firms with 10–19 Workers, Manufacturing Establishments

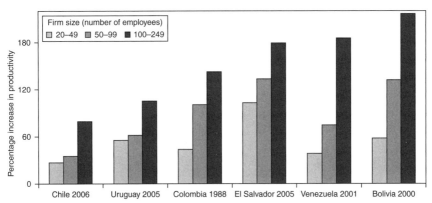

Sources: Bolivia, Machicado and Birbuet (2009); Chile, Busso, Madrigal, and Pagés (2009a,b); Colombia, Camacho and Conover (2009); El Salvador, Atal, Busso, and Cisneros (2009); Uruguay, Casacuberta and Gandelman (2009), Venezuela, authors' calculations based on Venezuelan Annual Industrial Survey, INE (2001).

Note: See notes in Figure 4.1.

Figure 4.3 Distribution of Firm Productivity in Mexico and El Salvador. All Manufacturing Establishments

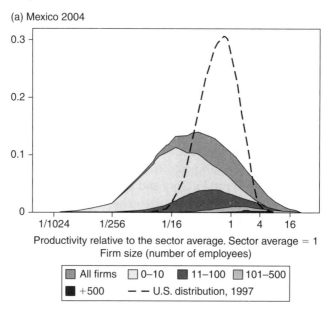

(a) Mexico 2004

Productivity relative to the sector average. Sector average = 1
Firm size (number of employees)

All firms | 0–10 | 11–100 | 101–500
+500 | – – U.S. distribution, 1997

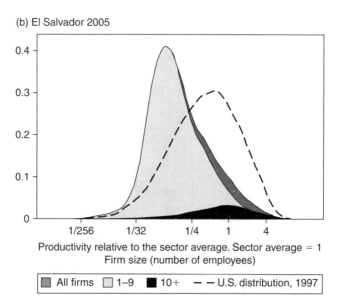

(b) El Salvador 2005

Productivity relative to the sector average. Sector average = 1
Firm size (number of employees)

All firms | 1–9 | 10+ | – – U.S. distribution, 1997

Source: El Salvador: Atal, Busso, and Cisneros (2009). Mexico: INEGI (2004, 2005).

Note: Productivity measured as a fraction of each industry average. Industries defined at four digits of disaggregation.

and El Salvador (Panel b), the only countries in Latin America for which data for manufacturing firms were available to the authors. Among small firms, some are quite productive relative to the industry average—particularly in Mexico. Among large firms, some are quite unproductive, again relative to the relevant sector average. Yet the low tail of the distribution of productivities is dominated by small firms, suggesting that part of the problem of low productivity in Latin America may be associated with the inordinate weight of small, unproductive firms.

Comparisons with the United States also give some credence to the "missing middle" hypothesis. It is quite noticeable that in both Mexico and El Salvador, there are many more manufacturing firms at the lower end of the distribution of productivity, and fewer around the average (with a productivity relative to the average of their sector equal to 1) compared to the United States (dotted line in Figure 4.3). This is particularly clear in Mexico, where the share of high productivity firms relative to the average is higher than in the United States. In El Salvador, medium and high productivity firms are missing.

A Region of Small Firms

The evidence also reveals that Latin America is a region of very small firms, compared to the United States.[7] When comparing the subsample of manufacturing establishments with ten or more workers, the size distribution of firms across Latin American countries and the United States is quite similar. Only in Bolivia, Argentina, Mexico, and El Salvador is the share of small establishments (10–49 workers) larger than in the United States, while in five countries in Latin America this share appears to be at similar levels or lower (Table 4.1).

Differences across Latin America and the United States appear starker once the smallest firms are also considered. Data for manufacturing, including microestablishments (consisting of fewer than ten workers), suggest a much larger share of the smallest firms in Latin America. In Mexico and Bolivia, 91 percent of manufacturing establishments employ fewer than ten workers. These figures are lower in Argentina or El Salvador, but still considerably above the percentage of microfirms in the United States (Table 4.2).

The share of employment for very small firms is considerably larger in Latin America than in the United States at about 43 percent of manufacturing employment in Bolivia and around 20 percent in Argentina, El Salvador, and Mexico compared to a mere 4.2 percent in the United States.

Table 4.1 Distribution of Firms and Employment in Manufacturing by Firm-Size Category, Firms with Ten or More Employees (percent)

Firm size	Argentina (1993)		Bolivia (1992)		Chile (2006)		Colombia (1998)		Ecuador (2005)	
	Firms	Employment	Firms	Employment	Firms	Employment	Firms	Employment	Firms	Employment
[10–19]	56.9	17.2	51.3	17.7	26.8	4.0	28.7	4.56	30.3	3.9
[20–49]	21.6	14.4	31.6	24.0	34.3	10.6	31.6	11.07	31.2	8.9
[50–99]	15.4	24.3	9.9	17.5	17.3	12.3	18.2	14.49	16.0	10.2
[100–249]	2.9	10.6	7.2	40.8	12.5	19.8	13.9	24.48	13.4	19.8
[250+]	3.3	33.5			9.2	53.3	7.6	45.4	9.1	57.3

Firm size	El Salvador (2005)		Mexico (2004)		Uruguay (2005)		Venezuela (2001)		United States (2005)	
	Firms	Employment	Firms	Employment	Firms	Employment	Firms	Employment	Firms	Employment
[10–19]	40.8	8.1	44.3	7.1	15.4	2.1	16.5	1.5	31.9	5.0
[20–49]	29.4	13.4	28.1	10.4	34.9	11.2	25.3	5.2	32.4	11.5
[50–99]	14.3	15.0	11.4	9.7	23.4	16.0	15.9	7.0	16.2	12.9
[100–249]	9.5	23.0	9.3	17.3	17.5	25.2	25.1	26.9	12.8	22.2
[250+]	6.0	40.5	6.9	55.5	8.8	45.5	17.3	59.4	6.8	48.4

Sources: Argentina, Neumeyer and Sandleris (2009); Bolivia, Machicado and Birbuet (2009); Chile, Busso, Madrigal, and Pagés (2009a); Colombia, Camacho and Conover (2009); Ecuador, Arellano (2009); El Salvador, Atal, Busso, and Cisneros (2009); Mexico, Hsieh and Klenow (2009); Uruguay, Casacuberta and Gandelman (2009); Venezuela, authors' calculations based on Venezuelan Annual Industrial Survey, INE (2001); United States, BLS (2005).

Note: Categories of firm size in Argentina are: 11–25, 26–40, 41–50, 51–150, 250+.

Table 4.2   Distribution of Firms and Employment in Manufacturing by Firm Size Category, All Manufacturing Firms (percentage)

Firm Size	Argentina (1994)		Bolivia (1992)		El Salvador (2005)	
	Firms	Employment	Firms	Employment	Firms	Employment
[1–9]	84.0	22	91.7	43.6	82.0	17.7
[10–19]	12.9	25	4.2	10.0	8.3	6.2
[20–49]	2.5	19	2.6	13.6	3.9	6.2
[50–99]	0.8	35	0.8	9.8	2.8	10.2
[100+]	0.2	18	0.6	23.0	2.9	59.7

Firm Size	Mexico (2004)		United States (2005)	
	Firms	Employment	Firms	Employment
[1–9]	90.5	22.7	54.5	4.2
[10–19]	4.2	5.5	14.5	4.8
[20–49]	2.7	8	14.7	11
[50–99]	1.1	7.5	7.4	12.3
[100+]	1.6	56.3	8.9	67.7

Source: Argentina, Neumeyer and Sandleris (2009); Bolivia, Machicado and Birbuet (2009); El Salvador, Atal, Busso, and Cisneros (2009); Mexico, Hsieh and Klenow (2009); and United States, BLS (2005).

Note: Categories of firm size in Argentina are: 11–25, 26–40, 41–50, 51–150, 250+.

While very few countries have data for all sectors of the economy, data, when available, suggest that the percentage of microenterprises is even higher outside manufacturing. In Mexico, 97 percent of retail establishments and 94 percent in the services sector employ fewer than ten employees, with an average of 95 percent for the whole economy. In retail, 72 percent of the establishments have two workers or less (Hsieh and Klenow 2009). This higher prominence of smaller firms may help account for the greater dispersion in productivity in the service sectors. Yet the prominence of very small firms is underestimated in establishment-level data, even if it comes from a census, as in this case, since it takes into account only establishments with a fixed location. Itinerant businesses or street vendors are not usually included in census data. In Mexico, establishments covered by the economic census account for only 40 percent of the labor force. Another 26 percent is employed in sectors, such as agriculture or government, that are not surveyed. This leaves a very sizeable 13.6 million workers (33.5 percent of the labor force) unaccounted for. Data from employment surveys (Encuesta Nacional de Ocupación y Empleo [ENOE]; INEGI, 2003) indicate that these workers work in mobile locations without a fixed establishment, of which 5 million work on their own and 6 million in firms with fewer than five workers. By sector, the percentage of workers without a fixed establishment not accounted for in the census is 8.4 percent for manufacturing, 17 percent for retail and commerce, and 95 percent for nonfinancial services.[8]

The prominence of very small firms and self-employed workers, added to their much lower productivity, can be an important factor explaining why the average TFP in the region is low. And there is no sign that this prominence is tapering off. In Mexico, for example, the share of microestablishments, constituting about 95 percent of all businesses, has remained stagnant since 1988. Similarly, the percentage of workers in self-employment or in microenterprises has not changed much during the last 15 years throughout the region.[9] Considering their prominence and their low levels of productivity, coupled with the fact that small firms are less likely to innovate (see Chapter 10) or train their workers,[10] it is perhaps not that surprising that productivity in the region has remained stagnant.

Size Matters

A couple of counterfactual exercises show the importance for aggregate productivity of the fat lower tail of very low productivity firms in the region. The first exercise assesses what would happen to average productivity if a country had the same shares of low, medium, and high productivity firms as the United States, while leaving the productivity levels of low, medium, and high productivity firms unchanged. Note that this exercise focuses on shifting the shape of the distribution of firm productivities, which in the case of Mexico implies increasing the share of firms with medium levels of productivity, and for El Salvador increasing the share of medium and high productivity ones. These adjustments would increase average productivity by about 90 percent in El Salvador and by approximately 120 percent in Mexico, enough to close the productivity gap with the United States.[11] The results strongly suggest that the productivity problem of the region is one of a deficit of medium, or of medium and high productivity, firms, rather than low levels of productivity across all firms.

A second simulation assesses how aggregate productivity would rise if policies to raise productivity were to target the lower end of the productivity distribution. It estimates how much productivity would increase if the productivity of the least efficient firms increased (with technical assistance or innovation promotion policies targeted to the least productive firms) to just above a certain minimum level, denominated *x,* expressed as a percentage of the average of the sector: for example,

Figure 4.4   Effect on Aggregate Productivity When Raising Productivity in the Least Productive Manufacturing Firms

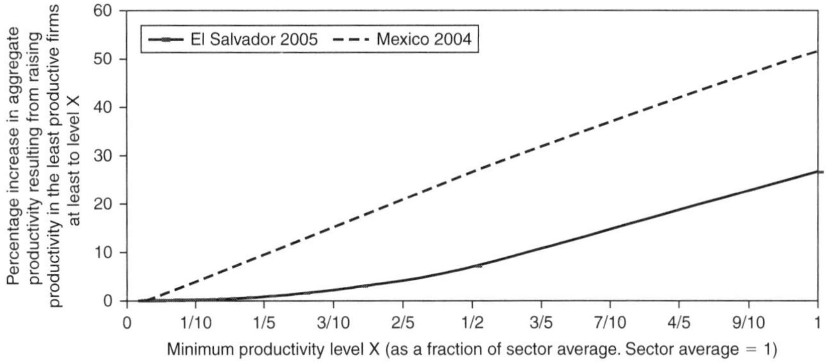

Source: El Salvador, Atal, Busso, and Cisneros (2009); Mexico, INEGI (2004, 2005).

Note: This figure plots the resulting increase in aggregate productivity from raising productivity of all firms with productivity below X to a minimum level X (expressed as a fraction of average productivity in industry).

one-tenth of the sector average. The exercise then assumes that all firms with productivities below, say, one-tenth of their sectors' average are "given" a productivity of one-tenth of the average. The results, presented in Figure 4.4, show the TFP gains of performing this exercise for different values of *x* in El Salvador and Mexico. As expected, raising the efficiency of the least productive firms raises average productivity. However, the remarkable part is how small these gains are, which reflects the fact that the contribution of the least productive firms is very small. As the minimum threshold is pushed upward and the least productive become more productive, aggregate output increases faster. Raising all low productivity firms to a minimum level of, say, one-tenth of the average of each industry would increase aggregate TFP in manufacturing in Mexico by 3.8 percent, while in El Salvador this gain would be close to zero.

Thus, because of the low levels of productivity of the least efficient firms, a certain policy or intervention can substantially boost productivity in percentage terms, but still leave a firm with very low productivity and not be cost-effective. Unless policies directed to improve the productivity of the smallest, least efficient firms achieve huge productivity gains, they will do little to improve productivity in the aggregate. From a policy point of view, perhaps a more relevant issue to understand is why so many small unproductive firms persist and under what conditions they could disappear, so that those firms' capital and labor could be used more productively.

Misallocation: An Untapped Productivity Potential in Latin America?

This chapter opened by stating that in economies where workers and capital are poorly allocated across firms, improving the allocation of resources could provide a boost to productivity comparable to decades of technological growth. Does this potential exist in Latin America?

To answer this question, it is first necessary to understand how resources are allocated across firms, and how resources end up in the wrong places. As stated, when markets work relatively well, workers and capital are allocated in ways that favor the growth of more productive firms. By virtue of their superior technologies or better management, more productive firms can squeeze more output out of every unit of input, and therefore sell their products at a lower price. Lower prices (adjusted for quality) translate into more sales and larger firm size, with a greater share of resources allocated to more productive firms. Firms do not grow indefinitely because in order to sell more, they would need to cut prices to a point where they would make lower profits.

Yet the relationship between firm size and productivity breaks down or becomes weaker if market or government failures favor some firms over others, allowing some firms to gain market share (size) even if they are less productive, or preventing some firms from gaining market share even if they are highly productive. This distorts the allocation of resources across firms reducing the output that can be attained with existing capital and labor.

What are the potential sources of misallocation? One of the most obvious culprits of resource misallocation is the financial market. As described in Chapter 6, financial markets in Latin America are underdeveloped and leave many firms underserved. If financial institutions are unable or unwilling to provide credit to firms that are highly productive but that have no credit history or insufficient guarantees, then these firms cannot expand as far as their ideas/projects could take them if markets worked properly. In an economy where good firms are credit-constrained, transferring additional resources to these firms can yield very high returns. Resource misallocation can also occur if directed credit provides cheap credit to inefficient firms, thereby allowing inefficient firms to expand.[12]

The second suspect in resource misallocation is the tax collection system. The combination of high taxes and poor enforcement creates strong incentives for tax evasion in Latin America. Moreover, in many countries, tax authorities searching for ways to improve the efficiency of tax collection focus their enforcement activity on the largest and most productive firms, virtually ignoring tax collection from micro-, small, and medium enterprises

(MSMEs). Since the sum of taxes and regulation compliance may be high in Latin America (particularly in the highest-income countries), noncompliance with taxes is equivalent to a substantial subsidy to noncompliant, less productive firms. Since large firms tend to be more productive than smaller firms, selective noncompliance amounts to a potentially large subsidy to less productive, smaller firms, thereby artificially increasing their size and weight in the economy, while constraining the size of larger, more productive firms.

The third suspect villain in the resource misallocation caper is the poor enforcement and incomplete coverage of social security systems. In addition to leaving many workers unprotected against the risks of old age, poverty, sickness, or unemployment, incomplete coverage of social security programs across all workers, and uneven enforcement of those who are covered, can also have negative effects on resource allocation and productivity. By evading taxes, some firms can save on a number of costs associated with taxes and regulatory mandates, and therefore compete on unfair terms with more productive firms. To the extent that firm evasion is triggered by a deliberate intent to compete with more productive firms, resources may be diverted from the best firms, promoting instead the expansion and or survival of less efficient ones.

These effects can be magnified by the fact that governments increasingly provide some benefits (health, pension) free of charge to workers conditional on their not being affiliated with social security.[13] While the benefits of such programs for the underserved population may be large, the adverse effects on productivity may also be sizeable if they simply fuel the fire, and help many workers—not satisfied with the value of services offered by social security—to switch toward self-employment, where they can avoid paying social security contributions and still get some of the benefits free of charge, provided that they remain informal. This is not to imply that governments should not help unprotected workers. It just means that they should not make program coverage conditional on participants being informal. Otherwise, well intended programs may contribute to the proliferation of many small or one-person firms that are not necessarily very productive but that benefit from not paying into social insurance programs and complying with labor regulations. Chapter 8 describes this problem in more detail and suggests avenues for reconciling protection with productivity.

At the practical level, assessing the extent of resource misallocation in a given economy involves gauging how far that economy is from efficient allocation—which is attained when moving labor or capital across firms does not change aggregate productivity. In efficient allocation, the revenues that result from an additional unit of labor or capital—what economists call marginal revenue product of labor or capital—are equated across all firms. In contrast, if policies or market failures prevent high productivity firms from expanding, an extra unit of labor or capital in these firms can yield more than others. Thus reallocating resources from firms with low returns to firms with high returns provides ways to increase output just by using the same resources differently. Similarly, if the operation of a firm has been subsidized by directed credit or by turning a blind eye to tax evasion, these firms may be using too many resources relative to efficient allocation, implying that the return of an extra unit of labor or capital would be lower than in other firms. In this case, transferring one unit of labor or capital away from this firm raises TFP in the economy as a whole.

Given this line of reasoning, the dispersion of the marginal revenue product of labor and capital across firms is an appropriate measure of misallocation. In an efficient allocation, marginal returns are equated across firms and therefore the dispersion of marginal returns would be zero. Higher dispersion indicates more misallocation. Clearly, according to this metric, Latin America suffers from a substantive degree of misallocation. Marginal products of labor and capital are computed following Hsieh and Klenow (forthcoming). Figure 4.5 compares dispersion in marginal products of capital and labor across firms within a given industry in selected Latin American countries, relative to the United States and China. Dispersion in marginal revenue products is lower in the United States, indicating a lower level of misallocation in this country. Within Latin America, dispersion is higher in Venezuela, Colombia, Uruguay, and Mexico, all with differences between high and low marginal products above 200 percent. This extensive dispersion is not the result of comparing apples with pears, as differences are calculated within each sector (at four digits of disaggregation). Therefore, high levels of dispersion highlight potential gains in productivity that could be achieved by moving factors from low to high marginal revenue products.[14]

The next section examines which government or market failures may be responsible for resource misallocation across the set of countries in the region for which firm-level data are available for this study. Yet prior to that, it is useful to quantify how costly misallocation is for aggregate productivity in Latin America. It turns out that by reallocating existing capital and labor across firms, aggregate productivity in most countries of Latin America could increase by approximately 50–60 percent (Figure 4.6). These calculations follow the methodology of a recent study assessing the potential gains of resource reallocation for China, India, and the United States (Hsieh and Klenow forthcoming). As in the seminal study, these gains consider reallocation only *within* four-digit industries. There could

Figure 4.5   Dispersion of Marginal Revenue Product of Labor and Capital in Manufacturing, Selected Countries, Firms with Ten or More Workers

Percentage difference in marginal returns between the 90th and 10th percentiles

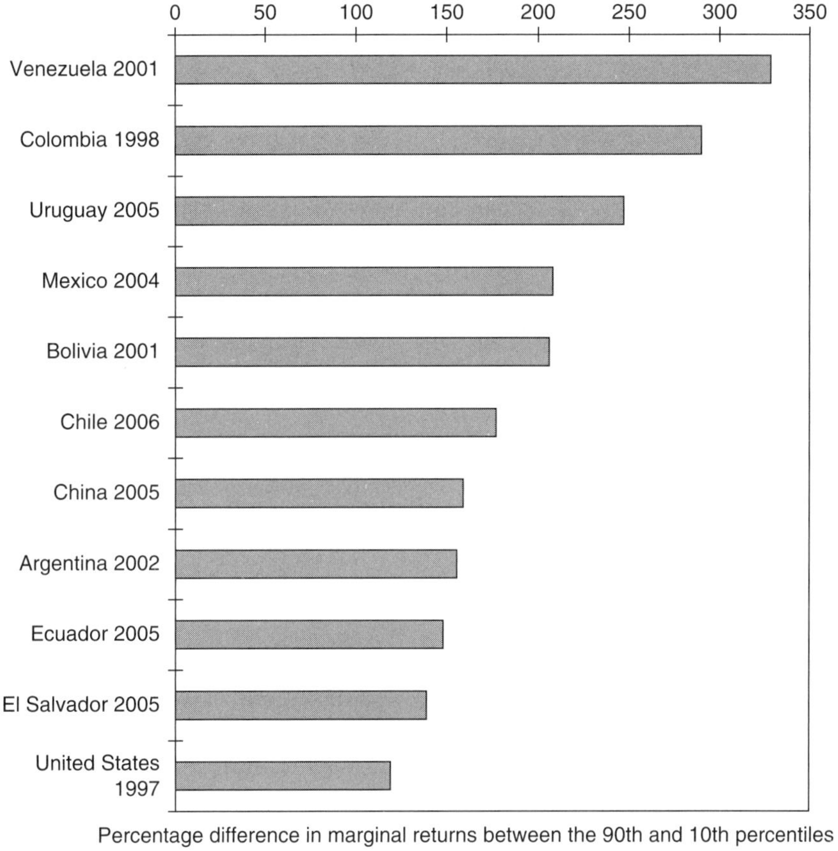

Source: Argentina, Neumeyer and Sandleris (2009); Bolivia, Machicado and Birbuet (2009); Chile, Busso, Madrigal, and Pagés (2009a,b); Colombia, Camacho and Conover (2009); Ecuador, Arellano (2009); El Salvador, Atal, Busso, and Cisneros (2009); Mexico, authors' calculations based on 2004 Census Data; Uruguay, Casacuberta and Gandelman (2009); Venezuela, authors' calculations based on Venezuelan Annual Industrial Survey, INE (2001); and China and the United States, Hsieh and Klenow (forthcoming).

Note: Data are for firms with ten or more workers. The length of the bars represents the dispersion in firms' marginal revenue product of labor and capital. A longer bar implies more dispersion. Data for the United States cover all manufacturing firms, for China only plants with sales above US$600,000 a year.

be further, sizable gains from reallocating *across* industries—for example, away from agriculture to manufacturing, as described in Chapter 3.

These estimates suggest that the potential gains of reallocation are larger in most countries in Latin America than in the United States—where the comparable figure is 30–43 percent (Hsieh and Klenow forthcoming)—but smaller than in China.

To put these numbers in perspective, the estimates presented in Chapter 2 suggest that to close the productivity gap with the United States,

Figure 4.6   Aggregate TFP Gains from Reallocating Resources in Manufacturing (as a percentage of initial productivity)

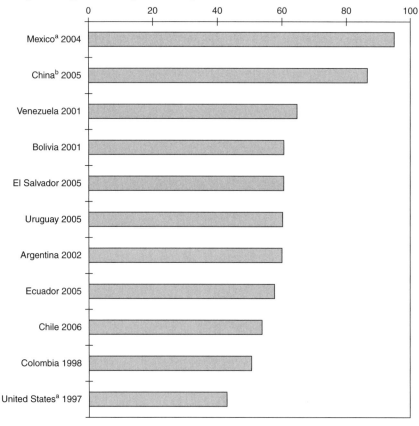

Percentage of TFP gain

Source: Argentina, Neumeyer and Sandleris (2009); Bolivia, Machicado and Birbuet (2009); Chile, Busso, Madrigal, and Pagés (2009a,b); Colombia, Camacho and Conover (2009); Ecuador, Arellano (2009); El Salvador, Atal, Busso, and Cisneros (2009); Mexico, Hsieh and Klenow (2009); Uruguay, Casacuberta and Gandelman (2009); Venezuela, authors' calculations based on Venezuelan Annual Industry Survey, INE (2001); China and the United States, Hsieh and Klenow (forthcoming).

Notes: Data are for firms with ten or more employees.
a. Data for the United States and Mexico cover all manufacturing establishments.
b. Data for China cover only plants with annual sales of more than US$600,000.

productivity in the region must double. Yet differences across countries in manufacturing productivity are lower than for the aggregate (Duarte and Restuccia forthcoming), indicating that the gap in productivity between Latin America and the United States in manufacturing is less than 50 percent. The magnitude of these figures suggests that improving the allocation of resources would close an important part of the gap between Latin America and the United States, particularly in the case of Mexico.

Moreover, the gains in TFP brought about by an improvement in the allocation of resources are likely to motivate an increase in the investment rate, as higher productivity is associated with higher returns of capital and labor. In that case, the overall effect would be much larger: on the order of 90 percent (rather than 60 percent).[15]

Untapped growth opportunities are even larger outside manufacturing, particularly in the service sector, identified in Chapter 3 as having the biggest productivity gaps with the world frontier. In Uruguay, the largest gains arise in commerce (75 percent) and transportation (52 percent). In Mexico, the potential gains of transferring resources across firms in the service sector are huge—on the order of 267 percent in retail and 246 percent in personal and community services. Similarly, in the retail sector of Brazil, the potential gains of reallocating resources toward the most efficient retailers are enormous—on the order of 257 percent.[16] These large gains underscore that a good part of the extremely low productivity in services lies not only in the low productivity of firms, but also in the poor way resources are allocated across them.

Market failures and/or poor policies tend to be more concentrated in the service sector, which may explain why, around the world, there is more convergence to the frontier in manufacturing than in the service sector. Given the growing importance of the service sector in all economies and the more rapid growth in productivity of the service sector in the developed world, failure to improve allocation in this sector will contribute to enlarge the gap in aggregate productivity relative to higher-income countries (Chapter 3). Duarte and Restuccia (forthcoming) point to the lower degree of competition in the service sectors in relation to manufacturing as one potential reason why the service sector has failed to catch up. Services are generally nontradable, and often heavily protected by a myriad of regulations; moreover, variables like location play a much more important role in services than in manufacturing. Together, these factors shield services from competition, which is often credited as an important engine of productivity growth. Extensive misallocation is a symptom of lack of fair competition for resources, as policies, market failures, or location advantages favor some firms relative to others for reasons other than their relative efficiency. The next section explores in more detail what may be driving this misallocation.

Explaining Low Productivity and Resource Misallocation: The Role of Market and Policy Failures

As stated at the outset of this chapter, low productivity in Latin America can be explained by two important factors. First, there are too few firms with medium levels of productivity. Second, resources are poorly allocated across existing firms, particularly in the service sector. It is now time to return to the question of what explains these two fundamental drivers of the low aggregate productivity levels in the region.

Drivers of Resource Misallocation

Misallocation signals that labor and capital have been allocated across firms in ways that do not correspond to firms' relative productivity. While many policies and market failures can alter the allocation of resources, three main candidates stand out: financial market failures; disparities in tax regimes and enforcement; and uneven coverage and enforcement of social and labor policies. Each is the basis of a separate chapter in this book; much of the detail on how these policies operate and their potential impacts on productivity can be found in those chapters. The objective here is to discuss how different market and policy failures relate to the TFP losses resulting from the misallocation documented above (or alternatively, the potential gains derived from reallocating resources). The three possible drivers of misallocation—poorly functioning financial markets, tax systems, and social security mandates—generate predictions regarding the relationship between misallocation and firm size that can help identify the source of misallocation. If misallocation is due to financial market failures, this would be reflected in the presence of many small firms that have difficulty growing—even though they have good projects—because they cannot secure access to credit. For these firms, the returns of additional capital would be very large—much larger than for firms whose demands for funding have been met by the capital market and therefore do not have any high return projects left to fund. If credit markets are the problem, then on-average returns to additional factors would be higher in small firms than in larger ones.

On the other hand, if distortions are due to unequal enforcement of taxes, social security contributions, or labor regulations, then the returns of additional capital and labor would be expected to be lower in smaller firms. This is because noncompliant firms are generally small, and tax evasion works as a subsidy that helps them expand beyond what they would have had they paid taxes, lowering the marginal returns of factors relative to compliant firms.

What does the relationship between marginal products of factors and firm size reveal about the origins of misallocation? This relationship varies across countries, but, more often than not, returns are increasing in relation to firm size. In some countries, such as Colombia, El Salvador, and Mexico, the marginal revenue product of an extra unit of resources tends to be larger in medium and large firms than in the smallest ones. In these countries, evidence suggests that, on average, providing extra resources to medium or large firms would yield higher returns than providing resources to smaller ones. The implication is that in these countries, most small firms are not too small, but rather too large relative to what they should be in an efficient allocation. In contrast, medium and large firms appear to be too small relative to what they would be if resources were assigned following relative productivities. In these countries, it is difficult to argue that the main source of such distortions are capital market constraints, unless it can be shown that the medium or large firms are the most constrained by lack of financial access. Instead, it might well be that small firms are credit-constrained, but they compensate for these higher costs, or for the greater difficulty of accessing credit, by not paying taxes and circumventing regulations. This latter effect seems to dominate. In this set of countries, tax evasion and informality, which are concentrated in the smallest firms, are very plausible sources of misallocation.

The data presented in Figure 4.7 correspond to manufacturing, but patterns are similar across economic sectors. In Mexico, the returns to an extra unit of labor and capital are also larger in medium firms (50–99 workers) in retail, while in services they increase monotonically with firm size, peaking in the 500–999 size category. Tax and social security evasion could explain why distortions are more prevalent in the service sector, where evasion is more rampant.

Patterns differ in some countries, however. Credit market constraints seem a more likely source of distortions in Chile and Uruguay. In these two countries, the returns to an extra unit of capital and labor tend to decline with firm size, indicating that the smallest firms tend to be size-constrained, while the largest firms appear subsidized, given their productivity. The lower level of evasion and higher level of formality in Chile and Uruguay may also explain why in these two countries small firms are relatively more size-constrained, as they cannot easily compensate for low access to credit with tax and social security evasion. However, tax evasion favoring the largest firms could also explain these patterns. In Chile, larger manufacturing firms appear to evade more taxes and receive more state subsidies than smaller ones (see Chapter 7; and Busso, Madrigal, and Pagés 2009b).

The evidence presented provides some interesting clues as to the likely sources of misallocation in Latin America. Contrary to popular wisdom, there is not much evidence for the hypothesis that very small firms are too small, or are size-constrained. Only in Chile and Uruguay are marginal

Figure 4.7 Marginal Revenue Product of Capital and Labor by Firm Size, Selected Latin American Countries, Firms with Ten or More Employees

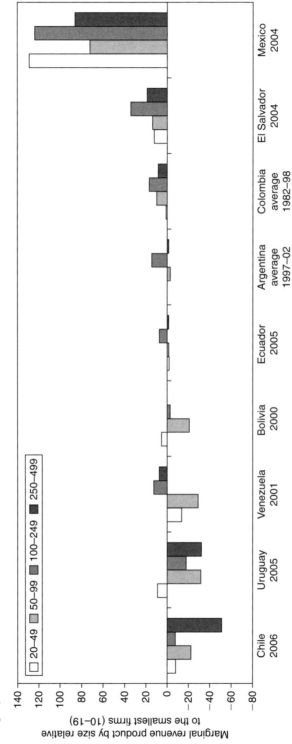

Sources: Argentina, Neumeyer and Sandleris (2009); Bolivia, Machicado and Birbuet (2009); Chile, Busso, Madrigal, and Pagés (2009a,b); Colombia, Camacho and Conover (2009); Ecuador, Arellano (2009); El Salvador, Atal, Busso, and Cisneros (2009); Mexico, Hsieh and Klenow (2009); Uruguay, Casacuberta and Gandelman (2009), Venezuela, authors' calculations based on Venezuelan Annual Industrial Survey, INE (2001).

Note: Data are for firms with ten or more employees. Data for Mexico cover all establishments. Data for Argentina show results for 80–200 workers and more than 200 categories. Figures in the vertical axis denote the average marginal revenue product by size relative to the average of the smallest firms in the sample (10–19).

products of capital clearly declining in size, as this hypothesis would imply, and in Chile tax avoidance of larger firms can also account for this pattern. As indicated, even if small firms suffer from capital access constraints, other factors, such as their partial or total noncompliance with taxes and social security mandates, provide them with an implicit subsidy that allows them to be larger than the size that would be warranted by their productivity.

Explaining the Mix of Firms

So far the discussion has focused on the channels by which policies and market failures can bias the allocation of resources across firms of given productivities, *taking the mix of active firms as given*.

Yet, as indicated above, a key factor that accounts for much of the difference in productivity across Latin America and the frontier relates to the actual mix of firms in Latin America. There are seemingly too many low productivity firms and too few firms with medium levels of productivity. Which firms survive in the market is determined by the rewards and incentives provided by policies and market conditions, which matter because aggregate productivity is the average productivity of all active firms. What conditions allow very unproductive firms to survive in one country and perish in another? What conditions allow high productivity firms to enter the market in some countries while not allowing the same in others?

Some of the policies that lead to resource misallocation can also explain the selection of firms. The evasion of taxes, social security contributions, and labor regulations can help many low productivity firms capture market share, and at the same time enhance their probabilities of surviving and competing with much more productive firms. While this may seem acceptable from the viewpoint of the owners of such firms, it represents important costs in the aggregate, as productivity declines due to the inordinate weight of low productivity firms and the constriction of the most productive ones.

Low exposure to international trade and/or high transportation costs also protect low productivity producers from the competition of geographically distant producers, allowing less efficient producers to survive. Greater exposure to international trade (or lower transportation costs) steps up the rate by which low productivity firms exit the market, thereby providing a channel for productivity to increase (see Chapter 5).

Expensive and cumbersome bankruptcy regulations and high firing costs also improve the survival rate of low productivity firms and slow down the process of reallocating workers and capital across firms.

In contrast, credit market failures seemingly play a limited role in explaining the survival of low productivity firms, as directed credit is not prevalent in Latin America and only a fraction of the small, least productive firms receive any form of credit.

Perhaps more important than identifying the reasons for the survival of very low productivity firms is assessing what impedes the entry of medium or high productivity firms. Here again, the presence of high informality levels and high tax rates could explain the "missing middle," as only very productive firms can compete with the relative cost advantage created by the evasion of taxes and social security.

While the region has an excess of low productivity firms to shed, the entry of more productive firms and the exit of the least productive ones accounts for only a slightly higher fraction of productivity growth than in the United States (Figure 4.8), suggesting that the previously discussed barriers to entry and exit are indeed taking a toll. Chile is an exception, as the entry-exit component of productivity growth is larger than in the other countries in the region. This is seen in Figure 4.8, in which the net entry effect is larger than for the other countries.[17]

Technology Upgrades and Firm Dynamics

In addition to affecting the allocation of resources and/or the selection of firms, policies and market failures are also likely to affect firms' incentives to invest in acquiring or developing new technology.

Tax evasion distorts the allocation of resources away from compliant firms and *at the same time* reduces those firms' incentives to invest in better technologies leading to lower productivity growth. Allowing for the combination of static and dynamic effects, tax evasion can reduce aggregate productivity by 40 percent, a factor large enough to explain the bulk of the productivity differences between the United States and Latin America (Restuccia 2008; Restuccia and Rogerson forthcoming).

Credit constraints can limit the ability of entrepreneurs to acquire better technologies and therefore limit firms' productivity growth (Banerjee and Duflo 2005; Jeong and Towsend 2007). Poor access to capital would then reduce average productivity by both lessening the economic weight of highly productive but capital-constrained firms, and also by increasing the share of low productivity and backward firms.

Finally, low exposure to trade and/or high transportation costs constrain productivity growth by reducing competition from higher productivity firms abroad, or in the same country but in a geographically distant location.

Figure 4.8 TFP Decompositions, Manufacturing Firms with Ten or More Employees, 1997–2006

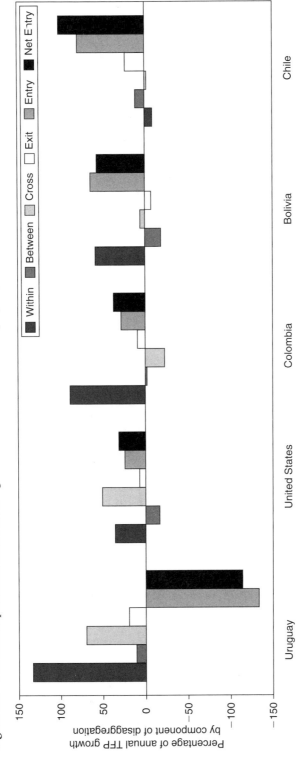

Source: Busso, Madrigal, and Pagés (2009a); for the United States, Foster, Haltiwanger, and Syverson (2008).

Note: Decompositions based on Foster, Haltiwanger, and Krizan (2001) using employment weights. Data for Uruguay are for 1997–2005. Data for the United States are for 1977–97. Data for Bolivia are for 1998–2001.

How important are technology upgrades in explaining productivity growth in the region? With the exception of Chile, this factor weighs more on overall productivity growth in Latin American countries than in the United States. This is seen in Figure 4.8 where total productivity growth in manufacturing establishments tends to be explained by the growth in TFP of each firm (weighted by the employment share of each firm in the economy). Yet, Chapter 10 documents the lower incidence of innovation in the region compared to higher-income countries. This again provides evidence that, in addition to innovation, the other two channels of growth—improved resource allocation and better firm selection—have been underutilized in the region.

Conclusion

Latin America is characterized by large disparities in productivity and substantial resource misallocation, which together open important avenues for productivity growth. While the gains from improving resource allocation and the mix of firms would provide only temporary sources of growth, they could provide a huge leap forward similar to what the region enjoyed during the period of rapid urbanization and structural transformation during the 1950s and 1960s (see Chapter 3). This transformation would require reforms aimed at reducing the distortions created by differences in tax codes and uneven enforcement of taxes and regulations, improving social insurance policies, improving the functioning of capital markets, and stimulating competition, particularly in the service sectors. The next chapters examine each of these aspects in more detail.

Improving the allocation of resources and the mix of firms can create many winners but also some losers. Appropriate compensation and risk amelioration measures must be put in place so the welfare of those who stand to lose is protected and reforms that provide important societal gains are not blocked. This implies improving unemployment compensation, intermediation, retraining programs, and firm bankruptcy policies.

Notes

1. See Busso, Madrigal, and Pagés (2009a) for a detailed description of the data used, the methodology employed, and additional results characterizing productivity dispersion and misallocation for Latin America.
2. In order to make a comparison among firms that produce similar goods (say meat products), productivity for each firm is computed as the ratio of

productivity of the firm relative to the average of the sector to which the firm belongs. Sectors are defined at the four-digit level of disaggregation.

3. Dispersion figures for Mexico and El Salvador, when also including manufacturing establishments of fewer than ten workers, are 389 and 288, respectively. Thus, in Mexico, the measured dispersion in productivity increases when the sample of microenterprises is included alongside the sample of establishments of ten or more workers. In El Salvador, however, productivity heterogeneity is lower for the whole sample than for the subsample of firms with ten or more workers. This reflects the lack of dispersion within the group of microenterprises (they all have low levels of productivity); and the group of ten or fewer workers constitutes the majority of establishments. Figures for Mexico and El Salvador are based on establishment census data that cover all establishments with a fixed location. Establishments without a fixed location, such as mobile vendors, are not represented in census-type data. The data from the United States exclude non-employer firms (typically the self-employed), while the data from El Salvador and Mexico include self-employed firms. Results are virtually unchanged, however, when self-employed establishments are excluded from the calculations for these two countries.

4. Following Hsieh and Klenow (Forthcoming), the estimates of firm productivity account for differences in human capital of workers across firms, by using the wage bill as a measure of labor.

5. Casacuberta and Gandelman (2009); and Hsieh and Klenow (2009).

6. The argument is that productivity determines size, with more productive firms growing to be larger, rather than the other way around: that larger firms become more productive as a result of their size. Yet a positive relationship between TFP and size can also be driven by economies of scale. This is because most methods of computing TFP assume constant returns to scale; therefore, increasing returns to scale would wrongly show up as higher TFP for bigger firms.

7. The data for the selected group of countries presented here also suggest that in addition to size, productivity increases with age and with exporting status.

8. Calculations from INEGI (2002).

9. Cedlas and World Bank (2009). Microenterprises are defined as those with five or fewer employees, and in some countries four or fewer.

10. For example, data collected from the Enterprise Survey by the World Bank for 15 countries in Latin America in 2006 shows that, on average, only 33 percent of firms with fewer than 20 workers provide formal training for their workers, while the corresponding figure for firms with 100 or more workers is 75 percent.

11. This is assuming a productivity gap in manufacturing that is equal to the overall productivity gap identified in Chapter 2 between Latin America and the United States. Results also assume 33 productivity brackets. The computation assumes that the average levels of productivity (relative to the sector average) in each bracket remain unchanged, but the shares of firms in each bracket are changed to match those in the United States.

12. Another reason a firm may be inefficiently small is that it exerts some form of monopoly power.
13. Levy (2008).
14. Again, care should be taken in comparing countries with different data coverage (see Box 4.1). In this case, comparisons for Mexico and El Salvador, including and excluding the smallest firms, suggest that including these firms may increase or reduce the estimated degree of misallocation. In Mexico, for example, the dispersion in marginal revenues is 227 when all firms are included and only 208 for firms of ten or more employees. In contrast, in El Salvador, dispersion is 135 for all firms and 138 for firms of ten or more employees.
15. This calculation assumes that the share of capital share in value added is of one-third.
16. Casacuberta and Gandelman (2009) for Uruguay; Hsieh and Klenow (2009) for Mexico; and de Vries (2009) for Brazil.
17. Figures obtained by decomposing TFP growth in five components: within firm growth, between firm growth, cross-term, entry of firms, and exit of firms, following Foster, Haltiwanger, and Krizan (2001).

5

Trade and Productivity:
A Route to Reallocation
with a High Transport Toll

Plenty of ink has been devoted to the topic of trade and productivity, particularly in Latin America and the Caribbean. Even though the results are mixed when country and sector data are used, most of the more robust evidence at the firm level seems to confirm what professional economists have known for centuries: trade boosts productivity (see IDB 2002; Fernandes 2007; López-Córdova and Mesquita Moreira 2004; Muendler 2002; and Pavcnik 2002).

The governments of the region, with a few exceptions, do not seem to doubt this conclusion. Most countries have undergone sweeping trade liberalizations and some of them are actively pushing the boundaries of this process by signing comprehensive bilateral trade agreements with countries such as the United States and China. While the region's failure to significantly boost productivity after the trade reforms and the pressures brought about by the recent financial crisis have provided fodder for a protectionist backlash, such reversals have been few and far between so far. Thus, the question is what is the point in revisiting this issue? Or, to put it bluntly: where's the beef?

The motivation is threefold. First, since the first wave of studies, some important theoretical advances have shed new light on one of the often overlooked channels through which trade affects productivity—the so-called reallocation channel (Bernard et al. 2003; and Melitz 2003). Most of the attention so far has been on the impact of trade on productivity within firms. Yet trade has also a Darwinian effect, weeding out low productivity firms and boosting high productivity ones and in the process, raising the economy's average productivity. By overlooking reallocation, most of the previous studies have probably underestimated the positive effect that trade has on productivity.

The second motivation arises from another overlooked factor: the role of transport costs. It is a time-honored tradition in economics, particularly in fields such as international trade, to regard the cost of transporting goods as a nuisance and to assume they are zero for the sake of simplicity. That attitude also prevailed in the first wave of studies on trade and productivity. It just so happens, however, that rather than an annoying residual, transport costs have become arguably Latin America's most important obstacle to trade (Mesquita Moreira, Volpe, and Blyde 2008). In practical terms, this means that the impact of trade on productivity cannot be fully understood without accounting for a trade cost that not only seems to matter, but that differs from import tariffs in nature, impact, and policy implications.

The third motivation is purely policy-driven. The region's productivity performance after the trade reforms has been well below expectations—a main outcome of aggregate, economy-wide estimates of productivity that has been discussed at length in previous chapters. This naturally prompts the question: what happened to all those productivity gains attributed to trade that economists have been finding in firm-level studies?

This is less of a puzzle once it is pointed out that those studies focused only on the tradable, manufacturing side of the economy, where productivity growth did resume after the reforms and where, by definition, the trade impact could be expected. Moreover, most Latin American economies have a large, nontradable service sector, where productivity has been flat or even declining, with a few exceptions. Finally, even in the tradable sector, notwithstanding the rhetoric that has accompanied reform, there are no theoretical or empirical grounds to expect that trade alone can do the job. Productivity has many other determinants that go well beyond trade.

As strong as these arguments are, they do not let trade economists entirely off the hook. Despite the recovery, productivity growth even in the manufacturing sector has been disappointing, often with rates that are well below what countries experienced in the heyday of their inward-oriented regimes and clearly below the estimates usually associated with East Asia or India. While other factors might be at play, it is not clear whether the reallocation channel in Latin America has been working as expected, or if there are policies or market failures that may be undermining its effectiveness. Likewise, shipping costs are on average higher than tariffs and substantially higher in Latin America than in the developed world, yet there is not much analysis to understand the links between trade, transport costs, and productivity. Governments in the region continue to think of trade policy as a matter of just tariff and nontariff barriers.

This tightly knit combination of academic and policy-related factors is important enough to make revisiting trade and productivity a worthy proposition. This chapter seeks to use these theoretical and methodological advances to shed some light on the reallocation and transport cost "black holes" that still remain in the trade-productivity relationship in the region, and with that, help advance a policy agenda focused on raising the region's productivity growth.

The Reallocation Effect and Productivity

Trade costs can impact a country's productivity by affecting firm-level productivity directly or by distorting the reallocation of resources across the economy. The impact on firm-level productivity in turn can arise through various mechanisms. One of them is through the so-called import-discipline effect. This channel refers to the notion that lower trade barriers foster more competition from abroad, forcing domestic firms to reduce the gap between actual productivity and the maximum productivity achievable, known as X-inefficiency, by improving existing processes and cutting the slack in firm management (Martin 1978). Stronger import competition can also stimulate innovation through so-called Schumpeterian incentives,[1] leading to gains in productivity. A different mechanism involves the inputs of the plant. Reducing trade costs can improve plant productivity when high-quality equipment and foreign intermediate goods allow firms to adopt new production methods or when the expansion in the number of intermediates allows a better match between the input mix and existing technology (Ethier 1982).

Lower trade costs can also lead to higher plant productivity by expanding exports, as exporting may allow producers to access foreign know-how from knowledge buyers (Grossman and Helpman 1991) or exploit economies of scale. Yet another channel relates to foreign direct investment (FDI). Plant productivity could rise from the stronger competition of world class competitors at home or through the spillovers and linkages between foreign and local firms.

A rich empirical literature has evolved to explore the evidence behind many of these channels. The evidence available for Latin America has been reviewed in detail by López-Córdova and Mesquita Moreira (2004) and IDB (2002). Generally, the results suggest a positive impact of trade on productivity, with consistent support for the import-discipline channel and more mixed evidence for the other channels.[2]

But trade might affect productivity (hereafter, also referred to as total factor productivity, or TFP) not only through its impact on the plant; it may also impact aggregate TFP—even without changing the productivity of the plant—by affecting the reallocative process across plants of different productivity levels. Recent trade models with heterogeneous firms

(Bernard et al. 2003; Melitz 2003) show how lower trade costs can augment aggregate productivity either by forcing lower productivity firms out of the market—cutting off the lower tail of the productivity distribution—or by fostering the expansion of high productivity plants through export.

While evidence of these effects has been reported for developed countries (see Bernard, Jensen, and Schott 2006), not many studies for Latin America and the Caribbean have empirically tested the existence of these trade-induced reallocation channels. Some exceptions are Tybout (1991) and Pavcnik (2002), who show that shifting market shares toward more efficient plants contributes significantly to productivity growth among the tradable sectors. Building on this existing literature, this section provides new evidence for the region on the links between trade and productivity through the process of resource reallocation.

New trade models predict that when trade costs fall, aggregate productivity rises both because low productivity, non-exporting firms exit and because high productivity firms are able to expand through exporting.[3] The exit could be driven by the stronger competition from abroad or by the expansion of more productive firms, bidding up real wages and forcing the least productive firms to exit.[4] Using data for Brazil and Chile, Figure 5.1 provides some preliminary evidence of the necessary mechanisms that are key for the trade-induced reallocation effects to take place: namely that the plants that normally exit are on average less productive than the plants that do not exit and that the plants that export,

Figure 5.1   Difference in Average Plant Productivity across Comparative Groups

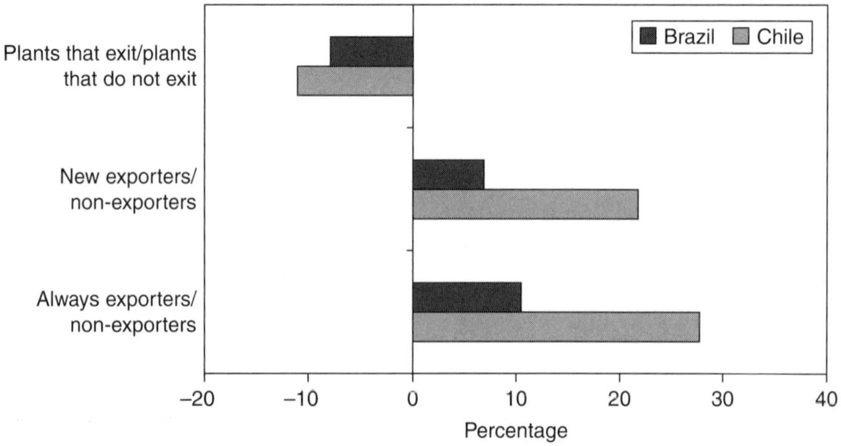

Source: Authors' calculations.

Note: The figure shows differences in average plant productivity across comparative groups after controlling for differences in plant size and industry characteristics. The data for Brazil refer to the period 1996–2000 and the data for Chile refer to the period 1995–2006.

Table 5.1   Correlations between Trade Costs and Market Selection: Summary of Econometric Results

	Probability of exit		Probability of exporting	
	Brazil	Chile	Brazil	Chile
Total trade costs	Negative	Negative	0	Negative
Ad valorem tariff	Negative	Negative	0	0
Ad valorem freight	0	Negative	Negative	Negative

Source: Authors' calculations.

Note: The table summarizes the impact of changes in trade costs on the probability of exit and on the probability of becoming an exporter for Brazil and for Chile. The results of the regressions where the trade costs are included as the sum of ad valorem tariffs and freight rates are reported in the first row. The results of an alternative specification where the tariff and freight rates are included separately but in the same regression are reported in the second and third rows. "Negative" indicates that the change in trade costs and the respective probability are inversely related. "0" indicates that the relationship is not statistically significant. All the regression include other variables as controls.

or eventually become exporters, are usually more productive than the plants that do not export. For example, plants that exit are on average 8 percent less productive than plants that do not exit in Brazil, while they are 11 percent less productive in Chile.[5]

Given this evidence, the relevant question is whether lower trade costs have been helping to weed the inefficient plants out of the market. Equally relevant is the question of whether a reduction in trade costs gives prospective exporters a better chance of servicing foreign markets. Table 5.1 summarizes the main findings of an econometric exercise undertaken in conjunction with this study. The general results for Brazil and Chile (first row) indicate that plants in industries with larger declines in total trade costs exhibit higher probabilities of exit.[6] The impacts are far from negligible. A 10-percentage-point decline in trade costs increases the probability of exit by approximately 7 percent for Chile and by around 3 percent for Brazil. Results from Chile also show that the chance of becoming an exporter is higher in industries with greater declines in trade costs, as implied by the literature. A 10-percentage-point decline in trade costs, for example, raises the probability of exporting by around 7 percent.[7]

Colombia provides another example of trade-induced reallocation effects. Using a slightly different methodology than the one used in the econometric study, Eslava et al. (2009) show that the tariff reduction of around 35 percentage points that took place in Colombia during the first half of the 1990s resulted in a more than 10 percent increase in the exit rate. Box 5.1 describes this study in more detail.

Having shown that trade costs affect resource reallocation, it is important to analyze how relevant these effects are to the productivity of the

Box 5.1   Trade Reforms and Market Selection in Colombia

Like other countries in Latin America, Colombia liberalized trade sub-stantially during the first half of the 1990s. The average nominal tariff declined from 27 to 10 percent overall, and from 50 to 13 percent in manufacturing. The dispersion of tariffs also fell considerably. This epi-sode provides an excellent opportunity to evaluate the effect of a trade reform on market selection by exploiting the cross-sectional variation in tariff reductions. Eslava et al. (2009) pursue precisely this objective, using detailed data from the Colombian Annual Manufacturing Survey (AMS).

The authors estimate a probit model to measure the impact of vari-ous factors that determine the establishment's profitability on plant exit. The availability of price data at the firm level allows them to decompose the plant's profit margin into four parts: productivity, demand shocks, markups, and input costs. Then they exploit the variation across sectors in tariff changes after the trade reform to evaluate how the liberaliza-tion affected the impact of these market fundamentals on plant exit. The results show that the stronger international competition generated by the trade reform magnified the impact of productivity and other market fundamentals on plant exit. For example, a plant with low pro-ductivity was more likely to exit after the trade reform took place. Using counterfactual exercises, the authors measure what would have been the average productivity level if plant survival had continued with the ini-tial tariff rates compared to the actual tariffs. They found that average productivity is 3.3 percentage points higher than it would have been in the absence of improved market selection.

Source: Authors' summary based on Eslava et al. (2009).

whole economy. This is far from a trivial task. This type of analysis typically involves simulations with simplified assumptions that may not reflect the reality on the ground. Yet they are useful in providing at least an order of magnitude estimate of the importance of these effects. For instance, Eslava et al. (2009) use this method to estimate what the average productivity level in Colombia would have been if no changes in plant survival had occurred after trade liberalization. They find that improved market selection following the decline in the tariff rate was associated with a gain in average TFP of approximately 3 percentage points between 1992 and 1998. This is substantial considering that during this period, aver-age industry TFP in Colombia increased by around 12 percentage points (Eslava et al. 2004).

Similar simulations can be used to estimate the gains in average TFP from a hypothetical reduction in Chile's tariffs and freight rates to U.S. levels. As in Colombia, improved market selection from the increase in the exit rate can have an important impact on productivity: average TFP in Chile could gain 2.4 percentage points over five years after the decline in freight rates and an additional 1 percentage point from the cut in the tariff rate.[8]

Transport Costs and Productivity

While tariffs are certainly the most visible obstacles to trade, they are not the only ones. Broadly defined, trade costs include all the costs incurred in getting a good to its final user, including expenses arising from transportation, regulation, and differences in currencies or languages (Anderson and van Wincoop 2004). The empirical literature tracing the effects of many of these nontariff costs on trade flows is long and diverse, although often beset by difficulties in measuring the barriers properly. Most studies, however, are unequivocal as to both the statistical and economic importance of these costs in restricting trade flows, be they technical barriers, such as health, sanitary and environmental regulation, or quality, safety, and industrial standards (Baldwin 2000; Hufbauer, Kotschwar, and Wilson 2002; Chen, Wilson, and Otsuki 2008; Wilson 2008); business regulations (Freund and Bolaky 2008); or currency effects (Rose 2000; Glick and Rose 2002; Micco, Stein, and Ordóñez 2003; Frankel 2008).

While many of these factors certainly limit the prospects of trade and integration and its capacity to foster productivity, this chapter concentrates on one of these barriers, transport costs, for both pragmatic and analytical reasons. The pragmatic reasons relate to the difficulty of obtaining accurate measures of all nonpolicy components. The analytical reasons center on the prominence of transport costs among the nontariff barriers and the growing evidence that transport infrastructure is an important constraint on the growth of Latin America's trade.

Economists usually see transport costs as having an impact on trade, and therefore on productivity, similar to that of tariffs. Yet in the real world, things are not that simple. At least three factors set transport costs apart from tariffs (Mesquita Moreira, Volpe, and Blyde 2008).

First, unlike tariffs, transport costs are highly variable over time. The uncertainty associated with these fluctuations can hurt trade, particularly if transport costs are high.

Second, unlike tariffs, transport costs are not a simple, fixed proportion (ad valorem) of the price of products. Transport costs have a per-unit component determined by a number of characteristics such as weight, volume, and perishability. These characteristics vary considerably across products and, therefore, have very different implications for the way trade can impact productivity, particularly when combined with the country's geography and infrastructure. For instance, a producer of a good with no import tariff may not be subjected at all to "import discipline" if transport costs are high enough to deter competition because of the intrinsic characteristics of the good, the country's bad infrastructure, or a combination of both.

Third, unlike tariffs, transport costs are not fixed by fiat, but respond to variables such as trade flows, the quality of the countries' infrastructure, and the degree of competition in the transport industry. Bringing transport costs down, therefore, goes well beyond the political economy of protection and requires more complex policy actions than those involved in a typical trade liberalization.

These distinct characteristics would be enough to justify a closer look at how transport costs impact the relationship between trade and productivity. In Latin America, this issue assumes even greater importance for two main reasons. First, the region's exports are heavily dependent on "transport-intensive" goods (transport costs make up a large share of the CIF price), be they natural resources (such as minerals and grains) or time-sensitive goods (such as fruits, cut flowers, or apparel).[9] Second, the region suffers from well-known deficiencies in its infrastructure.

How exactly does this complex relationship between transport, trade, and productivity play out in the region? One way to look for answers is to assess the specific impact of transport costs on both reallocation and on within-firm productivity. The results of an exercise focused on reallocation in Brazil and Chile are presented in the third row of Table 5.1. To put things into perspective, the results for tariffs are also presented in the second row. Even though there is some variation in type of market selection effect and country, the estimates in general suggest that both types of trade costs matter for reallocation. For instance, in Chile, not only tariffs, but also freight rates are found to be related to plant exit. A 10-percentage-point cut in tariffs increases the probability of exit by approximately 2.1 percent, while a 10-percentage-point cut in the freight rate boosts the probability of exit by an additional 1.5 percent. High shipping costs also negatively impact the possibility of entering the export market. The high costs of transportation hurt the chances that a plant becomes an exporter in both Brazil and Chile.

The importance of transport costs becomes clearer when the relative magnitudes of tariffs and shipping rates are compared. Panel (a) in Figure 5.2 presents an example for the manufacturing industry in Chile. Ad valorem transport costs are currently more than four times higher than the ad valorem tariffs, implying that the scope for reducing these costs—and their potential effects—is also considerably larger. This is confirmed

Figure 5.2   Trade Costs in Chile and Changes in Exit Rate from Reducing Tariffs and Freights to U.S. Levels

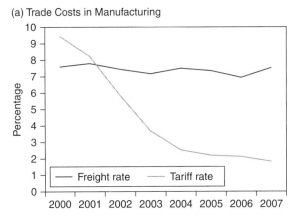

(a) Trade Costs in Manufacturing

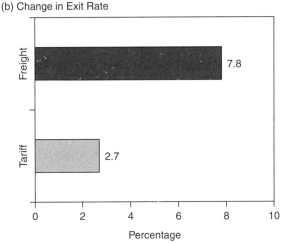

(b) Change in Exit Rate

Source: Authors' calculations.

Note: Ad valorem freights and tariffs are the ratios of freight expenditures and tariff revenues to imports, respectively. Trade costs are derived from product-level data collected at the border and aggregated using imports values.

by an exercise shown in panel (b) of the same figure, which measures how much the average exit rate in Chile would increase if the tariff and freight rates fell to U.S. levels. The increase in the exit rate arising from a reduction in freight costs would be nearly three times higher than that triggered by a cut in tariffs. This occurs even when the marginal effect of the tariff is higher than the marginal effect of the freight rate because the required decline in freight rates (around 50 percent) is much greater than the required reduction in the tariff rate (around 10 percent). The example illustrates a key point: that transport costs are important in Latin America in large part because they represent a higher trade barrier today than the tariff rate. This is not an exclusive feature of the Chilean economy but a prominent characteristic across the region.

With respect to within-firm effects, the econometric exercise conducted as part of this study explores whether the effects on plant productivity arise not only from tariffs but also from transport costs. The exercise expands the specification from López-Córdova and Mesquita Moreira (2004) to include not only the tariff rate and the import penetration ratio, a variable that is frequently added to proxy for nontariff barriers, but also the ad valorem international freight rates.[10]

The findings indicate that both trade costs are important. For Brazil and Chile,[11] a 10-percentage-point reduction in tariffs increases plant productivity by around 1.8 percent and 4 percent, respectively, while a 10-percentage-point reduction in the freight rate raises plant productivity by an additional 0.5 percent and 0.7 percent, respectively. The marginal effects from the tariff seem to be larger than those from the freight rate. However, this does not invalidate the argument that transport costs matter. The significance of transport costs for the region centers on two aspects: that their impact is far from negligible and that the scope for reducing them today is much larger than for tariffs.

How High Are Transport Costs in Latin America and the Caribbean?

The evidence reviewed thus far shows that trade costs affect reallocation, and therefore the productivity of the whole economy, both by protecting inefficient producers, which lowers their likelihood to exit, and by limiting the expansion of efficient plants, which lowers their likelihood to export. Moreover, these costs have a negative impact on firm productivity by undermining competition. Finally, tariffs are not the only trade cost with which policymakers should be concerned. Transport costs can also be an important impediment to competition and to an efficient allocation of resources across firms.

The case for focusing more attention on transport costs in both research and policymaking becomes even more compelling when tariffs are compared with freight rates across the region and when transport costs in Latin America are compared with those of the developed world. The first exercise in this section clearly shows that Chile is not an exception. Transport costs are significantly higher than tariffs for most countries in the region. Figure 5.3 gives a broad picture of both intraregional and

Figure 5.3 Relationship between Ad Valorem Freights and Tariffs in Latin America, 2006

(a) Intra- and Extraregional Imports

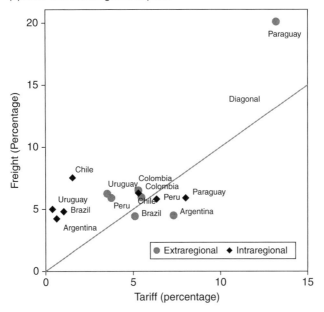

(b) Intraregional Exports and Exports to the United States

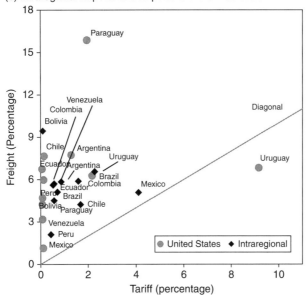

Source: Authors' calculations based on Asociación Latinoamericana de Integración (ALADI) dataset and U.S. Census Bureau dataset on U.S. Imports of Merchandise (various years).

Note: Freight is the ratio of freight expenditures to imports. Tariff is the ratio of tariff revenue to imports. Import data for Paraguay and Colombia are for 2000 and 2003, respectively. Intraregional exports include Argentina, Brazil, Chile, Peru, and Uruguay.

extraregional trade in Latin America. In the case of imports, shown in panel (a), transport costs are higher than tariffs by a large margin: thus most countries lie to the left of the diagonal. Even for the few exceptions that lie to the right of the diagonal, the ratio of tariff to freight costs is too small to justify a trade agenda that is focused primarily on policy barriers.

Panel (b) presents the case for exports. Since the product and market composition of these two flows are markedly different, export data could tell a different story. Unfortunately, data on trade costs for exports are available only for the United States and five Latin American countries. It is clear that the dominance of freight costs over tariffs is even more pronounced, with all countries' exports positioned to the left of the diagonal, except for Uruguay's exports to the United States. Clearly, the region, after a wide-ranging process of liberalization, now faces a different reality than the one that existed two decades ago when policy barriers were the main obstacle to trade.

The second exercise—an international comparison of Latin America's freight rates—addresses a critical question: whether or not there is room to cut transport costs in the region. As suggested, freight rates, unlike tariffs, are not just the product of (bad) policies. Factors such as geography and the composition of trade matter; contrary to what economists used to do to simplify their analyses, governments cannot simply eliminate these costs. It is important to know whether there is significant room for policy action and to identify the main sources of the problems.

It is not easy to answer these questions definitively because few countries in the world collect data on international trade freight, let alone on domestic freight rates. The United States is one of the few exceptions and provides a rare opportunity to get some international perspective on Latin America's freight costs. Figure 5.4 offers a preliminary answer to the question and suggests that the region as a whole spends nearly twice as much as the United States to import its goods: Argentina has the lowest costs and, not surprisingly, landlocked Paraguay has the highest. With data alone, it not possible to determine what is driving the results: geography, trade volume or composition, or other policy-related issues such as the quality of the infrastructure.

Figure 5.5 uses data to compare Latin America's transport costs with those of other exporters to the United States. As with import freights, little can be said about the determinants of these results. Nevertheless, the comparison provides interesting insights that confirm the findings using imports. The general conclusion is that proximity does not always translate into lower freight rates. Most Latin American countries have higher freight rates than countries in the Far East and Europe. This is striking,

Figure 5.4 Total Import Freight Expenditures as a Share of Imports, United States and Selected Latin American Countries, 2006

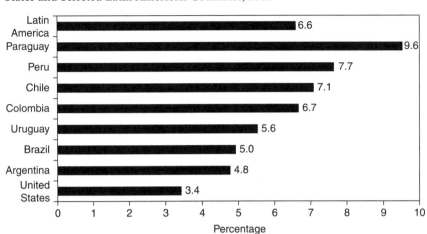

Source: Authors' calculations based on Asociación Latinoamericana de Integración (ALADI) dataset and U.S. Census Bureau dataset on U.S. Imports of Merchandise (various years).

Note: Latin America is the simple average of Argentina, Brazil, Chile, Colombia, Paraguay, Peru, and Uruguay.

particularly when considering countries that are very close to the United States, like those in the Caribbean. As expected, most of the countries of the Southern Cone lie at the higher end of the range, but even these countries, as well as some countries from Central America that are very close to the United States such as Guatemala and Panama, exhibit freight rates that are higher than China or Oceania.

The evidence suggests that Latin America's transport costs are relatively high, but how are these costs evolving over time? Is the situation improving or deteriorating? Mesquita Moreira, Volpe, and Blyde (2008) assess the region's trends in transport costs by mode of transportation after controlling for changes in trade composition. Aside from some nuances across countries, the general finding is that ocean freight costs in the region have been converging to those of the developed world but when it comes to the increasingly important air freight, the gap has been growing.

The burning question is, what drives the high level of transport costs in Latin America? Answering this question involves isolating the role of a number of complex and interrelated issues, ranging from the quality of infrastructure services to distance, scale, and market structure. Fortunately, the literature has benefited from a number of recent contributions using micro data that have provided very useful insights (see Hummels 2001; Clark, Dollar, and Micco 2004; Micco and Serebrisky 2006; Hummels,

Figure 5.5   Freight Expenditures as a Share of Exports to the United States, 2006

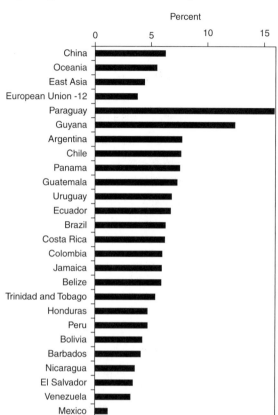

Source: Authors' calculations based on U.S. Census Bureau dataset on U.S. Imports of Merchandise (various years).

Note: European-12 countries are Austria, Belgium, Denmark, Finland, France, Germany, Ireland, Italy, Luxembourg, the Netherlands, Sweden, and the United Kingdom.

Lugovskyy, and Skiba 2009). Inspired by this literature, Mesquita Moreira, Volpe, and Blyde (2008) provide a series of econometric exercises to analyze what factors explain the higher transport costs in Latin America relative to other regions. The analysis is done by mode of transportation and trade flows. Box 5.2 summarizes the case for ocean freight costs in export flows.

Beyond the nuances of mode of transportation, country, and trade flow, some general findings are worth stressing. A large part of the higher transport costs in Latin America relative to the developed world is explained by differences in composition. The goods that the region imports and exports—particularly exports—are considerable "heavier" than those of the United States or Europe. Grains, minerals, and commodities in general

are very "heavy" products because they have very high weight-to-value
ratios. Since freight costs have been shown to be directly proportional
to weight-to-value ratios (Hummels 2001), natural resource exporters
pay relatively more to transport their goods. The implication of this is
clear: poor and costly transport infrastructure can severely undercut the
rents that countries can extract from their natural resources, transferring
income from producers to monopolistic and inefficient freight-forwarders
or port, road, and airport operators. Rather than just an inevitable fact,
differences in composition is a powerful reminder of the strategic importance of transport infrastructure for the countries of the region.[12]

Composition, however, does not tell the whole story. Once its influence is netted out, factors related to the efficiency of the infrastructure in
ports and airports generally explain about 40 percent of the difference in
shipping costs between Latin America and the United States and Europe.[13]
Many factors affect port and airport efficiency. In the case of ports, for
example, their efficiency is related not only to the quality of their physical
facilities, but also to various other support activities, such as pilotage, tow-
ing and tug assistance, and cargo handling. Port efficiency also depends on
aspects such as the clarity of port procedures, the accuracy of their information systems, and the existence of legal restrictions, such as requiring
special licenses to perform loading and unloading operations, which can
influence the port's performance (Fink, Mattoo, and Neagu 2002). The
degree of airport efficiency depends on similar aspects.

Detailed data on port and airport efficiency are hard to find. The literature on the determinants of transport costs—including the exercise shown
in Box 5.2—often relies on econometric analysis to recover a parameter
that captures the efficiency of the port or the airport (see also Blonigen
and Wilson 2006). Aggregate data at the country level are more commonly available (e.g., as in *The Global Competitiveness Report*), but such
information typically relies on subjective opinions. Figure 5.6 presents
two productivity measures based on hard data at the port level taken from
Drewry (2002), a rare dataset that compiled information from around 600
ports around the world. The figures are aggregated at the regional level for
comparison. Note that productivity is measured in a conventional way: the
level of output (number of containers per year handled) compared to the
level of inputs, such as numbers of cranes (see "X" axis) or meters of quay
(see "Y" axis). The measures confirm that Latin America lags behind many
other regions in terms of the productivity of its port systems.

The analysis in Box 5.2 also reveals a third—albeit lesser—factor contrib-
uting to higher transport costs in Latin America: the lower degree of competition among shipping companies. A similar result is found in Hummels,
Lugovskyy, and Skiba (2009). The benefits to transport costs of increasing

---

Box 5.2   Explaining Differences in Ocean Freight Costs between Latin American Countries and Other Countries

Several factors explain international freight costs. The first and most studied determinant is geography, particularly distance. A second obvious determinant is the transportability of the good. Holding value constant, heavier goods normally command higher ad valorem shipping prices. The volume of imports is another factor that affects transport costs, as the transport industry is generally associated with scale economies. Trade imbalances between markets can also affect shipping prices. When a ship is forced to travel empty in one direction, freight rates tend to be higher, as the shipper normally pays for forgone capacity on either the inbound or the outbound trip (Clark, Dollar, and Micco 2004). Shipping prices depend on the degree of competition on the commercial route, as well. Price discrimination is also a characteristic of the shipping industry. For instance, it has been shown that larger markups are expected on goods with relatively inelastic import demands and with larger tariff rates (for details, see Hummels, Lugovskyy, and Skiba 2009). Two other determinants of ocean freight rates are the quality of port infrastructure and the level of containerization.

Mesquita Moreira, Volpe, and Blyde (2008) provide details of an econometric estimation that relates transport charges paid by U.S. imports from several ports around the world with proxies for all the variables cited above. Using the results from this estimation, they perform a decomposition exercise based on Hummels, Lugovskyy, and Skiba (2009) to compare Latin America's export freights to the United States with those of the Netherlands.[a] The exercise is done for 11 Latin American countries. The figure in this box depicts graphically the results for the simple average of the region. Latin America's exports to the

---

competition in the sector might not be limited to actual transportation services. A whole array of auxiliary port and airport services, such as storage and warehousing, provisioning, repairing, and fueling, can be allocated competitively. In this aspect, competition and port efficiency become interrelated.[14]

Thus far, this chapter has focused on the international dimension of transport costs: the costs incurred in moving merchandise from at the carrier at the port (or airport) of exit and placing it at the carrier at the port of entry. The main reason for this international focus is analytical convenience, because collecting data on domestic freight costs is a challenging exercise, to say the least. But counting transport costs only between borders is clearly arbitrary. Like international transport costs, high transport costs within

(continued)

United States command freight rates that are 70 percent higher than those from the Netherlands, on average. The main factors explaining this difference are the weight-to-value ratios and port efficiency, followed by the levels of competition among shipping companies and, to a lesser degree, the volumes of trade.

Box 5.2 Figure   Decomposing Differences in Ocean Freights between Latin America and the Netherlands: Exports to the United States, 2000–2005

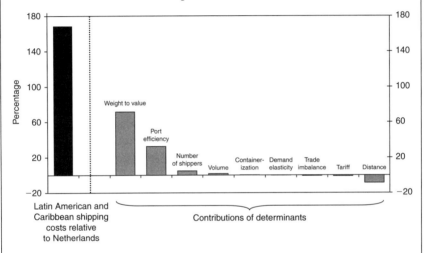

Source: Authors' calculations based on Mesquita Moreira, Volpe, and Blyde (2008)

[a] The Netherlands is selected as a benchmark because the country is often recognized for the quality of its port facilities. The results, however, remain qualitatively the same if other benchmarks are used.

a country can undermine the positive impact of trade on productivity, whether through reallocation or import discipline, or both.

Lower domestic transport costs can improve the allocation of resources across the regions and sectors of an economy, and thereby increase aggregate productivity along the lines of the classical gains from trade. Empirical evidence supporting this effect is found in Herrendorf, Schmitz, and Teixeira (2007), which analyzes the impact of the nineteenth-century improvements in the U.S. transportation system. The authors show that declining transport costs for internal commerce encouraged specialization in production between regions in the United States, which, in turn, led to large increases in gross domestic product (GDP). Syverson (2004) also shows that lower internal transport costs can increase spatial

Figure 5.6   Port Productivity Measures, Regional Averages, 2001

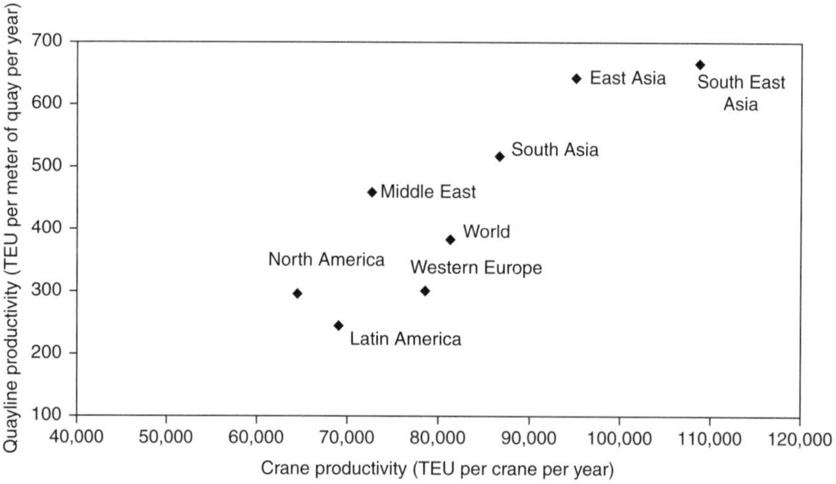

Source: Drewry (2002).

Note: The figure reports regional average productivity measures for ports with container terminals. TEU, or twenty-foot equivalent unit, refers to the size of containers used in maritime transportation.

substitutability in the product market, making it easier for consumers to switch between suppliers. This effect makes inefficient producers more likely to exit, which in turn improves aggregate productivity.

Even within city limits, the benefits of urban density, generated through agglomeration externalities, can quickly diminish with congestion and potentially lead to agglomeration diseconomies (see Graham 2007). Traffic in many large cities in Latin America is congested, which directly increases the costs of moving people and commodities. In Brazil, for example, traffic congestion is estimated to increase public transport operating costs by 15.8 percent in São Paulo, but only by 0.9 percent in Brasília, a mid-size city with abundant highway space (ANTP 1999). Estimates for Chile suggest that a reduction of the average speed of private car journeys and public transportation by 1.0 km/hr and 0.5 km/hr, respectively, would amount to costs equivalent to 0.1 percent of GDP (Thomson 2000). Besides these direct costs, traffic congestion also generates indirect costs associated with lower interactions among suppliers, buyers, workers, and firms, capping the potential productivity gains from scale and agglomeration and limiting the prospects for trade.

Box 5.3 illustrates the importance of domestic transport costs in Latin America, presenting two case studies covering exports of soybeans in Brazil and cut flowers in Ecuador. The studies examine the logistic chains of these products and identify the main problems and bottlenecks. The study for Brazil, for example, reveals that the erosion of competitiveness in exporting soy, when compared to the United States, is driven mainly by the high costs of domestic transportation. The two analyses point to issues such as regulation, the quality of infrastructure, and the lack of competition in the transport industry as the main factors behind these costs.

What Governments Can Do

Clearly, Latin America's high transportation costs undercut its trade-related productivity gains and the relatively poor quality of its infrastructure plus the inefficiency of its transport services are largely to blame for these costs. What can governments do? While an exhaustive list of policy recommendations is beyond the scope of this chapter, a number of general issues are worth noting.

With respect to ocean freight, the region has already made progress toward reducing shipping costs by moving forward on liberalizing the industry (Hoffman 2000). Several countries have eliminated cargo reserves for state-owned shipping companies, privatized national flag carriers, and granted concessions to several port operations. Not all countries, however, have moved at the same pace. Many ports in Central America, for example, have yet to learn from the experience of countries like Colombia, in which concessions to private terminal operators were accompanied by modern port operating practices,[15] resulting in significant reductions in ship waiting and turnaround time and increases in berth productivity.

Liberalizing the industry and decentralizing port operations might not be enough, however. Some investments might not take place without government intervention, such as dragging a channel to allow for larger vessels with lower operating costs to enter a port. The effective regulation of the market is another area in which governments should be active, as anticompetitive practices by carriers and shipping lines across the region are not uncommon (Sánchez and Wilmsmeier 2009). Another problem, particularly for several island countries in the Caribbean, is the atomization of port operations, with many small private terminals operating without the oversight of a unifying port authority (World Bank 2009a). Since cargo agglomeration is important to lower shipping costs through scale economies, governments in these countries would be well advised to encourage some consolidation or coordination of small private operators. Small countries should also gain from coordination among governments to facilitate growth in transshipment, where intermediate hub ports are used to move cargo to its final destination.

With respect to air freight, issues of airport efficiency and regulation lie at the heart of the region's problems. Regulation seems to be particularly dysfunctional (Ricover and Negre 2003). Based on old bilateral agreements with stringent limitations on market access, the regulation of air transport

---

Box 5.3   Domestic Transport Costs and Trade: Case Studies from Brazil and Ecuador

Case studies of two industries in Brazil and Ecuador provide vivid examples of how shortcomings in internal logistic and transportation systems can impose a heavy burden on trade.

Soybeans in Brazil. Brazil is the world's second largest producer and exporter of soybeans, after the United States. The source of this advantage lies in production and land costs that are much lower in the center and west of this country than in many other parts of the world, including the United States. Yet a significant share of this cost advantage is eroded by high domestic transport costs. Comparing the costs of production and internal transportation of soybean in Brazil (North Mato Grosso) with those in the United States (Minneapolis, Minnesota) provide a vivid illustration. The farm value of soybean is lower in Brazil than in the United States, but this initial advantage is eroded once the domestic transport cost of placing the soy at the port of exit is added. Domestic transport costs represent 32 percent of the farm value of soy in Brazil, but only 18 percent in the United States. When transport and production costs are combined, soybeans cost virtually the same in both countries at close to $250/ton. Short of doing a formal econometric analysis, it is worth noting that the distance from Minneapolis to the Gulf of Mexico is roughly similar to the distance from North Mato Grosso to the port of Paranaguá (approximately 1,300 miles). Therefore, it is hard to attribute these differences to distance alone. The high costs in Brazil are mainly the result of the lack of intermodal competition and the low quality of the roads. In Mato Grosso the rail system is almost nonexistent; thus the grain must be moved by

---

services in the region has failed to move in tandem with liberalization efforts in other parts of the world, which have been mostly undertaken through "open skies" agreements.[16] These agreements have helped reduce the costs of air transportation significantly. Micco and Serebrisky (2006), for example, show that the open skies agreements signed by the United States have reduced air transport costs by 8 percent, on average.

While some countries in Latin America have signed bilateral open skies agreements with the United States, very few agreements exist within the region (WTO 2005). Countries in the region could pursue similar bilateral agreements. A bolder liberalization approach would be a multilateral open skies agreement with the objective of creating a truly regional integrated

(continued)

trucks either directly to port or to railway—or waterway—transfer terminals far from the farms. The situation is exacerbated by the poor conditions of the roads, many of which are unpaved.

Cut Flowers in Ecuador. Although Ecuador has successfully developed a cut flowers industry, the country remains at a disadvantage relative to competitors like Colombia. This disadvantage is mainly due to factors related to the country's internal infrastructure. The first factor is somewhat exogenous and is related to geography. Located at about 2,814 meters above sea level, Quito's international airport can receive only short- to medium-range aircraft, and planes cannot take off fully loaded. The transport capacity constraints are exacerbated by the limited number of carriers operating on major routes. This is particularly problematic during the peak season. Another shortcoming has been the limited size area for refrigerated storage that is available at the airport. It is not uncommon to see boxes of flowers stored on the airport's tarmac at temperatures well above what is required. A final shortcoming is related to the airport's landing and other fees, used in part to finance the construction of a new airport,[a] but also to cross-subsidize the provision of air navigation services at small and rural airports with little or no regularly schedule service. At $2,211 per flight, this fee is one of the highest in Latin America.[b]

Source: Authors' summary based on Batista (2008) and Vega (2008).
[a] A new airport is scheduled to open in 2010 and is being built at 2,400 meters above sea level.
[b] Figure for March 2007, according to International Air Transport Associated (IATA).

market. Brazil has recently proposed an open skies agreement for South America, for example.[17]

Another area for improvement is airport services. With the exception of a few operational services, such as meteorological services, most commercial and handling operations can be subject to competitive forces. Indeed, to promote airport efficiency, the traditional public ownership model that existed in most of the world until the mid-1980s has gradually been replaced by various privatization schemes and concession contracts. The privatization trend has been significantly slower in Latin America than in many other parts of the world, particularly in industrialized countries or in the Asia-Pacific region. For example, the percentage of non-aeronautical revenues in Latin America's airports is only 28 percent, about half the percentage in North America. This is mainly the result of the limited retail concessions and commercial operations available in the region's airports (ACI 2008).[18]

While airport privatization throughout the world has generally led to improvements in efficiency, the transfer of ownership has not always generated the expected results (WTO 2006). One reason has been the lack of adequate regulation in the airport industry (ACI 2004). This gap highlights the important role of governments in establishing proper regulatory policies to deal with aspects like safety and the quality of services (Betancor and Rendeiro 1999).

Another area in which governments can actively work to reduce the costs of moving goods internationally is by reducing inefficiencies related to customs. Trade costs from custom delays can significantly add to the logistic costs of shipping goods across countries (see Mesquita Moreira, Volpe, and Blyde 2008). Custom inefficiencies can arise from complex custom declaration forms, procedures, and clearance to lack of coordination between phytosanitary and customs services within a country to lack of collaboration between custom agencies in neighboring countries (World Bank 2009a). Reducing these inefficiencies can save considerable time and money, which is important particularly for time-sensitive goods.

Another factor that can represent a significant share of the costs of trading goods across countries is inland transport costs, as discussed in Box 5.3. Lack of modal competition is part of the problem. However, the main cause is poor road quality. The importance of investing in roads to reduce the burden of excessive land transport costs cannot be overemphasized. It is well known that the present value of maintaining a road regularly is significantly lower than the cost of engaging in major reparations sporadically.

Reducing traffic congestion in urban centers across Latin America should also be a policy goal. Besides the obvious problem of reducing the quality of urban life, congestion interferes with a city's economic efficiency, decreasing the synergies arising from the concentration of services and ultimately reducing the capacity of firms to compete internationally. Several measures have been proposed to tackle this problem. On the supply side, suggestions vary from improving road markings and signs to synchronizing traffic lights, reversing traffic flow direction, establishing segregated bus lanes, and the most obvious, but also the most expensive, constructing new roads or widening existing ones. On the demand side, measures may involve applying regulations and restrictions or using rewards or disincentives for adopting forms of conduct that reduce congestion (ECLAC 2003). The right mix of measures will depend on the idiosyncrasies of the city, including the capacity of the relevant authorities to enforce certain regulations. In the longer term, a strategic vision of how the city should develop is also fundamental. Achieving results in many of these areas is conditioned, to a large extent, on how transport authorities are organized. The task can be made easier, for example, when town-planning officials and transport authorities across municipalities are well-coordinated or when there is a single unified entity for the metropolitan area (ECLAC 2003).

Still, transport costs are just one factor related to a country's infra-structure that can have an impact on productivity. As a report by the Corporación Andina de Fomento (CAF 2009) shows, other areas such as energy or telecommunications can also play an important role, and therefore also deserve to be part of a broad agenda to boost the region's productivity.

Conclusion

The relationship between trade and productivity, in general, and in Latin America, in particular, is more intricate and far-reaching than captured by previous studies. Trade costs have a negative effect not only on firm pro-ductivity, but also on how resources are allocated across firms. It is not just that import competition, for instance, pushes firms to increase productiv-ity; trade also helps markets select the most efficient firms, improving the economy's overall productivity. A number of empirical exercises have shown that this is the case in Latin America and the Caribbean.

Another important element that has been overlooked is the role of trans-port costs. Trade costs are not just about tariffs. This is particularly impor-tant for Latin American policymakers, given the types of products the region exports and the quality of its infrastructure. Bringing tariffs down, as most of the countries in the region have done in the last few decades, will by itself be insufficient to maximize the positive effects of trade on produc-tivity. Transport costs must be reduced in tandem to allow stronger import competition, greater export opportunities, and faster and more efficient resource allocation among firms. There is plenty of room to bring these costs down in line with costs prevalent in the developed world. The outline of an agenda to fulfill this task is also clear. The utmost priority should be given to improving the efficiency of ports and airports and to reshaping the regulatory framework to promote investment and competition.

The agenda, though, is not restricted to freight costs and does not stop at the border. Other trade costs, such as custom procedures and technical regulations—usually part of the catchall term "trade facilitation"—also deserve the watchful eye of governments and researchers if the objective is to maximize trade flows and their positive impact on productivity. The logistic networks that take goods to ports, airports, and border crossings must also be an integral part of the system; otherwise, the gains made in reducing international freight costs can easily be dissipated because of congested and ill-kept roads or the lack of more cost-effective modes of transportation, such as railways.

The timing of such an agenda could not be more opportune, given that the region is still struggling to raise productivity and consolidate its recent reencounter with growth. Trade surely cannot provide all the answers to the productivity puzzle, but the region has yet to lay all the groundwork to fully extract the productivity benefits that trade can yield.

Notes

1. Schumpeterian incentives refer to the notion, popularized by Schumpeter, that a firm, faced with stronger competition, invests in innovation to put some technological distance between the firm and its competitors.
2. A more recent analysis by Casacuberta and Zaclicever (2009) also provides strong support for the import-discipline channel in Uruguay.
3. The theoretical models contemplate symmetric reductions in trade costs: that is, both the trade costs of importing and exporting change in the same way.
4. See Melitz (2003) for details on these effects.
5. Similar evidence has been found by others. See, for instance, Álvarez and López (2005) for the case of exporters in Chile.
6. Total trade costs refer to the sum of both ad valorem tariffs and freight rates.
7. The potential increase of aggregate productivity through the expansion of high productivity plants via exporting could also take place when firms that are already in the export market increase their sales as a result of the decline in trade costs. The results for Brazil and Chile, however, do not provide empirical support for this particular channel.
8. See Blyde, Iberti, and Mesquita Moreira (2009) for details. The evidence presented in this section is in line with results from Tybout (1991) and Pavcnik (2002).
9. Time-sensitive goods are those whose costs are extremely sensitive to shipping times because of an accelerated depreciation driven, on the supply side, by the physical characteristics of the product (e.g., perishable goods such as fruits, fresh produce, and cut flowers) or by the fast pace of technological progress (such as semiconductors); and, on the demand side, by stringent time requirements (such as inputs to just-in-time assembly) or by unpredictability and volatility of the customers' preferences (such as holiday toys and high fashion apparel) (Hummels 2001).
10. The tariff rate and the import penetration ratio are potentially endogenous to the productivity variables; therefore, the regression is estimated using instrumental variable (IV) techniques. The tariff rate is instrumented using the Mexican most-favored tariff; the two variables have a 0.5 correlation coefficient and it is unlikely that Brazilian producers adjust their efficiency

levels to Mexican protection. The import penetration ratio is instrumented using a gravity equation approach, as in Frankel and Romer (1999). See López-Córdova and Mesquita Moreira (2004) for details.

11. The Chilean tariff rate is instrumented using the most-favored tariff rate from the Philippines. The evolution of both tariff schedules follows very similar patterns over time. The correlation of the Chilean and Philippine tariff rates of 0.54 is one of the highest that can be found, while the two countries engage in very little trade. This suggests that it is unlikely that producers in Chile would adjust their efficiency levels to the protection in the Philippines. The import penetration variable is instrumented using the same gravity equation approach used for Brazil.

12. The composition of trade is not exogenous to transport costs. For instance, if transport costs are high, exporters could avoid shipping heavy goods. However, this is not the case in Latin America because many other factors affect what goods are produced and traded, and comparative advantages in natural resources play a significant role in the region. The nuance of this argument, however, is that declining transport costs in the region could make trade shift even more strongly to high weight-to-value goods. But even if this were to occur, the rents that the countries extract from their natural resources would not be wasted on inefficient transport-related systems.

13. Port efficiency was also found to be an important determinant of maritime transport costs in Clark, Dollar, and Micco (2004).

14. The analysis in Mesquita Moreira, Volpe and Blyde (2008) also reveals that factors like distance, volume, containerization levels, and the import elasticity of the good are important determinants of transport costs. However, *differences* in these factors generally do not contribute much to explain *differences* in transport costs between Latin America and other countries.

15. Examples of these practices are the introduction of electronic tracking of containers and modern cargo handling equipment, such as labor-reducing and time-saving gantry cranes (World Bank 2009a).

16. The term "open skies" was coined in 1992 when the United States signed a bilateral agreement with the Netherlands containing provisions that were much more liberal that the existing agreements. Since then, the term has been used for agreements that are also more liberal.

17. "ANAC quer Tratado de Céus Abertos na America do Sul," http://oglobo. globo.com/pais/mat/2008/03/03/anac_quer_tratado_de_ceus_abertos_na_ america_do_sul-426054295.asp (accessed March 2008).

18. The trend toward airport privatization in Latin America, even at its lower rate, has continued. Brazil, for example, has recently announced the privatization of the Rio de Janeiro (Galeão-Antônio Carlos Jobin) and São Paulo (Viracopos/ Campinas) international airports. The decision was mainly driven by the preparation for the 2014 World Cup and a bid to host the 2016 Olympics, but it was also coupled with the urgent need for renovations at both airports (ACI 2008).

6

Why Credit Matters for Productivity

An economy without credit is like a car without fuel: it simply cannot move forward. There is abundant evidence that credit is an important driver of economic growth.[1] At the most basic level, credit is the mechanism through which savers in the economy connect to borrowers, enabling them to carry out investment projects that are the basis for the process of capital accumulation. But credit does not only foster economic growth through investment. Credit also promotes productivity growth in a number of ways. Indeed, the "productivity channel" through which credit impacts economic growth is an amply studied mechanism.[2]

Accessing credit markets allows individual firms to purchase certain types of goods—mostly capital goods—that would be unavailable without proper funding. It also helps firms sustain long gestation periods when developing new technologies or processes. Thus, in order to upgrade their technologies or processes and achieve higher productivity, firms need to borrow and spread costs over time. Whether firms upgrade and, therefore, improve their productivity, or not, depends to a large extent on whether they have proper access to finance.

Credit markets also improve aggregate productivity by fostering a better allocation of resources across firms. The basic idea dates back to at least Bagehot (1873) and Schumpeter (1912). The argument is that credit enhances productivity through efficient capital reallocation. In poorly developed capital markets, the scale of entrepreneurial activities is determined by entrepreneurs' wealth, not by the quality of their projects. Productive projects may be insufficiently funded due to lack of financing. Conversely, bad but wealthy entrepreneurs may be in business because they cannot transfer their resources to other, more talented entrepreneurs. Deeper financial markets allow more talented entrepreneurs to step into the production arena. They are also more efficient in filtering the best projects and the best entrepreneurs. Larger financial systems play an important role in shuffling and reshuffling funds from firm to firm or from sector to sector so that higher aggregate productivity is achieved. Aggregate productivity increases because high productivity firms/industries can grow while low productivity projects either shrink or go out of business.[3]

Credit can also have positive effects on productivity by reducing the incidence of informality, understood as lack of firm or workers registration, or tax evasion, and social security registration avoidance. One of the costs of informality is not having access to formal credit markets; the greater the supply of credit, the higher the opportunity costs of being informal.

Finally, access to credit allows firms to cope better with macroeconomic volatility. Access to credit during systemic financial crises can be a matter of life or death for distressed firms—even for those that are quite productive; lack of information on the quality of projects can cause credit to be misallocated, leading to the shedding of more productive firms in order to save less productive ones with better connections to credit markets. But volatility can also impact productivity in other ways. For example, it provides incentives for investors to adopt more "malleable technologies" that enable them to accommodate more easily to abrupt and frequent changes in relative prices, but at the cost of preventing the discovery or use of more efficient methods of production. This investment allocation effect, in turn, is stronger in economies with underdeveloped financial markets, as firms in these countries have fewer opportunities to diversify away those risks.[4]

Against this backdrop, low financial depth in Latin America is an important source of concern. It is therefore important to assess whether the largely underdeveloped financial markets in the region can account for the chronically low rates of productivity growth documented in Chapter 2.

Does Credit Really Matter? A Glance at the Evidence

In deeper credit markets, aggregate productivity increases thanks both to a boost in individual firms' productivity and to reallocation effects. In this light, Latin America's underdeveloped credit markets are a serious problem (IDB 2005). While other developing countries also suffer from this problem, East Asia does not.[5] Over the last four decades, the average share of credit to the private sector as a percentage of GDP (77 percent) in East Asia—a widely used measure of credit availability—was comparable to industrial countries (74 percent) and twice that of Latin America

Table 6.1   Financial Development and TFP Growth by Region, 1965–2003

Region	Number of countries	Credit to the private sector (percentage of GDP)	TFP growth (percent)
East Asia	7	77	1.3
Industrial countries	22	74	0.6
Africa	16	18	−0.1
Latin America	18	31	−0.5

Source: Credit to the private sector: World Bank (2009d); and TFP: Fernández-Arias and Daude (2010).

Note: Values are simple averages for the regions in the period between 1965 and 2003. Latin American countries include Argentina, Bolivia, Brazil, Chile, Colombia, Costa Rica, the Dominican Republic, Ecuador, El Salvador, Honduras, Jamaica, Mexico, Nicaragua, Panama, Peru, Paraguay, Uruguay, and Venezuela. East Asia is comprised of Hong Kong, Indonesia, Malaysia, the Philippines, the Republic of Korea, Singapore, and Thailand. Industrial countries are Australia, Austria, Belgium, Canada, Germany, Denmark, Finland, France, the United Kingdom, Greece, Ireland, Italy, Japan, the Netherlands, Norway, New Zealand, Portugal, Spain, Sweden, Turkey, the United States, and South Africa. Finally, African countries are Algeria, Benin, Cameroon, Ghana, Kenya, Lesotho, Mali, Malawi, Mozambique, Niger, Senegal, Sierra Leone, Togo, Tunisia, Uganda, and Zambia.

(31 percent).[6] Over the same period, average aggregate productivity growth, measured as total factor productivity (TFP) growth, in Latin America has underperformed compared to industrial countries and, even more dramatically, in relation to East Asia (Table 6.1).

The cross-country correlation between financial depth and TFP growth is very strong. Figure 6.1 plots the relationship between the mean shares of credit to the private sector over GDP with mean aggregate TFP growth rates by country. The correlation is significantly positive, and regression estimates show that it persists after correcting for GDP per capita levels. As shown in this figure, countries in Latin America are concentrated in the lower left quadrant of the chart, meaning that low financial depth coexists with low TFP growth rates.

The levels of financial depth and TFP have correlated very strongly over the past four decades and may explain a portion of the gap that has developed between Latin America and East Asia. Figure 6.2, taken from a study by Arizala, Cavallo, and Galindo (2009), plots the average level of manufacturing sector TFP and the average level of financial depth for Latin America as well as for East Asia relative to industrial countries. The figure shows that the average TFP levels in Latin America were considerably higher than in East Asia in the late 1960s and early 1970s. This pattern persisted until Latin American countries began a secular decline around the time of the debt crises that beset the region in the early 1980s. The process was temporarily reversed in the 1990s, a period of major market-oriented reforms, until the latter part of the decade when a new wave of financial

Figure 6.1 TFP Growth and Financial Development, 1965–2003

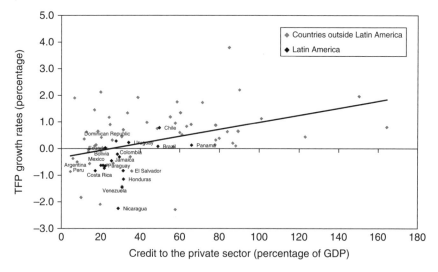

Source: Credit to the private sector, World Bank (2009d) and TFP, Fernández-Arias and Daude (2010).

Figure 6.2 TFP and Financial Development Levels Relative to Industrial Countries, 1965–2003

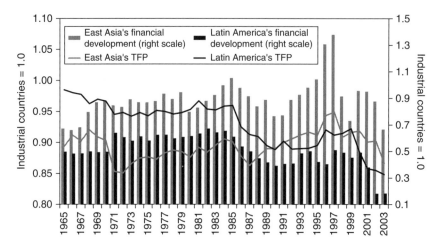

Source: Authors' calculations based on Arizala, Cavallo, and Galindo (2009).

Note: Values are simple averages for the regions for the period of 1965–2003. Latin American and Caribbean countries included are Argentina, Bolivia, Brazil, Chile, Colombia, Costa Rica, the Dominican Republic, Ecuador, El Salvador, Honduras, Jamaica, Mexico, Nicaragua, Panama, Peru, Paraguay, Uruguay, and Venezuela. The East Asia region is comprised of Hong Kong, Indonesia, Malaysia, the Philippines, the Republic of Korea, Singapore, and Thailand. Industrial countries are Australia, Austria, Belgium, Canada, Denmark, Finland, France, Germany, Greece, Ireland, Italy, Japan, the Netherlands, New Zealand, Norway, Portugal, South Africa, Spain, Sweden, Turkey, the United Kingdom, and the United States.

crises—starting with Asia and Russia in 1997 and 1998, respectively—hit the region with full force and TFP collapsed. Instead, East Asia suffered stagnation and even a small decline in the early 1980s that washed out part of the gains achieved during the previous decade. But in the mid-1980s it began a process of rapid catch up that persisted until the financial crises of 1997. This impressive growth likely earned the region its nickname of the "Asian Tigers."[7]

The availability of credit to the private sector is relatively low in Latin America and has been quite fickle. Figure 6.2 also plots the evolution of the average levels of credit to the private sector over GDP in Latin America and East Asia vis-à-vis that of industrial countries during the same period. The patterns closely mimic those of TFP: in East Asia, during the period of high relative TFP growth rates, particularly in the early 1990s, credit availability also increased to levels that even surpassed the average for industrial countries prior to the financial crises of 1997. The pattern changed after the crisis, when both TFP growth and credit collapsed. In Latin American countries, the average levels of relative financial development show a declining trend over time, beginning in the early 1980s (with a short-lived lapse in the early 1990s), similar to the trend of TFP. Overall, the simple correlation for TFP and financial depth series is 75 percent for Latin America and 67 percent for East Asia. These figures also point to the role of financial crises—and the associated crisis volatility—as an important factor underlying the co-movement of credit and TFP. Since financial crises hit emerging markets in 1997 and 1998, affecting Asian countries particularly hard, TFP performance in that region has been fairly disappointing.

While correlations are no proof of causality, they are indicative of aggregate relationships that warrant closer inspection. Arizala, Cavallo, and Galindo (2009) focus on how industries with different characteristics in different countries respond to changes in a country's supply of credit. One of the key features that distinguish industries from one another is the amount of credit needed for each typical production process. Firms in some sectors require more credit than firms in others for, among others, technological reasons. The pharmaceutical industry, for example, is very intensive in research and development. Finding the right drug may take years of research that require extensive financing. Firms in other sectors may have a faster return of their cash flow and can thus fund most of their activities with little or no credit. Deeper credit markets thus have a stronger impact on firms in industries that need credit the most.

Having access to credit markets is a key element in boosting productivity. In fact, as shown in Figure 6.3, an increase in the depth of credit markets can have an important impact on the growth rate of a sector's productivity. On the vertical axis, Figure 6.3 plots the yearly increase in

Figure 6.3   Impact of Increase in Credit on Productivity Growth

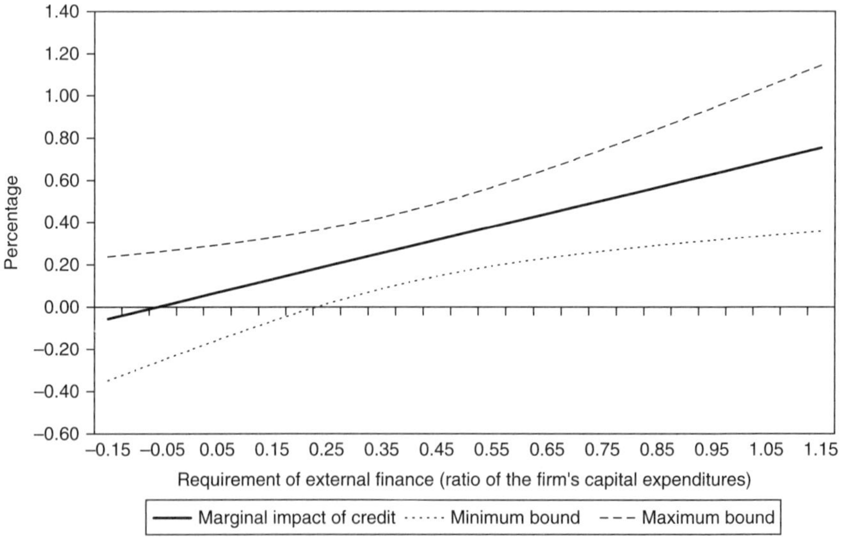

Source: Authors' calculations based on Arizala, Cavallo, and Galindo (2009).

the growth rate of TFP that results from a rise of 35 percentage points in the size of credit markets.[8] This is roughly what it would take to bring the level of financial development in Bolivia to the one prevailing in Portugal. The horizontal axis plots a measure of financial requirements by economic sector that is computed as the difference between the investment needs of firms (capital expenditures) and their cash flow divided by capital expenditures.[9] Greater values of this measure indicate that firms in that sector need more external finance to keep their operation going. In short, the graph indicates that credit boosts productivity growth most in those firms with the greatest credit needs. As external capital needs increase, so does the importance of financial development in explaining productivity growth. For example, for an industry with the median level of finance requirements of 0.53 (i.e., the glass industry), the estimated effect of a 35-percentage-point increase in financial development is an acceleration of TFP growth of approximately 0.4 percent per year. The average TFP growth in that sector has been around 1.2 percent per year. Thus, the estimated increase is equivalent to accelerating the TFP growth rate in this particular sector by approximately 33 percent with respect to the prevailing level. For industries with higher external financial requirements, the boost in TFP growth is even greater. In short, enhancing access to credit has a large impact on productivity growth.

How Does Credit Matter?

Credit matters for productivity growth, and it matters a lot. The mechanisms through which it operates vary from country to country. The results shown above do not shed light on how credit impacts productivity. They suggest that more credit leads to higher productivity within an economic sector, but say little about why this happens. Is it because deeper credit markets allocate resources in a more effective way? Is it because when more credit is available individual firms can increase their own productivity? Is it a combination of both?

Answers to these questions are scarce. A study by Bergoeing et al. (2002) points to the importance of financial reforms for TFP growth by contrasting the differences in Mexico and Chile following the debt crises of the 1980s. While both countries experienced severe economic crises, Chile recovered much faster and more solidly than Mexico. Using growth accounting, a calibrated growth model, and other tools, they found that the crucial difference between the two countries was the earlier and more decisive reforms in banking and bankruptcy procedures in Chile, which led to productivity growth. The key differentiating element was financial deepening, which was higher in Chile than in Mexico. With more developed financial markets, there is less room for misallocating resources. One of the regulatory elements that supported deeper financial markets in Chile was the proper design of bankruptcy rules. The institutional setup behind bankruptcy procedures led to higher aggregate productivity by encouraging poorly performing firms to exit production.

A study on Thailand by Jeong and Townsend (2007) emphasizes occupational choices as an important channel connecting financial development and TFP growth. In the model, productivity growth comes from improving the allocation efficiency of labor, which in turn depends on the distribution of wealth and the efficiency and depth of the financial system. People can choose occupations that employ either traditional or modern production technologies. Modern technologies are better suited for talented people and are more productive. While technological blueprints are available to everyone, modern technologies are costly and thus talented but poor entrepreneurs without access to credit may be forced into less efficient occupations that use less costly traditional technologies. Limited access to credit generates a mismatch between talent and wealth in occupational choice. Therefore, access to credit helps poor people relax the borrowing constraint on their occupational choices, enabling the talented poor to access modern technology. In the case of rich but less talented people who are not credit-constrained, access to credit, by virtue of shifting factor prices in the economy, might end up discouraging the choice of modern technologies for which they are not well suited. Aggregate productivity thus depends on efficiency in allocating talent in the economy, which improves as the financial sector expands.[10]

In addition, a recent study by Eslava et al. (2009) tackles some of the questions mentioned above by using a very rich data set of manufacturing firms in Colombia. Although it is difficult to generalize results, they provide a reference for understanding how credit markets affect productivity.

In Colombia, when credit increases, the productivity of firms in the sector that receives it generally rises as well. This result is similar to the one highlighted above for a larger set of countries—but with a caveat. The relationship between aggregate productivity of the sector and credit availability depends on the average size of firms in that sector. The smaller the firms in the sector, the stronger is the link between access to credit and aggregate productivity in that sector. A possible explanation is that deeper credit markets are better able to reallocate resources from less to more productive firms in that sector. In this vein, industries with smaller firms that are typically more credit-constrained than larger firms, are likely to have more space for the reallocation mechanism to work, as credit can now be allocated to constrained units with a higher marginal product of capital. Given these characteristics, credit is expected to have a higher impact on industries with smaller firms than on industries with large ones.[11]

Figure 6.4 summarizes these findings. The horizontal axis plots the average size of firms in the sector, while the vertical axis measures the impact of increasing credit in one standard deviation (14 percent in the sample studied). In sectors with small firms, the impact is very large. A 14 percent increase in credit can lead to a greater than 50 percent jump in productivity. As the average size of the firms in the sector rises, the impact of credit fades away. The impact is positive and statistically different from zero (that is, the lower-bound estimate is greater than zero) for sectors in which the average firm has fewer than 40 workers.[12] For sectors with larger firms, accessing credit does not impact productivity significantly. When decomposing the rise in productivity into the part attributed to the increase in the average firm size in the sector and the reallocation component, the study finds that most of the action of increasing credit in Colombia comes through the reallocation effect.

These results say much about credit's role in enhancing productivity. Deeper financial systems have the virtue of identifying profitable opportunities and allocating resources in that direction. Evidence for Colombia shows that this may be particularly relevant for smaller firms, which are typically more credit-constrained.

Figure 6.4   Impact of Increase in Credit on Productivity in Colombia

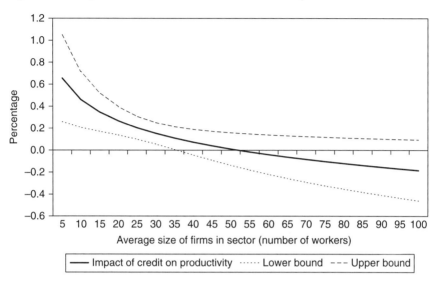

Source: Authors' calculations based on Eslava et al. (2009).

Does Size Matter?

The discussion above suggests that size matters, too. The impact of getting credit differs across different types of firms. The same Colombian study mentioned above estimates the impact of an increase in credit on an individual firm's productivity and finds that it is positive and relevant up to a certain firm size.[13] A study using surveys carried out by the World Bank in 43 countries, including 17 from Latin America and the Caribbean, yields similar results and finds that access to credit is correlated with productivity in different ways depending on the size of the firm receiving the credit. Undoubtedly, using some data sets to analyze causality, that is inferring that one thing, such as having credit, leads to another, such as raising productivity, is very tricky. It is possible that credit raises productivity, or that because productivity is high, firms receive credit. Unfortunately, in many cases it is not possible to identify whether the egg or the chicken came first, and at best, it can be said that the two events occurred simultaneously or that they were correlated. This is the case here.

Identifying causality is not the only problem faced when analyzing these data. In addition, the information available to measure productivity is limited. These two caveats suggest the need for great caution when interpreting the correlations between measures of access to credit, firm size, and productivity. However, using survey data to measure revenue productivity, which is the difference between the value of the output and the value of the combination of inputs in a production function, access to credit correlates strongly with productivity.[14] Of particular interest is the relatively greater correlation between credit and productivity in smaller firms than in larger ones.[15]

One way of interpreting this finding—closely related with the story told previously—is that large firms are less credit-constrained than smaller ones. When the constraint is relaxed in small- and medium-sized firms, they can adopt new technologies that raise their productivity. Large firms may already be highly productive. They may access credit or other sources of financing and grow maintaining their high productivity, in which case they will be even larger but not necessarily much more productive.

Increasing access to credit to small firms could raise their productivity. But not all credit is the same. The "quality" of credit varies. Usually smaller firms access different types of credit and under different conditions than larger firms. Table 6.2 uses survey data to show how firms finance their investment needs in Latin America compared to other regions of the world. A few results are worth highlighting.

First, firms in Latin America have less access to credit provided by financial institutions than their counterparts in advanced economies and other emerging markets. This is true for firms of almost all sizes, but the gap between the share of investment financed through financial institutions in Latin America with respect to advanced economies is wider for larger firms.

Second, in Latin America, firms resort to trade credit more than in other regions of the world to finance investment. This happens in firms of different sizes, and should raise flags given the nature of this type of funding. Usually trade credit is a very short-term financial instrument. Investment decisions that enhance firm productivity tend to be long-term enterprises. Financing such activities with short-term credit may signal a low-quality investment, or expose firms to the possibility of interruptions in their investment plans.

Third, capital markets in Latin America are not a significant source of funding for firms. Firms in the emerging world need to rely more than their counterparts in advanced economies on other sources of funding, most of them informal. As expected this is more common among smaller firms than larger ones. Informal sources are usually far more expensive than formal sources, meaning that smaller firms not only have less access to external funding, but also pay a disproportionately higher cost to access funds.

Table 6.2 Firm Financing of Investment

Firm Size	Advanced economies	Emerging markets	Latin America
		Region	
	Share financed with financial institutions (percentage)		
Small	24.1	18.7	20.2
Medium	33.6	24.3	22.5
Large	34.2	32.9	26.7
	Share financed with trade credit (percentage)		
Small	2.7	2.5	7.3
Medium	2.4	3.9	8.2
Large	2.7	3.2	6.5
	Share financed with sales of stock (percentage)		
Small	5.9	7.7	0.8
Medium	7.3	5.7	1.5
Large	5.9	4.9	1.2
	Share financed with other sources (percentage)		
Small	3.3	5.8	4.5
Medium	0.4	6.7	3.8
Large	0.7	2.6	1.8

Source: World Bank (2009c).

Note: Small firms are those with fewer than 20 workers, medium with more than 20 and less than 100, and large with more than 100. Countries in sample—Advanced economies: the Czech Republic, Germany, Greece, Ireland, Portugal, and Slovakia; Emerging Markets: Algeria, Bulgaria, China, Croatia, Egypt, Georgia, Hungary, India, Indonesia, Kazakhstan, Lebanon, Malaysia, Montenegro, Morocco, Pakistan, the Philippines, Russia, Serbia, Turkey, Ukraine, and Vietnam; Latin America: Argentina, Bolivia, Brazil, Chile, Colombia, Costa Rica, the Dominican Republic, Ecuador, El Salvador, Guatemala, Honduras, Jamaica, Mexico, Nicaragua, Panama, Paraguay, Peru, Uruguay, and Venezuela.

How does this relate to the discussion on productivity? As stated above, access to credit is a crucial ingredient for productivity growth. Thus, if there are important differences between the way firms of different sizes fund themselves, then there may be disparities in the role of credit for each type of firm. Smaller firms have less access to formal sources of credit. Due to information problems, credit is usually more expensive for them and probably of "lower quality." Likely, the quality of the credit they can access (mostly short-term) is not the best for achieving the best possible investment in productivity-enhancing activities.

Increasing access to formal credit markets and to credit with longer maturities is desirable to secure a bigger bang for the buck. Market and regulatory failures usually deter smaller firms from accessing the right type of credit. This can be corrected.

Does Credit Induce Formalization in Labor Markets?

Credit can also enhance productivity by affecting firms' incentives to be informal. As discussed in other chapters in this book, the presence of widespread informality tends to undermine allocation efficiency, with potentially important consequences for productivity. If informality results from optimizing decisions made by rational agents, then explaining the phenomenon boils down to weighing the costs and benefits of going informal. A major cost of being informal is the inability to tap into formal credit markets.[16] This opportunity cost rises as financial markets deepen and credit is more abundant, cheaper, and, in general, more accessible.

Catão, Pagés, and Rosales (2009) find strong evidence of the credit-formality-productivity link in Brazil. Between mid-2004 and the first half of 2008, formalization—as measured by the share of urban workers with a formal labor contract—rose from 38 to 45 percent of the urban labor force; during the same period, bank credit rose from 25 to 38 percent of GDP, with credit to formal firms rising from 15 to 24 percent.[17] The study relates the needs of each industry in terms of external funding to the availability of a larger credit supply. It tests whether formalization rates increase more in industries with a greater need for external funding when the supply of credit increases, and finds that the relationship between financial deepening and formal employment is stronger in sectors that rely more on credit.

Promoting registration and formalization of firms—which in turn positively impacts productivity by reducing the incentive for firms to remain small and invisible to authorities—levels the playing field, as it reduces the implicit subsidy that noncompliance provides to a substantial number of firms at the expense of larger, more productive ones that comply with tax laws and regulations.[18]

Do Volatility and Crises Matter?

Underdeveloped credit markets are not only related to lower amounts of credit, but also to macroeconomic volatility. High volatility is correlated to poorer TFP growth performance in the cross-section of countries. Figure 6.5 plots the relationship between the average volatility of the real exchange rate by country (a key measure of crisis volatility) and the TFP growth rates by country.[19] Note that the simple correlation is not as strong (in absolute value) as in the case of financial depth. However, it is quite relevant when it comes to emerging markets, bringing the correlation up to 65 percent. Regression estimates (not reported) show that the association between the variables is positive for the subsample of industrial countries

Figure 6.5   TFP Growth and Volatility of the Real Exchange Rate, 1965–2003

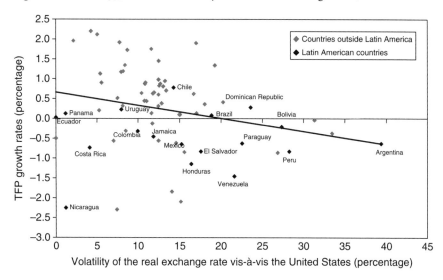

Source: Volatility, authors' calculations based on International Monetary Fund (2009a) and TFP, Fernández-Arias and Daude (2010).

and negative for emerging market economies, suggesting that advanced countries are able to cope with volatility better. Furthermore, it suggests that volatility per se is not detrimental to TFP growth, but when combined with other frictions, it can compound to generate negative effects.

A key characteristic of emerging markets is that while most of the time they enjoy the benefits of financial integration, they are also susceptible to periodic financial crises that typically come hand in hand with a disruption of the banking system (see IDB 2005). As a matter of fact, Latin America has historically been the region with the largest share of systemic banking crises, as well as the largest share of countries that backslide into banking crisis mode—at least until recently. Indeed, Latin America has withstood the current global financial crisis so far with unusual resilience. Two factors highlighted by the literature on financial crisis may help explain this resilience: liability dollarization levels are low, particularly compared to the late 1990s when the Russian crisis wreaked havoc on the region, and the average current account balance position is much better than in the past, suggesting that potential changes in the real exchange rate to accommodate a sudden cut in external financing are less severe.[20] This is good news since avoiding a financial crisis keeps the specter of large real exchange rate depreciation and associated balance-sheet effects at bay. It may actually be the first time in a long time that Latin America finds itself in this relatively advantageous position.

Figure 6.6   TFP Behavior in Emerging Markets during Systemic Sudden Stops

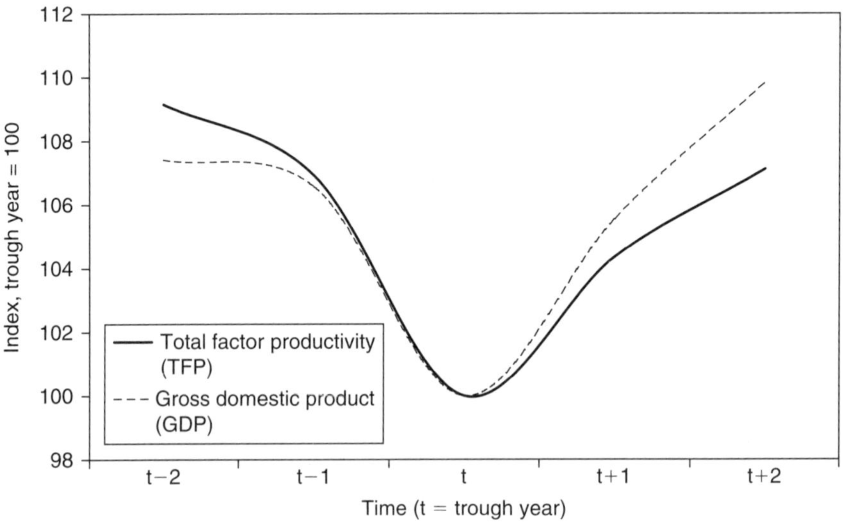

Source: Calvo, Izquierdo, and Talvi (2006).

However, previous performance in the region has been largely influenced by external fluctuations and associated financial crises. Recent evidence suggests that output behavior in the region is highly susceptible to external factors, some of them real (such as terms of trade, G7 countries growth), but also financial, like international interest rates and global spreads.[21] The influence of external factors becomes more critical when systemic financial crises lead to a sudden stop in capital flows in any particular country. Not only does output collapse during those episodes, but most of the collapse can be explained by a dramatic fall in TFP. Figure 6.6, representing average GDP and TFP behavior for a pool of 22 systemic crisis episodes in emerging markets (drawn from Calvo, Izquierdo, and Talvi 2006), attests to this relationship. However, in apparently miraculous fashion, most output recoveries to precrisis levels occur relatively rapidly, with a concomitant increase in TFP to precrisis levels. Does this mean that countries should not, therefore, worry about the consequences of financial crisis on productivity? On the contrary, even though countries seem to recover to precrisis TFP levels relatively quickly, they almost never recover to precrisis trend levels.[22] Additional evidence indicates that output does not recover either to precrisis trends.[23]

One possible explanation for this behavior lies in the way recoveries are financed. During crisis episodes, lack of access to credit is compensated by a substantial fall in investment (on average 34 percent from peak to trough), thus liberating the necessary resources to finance working capital needs that put idle physical capital back to work.[24] However, this comes at a cost: postponing investment purchases and new technology adoption affects future TFP performance.

Another explanation rooted in microeconomic developments relates to firm performance during times of crisis. The standard view of the literature on productivity behavior during recessions is in some ways Schumpeterian in that a "cleansing" effect occurs when inefficient firms exit the market in bad times, thus raising average TFP.[25] However, things may be quite different in the presence of credit frictions, especially when efficient production arrangements are vulnerable to credit constraints.[26] In particular, systemic financial crises may be events in which access to financial markets could be vital for survival regardless of productivity levels. Credit constraints could have a negative effect on aggregate productivity during downturns via an allocation effect. Firms with relatively high productivity, but which are credit-constrained and therefore cannot face recessions successfully, may be forced to exit the market. Shedding of high productivity firms could be productivity-decreasing at the aggregate level. This channel is most likely to operate through young firms that are highly productive but have still not achieved an optimal size, in contrast to older, less productive firms that may be less likely to face credit constraints, particularly when credit is assigned according to the ability of firms to provide collateral rather than on the profitability of projects.

Eslava et al. (2009) provide evidence for this in work performed at the plant level in Colombia. For firms with similar levels of productivity, the probability of exit of a firm varies sharply depending on its size. Figure 6.7 shows the probability of exit of a firm at different TFP levels, both for firms with fewer than 20 employees—a standard measure separating small from larger firms—and firms with 20 or more employees. It shows that at the average productivity levels, a small firm is almost four times more likely to exit than a larger firm with the same level of TFP.[27] How much more productive does a small firm need to be to share the same probability of exit of a large firm? In order to keep, say, an exit probability of 10 percent, a smaller firm needs to be three-and-a-half times more productive than a larger firm. In other words, survival is not only about being productive; there are additional factors that influence that outcome. To the extent that size constitutes a measure of access to credit, it could explain differences in survival rates at similar productivity levels.

This becomes particularly clear when analyzing exit probabilities in crisis years vis-à-vis noncrisis years for small and large firms. Crisis years refer to the time of the Asian/Russian crisis of 1997–1998, when financial constraints gripped many countries and the region experienced a

Figure 6.7   Exit Probability of Small and Large Firms at Varying Total Factor Productivity (TFP) Levels

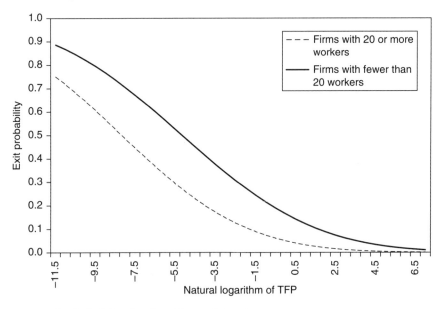

Source: Authors' calculations based on Eslava et al. (2009).

sudden stop in capital flows. During these times, access to credit can very well make the difference between "making it or breaking it." Figure 6.8 shows the difference in exit probabilities between small and large firms during crisis and non-crisis times. It demonstrates that the difference in exit probabilities between small and large firms balloons dramatically during crisis times, particularly at lower TFP levels, providing support to the hypothesis that higher productivity firms with scarce credit links may not have survived, whereas less efficient firms with better credit links may have made it.[28] To the extent that size is an indication of access to credit, and under the assumption that larger firms are loosely unconstrained relative to small firms, the difference in exit probabilities between small and large firms shown in Figure 6.8 can be a proxy for credit allocation distortions present during crisis episodes. Thus, firms that are similar in TFP levels but different in size may not have the same chance of survival, indicating the presence of an "uncleansing" effect of recessions when credit allocation is inefficient.

Thus far, the discussion has centered on the consequences of financial volatility, crises, and distortions in credit allocation on TFP performance. But what does the impact of volatility on TFP suggest about the future? Can a history of crises and volatility in relative prices affect the decisions

Figure 6.8   Difference in Exit Probabilities between Small and Large Firms in Recessionary vs. Nonrecessionary Times (at varying TFP levels)

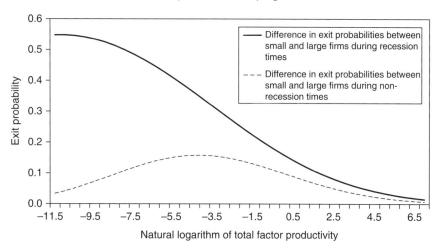

Source: Authors' calculations based on Eslava et al. (2009).

firms make regarding technology choices, thereby influencing future average productivity? A key characteristic of economies faced with systemic sudden stops in capital flows is their exposure to dramatic real exchange rate fluctuations.[29] Living in an economy that is periodically exposed to such turmoil in relative prices means that entrepreneurs face substantial uncertainty about the profitability of alternative projects. Under these conditions, a key asset is the ability to adapt to such a volatile environment. In the presence of incomplete markets where relative price insurance is not an option—as is often the case in emerging markets—one way of coping with such volatility is by privileging technologies that are highly malleable. The Latin American literature has long identified this idea as "speculative production," in that entrepreneurs, constantly speculating on relative price volatility, pick technologies that make it easy to switch from one product to another.[30] One of the clearest examples is transitory crop production in the agricultural sector, whereby producers may quickly switch crops depending on relative prices.

However, greater malleability may not be costless, given that constantly jumping from one task to another may prevent the discovery or use of more efficient methods of production.[31] Implicit in this statement is that specialization and focusing on narrow tasks are conducive to greater innovation or productive efficiency. As a result, more specialized, less malleable technologies tend to be more productive. To what extent does this hold? Although malleability is difficult to assess empirically, a shortcut is

Figure 6.9   TFP and Technology Flexibility as Measured by the Capital-Labor Ratio (industrial sector averages)

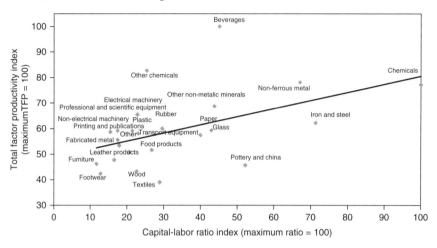

Source: Authors' calculations based on United Nations Industrial Development Organization (2008).

to consider capital intensity relative to labor as a proxy for inflexibility, under the assumption that labor is easier to reallocate than capital, which tends to be more specific to a particular production process. Figure 6.9 shows the relationship between an index of the capital-labor ratio and an index of TFP for a world sample of industrial sectors coming from United Nations Industrial Development Organization (2008) It indicates that more capital intensive, probably less flexible technologies are associated with higher TFP levels—the correlation between these two variables is 0.5—supporting the view that more productive technologies could, in fact, be more inflexible. If this is the case, then volatility could bias investment choices into technologies that are less productive but highly malleable. To the extent that expected volatility is a cloud on the investment horizon, economies could remain stuck in less productive environments than those of less volatile peers.[32]

The notion that volatility affects the composition of investment has been formalized by the literature in an allocation model of foreign direct investment.[33] In this framework, exchange rate volatility is shown to stimulate the share of investment activity located on foreign soil. However, this literature does not explore investment allocation based on the underlying productivity of technologies and their malleability. Recent work by Cavallo et al. (2009) marries the idea that macroeconomic volatility conspires against the choice of more productive technologies to the idea that volatility affects the composition of investment and asks: can volatility affect sectoral investment

Figure 6.10   Investment, TFP, and Volatility in Emerging Markets

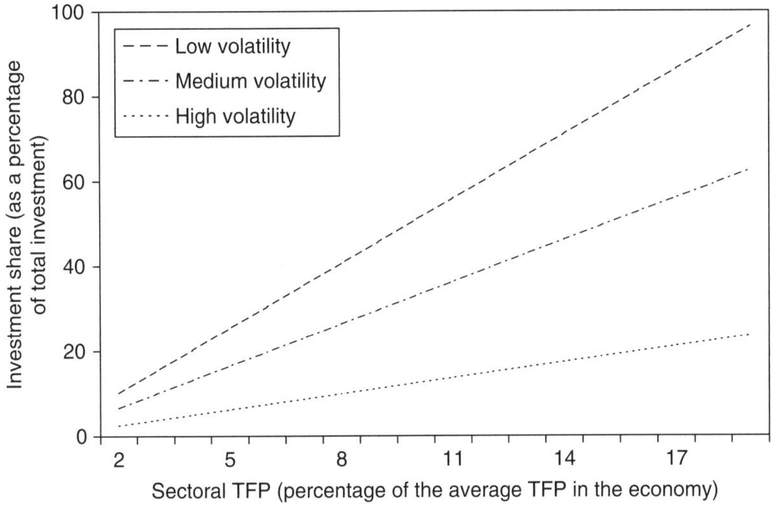

Source: Authors' calculations based on Cavallo et al. (2009).

allocation away from what TFP differences would indicate? The answer is affirmative for the case of emerging market economies.

Figure 6.10 shows the share of investment in a particular sector in total investment on the vertical axis, and relative productivity of that sector vis-à-vis the economy average on the horizontal axis. The relationship between these two variables is plotted for different levels of relative price volatility—defined here as real exchange rate volatility. With low volatility, there is a strong positive relationship between relative TFP and investment shares, meaning that—controlling for a set of other factors—investment tends to be allocated to more productive areas. However, as volatility increases, this relationship becomes less pronounced, suggesting that entrepreneurs may choose relatively less efficient (but more malleable) technologies in the face of volatility. To make this point more concrete, consider what would happen to the share of investment in a highly productive sector (at the 90th percentile of relative TFP) if volatility were reduced from the 95th to the 5th percentile. For this particular case, the increase in its share of total investment would be 11 percentage points. This difference can be interpreted as the inefficiency in production due to the presence of volatility. However, from the point of view of an entrepreneur, this may be perfectly optimal. In this case, volatility acts as a negative externality that hinders more productive investment allocation.

Interestingly, these results are statistically significant for emerging markets, but are not for either developed countries or developing countries not included in the emerging market group. Apparently, volatility hurts the most in countries that, while integrated to international capital markets, may lack sufficient institutional arrangements to cope with it. This result is echoed in recent findings that relate the probability of facing a sudden stop in capital flows—a major culprit for real exchange rate volatility—to levels of financial integration.[34] Countries with low levels of financial integration face only a small probability of a sudden stop, but so do developed countries that, while being vastly integrated, possess sophisticated volatility coping weaponry and are not subject to liability dollarization—a killer when the real exchange rate depreciates. However, emerging markets with higher levels of financial integration but more precarious volatility coping mechanisms than developed countries, face the highest probability of a financial crisis and, as such, are much more exposed to real exchange rate fluctuations stemming from financial turmoil. Of course, this does not mean that greater integration is necessarily bad. On the contrary, recent literature has highlighted the benefits of greater integration despite heightened proneness to crisis.[35] However, it implies that emerging markets are probably the most affected by real exchange rate volatility given their higher chances of facing financial crises. The threat of living in a potentially volatile environment may lie behind the choice of less productive technologies and lower levels of average TFP vis-à-vis more stable regions.[36]

At the microdata level, the notion that volatility conspires against the choice of productive technologies is consistent with results reported in Banerjee and Duflo (2005). They show that the inability to smooth consumption against variations in income due to underdeveloped insurance markets in many developing countries, may lead households to choose technologies that are less efficient, but also less risky.[37] In particular, lack of insurance may lead households to use productive assets as buffer stocks and consumption-smoothing devices, which would be a cause for inefficient investment and misallocation of productive resources.

In summary, there are two financial elements that combine to help explain Latin America's relative underperformance in TFP vis-à-vis industrial countries and East Asia. On the one hand, the region is more prone to financial turmoil. But volatility per se is not enough to explain the relative divergence, as some countries cope with it better than others. The key compounding factor is underdeveloped financial markets. In that context, insurance mechanisms that enable other countries to cope with crisis volatility are missing in the region.

More Credit: How?

Credit is good for productivity. But how can deep, stable, credit markets develop? As with almost everything, there is no single recipe for building up credit markets. Countries around the world and even within Latin America differ in many dimensions. A myriad of coexisting conditions has limited the development of financial markets in many different ways. However, some countrywide studies have identified common factors that repeatedly affect credit markets.

Macroeconomic Instability

In Latin America, macroeconomic instability has been one of the greatest barriers to developing financial markets. Many of the current characteristics of the region's financial markets are strongly rooted in its macroeconomic history. Episodes of hyperinflation and fiscal disarray in the 1970s and 1980s led to a great deal of volatility and uncertainty, limiting the flow of financial resources into countries as well as the space for contracts to flourish. Subsequently, the financial liberalization policies of the 1990s had the unintended side effect of provoking capital market volatility, which also took its toll on financial sector development.

Recently, the region has made significant progress in macroeconomic management. Inflation has been contained in most countries, fiscal conditions have strengthened, and structural weaknesses associated with a greater likelihood of capital markets crises—such as the size of foreign currency denominated liabilities and an inadequate debt term structure—have been reduced. While many weaknesses persist and the state of the macroeconomy may still not be as strong as desired, noteworthy improvements have certainly been made. Thanks to these improvements, the ongoing international capital market crisis has hurt Latin America less than other regions in the world.

Maintaining these achievements and the region's credibility in taming inflation while continuing to address underlying vulnerabilities, particularly fiscal weaknesses, is crucial for financial markets to flourish.[38] However, reducing macroeconomic volatility is not an easy task that can be accomplished overnight. What can be done in the meantime? Can volatility-coping strategies be developed while volatility is reduced? The answer is yes, if insurance markets are developed. If firms have access to insurance instruments that provide a safeguard against large swings in profitability due to relative price fluctuations, they may be better positioned to engage in less malleable but more productive technologies. However, the cost of such insurance mechanisms—if they exist at all—can be prohibitively high in emerging markets. Until recently, insurance in forward exchange rate markets was not common practice. Therefore, thought should be given to ways of developing insurance markets as a first attempt to cope with volatility. The resilience of the region to the first round of shocks of the global crisis without dramatic real exchange rate depreciation and financial collapse at home may provide new opportunities for developing cheaper insurance, particularly since extreme episodes of financial crises, so dreaded by insurance providers, have not materialized this time around.

Even this, however, is not enough; imperfections and frictions at the microeconomic level in the way credit markets work call for policies specifically designed to promote financial development and stability. These policies should go hand in hand with policies to reduce and cope with macroeconomic volatility.

Sector-Specific Policies

One of the main regulatory and institutional constraints for financial development in Latin America is the enormous difficulty involved in enforcing credit contracts. For financial relationships to thrive, the obligations of each involved party in a credit contract need to be explicit, and an enforcing agent must be ready to act if needed. Unfortunately, the effective protection of property rights in financial contracts in the region is weak.

The safeguard of creditors through rules and regulations that clearly dictate the ownership of assets in credit contracts and the efficiency of their enforcement are crucial areas to promote the development and stability of financial markets and increase the access of specific sectors to credit. Increasing the protection of creditor rights can have sizeable impacts on the depth of credit markets, increase credit market stability, and promote access to credit in sectors such as small-and medium-sized enterprises that have usually faced greater credit constraints.[39]

The lack of proper creditor rights enforcement, coupled with informational asymmetries, has in many cases led to inefficient credit allocation based on the availability of collateral instead of the quality of projects. This has on many occasions opened the door for the public sector to intervene in credit markets by creating public banks, which may work as a palliative until market inefficiencies are corrected. However, the impact of public bank intervention on productivity growth is unclear.[40]

In the meantime, while progress is made in boosting protection for creditor rights, work can advance on policies that increase the availability of collateral. In many countries, rules and regulations restrict the use of valuable assets as collateral in credit contracts. In some countries, the civil and commercial codes limit the scope of assets that can be collateralized. For example, there are cases in which movable assets (such as inventories, trucks, certain machines, crops, cattle, etc.) are not accepted as collateral, or if they are, the lender takes possession of the asset, thereby limiting the production process of the borrower. Often, revolving assets such as inventories are excluded as forms of collateral or a specific description of the secured assets is required for them to be pledged. In some countries, it is impossible to extend the security to products, proceeds, or replacements of the original assets pledged. This is particularly important, once again, for inventories. Additionally, laws tend to disfavor the use of specific parts of a business operation rather than the entire operation as a credit guarantee.

Bankruptcy rules and regulations also limit the usefulness of collateral. When a firm files for bankruptcy, the order in which secured creditors are paid is very relevant. Usually, secured creditors are only paid after tax and employee claims. In some countries they go further down the chain. In others the possibility of making claims effective is halted during bankruptcy procedures, which can often take years. This hiatus discourages the supply of credit. Another disincentive to credit is the bankruptcy rule that restricts the parties involved in a credit contract from solving their dispute out of court.

Finally, another institutional impediment to pledging collateral is the lack of organized collateral registries that allow lenders to track what assets have been pledged and on what terms. This is particularly notorious with movable sources of collateral such as machines, cattle, crops, inventories, etc.

Even when assets are pledged, lax rule of law and judiciary inefficiency in the region make securing property rights a costly and inefficient travail. Table 6.3 illustrates how Latin America lags behind advanced economies and other emerging market countries in the protection of creditor rights. The legal rights index in column 1 suggests that the legal conditions for pledging collateral in Latin America are precarious compared to other economies in similar stages of development and the advanced world.

The problems faced by Latin American countries relate not only to the rules and regulations on pledging collateral. Columns 2 and 4 of Table 6.3 deal with issues of enforcement. Both the number of procedures and the costs of enforcing contracts are very high. The combination of an unfavorable legal framework and an inefficient and costly judicial environment is a tragic one, and surely one that prevents financial markets from blossoming.

Improving creditor rights protection fosters productivity enhancements, not only by providing more resources for all types of firms, but also

Table 6.3   Institutional Credit Market Indicators

Region or economy	Legal rights index^a (0–10)	Procedures (number)^b	Duration (days)^c	Cost (percentage of claims)^d	Credit information index^e (0–10)
	(1)	(2)	(3)	(4)	(5)
Latin America	4.8	38.2	749.6	31.9	4.0
Other emerging economies	6.6	34.9	609.3	28.8	4.7
Advanced economies	6.6	31.2	474.6	19.7	4.9

Source: World Bank (2009b).

Notes: (a) Legal rights index measures eight aspects of regulation that protect creditor rights. Higher values correspond to greater creditor rights protection. (b) Procedures are the number of procedures from the moment the plaintiff files a lawsuit in court to the moment of payment in a dispute. (c) The number of days to resolve the dispute. (d) The cost in court fees and attorney fees as a percentage of the debt value disputed. (e) Credit information index measures rules affecting the scope, accessibility, and quality of credit information available through either public or private credit registries. Higher values correspond to greater credit information.

   Countries in sample—Latin America and the Caribbean: Argentina, the Bahamas, Belize, Bolivia, Brazil, Chile, Colombia, Costa Rica, the Dominican Republic, Ecuador, El Salvador, Guatemala, Guyana, Haiti, Honduras, Jamaica, Mexico, Nicaragua, Panama, Paraguay, Peru, Suriname, Trinidad and Tobago, Uruguay, and Venezuela; other emerging economies: China, Egypt, Hong Kong, Hungary, India, Indonesia, Israel, Korea, Malaysia, Pakistan, the Philippines, Singapore, South Africa, Thailand, and Turkey; advanced economies: Australia, Austria, Belgium, Canada, Denmark, Finland, France, Greece, Ireland, Italy, Japan, the Netherlands, New Zealand, Norway, Portugal, Spain, Sweden, the United Kingdom, and the United States.

by helping smaller, but productive, firms achieve a greater scale and adopt new and more efficient technologies. Unfortunately, the political economy of pushing through these types of reforms is very complex. Enhancing the protection of creditor rights is frequently interpreted as a mechanism to transfer power to lenders to use against the common citizen. Frequently, politicians ask if enhancing creditor rights can be associated with increasing the risk of a single female head of household losing her property to banks. The right answer is that it really increases the probability of more single-female headed households owning property. Unfortunately, many debates of this nature end up magnifying the downside risks rather than rationally evaluating the benefits, and ultimately very few countries decide to reform this crucial area.

   Certain types of firms may not have access to the types of goods that are usually pledged as collateral, or may be at a stage of development in which assets have yet to be purchased and hence do not have much to pledge. For these firms, the most valuable source of collateral available is information about their credit history. Credit bureaus or credit information registries have been around in the region for over one hundred years. In some countries, credit information is abundant; in others it is scarce because they lack a culture of sharing credit information or because the legal environment does not favor the storage and exchange of this valuable resource. As shown in column 5, on average the regulatory framework is less conducive to information sharing in Latin America than in other regions of the world. A reform to foster credit information sharing is a useful tool to enhance credit access for smaller firms, particularly microenterprises or the smallest segments of Small and Medium Enterprises (SMEs).

But, as the ongoing international financial crisis has once again proven, credit expansions must be accompanied by prudential policies that guarantee stability. An adequate financial framework that supports risk taking in a responsible way is needed. Currently, an important and lively discussion is taking place on the future of financial regulation and on the best possible organization of supervisors and international cooperation among them. Discussions advance on the need to improve the way credit, liquidity, and risks associated with securitization are monitored, on the way risks are consolidated for supervisory purposes, and on the need to strengthen capital requirements attached to some risks. The debate on strengthening prudential regulations in Latin America is not new, and has been ongoing since the early 1990s. Some countries have moved much faster than others toward new regulatory and supervisory schemes conducive to more stable financial systems, but there is still a long road ahead. Current advances will surely be accompanied by developments in international mechanisms for supervisory cooperation.

Regarding credit allocation policies, there has been a long and ongoing discussion on the benefits of directing credit toward specific sectors. Directing credit toward agricultural activities, SMEs, microfirms, and many others has been on the policy agenda in many countries in Latin America. The early 1970s witnessed laissez-faire financial policies throughout much of the region, which led to massive bankruptcies and generalized financial crises. The strategy was reversed in the 1980s and early 1990s when most banking systems were nationalized and credit-targeting practices were adopted. Later, in the 1990s, a new wave of liberalization followed, this time accompanied by stronger prudential regulation. Since then, the region has faced several crises, and the response until now has been to strengthen prudential regulation rather than promote credit-targeting practices. According to several studies, this has been the right approach to promote economic growth and efficiently allocate investment toward its most productive returns.[41]

Directing credit to SMEs is certainly a critical policy and one that is currently being implemented in many countries throughout the region.

There may be many reasons to do so from a social or political perspective, but whether this is the right policy to boost productivity is a question with no definite answer. The overall impact of directing credit to specific sectors on individual and aggregate productivity depends on many country, sector, and firm-specific characteristics. Much of the research reported in this book suggests that there are advantages in providing credit to small firms if there is evidence that they are productive but credit-constrained, and therefore have not being able to reach their optimal size, or that they can productively use the loaned funds to upgrade their technologies and processes. Identifying these firms is not an easy task, but many programs have thought up clever ways of doing so. In such cases, providing credit to these firms will certainly either boost their productivity or the aggregate productivity of the sectors to which they belong.

Yet, directing credit to SMEs can also have adverse effects on aggregate productivity if it is given to firms that are of low productivity or are not able to make use of loans to upgrade their productivity. In that case, this policy may create distortions that shuffle scarce resources out of highly productive and possibly larger firms into less productive smaller ones, and may harm aggregate productivity.

Several challenges lie ahead in Latin American's agenda to promote productivity growth through credit strategies. The policies suggested herein clearly state that using financial depth as an instrument to increase productivity is a multidimensional problem with constraints that must be tackled on several fronts. A key concern is that policies that aim at increasing productivity through the credit channel call for a much deeper knowledge that links tangible measures of firms' access to credit with deviations from optimal production scales. Regrettably, the availability of detailed microeconomic and financial data to develop that knowledge is an area in which the region lags behind. A credit strategy to promote productivity growth also calls for policies at the macroeconomic level that stimulate credit growth and foster its stability. The benefits of larger financial integration and financial deepening will not be fully exploited until that depth is sufficiently stable and persistent.

Notes

1. Most of the studies showing strong links between financial development and growth are based on cross-sectional growth regressions (see, for instance, King and Levine 1993a,b; Levine 1997; Levine and Zervos 1998); others are based on pooled time series-cross-sectional country level data (see Beck, Levine, and Loayza 2000; and Levine, Loayza, and Beck 2000). At the macro

level, depth of access is negatively correlated with poverty rates (Levine 1997; Honohan 2004)

2. As discussed by Levine (2004), the channels through which finance operates include higher savings rates, greater investment, technological innovation, and productivity gains.

3. Several papers provide an analytical basis for this idea. See Levine (1997) and Bencivenga, Smith, and Starr (1995) for a general discussion. Also, Buera and Shin (2008); Buera, Kaboski, and Shin (2008); Jeong and Townsend (2007); Aghion et al. (2005); and Greenwald, Kohn, and Stiglitz (1990), are examples of models describing how financial restrictions lead to an inefficient allocation of resources either across sectors or across activities with differential productivities.

4. For example, Aghion et al. (2005) show that when firms face tight credit constraints, long-term investments such as Research and Development become procyclical.

5. East Asia region is comprised of the so-called "Asian Tigers": Hong Kong, Indonesia, Malaysia, Philippines, the Republic of Korea, Singapore, and Thailand.

6. Alternative measures of financial development such as "credit and market capitalization" yield a similar picture. See IDB (2005).

7. Earlier studies suggested that East Asian growth came mainly from a capital surge, but Hsieh (2002) shows that productivity growth was an important factor behind the surge.

8. This is not a magical number. It corresponds to the standard deviation of the ratio of credit to the private sector to GDP in the sample of countries analyzed in the aforementioned study.

9. This ingenious measure was crafted by Rajan and Zingales (1998), and has been widely used since then. It was constructed using data for U.S. firms.

10. They calibrate their model to Thailand and find that financial deepening and occupational shifts explain 73 percent of aggregate TFP growth in Thailand for the two decades between 1976 and 1996.

11. It is important to note that these calculations do not include microfirms or informal firms. Alternatively, since smaller, credit-constrained firms are unable to update technologies at the same pace as larger, less-credit constrained firms, relaxing credit constraints in industries with smaller firms would also lead to faster productivity growth.

12. This covers a large portion of firms. The average size of firms in the Colombian sample is 24 workers; the median size is 20.

13. For the Colombian study, productivity is calculated using specific price measures for each individual firm, a peculiarity of the data set that yields a very precise measure of a firm's TFP.

14. In these exercises, access to credit is measured as having an overdraft facility.

15. Technically, this result is obtained exploring the partial correlation of a regression between measures of productivity per firm, access to credit per firm, size indicators, interactions of these and access to credit, country industry effects,

and a series of relevant firm-level controls. The differential correlations between productivity and access to credit across firms of different sizes does not appear when measuring productivity adjusting for differences in prices as suggested by Hsieh and Klenow (2007).

16. To be able to borrow from banks or from other regulated financial intermediaries, a firm needs not only to be formally registered (or in some cases legally incorporated as a limited liability company), but also comply with a wealth of information requirements about its balance sheet positions and income flows so as to allow at least some monitoring of its activity by financial intermediaries and enforcement authorities. Such requirements to tap formal credit markets have in general become more binding in recent years, as governments in most countries can now more easily cross-check information from different enforcement agencies and thus more effectively clamp down on illegal borrowing and lending practices and attendant tax evasion associated with informality.

17. Since real GDP growth accelerated during this period, credit growth has been especially strong, expanding at double-digit figures. Importantly, this credit expansion has taken place at rapidly declining interest rates in the cases of credit given to (legal) firms as well as for personal credit that allows the bank to be repaid via direct payroll deductions ("credito consignado").

18. A detailed discussion of taxation and productivity is found in Chapter 7.

19. Periods of financial crises are associated with large real exchange rate volatility. See Calvo, Izquierdo, and Loo-Kung (2006).

20. See for example, Calvo, Izquierdo, and Mejía (2008).

21. See for example Izquierdo, Romero, and Talvi (2008); or Österholm and Zettlemeyer (2007).

22. See Blyde, Daude, and Fernández-Arias (2009).

23. See Cerra and Saxena (2008).

24. See Calvo, Izquierdo, and Talvi (2006); and Izquierdo, Llosa, and Talvi (2009).

25. See Caballero and Hammour (1994).

26. For a theoretical treatment, see Barlevy (2003).

27. This result does not discriminate exit probabilities by sector.

28. This is equivalent to saying that the probability of exit for small firms during recessions—particularly at low TFP levels—becomes proportionately higher than for large firms.

29. See for example, Calvo, Izquierdo, and Mejía (2008).

30. See Ocampo (1984).

31. This idea is embedded in Calvo (2005), together with the consequences of real exchange volatility on the choice of technologies.

32. This is precisely the point explored in Calvo (2005).

33. See Goldberg and Kolstad (1995).

34. See Calvo, Izquierdo, and Mejía (2008).

35. See for example, Rancière, Tornell, and Westermann (2008); or Calvo and Loo-Kung (2009).

36. For related evidence see Demir (2009a,b) and Arza (2008).

37. Banerjee and Newman (1991) argue that the uneven availability of insurance at different locations may lead to inefficient migration decisions, since some individuals with high potential for one location (i.e., the city) may prefer to stay elsewhere just to remain insured.

38. Discussions on the underlying macroeconomic weaknesses, vulnerabilities, and policy options to deal with them can be found in IDB (2008a) and IDB (2009b).

39. See IDB (2005).

40. For instance, a recent study by Ribeiro and De Negri (2009) using data from Brazil's BNDES (Banco Nacional de Desenvolvimento Econômico e Social) explores the impact of Finame—a credit line targeted at machinery acquisition—on manufacturing firms' TFP. The Finame lending program has two important characteristics: it offers credit at longer terms than private markets usually offer in Brazil (up to five years) and at subsidized interest rates. These credit lines play an important role in creating employment and strengthening firms. However—and it must be stressed that it is not the purpose for which the program was originally defined—it does not raise the productivity of individual firms. A possible explanation is that credit is directed toward firms that are already productive but constrained by lack of credit. Firms are then not buying better technologies, but rather buying more capital to expand their scale of operations. In a sense, BNDES would be acting responsibly by safely directing taxpayer's money to activities that are profitable but that have somehow been ignored by private banks.

41. Detailed discussions of these studies can be found in Galindo, Schiantarelli, and Weiss (2007); and Galindo, Micco, and Ordóñez (2002).

7

Taxes and Productivity: A Game of Hide and Seek

High taxes—and high tax evasion—characterize business taxes in Latin America: a fact that is often considered part of a natural state of affairs. This chapter will argue that the combination of high taxes and widespread evasion has adverse consequences for productivity. High evasion may be a survival strategy for firms that would otherwise fail because of onerous and cumbersome regulations. Yet the combination of high taxes and high evasion distorts the investment decisions of firms, reduces the efficiency of markets, and diverts governments from investing in key public goods—all of which harm the productive possibilities of a society. From this viewpoint, tax evasion is both a consequence and a cause of low productivity and must be addressed directly if productivity is to increase in the region.

High and cumbersome taxes combined with widespread tax evasion affect productivity in a number of ways. High taxes can lessen firms' incentives to invest in technology and other productivity-enhancing strategies because taxes reduce the potential profits generated by those investments. Tax evasion also lowers a government's ability to invest in productivity-enhancing public goods, such as roads and education.

In addition to these two channels, this chapter examines two other, less explored ones. First, the coexistence of taxpaying and tax-evading firms creates difficulties for tax-abiding firms, which face high taxes and competition from tax-evading firms. Thus, contrary to the view that tax-evading firms (or outright informal ones) pose no threat to taxpaying firms (La Porta and Shleifer 2009), this chapter argues that tax evasion can amount to a large subsidy for low productivity firms.[1] This effective subsidy has consequences for the quality of jobs created—with most jobs created in low productivity firms—and on aggregate productivity, which is reduced by the increasing weight of low productivity firms.

The second channel concerns the usual remedies for the problem of high tax evasion—a cure that may be worse than the disease. A myriad of special regimes aimed at lowering taxes for micro- and small firms have created obstacles to the growth of productive firms. This, in turn, lowers aggregate productivity because it lessens the economic weight of productive firms.

This chapter aims to put these issues in perspective, comparing the situation in various countries in the region, as well as between Latin America and other regions in the world, and specifying the steps needed to make tax policy a means for raising productivity in the region, rather than lowering it.

The Current Tax Picture

Tax revenues in Latin America are low by international standards. Tax revenues excluding social contributions were about 17 percent of gross domestic product (GDP) in 2005. This figure has remained practically unchanged for the last ten years, despite a number of reforms that have been carried out during that period (Lora 2008). By contrast, tax collection in industrial countries reaches about 36 percent of GDP. In particular, it hovers around 27 percent in the United States (Cetrángolo and Gómez-Sabaini 2007).

Despite low tax collection, tax rates in Latin America are high and are typically associated with high transaction costs. According to data from the World Bank's Doing Business report (2009e), tax rates for Latin America are higher than those in several other regions. In particular, taxes on profits are on average the second highest after sub-Saharan Africa. The combination of low tax revenues and high tax rates points to the high incidence of tax evasion (Figure 7.1).

It is usually argued that taxes on profits, mostly capital income, are inefficient because the supply of capital is highly responsive to taxes; on the other hand, taxes on labor income are less so because labor supply is less flexible. This argument is less valid in Latin America because tax evasion is likely to make labor income highly sensitive to tax rates. Nonetheless, to the extent that the supply of capital remains responsive to taxes in the region, high tax rates are probably an inefficient way to tax firms.

This unfavorable situation is aggravated by the fact that transaction costs related to taxes in the region are also among the highest in the world (see Figure 7.2). For instance, concerning the number of annual transactions

Figure 7.1   Tax Rates in Latin America Compared to Other Regions, 2007

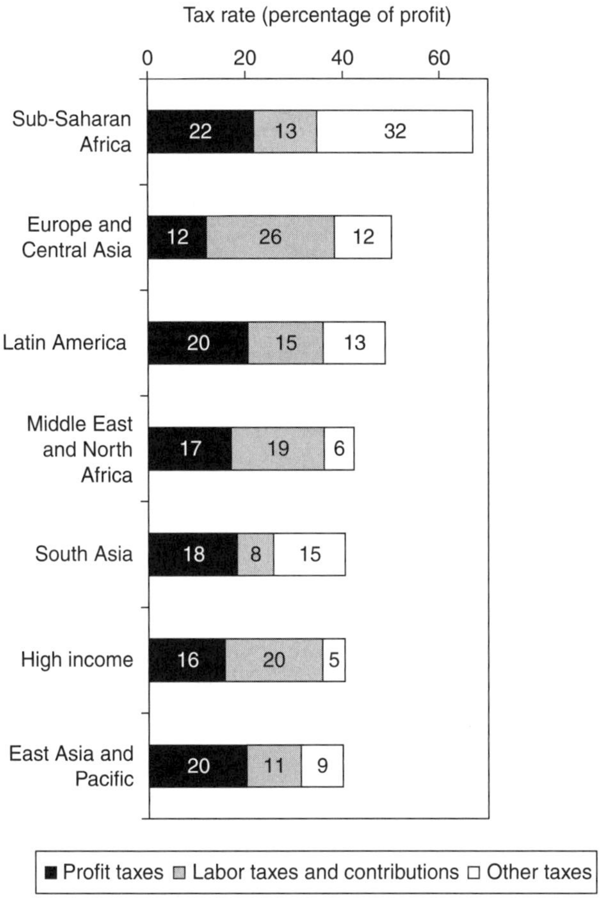

Tax rate (percentage of profit)

Sub-Saharan Africa	22	13	32
Europe and Central Asia	12	26	12
Latin America	20	15	13
Middle East and North Africa	17	19	6
South Asia	18	8	15
High income	16	20	5
East Asia and Pacific	20	11	9

■ Profit taxes ▨ Labor taxes and contributions ▢ Other taxes

Source: Authors' calculations based on World Bank (2009e).

Note: Information based on 181 countries, with data from January to December 2007.

that it takes for firms to make tax payments, Latin America ranks close to sub-Saharan Africa, with 35 transactions per year. Countries in the region vary widely on this measure, however. At one extreme, Nicaragua and Venezuela require 64 and 70 tax-related transactions per year, respectively. At the other end, Argentina, the Dominican Republic, Ecuador, and Peru require fewer than ten.

Greater numbers of transactions translate into more time spent by firms preparing, filing, and paying (or withholding) taxes. Latin America also ranks high on this measure when compared with other regions of

Figure 7.2   Number of Tax Payments Required, 2007

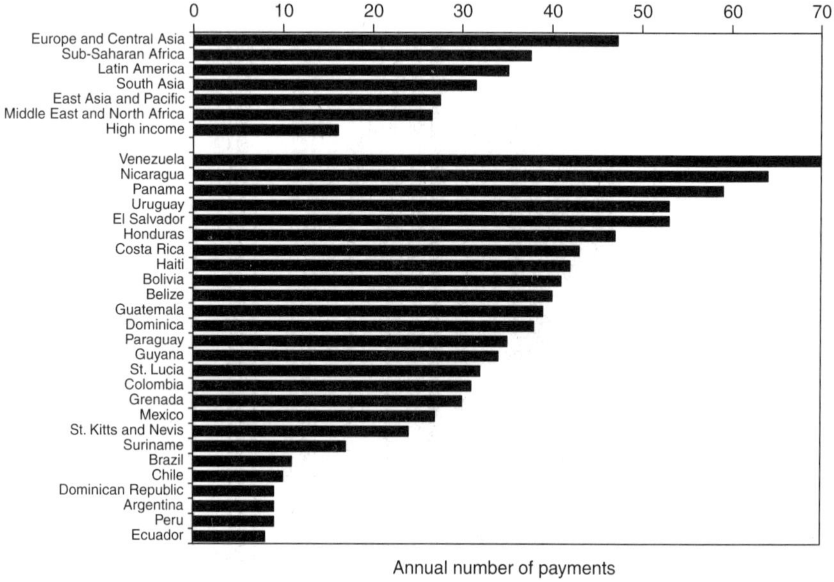

Annual number of payments

Source: Authors' calculations based on World Bank (2009e).

Note: The tax payment indicator reflects the total number of taxes and contributions paid, considering the method of payment, the frequency of payment, and the number of agencies involved for this standardized case.

the world (Figure 7.3), and the difference is not trivial. While firms in high-income countries spend an average of 177 hours a year in tax-related transactions, Latin American firms spend 320 hours, second only to those in Europe and Central Asia. Within Latin America, firms in Brazil and Bolivia spend the most hours in tax-related transactions (2,600 and 1,080, respectively).

As a result of these and other institutional distortions, the tax collection profile in the region looks dramatically different from other regions. While income tax looks very progressive in theory, it is not so in practice. During the mid-1980s, the marginal tax rates of income were about 50 percent. They are now below 30 percent, thus becoming less progressive. Meanwhile, the minimum taxable income has increased considerably, from 60 percent of per capita income in the 1980s to around 230 percent today. However, current collection of income taxes does not represent a significant percentage of total tax collection in the region because of exemptions, deficient collection systems, and outright evasion (Lora 2008). As a result, while tax revenues are low, the sources of revenues in Latin America are very different from other regions. In Latin America, 61 percent of tax revenues come from corporations.

Figure 7.3   Time Required to Complete Tax Payments, 2007

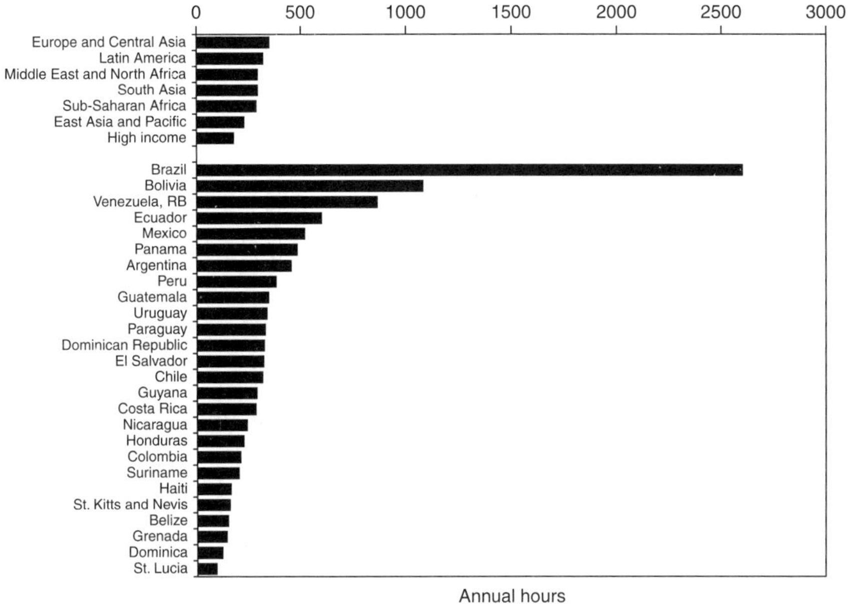

Annual hours

Source: Authors' calculations based on World Bank (2009e).

Note: Information based on 181 countries, with data from 2007–2008. Time is recorded in hours per year, and it measures the time to prepare, file, and pay (or withhold) three major types and contributions: the corporate income tax, value-added or sales tax, and labor taxes, including payroll taxes and social contributions.

In industrial countries, this percentage is only 25 percent (Cetrángolo and Gómez-Sabaini 2007). In short, corporate tax income is crucial to the tax collection system in the region, yet collection is very inefficient due at least to two factors: high evasion, particularly among small and microfirms, and a very large share of very small establishments.

Who Pays Taxes?

While tracking tax evasion of individual firms is notoriously difficult, the evidence indicates that evasion is particularly high for small firms and microenterprises, which in most cases are not registered, and thus are considered openly informal. But tax evasion is also high in medium and large firms, even when such firms are registered. This form of partial noncompliance is often referred to as the underground economy. Perry et al. (2007) find that firms underreport a large percentage of their sales for tax purposes, although the percentages vary considerably across countries.

Table 7.1   Tax-Related Informality in Mexico

Degree of tax-related informality	Firm Size (percentage)		
	Micro	Small and medium	Large
Openly informal (not registered)	67	n.d.	n.d.
Pays no taxes (less than 4 percent of what they should)	11	63	48
Semi-formal (pays 4–50 percent of what they should)	12	19	25
Formal (pays over 50 percent of what they should)	9	17	28
Total	100	100	100

Source: McKinsey and Company (2009).

Note: Estimates include only those firms with positive profits.
n.d. = no data.

Underreporting is the highest in Brazil and Panama, reaching 30–40 percent of sales, and the lowest in Chile, with less than 5 percent. Such figures, however, are obtained from firms' own estimates of how much *other* firms evade.

Surprisingly, figures based on *self-reported* tax payments in enterprise surveys for a few selected countries indicate similarly high, if not higher, levels of evasion. For instance, nearly 70 percent of microenterprises (firms with 10 or fewer employees) in Mexico report that they are not registered and hence do not pay any taxes (Table 7.1). Only 9 percent of microenterprises pay more than 50 percent of what they should (arguably, a very conservative measure of evasion). Furthermore, among small and medium firms, the largest share, 63 percent, are registered but report not paying taxes. In the case of large firms, the largest share, 48 percent, do not pay taxes (McKinsey and Company 2009).

The situation is even more dramatic in El Salvador. Only 1 percent of all microenterprises and 3 percent of all nonmicroenterprises are registered (McKinsey and Company 2009). While tax evasion is much lower in Chile, it is not negligible for some types of taxes. An estimated 66 percent of establishments with ten or more workers pay less than they should in value-added taxes (VAT), 58 percent underpay profit taxes and 34 percent underpay social security contributions (Table 7.2). While on average the percentage of social security contributions evaded is extremely low (around 1 percentage point of the tax base), average evasion of VAT and of profit taxes is around 5 percentage points. In an interesting departure from the conventional wisdom, tax evasion and state subsidies seemingly increase with size, as seen in Figure 7.4 (Busso, Madrigal, and Pagés 2009).[2]

Which firms do not pay taxes? Carpio and Pagés (2009) use a survey of microenterprises in urban areas of Brazil (IBGE 2003) to explore the characteristics associated with microenterprises that pay income taxes

Table 7.2   Tax Evasion in Chile

	Establishments with ten or more workers		
	Evasion (percentage of establishments)	Average evasion if evasion>0 (percentage of the taxable base)	Average legal tax rate
Social security contributions	34	1	19
Value-added taxes (VAT)	66	5	18–19
Profit taxes	58	5	17

Source: Busso, Madrigal and Pagés (2009).

Note: To calculate evasion, the legal tax rate in each year minus 3 percentage points was used.

Figure 7.4   Probability of Tax Evasion and Receiving Subsidies by Firm Size Relative to Firms with 10–19 Workers, Chile

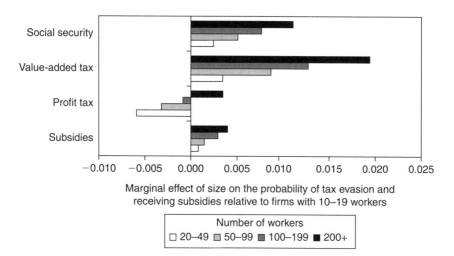

Marginal effect of size on the probability of tax evasion and receiving subsidies relative to firms with 10–19 workers

Number of workers
☐ 20–49   ▨ 50–99   ▦ 100–199   ■ 200+

Source: Busso, Madrigal, and Pagés (2009).

Note: Marginal effects were estimated using Pooled Tobit regressions. Dependent variables: reported evasion in social security, value-added tax (VAT), profit tax, and reported subsidies. Control variables are firm size, firm age, if the firm exports, percentage of unskilled workers, and year effects. Observations: around 22,000. All marginal effects are statistically significant at the 1 percent level with the exception of profit tax for 100–249 workers and 250 + workers categories. To calculate evasion, the legal tax rate in each year minus 3 percentage points was used.

(defined in the survey as firms with fewer than five paid workers). They find that the probability of paying income taxes increases with the size and age of the firm, and the education and degree of entrepreneurialism of the owner.[3] Interestingly, they find that the probability of paying taxes declines with the number of unpaid relatives in the firm, if the owner is self-employed, and with the difficulty in accessing financial services.

There is some evidence that credit is tightly linked to whether firms formalize and pay taxes. Catão, Pagés, and Rosales (2009) find evidence that formality rates increase with access to credit in Brazil. In particular, industries or economic sectors that are more credit-dependent tend to formalize faster in periods in which the supply of credit increases. They attribute this to the fact that banks normally require firms to register and, often times, to document tax payments in order to provide credit. When the supply of credit increases and firms' chances of obtaining credit rise, the incentives for firms to formalize increase as well.

A number of studies have examined the nature of informal firms in Colombia. Cárdenas and Mejía (2007) find that informal firms are much less likely to operate in a proper establishment, are younger and smaller, and are more concentrated in service sectors than formal firms. Similarly, Santamaría and Rozo (2008) find that informality is prevalent among small firms and tends to decline with firm size. They also emphasize differences in location and physical setup: most formal firms (around 75 percent) operate from commercial premises while many informal firms (around 42 percent) operate out of their own residence, use street kiosks, or conduct mobile sales. Arbeláez, León, and Becerra (2009a) also find that informal firms in Colombia tend to have lower revenues, expenditures, and profits; lower fixed capital investments; lower managerial capacity; lower integration with formal markets; and face tighter credit restrictions than formal firms.

Another important characteristic emphasized by many studies is the higher level of human capital among firm owners of formal firms (Arbeláez, León, and Becerra 2009a; La Porta and Shleifer 2008; Carpio and Pagés 2009).

Are Governments Hunting for Animals in the Zoo—or Fishing in a Fishbowl?

Taxing firms in a region where the majority of firms are small enterprises is not an easy task. As described in Chapter 4, 80–90 percent of manufacturing establishments employ fewer than ten workers, depending on the country. These figures are even higher in the service sector. For example, 97 percent of retail establishments in Mexico fall into this category. Many small firms imply a large number of establishments per capita, which makes collecting taxes from firms an operationally difficult and costly task for the state.

To facilitate formalization and tax collection, many countries have instituted special tax regimes for microenterprises and small firms, simplifying procedures and lowering tax rates for firms in this group. Yet tax collection

Table 7.3   Tax Collection in Simplified Tax Regimes (STR)

Chile	STR	Tax collection (percentage of total tax income)	Year	Taxpayers included in the STR (percentage of total registered taxpayers)	Year
Brazil	SIMPLES (Small)	4.0	2004	9.7	2004
Brazil	SIMPLES (Micro)	2.3	2004	57.9	2004
Uruguay	IPE	0.6	2007	n.d.	n.d.
Nicaragua	Unique Tax	0.5	2008	n.d.	n.d.
Peru	RUS/RER	0.2	2008	15.2	2008
Paraguay	Unique Tax	0.1	2007	62.9	2007
Chile	RS	0.1	2007	9.0	1998
Bolivia	RTS/RAU/RTI	0.1	2007	18.2	2006

Source: Arias (2009).

n.d. = no data.

from microenterprises and small enterprises represents a rather small percentage of the total tax revenues of a country, even though they constitute a significant proportion of the taxpayers (Arias 2009). This incongruence between the number of firms and their percentage contribution to tax revenue reflects the generally lower productivity and higher evasion of small firms. For instance, in Bolivia and Chile, taxpayers registered in simplified tax regimes for microenterprises and small firms represent nearly 20 and 9 percent of all taxpayers in the country, respectively, but contribute less than 1 percent of the total tax revenue in each country (Table 7.3). Most strikingly, in Paraguay, more than 60 percent of tax payers are microenterprises and small firms registered in simplified tax regimes, but they contribute barely 0.1 percent of total tax revenue. Given these low returns, tax agencies have little incentive to pursue microenterprises and small firms to comply with tax regulations.

The difficulty in making small firms comply with tax regulations, coupled with the relatively low return of enforcing compliance, means that the largest, most productive firms pay most of the taxes in Latin America. Such firms are closely monitored, as enforcement is highly concentrated among them. While this is a general pattern that also appears to be true elsewhere, the differential in time spent inspecting larger firms relative to the smallest ones is far more pronounced in Latin America (Figure 7.5).[4] Although there are far more small firms, they are difficult to track down, so tax authorities concentrate their efforts on the accessible large firms that already pay the lion's share of taxes. In other words, tax agencies are not hunting for animals in the jungle, but rather in the zoo. As Figure 7.5 shows, larger firms tend to spend more time dealing with state officials or are under inspection more than smaller firms.

Figure 7.5   Tax Enforcement by Firm Size Relative to Microfirms

Panel a. Time spent with officials   Panel b. Days of inspection

Management time spent with officials
(percentage) relative to micro firms

Natural logarithm (days of inspection)
relative to micro firms

Rest of the World   ■ Latin America

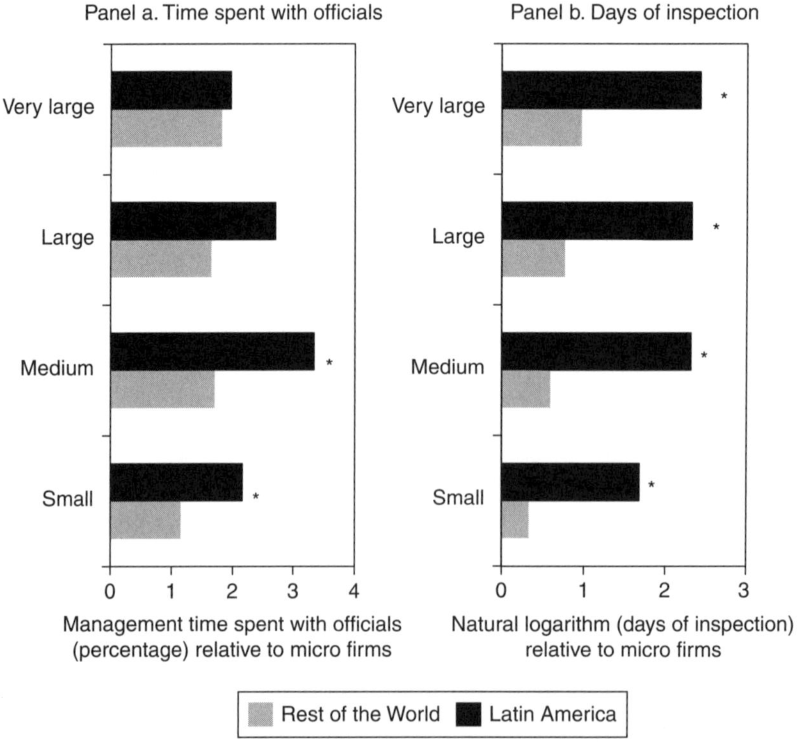

Source: Pagés, Pierre, and Scarpetta (2009).

Note: "*" Indicates that the differences between Latin America and the rest of the world are statistically significant.

The unevenness in tax enforcement between large and small firms has a bearing on how managers in both types of firms behave and, in particular, on how they allocate resources. The costs in terms of firm productivity are not trivial. If governments target larger, more productive firms, tax evasion becomes a subsidy for less productive firms and an additional burden for the most productive ones. From this point of view, tax evasion may be lowering average productivity, as the competition from tax-evading firms and informal firms reduces the market share of tax-abiding companies.

To illustrate this distortion, consider a situation in which consumers can purchase two types of food-preserving devices: ice bags, produced by low productivity, small, noncomplying firms; and refrigerators, produced by larger, more productive, and more tax-compliant firms. Ice bag producers can sell their product at low cost despite their low productivity because they do not pay taxes or comply with regulations. While ice is arguably less expensive to buy and use than refrigerators and thus more appealing to lower-income consumers, the price distortion created by tax evasion increases consumption of ice bags and reduces the consumption of refrigerators relative to a situation in which all firms comply with taxes and regulations. This reduces the demand for labor—and therefore the size—of the most productive firms, and with it aggregate productivity.

Are Informal Firms Parasites, Marginal, or Romantics?

The view of informal firms as parasites—in the sense of detracting market share from taxpaying firms—is not widely held. Two other prevailing views are the romantic view and the dual view.[5] In the romantic view (as described by La Porta and Shleifer 2008), informal firms are potentially productive but are held back by red tape/regulations (De Soto 2000). In the dual view, the informal sector is populated by firms engaged in highly inefficient marginal activities with very low productivity, such as street vendors, which exist in a parallel world that does not threaten formal firms (Harris and Todaro 1970). Thus the predictions of these three alternative theories are clear. In the *romantic* view, total factor productivity (TFP) of informal firms is large, but their size is small due to obstacles to their growth (high costs—both financial and bureaucratic—of registration, limited access to financing, and the like). In the *dual* view, TFP of informal firms is low—so low that they operate only in very marginal and segmented markets to which formal firms would never cater. In the *parasitic* view, TFP of informal firms is lower than that of formal firms, but they evade taxes and regulations as a way to compete with larger, more formal firms. The key difference between the parasitic and the dual view is that in the parasitic view, informal firms reduce the market share of formal firms—because informal firms produce goods that are close enough substitutes to the products produced by formal firms. Given the stark differences in the predictions of the three theories and their potential implications for productivity, as well as poverty and inequality reduction policies, it is important to ascertain which view is best supported by the evidence in Latin America.

La Porta and Shleifer (2008) state there is not much support for the parasitic view. However, they reach this conclusion based on the observation that informal firms are on average less productive than formal ones—an observation that would also be supported by the parasitic view. Moreover, their evidence is mostly for poor countries in Africa and Asia, where the role of the informal sector may be very different than in Latin America, as there is evidence that competition from informal firms in the region ranks high as an obstacle to the growth of formal firms.

Figure 7.6   Investment Climate Constraints, Latin America

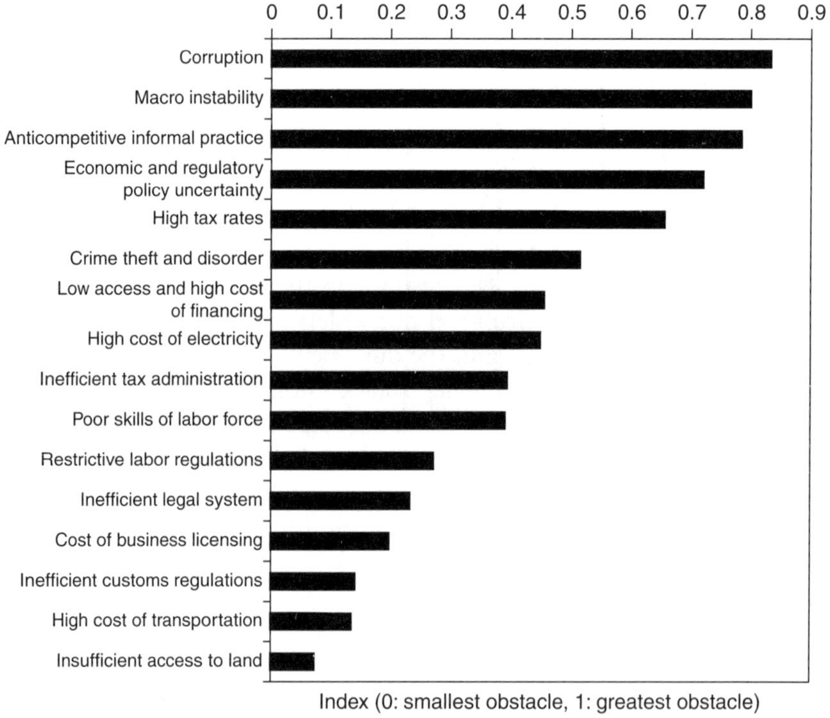

Index (0: smallest obstacle, 1: greatest obstacle)

Source: Pagés, Pierre, and Scarpetta (2009).

Note: The data for Brazil, Ecuador, El Salvador, Guatemala, Honduras, and Nicaragua are for 2003; Chile and Guyana, 2004; Costa Rica, 2005; and Argentina, Bolivia, Colombia, Mexico, Panama, Paraguay, Peru, and Uruguay, 2006.

Using data from the World Bank Enterprise Survey (WBES), Pagés, Pierre, and Scarpetta (2009) find that anticompetitive practices from the informal sector rank as the third most important constraint to formal firms' growth in Latin America, after corruption and macro instability, and ahead of other pressing issues, such as inefficient regulations, high tax rates, the economic cost of crime, high cost of electricity, or inefficient tax administration (Figure 7.6). Furthermore, according to these data, it appears that this concern is more pressing in Latin America than in other regions of the world where, typically, issues related with economic and regulatory policy uncertainty and macroeconomic instability are considered relatively more relevant (Figure 7.7).

Moreover, new evidence at the firm level for Brazil (Carpio and Pagés 2009) and Colombia (Arbeláez, León, and Becerra 2009a) suggests that while informal firms are less productive than formal ones in terms of TFP,

Figure 7.7   Investment Climate Constraints, Latin America and Other Regions

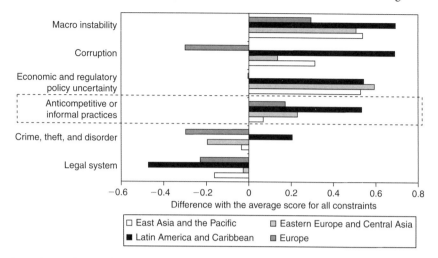

Source: Pagés, Pierre, and Scarpetta (2009).

Note: Investment climate constraints measured relative to average of responses to all obstacles. Obstacles of each country standardized to take values between 0 (smallest obstacle) and 1 (greatest obstacle).

tax avoidance can distort competition between the two types of firms. In both studies, the comparison between formal and informal firms is made only among small firms in order to isolate the effect of formality from the effect of size on productivity. The sample is for firms with fewer than five paid workers (Brazil) or ten paid workers (Colombia).

Figure 7.8 plots the distribution of individual firms' TFP expressed as a difference with the average productivity of the industry to which the firm belongs. A positive (negative) number on the horizontal axis implies a productivity that is higher (lower) than the average of all firms in that industry, whether formal or informal. This allows a comparison of firms relative only to those in the same industry, since comparing firms across industries (say, metal and fabric production) may not be very meaningful. The higher productivity of formal firms is illustrated by the fact that the distribution of productivity of formal firms is always to the right of the distribution of informal firms, which implies that more formal firms tend to be above average in their respective industries than informal firms. This pattern can be observed in both Brazil and Colombia.[6]

In Brazil, the average gap in TFP between informal and formal micro-firms is 55 percent. For the subset of firms that employ some paid labor, the gap is only 13 percent. For Colombia, the productivity gap between formal and informal firms is 80 percent. In comparison, the gap in TFP between the twenty-fifth and the seventy-fifth most productive firms in a

Figure 7.8   Establishment-Level Productivity, Average Productivity in Industry, Brazil and Colombia

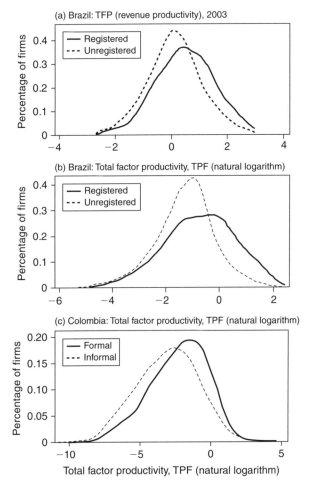

Sources: Carpio and Pagés (2009); Arbeláez, León, and Becerra (2009a).

Note: Productivity relative to the average of sector. Average sector = 0.

given industry among formal firms is 182 percent in Brazil and 266 percent in Colombia.[7] The corresponding numbers for the informal firms are 130 percent in Brazil and 279 percent in Colombia. This implies that there are more differences in productivity within formal firms or within informal firms than across formal and informal ones. This supports the conclusion that for any given micro formal firm, there are a number of micro informal firms in the same sector that are not that far off in terms of productivity—a finding that does not fit well with the dual view of informality.

The evidence for Colombia suggests that the market share of small formal firms is too small a world where all firms pay taxes (Arbeláez, León, and Becerra 2009a). This is illustrated by the fact that, at the margin, transferring capital and labor from informal to formal microfirms would yield gains in total output.[8] The flip side is that the market share of the informal, less productive firms is too large, thus affecting aggregate productivity through a composition effect. The study for Brazil also indicates that tax evasion allows informal firms—particularly productive informal firms—to expand their market share beyond what they would have if they paid taxes, eating into the market share of formal firms.

A study on producers of leather shoes in Bolivia (Birbuet and Machicado 2009) reveals great atomization in the subsector. Most producers are very small informal firms whose productivity increases with firm size. As in all other studies, productivity is higher in formal firms than in informal firms. Transferring resources (capital and labor) from informal to formal firms would increase aggregate productivity in the sector, as the marginal products of labor and capital are higher in formal firms.

In the case of Brazil, Lewis (2004) examines the retail sector and argues that more productive supermarkets cannot take advantage of their higher productivity by lowering their prices and thereby increasing market share because they must pass on the costs of paying taxes and of compliance, while traditional firms survive because they pay no taxes. He argues that Brazilian consumers, many of whom are very poor, would be better off if all firms paid taxes because their food prices would be lower. Similar results are found for supermarkets in Argentina (Sánchez 2009), where the tax burden is applied only to the relatively few formal supermarkets. This creates a vicious circle as ever fewer taxpayers further increase the tax pressure on the remaining formal chains and force many small formal self-service and traditional shops to move into informality. Moreover, many of the taxes, especially at the municipal level, are introduced or increased after the supermarkets have been established. This creates a problem of time inconsistency in tax policies, which may further deter expansion of formal supermarkets. These taxes act as an output wedge that mostly hurts the most productive firms.

Consider the case of the hotel industry in Colombia. Arbeláez, León, and Becerra (2009b) show that informal hotels have a large cost advantage relative to formal hotels, as formal hotels are obliged to pay income tax, VAT, wage tax, and other taxes exceeding 60 percent of sales. Furthermore, formal hotels register as commercial establishments, while informal hotels register as residences; thus, public utility rates for commercial establishments are almost twice as high for hotels. However, informal hotels are less productive as they cannot take advantage of the economies of scale common to hotel services because these would make the government take notice of them and tax them. When informal hotels grow, the consumption of public utilities increases, which attracts the attention of the utility service providers. Similarly, informal establishments cannot use branding, which eliminates potential economies of scale of chain-type arrangements. Because of these barriers, informal hotel services tend to grow through the proliferation of small independent firms. Furthermore, managerial capacity, which is fundamental in hotel services, is a scarce input. Hence, the more establishments there are in the market, the more probable it will be that many of them will lack adequate managerial capacity, and hence have low productivity.

A recent study by Hopenhayn and Neumeyer (2008) provides quantitative estimates of the effects of such distortions on aggregate productivity. In the context of a general equilibrium model, the authors assume that 20 percent of the firms produce 80 percent of the output, and calculate the effect of a corporate tax of 25 percent on profits paid by 75 percent of the most efficient firms, while the rest of the firms are in the informal sector. This scenario reduces output between 5 and 10 percentage points, depending on the level of labor taxes, the production function, the type of competition faced by firms, and the differences in the cost of capital between formal and informal firms.[9] These figures do not account for the indirect effects of a reduction in productivity yields on investment. As such, they underestimate the total effects on output.

In sum, the available evidence for Latin America suggests that informal firms are less productive than formal ones; nonetheless, they may be reducing the market share of formal firms because of their lower costs, which allow them to charge low prices in spite of their relatively lower productivity.

On the other hand, the evidence that informal firms are less productive than formal firms is compatible with the romantic view. In addition, there is little evidence indicating that most firms start as informal and then formalize; rather, they remain informal (Arbeláez, Leon, and Becerra 2009a). Similar evidence appears in the WBES for Latin America, a survey of registered firms. Only 9 percent of firms in this survey began operations as unregistered and were later formalized (La Porta and Shleifer 2008).

Yet the lack of formalization of informal firms may attest to very large registration costs. Some studies provide evidence that lowering the cost of formalization may induce a number of firms to formalize and grow. However, as reported by Perry et al. (2007), the magnitude of such effects is still a matter of discussion. Two studies (Fajnzylber, Maloney, and Montes Rojas 2006; and Monteiro and Assunção 2006) assess the impact of a program to reduce registration costs and taxes on new Brazilian microenterprises (SIMPLES) and find that it leads to a 6–13 percentage point increase in formalization. One of the studies (Monteiro and Assunção 2006) also finds that newly formalized firms in Brazil invested more and changed the composition of the expenditures toward long-run projects. However, a program to simplify registration in Mexico (SARE) yielded more ambiguous results. Bruhn (2008) finds that this program had a significant effect on formalization, although the inflow of formalized firms did not come from formerly unregistered self-employed workers, but rather from formerly relatively high-wage salaried workers who, it is presumed, were attracted by the lower costs of formalization. In contrast, Kaplan, Piedra, and Seira (2007) find that lower registration costs lead to very little new registration in the social security system. Such divergences might be due to the fact that the two studies use different formalization measures (registration in the commercial registry versus registration in the social security system); registration in the social security system is much more difficult than registration with tax authorities.

To conclude, the available evidence in Latin America indicates that informal firms may be capturing an undue market share thanks to tax and regulatory evasion. Nonetheless, there may be important differences across economic sectors. Two studies of Colombia (Arbeláez, León, and Becerra, 2009a,b) find evidence that while in some sectors the situation is best characterized by the parasitic view (hotels), in others (underwear manufacture), the situation conforms better to the dual view, with informal firms serving only residual market niches not covered by formal firms. In still other sectors, formal firms subcontract work to informal firms to gain flexibility in their production, and as a way to surmount extremely rigid labor market regulations. This diversity of findings implies that the relationship between informality and productivity needs to be evaluated carefully in each case.

Taxes and the Productivity of Formal and Informal Firms

In addition to the effects already described, the literature also emphasizes other channels by which taxes and noncompliance affect the productivity of formal and informal firms.

High taxes can hurt productivity by reducing the incentives of formal firms to develop or adopt new technologies. Yet the opposite could be the case, if existing or prospective formal firms are induced to innovate more to compensate for the cost advantages of informal firms. The way formal firms choose to go is likely to depend on the depth of their pockets, their cost/access to credit, and the relative probability of their gaining (and maintaining) a large share of the market with that investment.

The evidence suggests a negative relationship between corporate taxes and productivity at the firm level. Galindo et al. (2009) use individual firm-level data of formal firms from 42 developing countries from the WBES to examine the link between corporate taxes and productivity. Their methodology corrects for the possibility of reverse causality: that is, that firm productivity generates higher tax payments, instead of taxes generating productivity. Their findings also suggest that the impact of corporate taxes on investment and productivity increases as the size of firms increase. The larger the firm, the greater the negative impact of corporate tax rates on investment and productivity. These results suggest that tax policies may have significant consequences for economic development, and highlight the potential tradeoff between collecting revenue from firms and long-term growth.

Another important effect of tax evasion on productivity arises from the limited capability of the state to finance essential public goods that might improve the productivity of all firms, such as infrastructure. Chapter 5 emphasizes the importance of low transportation costs for productivity. This public good effect can account for a 12 percent reduction in output relative to an economy where the government can collect taxes from all firms (Robles 2009).

The economic literature also emphasizes the effect of noncompliance on the productivity growth of informal firms. By not formalizing, informal firms forgo a number of benefits and public goods, which hurts their productivity growth. By reducing firms' access to credit, tax avoidance limits the capacity of informal firms to finance the development or adoption of new technology. It also increases their incentives to remain small (to avoid detection)—and, if returns to scale are important, to become less productive as a consequence.

What is the evidence of these effects? On the one hand, most studies suggest that economies of scale tend to be small, which suggests that larger firms do not become more productive because of their size, but rather that productivity causes size, with more productive firms growing larger. This implies that informal firms are small due to their low starting level of productivity, but that they may not forgo much in productivity by remaining small. On the other hand, if firms could achieve large gains just by formalizing—and thereby gain access to credit and public goods—why would they not do so? Informal firm owners may simply be unaware of the benefits of formalizing—a plausible explanation given their lower levels of human capital.

A second explanation, more related to the central point of this chapter, is that when tax rates are high, and formalizing involves not only paying taxes but also making high social security contributions (see Chapter 8) and abiding by numerous regulations, the benefits of formalization may be quite large but taxes would deter firms from becoming formal, even if they are fully aware of the benefits. This implies that the higher the taxes and regulations, the higher the productivity benefits of formalization forgone by informal firms, with larger consequences for aggregate productivity.

Is the Cure Worse than the Disease? Simplified Tax Regimes

To deal with the low tax collection and high administrative costs of collecting taxes from numerous small firms, governments have adopted so-called special tax regimes that seek to broaden the tax base, increase tax revenues, and—through positive spillovers—set the stage to benefit the economy further. The basic reasoning behind the design and implementation of special tax regimes for smaller firms may be sensible. First, such regimes seek to simplify the taxation process and lower tax administration costs. Second, special regimes for smaller firms aim to promote formality as well as increase control of small taxpayers. Third, such regimes seek to reduce employers' labor contributions in order to stimulate employment and expand labor benefits to low-income workers. Finally, these simplified tax regimes for smaller firms are designed to help free up resources so that tax administration efforts can focus more on monitoring larger firms.

As sensible as these aims are, the obvious question is whether these special tax regimes actually work. To address this issue, it is best to separate it into two questions. First, do these programs increase formalization among microenterprises and small firms, thereby reducing some of the distortions described above? Second, are there unintended outcomes of these regimes that conspire against their original objectives? Before answering these two questions, it is useful to briefly review the characteristics of such programs.

Table 7.4 presents a summary of simplified tax regimes for many countries in Latin America. Of the 17 countries considered, 13 have at least one special tax regime. Two countries, El Salvador and Panama, simply exclude targeted firms from their general regime; these firms end up not being taxed. Venezuela and Ecuador are the only two countries that currently do not have simplified tax regimes for smaller firms (Arias 2009).

Most strikingly, many countries have more than one simplified regime; the number varies, depending on the industries and taxes affected. For instance, Peru has two simplified regimes, Bolivia has three, and Chile has four. Moreover, the word "*simplified*" is a euphemism: the requirements to qualify for these tax regimes are anything but simple. Requirements range from income and assets, to number of establishments, number of workers,

Table 7.4 Simplified Tax Regimes, Latin America

Country	Program name	Total	Income	Assets	Purchases	Area	Unit prices	Estab. (no.)	Employees (no.)	Other	Individuals	Sole proprietorship	Corporations
			Requirements to belong to a STR								Types of taxpayers	Firms	
Argentina	Simplified Regime for Smaller Taxpayers (Monotributo)	2	x				x	x	x	Electricity consumption	x	x	
	Simplified Regime for Eventual Taxpayers (RSCE)		x								x		
Bolivia	Simplified Tax Regime (RTS)	3	x				x			Capital	x		
	Integrated Tax Regime (STI)									No. of vehicles	x		
	Unified Farming Regime (RAU)					x					x		
Brazil	SIMPLES	2	x								x	x	
	Supposed Income Tax Regime		x								x	x	x
Colombia	Simplified Regime over the AVT (RS IVA)	1	x	x						Financial transactions	x	x	
Costa Rica	Simplified Tax Regime (RTS)	1			x			x	x		x	x	x
Chile	Simplified Regime over the Income Tax (RSIR)	4								Mining: no. of dependents. Handicraft: capital and no. of operations. Local fishing: no. of boats and weight	x	x	
Dominican Republic	Simple Estimation Regime (RES)	1	x								x	x	

Country	Regime	No.					
	Supposed Income Tax Regime—Farming Industry (RRPA)			x		x	x
	Simplified Tax Regime for Smaller Taxpayers (RTSPC)			x		x	
	Changing the Character in the VAT Regime (RCS IVA)		Fiscal valuation	x		x	
Honduras	Simplified VAT Regime (RSIV)	1	x	x		x	
Mexico	Small Taxpayers Regime (REPECOS)	4	x	x		x	
	Intermediate Regime (RI)		x	x		x	
	Simplified Regime for Agriculture, Farming, Forestry, and Fishing (RSAGP)		x	x		x	x
	Simplified Regime for the "Autotransporte" Sector (RST)		x	x		x	x
Nicaragua	Special Regime of Administrative Estimation (REEA)	1	Inventory	x		x	
Paraguay	Unique Tax (RSIV)	1	x	x		x	
Peru	Simplified Unique Regime (RUS)	2	x	x	x	x	
	Special Regime for Income Tax (RER)		x	x		x	x
Uruguay	Small Firm Tax (IPE)	2	x	x		x	x
	Monotributo		x	x		x	x

Source: Arias (2009).

and even surface area of establishments. Interestingly, of the 25 special regimes listed in Table 7.4, eight are issued only to sole proprietors,[10] while six extend to firms with more than one partner. Thus, effectively, when a sole proprietor of a microenterprise or a small firm decides to associate with another individual as a partner, the firm is forced to leave the simplified regime and choose between the underground economy and the general tax regime. This is not a trivial choice and is directly related to the tax profile in Latin America today.

Do these programs help resolve the thorny tax collection problem in Latin America and encourage greater formalization? The answer depends on whether the simplified regime is able to smooth the transition of firms toward registration and tax payments.

In general, it looks as if simplified tax regimes help reduce the large obstacle that may stop firms from starting to pay taxes. This is evident in Figures 7.9 and 7.10, which focus on Peru and Argentina, respectively, and depict a firm's profits as a function of sales for different tax regimes, based on the assumption that more sales are associated with higher profits.[11] The figures show the corresponding potential tax profit gap that a small firm faces when moving from not paying taxes (the solid line at the top) to paying taxes under different regimes. In all cases, paying taxes reduces profits—unless other factors not accounted for here, such as improved

Figure 7.9   Simplified Tax Regimes, Peru

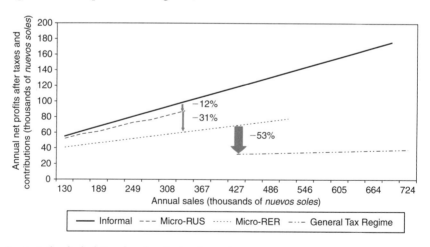

Source: Authors' calculations based on the taxation system.

Note: Annual replacement investment: 10 percent of sales. Inputs: 50 percent of sales. Annual depreciation: 10 percent. Annual sales are a linear function of the number of workers. Labor contributions are estimated according to the legislation that applies to the general and simplified tax regimes, and considering the legal monthly minimum wage of 50 *nuevos soles* monthly.

Figure 7.10 Simplified Tax Regimes, Argentina

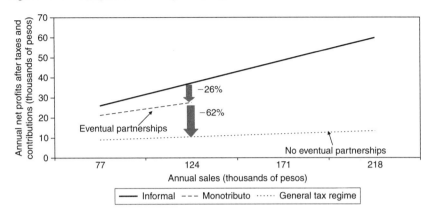

Source: Authors' calculations based on the taxation system.

Note: Annual replacement investment: 10 percent of sales. Inputs: 50 percent of sales. Annual depreciation: 10 percent. Annual sales are a linear function of the number of workers. Labor contributions are estimated according to the legislation that applies to the general and simplified tax regimes, and considering the legal monthly minimum wage of 980 pesos.

access to credit or public goods, compensate for taxes paid. Yet, if the smallest firms are taxed under the general tax regime (the dotted line at the bottom), profits drop even more.

Do more firms become formal as a result of simplified tax regimes? Unfortunately, the empirical evidence on this front is very sparse. Despite the large number of tax simplification programs listed in Table 7.4, their impact on registration and potential effects on firm behavior and productivity have scarcely been evaluated. One exception is the case of the SIMPLES program, already discussed, in which at least two separate studies found the program to have positive effects on formalization (between 6 and 13 percentage points). However, the effects of such programs will likely differ across countries. Enticing firms to pay taxes by simplifying and reducing tax obligations may not be enough if, by becoming formal, firms also face hefty additional costs associated with labor and product market regulatory mandates.

However, in spite of some favorable results at the margin concerning formalization, there are some unintended outcomes that may exacerbate and perpetuate the problems that such regimes were intended to fix. The main problem with these regimes is that they can stunt the growth of small firms. These regimes create gaps—or so-called non-linearities—which means that firms wanting to grow do not have the correct incentives to do so. Perhaps the best way of thinking about these gaps is to visualize a

Figure 7.11   Number of Companies and the Simplified Tax Regime, Mexico

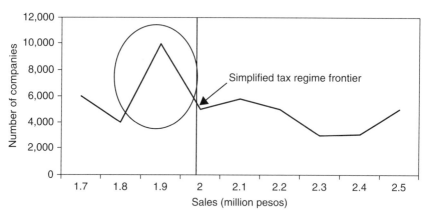

Source: McKinsey and Company (2009).

Notes: Informal firms pay less than 50 percent of what they should. In 2004, the simplified tax regime applied to those companies with annual sales of less than 2 million pesos and which were taxed at a rate of approximately 2 percent of income.

deficiently built highway with a section full of bumps and holes. It does not matter how good the automobiles are, or how smooth the asphalt is, or even how bad the traffic is; automobiles will be forced to slow down or stop the closer they come to the section full of bumps and holes.

These possible bumps are evident in Figures 7.10 and 7.11. For a Peruvian firm with sales around the threshold to move from the simplified tax regime to the general tax regime, growth in sales from say 400,000 to 450,000 *nuevos soles* implies a drop in profits of 53 percent, which is likely to render the increase in sales unprofitable. This large discontinuity in the marginal tax rate can create strong incentives to hover in the simplified tax regime, unless a firm faces an extraordinary growth opportunity that provides it with the means of bridging this rough and bumpy stretch. In Argentina, the growth discontinuity is even larger, since it implies a profit reduction of 62 percent.

Remarkably, these potentially adverse effects have gone largely unnoticed and thus there is a dearth of studies that empirically assess their consequences. A very recent study for Mexico, however, provides evidence that growth disincentives may be strongly at play (McKinsey and Company 2009). In 2004, Mexico had two tax regimes: a simplified regime and a general one. The first was designed for companies with yearly sales of less than 2 million pesos; they must pay around 2 percent of income as tax. The second system was designed for companies with yearly sales greater than 2 million pesos; they pay approximately 28 percent of profits as tax.

Using data from the 2004 national census of firms and the 2002 national survey of microenterprises, the study calculated the distribution of firms according to sales and found a significant concentration of firms right at the frontier of the tax regime change (Figure 7.11). This suggests that firms are getting stuck around the regime frontier.

A Better Tax Policy for Productivity

This chapter has reviewed the institutional setup of the Latin American tax system with particular emphasis on the productivity effects of tax regimes, tax collection, and tax-evasion patterns of firms. Tax evasion by firms is commonplace in the region, going well beyond the smallest firms; the chapter has provided evidence of significant tax evasion among large firms as well. The chapter then reviewed the different channels by which tax regimes, tax enforcement, and evasion affect productivity: by distorting the use of existing resources (and therefore reducing the potential productivity of existing resources in the region); reducing the provision of productivity-enhancing public goods; and curbing firms' appetite to invest in productivity-enhancing upgrades for both tax compliant and noncompliant firms.

The evidence indicates that most of these channels are at play. Taxes reduce formal firms' size and productivity, and evasion allows noncompliant firms to capture market share that otherwise would go to larger, more productive firms—all of which contribute to lower productivity levels and growth.

The very difficult policy conundrum is that tax evasion and, in particular, informality—the most extreme form of tax evasion—are survival strategies for many low-income households. In the short run, policies to better enforce tax collection may also increase unemployment. This highlights the difficulties of moving from the current situation to one where such households find better sources of income in larger, more productive firms. A possible strategy for the governments of the region is to focus first on particular sectors where it is clearer that informality is harming formal firms. Within a sector, increased enforcement could be directed first to the types of noncompliant establishments that are more likely to directly compete with tax compliant ones. In addition, temporary measures to help the transition of workers toward tax compliant, more efficient firms could be put in place.

There is also a need to truly simplify tax regimes, reducing the hurdles and the time required to comply with them. Tax systems should also minimize the large jumps between regimes for small and medium enterprises

(SMEs) and the general regime. At the least, the size of the bump could be reduced by increasing the number of sales brackets and making the tax rate increase more continuously until it merges with the generalized tax rate.

Another even more desirable alternative is to lower the general corporate tax rate so as to flatten the overall tax rate. In Latin America, a flat rate would be the most convenient as it would not require registries or other specific characteristics. However, such quotas should be set at more realistic levels (González 2006). This may have the double benefit of reducing the discontinuity between simplified and general tax regimes, and reducing evasion. To the extent that lowering the corporate tax rate entices more firms to pay, lower tax rates do not need to imply a reduction in tax revenues—something that the region could not afford.[12] Furthermore, lowering rates will reduce the incentives of small firms not to grow, and that of large firms to evade taxes.

In addition to reducing the cost of paying taxes, governments need to pay attention to enhancing the benefits of formality. Chief among them is the possibility of accessing credit. On the one hand, governments can increase the supply of credit and with it—as shown by Catão, Pagés, and Rosales (2009) for Brazil—improve the odds that firms become formal: either increasing the opportunity cost of firms of remaining informal or increasing the possibility for formal firms to grow and absorb workers from informal firms. As shown in Chapter 6, while the low supply of credit in the region responds partly to a history of volatile macroeconomic management, there is much room to expand credit supply, and with it, tax compliance, by improving the region's financial regulatory and policy framework. Yet it is also important to emphasize that the growing supply of microlenders can actually weaken the link between credit and formality if they provide lending without requiring firms to provide documentation of tax payments and proof of registration. To the extent that registered firms can access credit from other sources, it may be in the interest of microlenders not to ask for registration, which plays to firms' unwillingness to be registered. Yet this situation is inefficient from society's point of view and further steps to strengthen the link between microcredit and registration would be required.

Complementary policies concern the use of technology and simple organizational changes. An example of the former is to encourage firms to use the banking system.[13] An example of the latter is to make receipts mandatory. In addition to the operational reforms, countries that have sought to reduce tax evasion have emphasized information collection and data sharing and, above all, stronger penalties for noncompliance. For example, data exchange between the tax administration and relevant agencies could be improved. In terms of sanctions, countries could consider measures that provide for increased fines for noncompliance, larger penalties for failure to certify origin of goods or registration of employees, and the suspension of tax identification numbers (González 2006; Lewis 2004; World Bank 2009e).

Tax authorities should also try to rely less on corporate taxes and more on taxation of other sources, such as personal income. However, the many reforms that have tried—and to large extent failed—to do so attest to the difficulty of implementing this (and many other) productivity-enhancing changes.

Notes

1. Informal firms are defined in this volume as those that are not registered and that do not pay profit taxes or payroll taxes, such as social security.
2. An important caveat in the data for Chile, El Salvador, and Mexico is that they are computed based on applying mandatory tax rates to reported value added, profits, or wage payments, and hence they could underestimate some forms of legal exemptions, year-to-year carryovers, or other legal accounting allowances that create divergences between the taxable base and the reported figures.
3. They were able to differentiate between owners that created their firms to generate profit and growth and those that launched a firm because they lacked a job.
4. The definition of microenterprise varies across datasets and studies and is defined as fewer than five paid workers in the Brazilian Survey of the Urban Informal Economy (IBGE 2003), or fewer than ten paid workers in other datasets.
5. The labels *parasitic, romantic,* and *dual* were coined in La Porta and Shleifer (2008).
6. Measured differences in productivity between formal and informal firms depend on, among other factors, whether productivity is measured adjusting for the fact that informal firms tend to employ more unpaid laborers and operate with less human capital, or whether differences in prices charged at the firm level are accounted for. Yet results are quantitatively similar across alternative methods to measure productivity. Results are summarized in Carpio and Pagés (2009).
7. The figure for Brazil is for the year 2003 and for Colombia, 2006.
8. That is, the marginal revenue product of capital and labor is higher in formal than in informal firms.
9. Alesina et al. (2002) show that taxes have negative effects on profits. Cummins, Hassett, and Hubbard (1996) find that investment responds to tax changes in industrial countries. Alfaro, Charlton, and Kanczuk (2008) find that resource allocation determines differences in income. Chongvilaivan and Jinjarak

(2008) find that higher tax rates are associated with a lower number of firms. Dabla-Norris, Gradstein, and Inchauste (2008) and Chong and Gradstein (2008) find that the quality of the legal framework is crucially important to the size of the informal sector, whereas taxes, regulations, and financial constraints are less significant in the context of a well-functioning legal system.

10. Thus disallowing corporations.

11. A series of other neutral assumptions are also made: an annual replacement investment of 10 percent of sales; inputs, at 50 percent of sales; and an annual depreciation of 10 percent. Annual sales are a linear function of the number of workers. Labor contributions are estimated according to the legislation that applies to the general tax regime and the simplified tax regime in each country (RUR and RER for Peru; Monotributo for Argentina). Wages are the legal minimum (S/.550 monthly in Peru; Arg$980 monthly in Argentina).

12. A recent study by Djankov et al. (2009) provides evidence of an important association between the effective corporate tax rate and the size of the informal economy.

13. Argentina's current experience provides a cautionary tale about the use of the banking system to improve the monitoring of tax administration. A tax devolution scheme (a decrease of 3 to 5 percentage points of the VAT) for payments made with debit cards coexists with a tax on financial transactions at a maximum rate of 0.6 percent. One scheme cancels out the other.

8

Safe and Sound Social Policy: Reconciling Protection with Productivity

Societies need to protect their citizens against certain risks, especially current and future health problems, poverty, and labor shocks. In designing such social protection, most Latin American countries have followed the Bismarkian tradition of collecting in the labor markets the revenues needed for coverage. Unfortunately, this approach has not achieved universal coverage and important segments, especially the poor, remain vulnerable. Governments have tackled this problem by designing social protection policies to cover uncovered workers and their households through substitute public goods and services, such as free or low-cost health insurance, food vouchers, training vouchers, cash transfers, subsidized credit, and subsidized housing. While these policies may improve citizens' well-being, they may also encourage informality and have certain harmful effects on productivity (Levy 2008). This chapter argues that rather than eliminating social policies because of the collateral damage they may cause, they must be redesigned with productivity issues in mind.

Consider the case of free health insurance for families who are not entitled to it through formal employment. Two very different effects—one expected and the other unintended—occur. The most immediate and desirable impact is to mitigate the negative consequences of an illness or injury. However, free health insurance also reduces people's incentive to seek health insurance provided through formal employment and thus diminishes the likelihood that they will look for a quality job (or at least one covered by social security). When individuals have the option of being covered within or outside of labor markets (and one option is costly while the other one is free), wage distortions result, as equally productive individuals receive different wages, depending upon whether or not they are covered through the labor markets. Firms, in turn, face distorted labor prices and are induced to make decisions about labor allocation and scale of operations that may reduce total factor productivity (TFP) (see Chapter 4) and hamper productivity.

This chapter explores the extent to which social policies—either through spending or regulation—induce workers and firms to pursue informality, thereby incurring productivity losses. Before proceeding, however, it is important not to minimize the importance of social policies. Such policies play a central role in helping the state perform several key functions: coordinating the provision of public goods, filling in for missing markets (such as risk-pooling mechanisms), and mitigating the negative impact of power imbalances and distributional issues. In meeting these needs, social policies help maintain harmonious and cohesive societies. Such societies, in turn, are more conducive to productivity, reducing transaction costs and expanding business possibilities frontiers (IDB 2007). However, this chapter argues that some social policies inadvertently encourage informality and aggravate some of the maladies that limit the productive potential of economies. Thus, it is important to focus on the incentives some social policies generate and reassess their design and implementation to maximize their gains. Rather than eliminating social policies because of the collateral damage they may cause, they must be redesigned with their effects on productivity in mind.

Social Policies and Informality

Before delving into a discussion on the impact of social policies on informality, it is important to state some working definitions and establish the conceptual frameworks for these terms. As Kanbur (2009) notes, *informality* "is a term that has the dubious distinction of combining maximum policy importance and political salience with minimal conceptual clarity and coherence." To allow for cross-country comparisons, formal workers are defined here as all those who are effectively covered by government regulations (that is, mandated to be covered by social security and effectively compliant). Accordingly, the terms *effective coverage* and *formality* are used here interchangeably. This view combines the legalistic definition of informality with the notion of compliance. Evasion is an important element in this concept. Just as firms evade social security, they also evade taxes, as shown in Chapter 7 on taxation.

Throughout Latin America, the level of noncompliance and avoidance of the regulations that require employers to provide and pay for social services is high. For instance, more than two-thirds of the population lacks old-age insurance or pensions. As panel (a) of Figure 8.1 shows, coverage in many Latin American countries is not only lower than the developed countries, but also lower than other countries with similar income levels. While 68.5 percent of workers in Latin America are not covered by pension systems, 51 percent of workers lack access to pensions in countries whose gross domestic product (GDP) per capita is similar to Latin America's (ranging from $5,000 to $15,000 per year), while only 10.5 percent of workers lack coverage in advanced countries.

Not only is Latin America the land of the uncovered, but it is also the land of entrepreneurship and self-employment. As panel (b) of Figure 8.1

Figure 8.1   (a) Uncovered Labor Force in the World

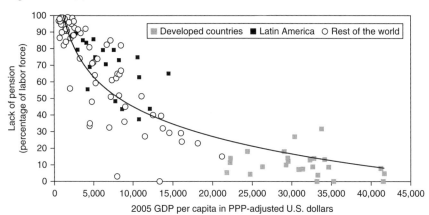

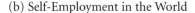

(b) Self-Employment in the World

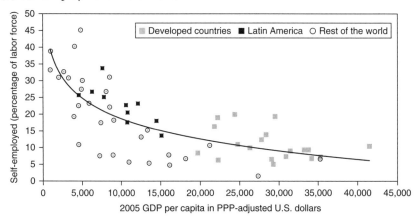

Source: Authors' calculations based on Perry et al. (2007) with data from ILO (2009a) and World Bank (2009f).

Note: Self-employment is measured as the percentage of self-employed workers with respect to total active population. Lack of pensions corresponds to the share of the labor force not covered by a pension scheme.

shows, the percentage of self-employed workers in the region is higher than in the rest of the world, even when compared to countries with similar incomes. In Latin America, about one in four workers is self-employed (23 percent), compared to one in six workers (17 percent) in countries with income levels similar to Latin America and slightly more than one in ten workers (11 percent) in developed countries.[1] As Kanbur (2009) notes, excessive self-employment can be seen as another form of strategic behavior on the part of individuals when used as a means of *avoiding* labor market legislation (which, in general, does not cover the self-employed).

Formality and productivity are linked in many ways. For instance, informal firms may operate at a suboptimal level because they lack access to credit and sources of innovation. Also, formal firms may suffer productivity losses due to competition with noncomplying firms. On another level, workers who are uninsured against poor health, old age, and other risks may be less productive, have fewer incentives to invest in human capital, or may engage in risk management strategies that conspire against long-term growth (such as selling productive assets, withdrawing children from school, or deferring use of preventive or curative health services). Moreover, a large informal sector that pays neither taxes nor social security undermines the ability of the government to provide public goods (such as institutions and infrastructure) and solve market failures (Perry et al. 2007).

Although all these channels are important, this chapter focuses only on how some social policies encourage an excess of informality,[2] which in turn induces individuals to allocate their labor in the wrong sectors, thereby lowering productivity in labor markets. This suboptimal use of labor is linked to a suboptimal use of capital as well, whereby capital is allocated to firms that exist only because they enjoy artificially low labor costs.

Social policies are understood as any actions by which the state intends to provide direct assistance to individuals to raise their living standards. The "direct" nature of the assistance is key, as many other policies (such as monetary policy and trade policy) can also be thought of as welfare-improving—but work indirectly. These direct policies can take the form either of government spending (education, health, conditional cash transfers [CCTs], food vouchers, health fairs) or regulations (the mandate to contribute to pension systems, health insurance, unemployment insurance).

Social policy is implemented through various channels and targeting mechanisms. One prominent approach has been to use labor markets as a channel to deliver services and the formality status as the targeting mechanism for coverage. This is the case with policies aimed at protecting against risks (health, social security) and policies with redistributive goals (e.g., housing and cash transfers, among others). These policies affect households' and individuals' incentives and, therefore, their behavior, particularly in labor markets (Levy 2008). This analysis will not cover policies such as those regarding universal education. Even though they aim to boost individual productivity by investing in human capital, their targeting mechanisms are generally not linked to the labor market and, therefore, they do not directly alter individuals' or firms' incentives in the allocation of labor.

Many social policies influence behaviors in labor markets. The degree and extent of that influence depends on key characteristics of their design, notably the targeting mechanism and eligibility criteria. These characteristics affect not only the efficacy and efficiency of the use of public resources, but also provide clear incentives for individual behavior. Social policies that provide household coverage through the formal labor market are referred to as *social security*. In Latin America and the Caribbean, with some variations across countries, salaried workers are entitled to a mechanism to save for their retirement, health insurance, unemployment insurance, severance payments, paid holidays, bonuses (such as a thirteenth or even fourteenth month's salary), child care, and housing finance, among others. These services are cofinanced by employers and employees, but the logistics of collecting payment is generally the responsibility of employers. In addition, employers must eventually pay for national training services and other solidarity taxes for their salaried workers. Of course, these benefits are not a free lunch. The costs of these benefits, plus the pure taxation on labor constitute the nonwage labor costs of formally hiring a worker. These costs vary across countries, depending on regulations. Table 8.1 presents estimates of these costs disaggregated in four components for a subsample of countries in the region.

Due to either legal avoidance (primarily through self-employment) or illegal evasion, many households do not have a family member in the labor market who receives protection against risks. The government has attempted to fill this gap by providing *social protection* to those uncovered families. Therefore, following Levy (2008), the distinction between *social security* and *social protection* depends on the coverage that households do, or do not, receive for their members' participation in labor markets. Note that this distinction does not depend on income, age, gender, type of work, or any other characteristic except formal attachment to the labor market. Social protection in the region has been implemented in different forms, ranging from noncontributory pension programs (such as Bolivida in Bolivia), to subsidized health care and insurance (as in the Subsidized Health Regime [SHR] in Colombia), to housing programs (as in Mexico).

Table 8.1 Nonwage Labor Costs (as a percentage of wages): Selected Latin American and Caribbean Countries

	Argentina	Bolivia	Brazil	Chile	Colombia	Costa Rica	Ecuador	El Salvador
Contributions and taxes[a]	39.7	22.2	29.0[c,d]	25.2[f]	36.8[g]	26.3	15.5	23.3
Holidays	4.2	4.2[b]	8.3	4.2	4.2	4.2	4.2	4.2
Grants	8.3	8.3	8.3	0	4.2	0	8.3	2.8[h]
Firing costs	2.1	3.2	8.0[e]	2.3	8.3	2.5	6.8	2.1
Nonwage labor costs	**54.3**	**37.9**	**53.6**	**31.7**	**53.5**	**33.0**	**34.8**	**32.4**

	Jamaica	Guatemala	Mexico	Nicaragua	Paraguay	Peru	Trinidad and Tobago	Venezuela
Contributions and taxes[a]	5.0	15.5	31.5	32.8	23.0	27.0	10.5	14.2
Holidays	4.2[i]	4.2	1.7[k]	8.3	3.3[l]	8.3	4.2[n]	4.2[i]
Grants	0	8.3	0	8.3	0[m]	16.7	0	0
Firing costs	1.2	3.8[j]	3.2	1.7	1.5	7.0	1.5	4.5
Nonwage labor costs	**10.4**	**31.8**	**36.4**	**51.1**	**27.8**	**59.0**	**16.2**	**22.9**

Source: Authors' calculations based on United States Social Security Administration (2008), Heckman and Pagés (2004), Kugler and Kugler (2009), Jaramillo (2004), Levy (2008), and ILO (2009b).

Notes:

a. Includes old age, disability and survivors, sickness, maternity, work injury, family allowances, unemployment, housing, and labor taxes.
b. For a worker with one to two years of tenure.
c. Assumes a contribution for pensions of 8 percent, corresponding to workers earning up to 2.2 times the minimum wage.
d. Assumes a contribution for work injury of 1 percent of gross payroll, which is the minimum contribution rate (depends on the assessed degree of risk).
e. Equals the contribution to the FGTS (Fundo de Garantia do Tempo de Serviço).
f. Assumes the minimum payment for work injury equal to 2.65 percent.
g. Assumes the lowest contribution for work injury (3.85 percent), which could go up to 8.7 percent (depending on the assessed degree of risk).
h. For a worker with one to three years of tenure.
i. Estimate based on World Bank, Doing Business database.
j. For a worker with less than ten years of tenure, and having worked 220 days or more.
k. For a worker with one year of tenure.
l. For a worker with between one and five years of tenure.
m. Excludes a payment of five percent of salary for each child.
n. No official number of mandatory holidays; assumption is 15 days.

Conditional Cash Transfers: What Targeting Mechanisms May Induce

Among social policies, CCTs have emerged as a prominent tool in recent decades, wisely linking current poverty alleviation with incentives for human-capital accumulation. These programs provide needy families with cash to be used to maintain their children's health and continue their education, for example, by taking their children to medical appointments and health fairs or sending them to school.

Many countries in the region have recently adopted proxy-means testing as the main targeting mechanism for their CCTs.[3] Interestingly, the way in which some of them are constructed explicitly incorporates the (lack of) social security coverage into the eligibility criteria. Such is the case, for instance, for the Ficha de Protección Social in Chile Solidario and the "SELBEN" in the Bono de Desarrollo Humano in Ecuador, among others. A comprehensive list of CCTs in the region and their targeting mechanisms is presented in Table 8.2.

In this way, even though CCTs are intended to provide needy families with the right incentives for human-capital accumulation, their targeting mechanisms could inadvertently induce unintended behavior in the labor markets. This would be the case whenever families are aware that their status as formal or informal workers is being used as the targeting criteria, and they act accordingly. It is important to emphasize that these CCT policies do not lie at the heart of the social security–social protection dichotomy that this chapter focuses on, but they do highlight the unintended consequences of some targeting mechanisms.

The Problem of Low Valuation for Social Security

Having paid nonwage labor costs, workers (with cofinancing from their employers) receive coverage in the form of promises for delivery of various social security services eventually (as in the case of health insurance) or more distantly in the future (as in the case of pensions). The literature has explored in detail why workers assign a lower utility to this coverage than to the current compensation they forego to pay their contributions (which is indeed the rationale behind the mandatory nature of contributions). Among the reasons for this incomplete valuation are: liquidity constraints; lack of knowledge of the systems (Cuesta, Millán, and Olivera 2009); myopia (Barr and Packard 2000; Packard 2002); financial illiteracy (Arenas de Mesa et al. 2006); limited access to benefits (Levy 2006a,b); poor program quality (Perry et al. 2007); undesired bundling with other social security

Table 8.2 Conditional Cash Transfers (CCTs) in Latin America: Main Components and Targeting Mechanisms

Program (Country)	Components	Targeting mechanism	Are beneficiaries questioned about their social security coverage in the targeting mechanism?
Plan Familias por la Inclusión Social (Argentina)	- CCT (on health and education) - Community development - Institutional strengthening	3 Sources: - Old beneficiaries of "Programa de Inversión en Desarrollo Humano" (targeted using a Quality of Life index) - Some of the old beneficiaries of "Programa de Jefes de Hogar" - Other vulnerable households	Indirectly as it once was for "*Programa de Jefes de Hogar*"
Bolsa Família (Brasil)	- CCTs (on health and education) with general and variable subsidies (depending on demographic characteristics of the families)	- Use of a unique roster (Cadastro Único) to select beneficiaries based on: geographical targeting and individual targeting	Not clear
Chile Solidario (Chile)	- Cash transfer - Psychological and legal support - Preferential access to social programs	- Social Protection Card: identifies vulnerable families through an assessment of their economic resources, daily needs and social risks	Yes
Familias en Acción (Colombia)	- CCTs (on health and education)	- Geographic targeting ("random" criterion at the early stage of the program) - Individual targeting: Sistema de Identificación de Potenciales Beneficiarios de Programas Sociales (SISBEN)	Yes
Avancemos (Costa Rica)	- CCTs (on health and education) - Saving incentives for students - Improvement of educational services for the poorest population	- Geographic targeting - Individual targeting: Ficha de Informacion Social (FIS)	Not clear

(continued on next page)

Table 8.2   Continued

Program (Country)	Components	Targeting mechanism	Are beneficiaries questioned about their social security coverage in the targeting mechanism?
Solidaridad (Dominican Republic)	- CCTs (on health and education)	- Geographic targeting (poverty map) - Individual targeting: Sistema Único de Beneficiarios (SIUBEN)	No
Bono de Desarrollo Humano (Ecuador)	- Conditional cash transfers (on health and education)	- Individual targeting : Sistema de Selección de Beneficiarios (SELBEN)	Yes
Red Solidaria (El Salvador)	- CCTs (on health, nutrition and education)	- Geographic targeting (poverty maps) - Individual targeting : Households in extreme poverty	No
Programa de Asignación Familiar (Honduras)	- CCTs (on health, nutrition and education)	- Geographic targeting (rural villages in extreme poverty) - Individual targeting: only restricted to those with at least one pregnant or breastfeeding woman, or at least one child younger than 13 years old	Not clear
Program for the Advancement through Health and Education (Jamaica)	- CCTs (on health, nutrition and education)	- Geographic targeting - Individual targeting	Not clear
Programa de Oportunidades (Mexico)	- CCTs (on health, nutrition and education)	- Geographic targeting - Individual targeting: Encuesta de Características Socio-Económicas de los Hogares.	Yes
Tekopora (Paraguay)	- CCTs (on health, nutrition and education)	- Geographic targeting (poverty maps): Índice de Priorización Geográfica - Individual targeting: principal components	*Yes (Health)*

(continued on next page)

Table 8.2   Continued

Program (Country)	Components	Targeting mechanism	Are beneficiaries questioned about their social security coverage in the targeting mechanism?
Juntos (Peru)	- CCTs (on health, nutrition, education, housing)	- Geographic targeting (poverty maps). Only rural - Individual targeting: Proxy-means test	Not clear
Asociaciones Familiares (Uruguay)	- CCTs (on health and education) - Pensions for poor adults	- Individual targeting: Índice de Carencias Críticas (ICC)	Yes, for retirees without pension

Source: Johannsen et al. (2009) and questionnaires from various social and economic surveys from Argentina: MTEySS (2003); Brazil: MDS (2001); Chile; MIDEPLAN (2007); Colombia: DANE (2003); Dominican Republic: Coordinación del Gabinete de Política Social (2005); Ecuador: MCDS (2006); Mexico: Sedesol (1997); and Paraguay: SAS (2005).

Note: Data are as of May 2009.

elements (Levy 2008; Perry et al. 2007); lack of government credibility (Perry et al. 2007); and poor design (for instance, minimum pensions or extended coverage for spouses who then have less of an incentive to contribute; Galiani and Weinschelbaum 2007).

Contributions to pension systems represent the largest share of nonwage labor costs in most of the region. Consequently, a key issue when analyzing whether incentives are to be covered or not by these systems is the value individuals place on the benefits received in exchange for contributions to the pension system. It is telling that pension system coverage among salaried workers has remained stagnant in recent decades (see Figure 8.2 and Rofman and Lucchetti 2006) and that participation and contribution rates among the self-employed are still extremely low (Auerbach, Genoni, and Pagés 2007), despite the overall transition toward fully funded schemes in the region—a shift aimed at reducing implicit labor taxes on formal employment to directly link contributions to benefits (see Lora and Pagés 2000; Corbo 2004; and Corbo and Schmidt-Hebbel 2003).

What drives this low rate of participation in and contribution to pension systems? The answer is complex. Besides the proliferation of old-age benefits in the form of social protection, the literature has emphasized both governments' low enforcement capability (Almeida and Carneiro 2005) and individuals' low valuation of social security benefits.

Figure 8.2   Share of Salaried Workers with Right to Pensions When Retired

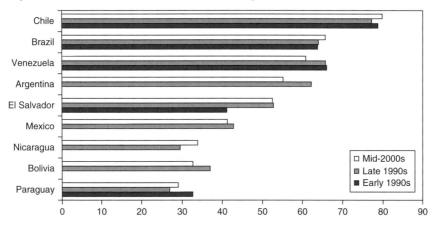

Source: CEDLAS and World Bank (2008).

Notes: Years considered – Argentina: 1998 and 2003; Bolivia: 1999 and 2005; Brazil: 1992, 1999, and 2004; Chile: 1990, 1998, and 2006; El Salvador: 1991, 1999, and 2005; Mexico: 1998 and 2006; Nicaragua: 1998 and 2005; Paraguay: 1995, 1999, and 2005; Venezuela: 1995, 1999, and 2006.

A recent IDB survey focusing on workers aged 25 to 55 in metropolitan Lima explored the reasons behind low pension coverage. In this city, pension coverage reached only 40 percent of the target population. Unsurprisingly, salaried workers, males, more educated, older, and wealthier persons are more likely to be affiliated with the system. Strikingly, 45 percent of respondents admit to not having thought about how to finance their old age at all. Moreover, among those who claimed to have thought about the financing of their old age, only 43 percent said they had taken concrete action in this regard. The statistic is even more dramatic among the less educated and the poor.

Another striking finding is the low share of noncontributors who would contribute if contribution rates were lowered. Nearly 60 percent of noncontributors responded that they would not contribute even if the contribution rate were halved. Overall, the valuation that people attach to social security coverage is low, which is in line with recent research that finds that in general, job satisfaction is not strictly related to coverage.[4]

Among those who do not contribute to their pension accounts, nearly half blame limited or irregular incomes for their decision. This justification is even more pronounced among the poor. However, another important share of those who do not contribute (25 percent) blames their lack of information about and trust in the system.[5] Indeed, financial literacy and knowledge about pension systems is strikingly low. When asked about six basic features of how the Peruvian pension systems function (such as the male and female retirement age, contribution amounts, commissions and who pays for them, and how benefits are calculated), nearly half the respondents were unable to answer a single question correctly. Hardly any of the respondents answered all six of them correctly. These results paint a picture of myopic behavior vis-à-vis protection for old age, accompanied by a widespread lack of information about the system (Atal et al. 2009).

Pension-related savings have shown low real rates of return (net of commissions) in some countries in the region (Colombia, Costa Rica, and the Dominican Republic are prominent examples). Thus, even for a fully informed and perfectly rational worker, evading social security contributions would be a tempting option. In this situation, pension contributions are likely viewed as a tax on formality and, as such, promote informal agreements in the labor market.

Recent research has found that workers are often paid lower wages to compensate for employers' social security contributions (Gruber 1997; Heckman and Pagés 2004; Betcherman and Pagés 2007), making workers' valuations for benefits a critical issue. Boosting valuation by promoting financial literacy and trust in the system may be one avenue to pursue, even though strong empirical evidence on its impact is still scarce.[6] Alternative or complementary measures may be to redesign the financing mechanisms, subsidize contributions for low-wage earners, or provide tax exemptions (IDB 2008b). These measures must be complemented by others aimed at boosting workers' valuations of the nonpension components of social security (such as health and unemployment insurance and severance payments). Along these lines, improving the quality of service delivery, including the availability of services and wait times, may work in the desired direction, although more research is needed to clarify the potential of these measures.

A Framework to Analyze Individuals' Incentives and Decision Making

How much productivity is lost as a result of the social security–social protection dichotomy? A simple static framework provides rough estimates of these losses. The analysis that follows assumes an *integrated markets* view, that is, individuals choose to be covered or not covered by social security by taking into account the costs and benefits of each alternative and have the flexibility to pick one alternative over the other. This view has prevailed in the recent literature for the region given the lack of strong evidence of a dualistic labor market in which informal workers are queuing for formal positions (see Maloney 2004; Galiani and Weinschelbaum 2007).

However, recent evidence supporting the dualistic approach has shown that informal workers appear to be involuntarily confined to their jobs, at least to some extent. Household surveys for Argentina, Bolivia, Colombia, and the Dominican Republic reveal that the inability to find a better job is the main reason informal salaried workers keep their current positions (Arias and Bustelo 2007; and Arias, Landa, and Yáñez 2007). Still, as noted by Perry et al. (2007), informal salaried workers who are unhappy with their jobs mainly tend to turn to independent employment rather than formal salaried employment.

There is also extensive mobility between covered and uncovered salaried jobs, supporting the lack of rationing between the two (IDB 2003; Bosch and Maloney 2007; Levy 2008; Pagés and Stampini forthcoming). Even though there is still no widespread consensus, the integrated markets view appears to be the most sensible framework for analyzing decision making in the covered-uncovered margin. Within this framework, the aim is to emphasize the role that social policies may play in shaping the decisions of both workers and firms regarding whether to fill positions that are covered or not covered by social security.

On the basis of the integrated markets view and the limited valuation of benefits discussed above, a convenient framework to analyze workers' and firms' decisions is proposed by Levy (2008). According to this framework, a covered worker receives wages (net of contributions) and benefits from *social security* as compensation for her/his labor. Wages are received immediately and in cash and are fully valued. However, social security benefits are valued at a discount for the reasons described above. Hence, the total valuation of covered workers' compensation is the sum of net wages and the discounted value of social security. Analogously, the total valuation of uncovered workers' compensation is comprised of wages and *social protection* transfers, which, in turn, may not be fully valued either. That is, the total utility for a worker in the uncovered sector is equal to the wage plus the discounted value of social protection. Workers compare the total valuation of a covered and an uncovered job and decide which one is in their best interest.

Social protection, which was created to protect those who are not covered by social security, can be understood as a deficient replica of social security. Governments' efforts to provide social protection to the uncovered population regularly fall short and the scale and scope of the services fail to reach all those who need it (regardless of their income level). Social protection and social security are imperfect substitutes. For this reason, it is important to distinguish individuals' valuation of social protection from that of social security.

When a firm decides to hire a worker and offer him/her coverage, it must pay net wages plus social security. Hiring the same worker without coverage would require only wage payment.[7] Total payments made by firms in each case differ, which reflects the fact that social policy distorts the labor market. Note that net wages are not necessarily the same in the covered and uncovered segments of the labor markets. For this reason, the individual distortion is not just equal to the nonwage costs but is actually equal to the sum of the formality gap in wages plus the extra, nonwage costs of formality.

According to the Levy model, individual distortion can be expressed as two additive components: one that arises from the cost of social security and its incomplete valuation (which takes the form of a tax on formal labor); and another that results from the value of social protection already in place (and takes the form of a subsidy to informal labor).

The focus of this simplified model is the covered-uncovered margin, leaving aside labor-market participation decisions resulting from the distortion created by the social security–social protection dichotomy. Recent empirical literature has found mixed evidence of the impact on labor participation. For instance, Yáñez-Pagans (2008) finds no effect on labor participation for a major noncontributory pension program in Bolivia (Bolivida). Similarly, Alejo et al. (2009) report only small reductions in labor supply as a consequence of CCTs in the region, mostly among women. On the other hand, Juarez (2007) reports less negligible negative effects on the labor participation of women caused by a nutrition transfer for senior adults in Mexico City. Gaviria, Medina, and Mejía (2006) find an important decline in participation rates among women as a result of the SHR in Colombia.

How Big Are the Distortions and Output Losses?

Adding up the individual distortions for all workers involved (i.e., the number of workers not covered by social security that would be covered in the absence of social protection policies) yields a proxy measure for the total output loss induced. What is the magnitude of this total loss? This section attempts to measure this loss for a sample of countries in the region.

As stated above, the individual distortion can be expressed as the difference in the compensation paid by firms for hiring a covered or uncovered worker. This distortion can therefore be expressed as a "formality gap in wages" (the difference in net wages earned by a worker depending on his formality status) plus the nonwage labor costs of formality. A first building block for estimating the output loss is to measure the formality gap in wages. The data sources for countries with available information are

National Household Surveys. A raw comparison of average wages for covered and uncovered salaried workers provides a first estimate of the gap. The problem with this first estimate is that it fails to take into account the differences in the human-capital characteristics of covered versus uncovered workers. Taking those differences into account provides better estimates of formality gaps, which are below the original raw estimates.

In countries for which panel data are available, more precise estimates for formality gaps can be obtained. Available evidence suggests that estimates obtained with these richer data are even smaller than those obtained from cross-sections and even statistically not significantly different from zero in many cases.[8] Hence, the most conservative scenario for an estimation of formality gaps would be to assume that they are equal to zero. A less conservative estimate, that accounts for the differences in characteristics with the technique devised in Ñopo (2008), ranges from 9 percent to 22 percent of the average wage in the corresponding country (column III of Table 8.3).

The second building block for estimating the output loss is a measure of the extra cost of formality, which was already provided in Table 8.1. In a sample of Latin American countries, nonwage labor costs in the region range between 23 and 54 percent of wages (see column II of Table 8.3). The average differences in marginal productivity for each country as a result of these extra costs range between 23 and 54 percent in a conservative scenario, which assumes no difference between formal and informal wages, and between 37 and 73 percent, assuming the wage gaps from column III (see column IV).

The third building block in this computation is the number of workers affected by this distortion. In a world with universal social security, there would be no informal (uncovered) workers and thus no difference in marginal productivity. The introduction of social security financed through labor markets and then coupled with social protection policies encourages workers and firms to enter into informal contracts. This exercise makes the counterfactual assumption that all uncovered dependent workers choose this option because of the distortion generated by social policies. Even if this estimate may exaggerate output losses by assuming that all uncovered workers opted for that because of the wage and nonwage distortions generated by social security and social protection, it does not account for those who opted for self-employment to escape from nonwage labor costs and to benefit from social protection.[9]

The individual distortions, which are represented as percentages of average wages, are then converted into monetary units by multiplying them by the average wages, which are calculated using the same household surveys. The total distortion is calculated by multiplying the individual

Table 8.3 Output Loss Estimates for the Region

Country	Year	Uncovered salaried workers (Millions of workers)	Uncovered salaried workers (Percentage of salaried workers)	Nonwage labor cost (Percentage of salary)	Covered/Uncovered wage gap (Percentage of average salary)	Difference in marginal productivity (Percentage of salary)	Annual GDP loss range (Percentage of GDP)
		(I)		(II)	(III)	(IV) = (II) + (III)	$(V) = 0.5 \times (I) \times (IV) \times$ (Average wage)/GDP
Bolivia	2002	0.9	75.0	37.9	8.72[a]	46.6	[3.6–5.1]
Brazil	2007	17.8	31.9	53.6	17.9	71.5	[1.8–2.5]
Chile	2006	0.9	20.1	31.7	13.5	45.1	[0.4–0.6]
Colombia	2005	2.4	31.8	53.5	19.9	73.4	[1.1–1.5]
Costa Rica	2006	0.2	18.1	33.0	12.5	45.5	[0.6–0.8]
Ecuador	2007	2.1	66.9	34.8	20.9	55.6	[2.1–4.1]
El Salvador	2005	0.6	49.0	32.4	12.5	44.9	[1.6–2.4]
Guatemala	2006	1.7	63.4	31.8	21.8[a]	53.6	[1.9–4.1]
Mexico	2002	13.6	50.7	36.4	14.0[b]	50.3	[1.4–2.1]
Nicaragua	2005	0.7	67.0	51.1	19.8	70.9	[3.9–6.3]
Paraguay	2006	0.9	83.3	27.8	15.0	42.9	[2.7–5.2]
Venezuela	2004	1.9	41.0	22.9	14.0	36.9	[0.4–0.8]

Source: Authors' calculations based on Table 8.1, IMF (2009b), and countries' household surveys from Bolivia: INE (2002); Brazil: IBGE (2007); Chile: MIDEPLAN (2006); Colombia: DANE (2005); Costa Rica: INEC (2006); Ecuador: INEC (2007); El Salvador: DIGESTYC (2005); Guatemala: INE (2006); Mexico: INEGI (2002); Nicaragua: INIDE (2005); Paraguay: DGEEC (2006); and Venezuela: INE (2004).

Notes: Column (III) shows the wage gap that remains after controlling for gender, age, education, living in the capital city, economic sector, and firm size. The lower bound in column (V) assumes that the covered-uncovered wage gap is zero. The upper bound in that column uses the result in column (III).
[a] Due to data availability, not controlling for either firm size or economic sector.
[b] Due to data availability, not controlling for firm size.

Figure 8.3 (a) Public Social Protection Spending Evolution: Countries with Increasing Social Protection (Percentage of GDP)

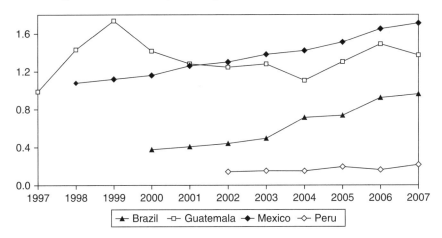

(b) Public Social Protection Spending Evolution: Countries with Decreasing Social Protection (Percentage of GDP)

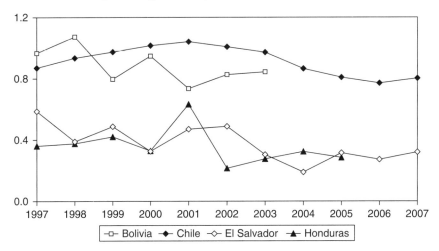

Source: Authors' calculations based on data from various government agencies: Bolivia–MEFP (2009); Brazil–MF (2009); Chile–MH (2009); El Salvador–MHS (various years); Guatemala–MFG (2009); Honduras–World Bank (2007); Mexico–SHCP (2009); Peru–TEP (2009).

income (up to a cap of 20 minimum wages), two thirds of which is paid by the employer. One-and-a-half percentage points of this contribution goes toward financing the SHR. As Cárdenas and Bernal (2003) document, these increases in nonwage costs have negatively impacted labor demand and raised unemployment. Kugler and Kugler (2009) analyze manufacturing plants and estimate that a 10 percent increase in payroll taxes reduces formal employment by 4 to 5 percent and formal wages by 1.4 to 2.3 percent.

Another problem is that the program is designed in a way that the benefits are comparable between the two regimes. Affiliates of the subsidized system have access to a basic benefit package known as *Plan Obligatorio de Salud Subsidiado* (POSS, the Mandatory Subsidized Health Plan), which covers health promotion and education, primary healthcare, basic hospital services, and treatment for a number of high-cost diseases (Panopoulu and Vélez 2001). The POSS also offers full coverage for maternity and child care, including some secondary and tertiary care in hospitals. Even though the POSS covers fewer services than the basic benefit package of the CHR (the *Plan Obligatorio de Salud,* POS) the benefits of the two packages were expected to converge by 2001. While they have not converged yet, a recent decree by the Constitutional Court mandates the adoption of measures to unify the benefits. In addition, even though both the POS and the POSS offer family coverage, only the POSS covers every member in the household, regardless of his or her relationship to the household head.[12] Services that are not covered by the POSS are supplied by public health providers with a 5 or 10 percent copayment (Gaviria, Medina, and Mejía 2006). As Cuesta, Millán, and Olivera (2009) note, individuals' valuation of both regimes is similar and homogeneously high across socioeconomic strata, although contribution rates differ substantially.

Finally, and beyond any social policy, the construction of the SISBEN index as a proxy-means test for a plethora of social policies may itself lure people into informality. Despite claims of manipulation problems in its early stages (Camacho and Conover 2008a), the SISBEN has proven to be an effective targeting mechanism (Bottia, Cardona, and Medina 2008). It is a tool that does an effective job of distinguishing the poor from the nonpoor. The problem, however, is that both access to social security and the size of the firm of the highest wage earner in the household are variables that form part of its construction (at least in its first version). Therefore, according to the way the index is computed, a formal worker is likely to lose eligibility to any other program beyond the SHR once he enters the formal sector. Also, there has not been free mobility between the two regimes as until 2003, it was not possible to move back to the SHR after entering the CHR. This, as Cuesta, Millán, and Olivera (2009) note, generates further distortive incentives.

Santamaría, García, and Mujica (2009a) provide evidence that the SHR encourages informality by showing that half the beneficiaries of the SHR in Bogotá, Bucaramanga, and Cali are unwilling to change their formality status and lose their SHR entitlement. They also document a noticeable increase in the share of self-employed workers after the reform, which they relate to the noticeable increase in nonwage labor costs (Santamaría, García, and Mujica 2009b).

Camacho and Conover (2008b) study the causal effect on the SHR on formality, and find robust effects of the SHR on social security coverage, with reductions that range from 1 to 4 percentage points. Also, Gaviria, Medina, and Mejía (2006) find that the SHR reduces labor-force participation by 25 percentage points and that the effect differs substantially by gender: female participation is reduced by as much as 34 points, while male participation remains unchanged. The authors argue that the SHR has a positive income effect, eliminating the need for a second income to cover health expenditures. Second, the fact that all beneficiaries in a family lose their entitlement to the SHR once one family member is enrolled, discourages workers from taking formal jobs that could be volatile. As a result, "the SHR ends up working as (an additional) labor market rigidity for the movement of individuals from the informal to the formal sector."

In summary, Colombia substantially expanded health insurance coverage and improved health standards among its population with this reform. However, in addition to this welcome social effect, the reform produced undesirable outcomes in labor markets. Among the most salient effects were lower participation and higher informality. The reform was designed in a distortive way when looked at through the lenses of the labor market.

Policy Implications

Social policies are necessary for societies, as they serve a plethora of objectives that improve well-being and facilitate social cohesion. However, some social policies induce a misallocation of resources, which in turn yields a productivity loss. The strategy of financing social security through labor markets, coupled with scanty enforcement of labor regulations and individuals' low valuation of social security benefits, fuel informal markets by encouraging both workers and firms to remain uncovered in order to avoid the cost of contributions. This, in turn, generates the need for social protection policies for those who are not covered by the formal mechanisms. This policy decision further reduces worker's willingness to search for jobs with social security coverage and distorts firms' decisions on labor allocation and scale of operations. In short, social policies push people into the informal sector, which has a negative impact on productivity.

The state has a social obligation to impose coverage against risks on people who do not seek protection on their own because they assign it a low priority. In a region characterized by low compliance with existing regulations (Kaufmann, Kraay, and Mastruzzi 2006), enhancing enforcement may be a straightforward solution to achieve the state's social goals and at the same time reduce the productivity loss depicted in this chapter. However, this strategy alone is not a promising answer to the big problem of protecting societies. Unless contributions and benefits are strongly aligned, individuals' valuation of social security will remain low and they will continue to seek ways of avoiding the costs of being covered. Therefore, the problem of low valuation must be addressed as well.

Strengthening the quality of services and directly linking individuals' benefits to contributions should work in the appropriate direction. One example of such a policy is the migration from defined-benefit to defined-contribution pension systems, as it improves individuals' incentives to contribute to their old-age savings. Still, the impact of this policy on contributions has been limited, probably in part because of widespread financial illiteracy.

The major problem revolves around the decision to provide social security through labor markets. A profound solution to the productivity problem posed by social policies would have to eliminate the social security–social protection dichotomy so that benefits (insurance and services) are delivered independently of an individuals' labor market status. As proposed by Levy (2008), a major reform to social policies in this direction would be to provide universal social entitlements regardless of the salaried/nonsalaried labor status and finance them out of consumption taxes. In this way, government's social objectives of providing coverage could be achieved without taxing formal labor and without subsidizing the informal sector, thereby eliminating the current distortions in allocating resources that harm productivity. Only the benefits specific to salaried workers, such as unemployment insurance and severance payments, should be reserved exclusively for them.

The package of benefits included in these universal social entitlements should only be one for which there is a clear rationale for state intervention, either because there are risk-pooling gains, good risk-management rationales, or market failures. Old-age pensions and life and health insurance clearly fall within these categories, but housing, child care (as in the case of Mexico), or early childhood development (as in the case of Colombia) seem to be beyond their scope.

Without nonwage labor cost revenues, consumption taxes to finance universal benefits will likely have to be increased. Beyond imposing its preferences, the government should maintain its goal of income redistribution toward the poor, which could be achieved with a pure income transfer to a subset of workers such that fiscal sustainability is assured. However, there are important targeting challenges. Governments need to improve their strategies for reaching those who are most in need, especially in urban areas. Red Juntos in Colombia and Chile Solidario are interesting and improved strategies for reaching the extremely poor and excluded (although as noted, targeting mechanisms must also take into account the incentives they pose).

In addition to the negative impact of some social policies on productivity, the design of some of these policies also conspires against their primary social goal of protecting those in need, as they encourage informality and the attendant evasion of coverage. Unfortunately, under these conditions economic growth alone will not solve the problem of informality. In fact, it is much the other way around. Economic growth is constrained because persistent informality chips away at productivity. Again, it is important to emphasize that social policies per se are not the cause of productivity problems; rather, their particular design and implementation are to blame for the distortive incentives they engender.

Many countries in the region are working to consolidate their social security systems and at the same time combat poverty and improve the living conditions of their populations through social protection. This chapter emphasizes that social policies must carefully consider both their social and economic goals. Understanding how social security and social protection policies interact and the incentives they each create has practical consequences on productivity.

Notes

1. Data on firms illustrate the same phenomenon; the share of very small firms is much larger in Latin America than in the United States. For examples see Chapter 3.
2. For more on the concept of excess informality see Levy, 2008.
3. See Johannsen et al. (2009) for a discussion of targeting mechanisms in the region. Proxy-means testing consists of using certain "easy to measure" variables to approximate household income or expenditures (as a way to approximate poverty) and in turn determine eligibility for social programs.
4. For instance, Madrigal and Pagés (2008) find that job satisfaction in uncovered jobs declines only for highly skilled workers (see also IDB 2008b).
5. Similar results were found by Arias and Bustelo (2007) and Arias, Landa, and Yáñez (2007) for Argentina, Bolivia, Colombia, and the Dominican Republic.
6. For the United States, Agnew et al. (2007) find that financial literacy plays a critical role in improving 401(k) savings behavior and underscores the importance of ongoing workplace education for both voluntary and automatic enrollment. They also highlight the important role that trust in fund administrators plays in enrollment. Also for the United States, Lusardi and

Mitchell (2006) show that those with higher financial literacy are more likely to plan for retirement, succeed in their planning, and save and invest in more complex assets. However, the problem of reverse causality of financial literacy and financial behavior is still to be addressed in these empirical findings.

7. Plus the expected fine of being caught, which is not modeled within this simplified context.

8. See Levy (2008) for a careful computation of estimates for the formality gaps using panel data for Mexico. Similar estimates for Chile are available from the authors upon request. See also Pratap and Quintin (2002) and Pagés and Stampini (forthcoming).

9. Incipient literature from the region tries to measure the actual effect of changes in social policy on informality. Results are mixed, suggesting some case-specific effects. For instance, Barros (2008) finds that a major expansion of health services to the population not covered by social security in Mexico did not result in a shift of workers to the informal sector. On the other hand, Gasparini, Haimovich, and Oliveiri (2007) suggest shifts to the informal sector generated by the program Jefes de Hogar in Argentina. Also, Camacho and Conover (2008b) find small but robust effects on the informality of the SHR in Colombia (this program is analyzed in detail below).

10. For details on the model see Levy (2008).

11. The difference depends on whether or not informal firms are confronted with capital wedges and two different ways of modeling the economy (monopolistic competition with constant returns to scale, or a perfect competition environment with decreasing returns to scale).

12. The POSS offers coverage to spouses or stable partners with at least a two-year relationship (and who are not directly enrolled in the CHR) and any economically dependent children of either spouse. The latter includes children under 18, full-time students under 25, and disabled dependents of any age. If the affiliate is single or has no children, the family group includes a parent who is a dependent.

9

Big Questions about Small Firms

L atin America has many small firms, and many of these suffer from low
productivity. Governments in the region have increasingly invested in
policies to support micro-,` small, and medium enterprises (SMEs). The
justification for these policies has been that SMEs face extraordinary challenges that hinder their productivity and growth, and thus their potential
to provide jobs and incomes for vast segments of the population. However,
despite the enthusiasm with which SME policies are often promoted,
little is known about their effectiveness or impact. This chapter provides a
framework for analyzing the rationale and potential impact of SME policies
on both firm performance and aggregate productivity.

Research confirms that large enterprises tend to be more productive than SMEs. Some determinants of this productivity gap are variations in access to credit, use of training, intensity of innovation, and
quality certification, all of which are related to firms' acquisition of
improved technologies. Thus policies that focus on increasing the provision of these technologies and services to SMEs could be expected to have
a potentially positive effect on the productivity of these firms. However,
the scarcity of actual evidence on their impact or cost-effectiveness
implies that caution should be exercised when interpreting these results.

The SME Sector and SME Policies: Objectives, Rationale, and Instruments

The SME Sector in Latin America

The definition of SMEs varies by country and region. All definitions use
a quantitative measure, such as number of employees. SMEs are defined

as those firms for which that measure lies below a certain threshold. However, not all countries use the same quantitative measure or threshold. The most commonly used criteria are number of employees and monthly or annual sales.[1]

The relative size of the SME sector varies across countries and is an endogenous characteristic of each country. Some countries may have endowments that give them a comparative advantage in goods that are produced efficiently in large firms, while other countries may have a comparative advantage in goods produced more efficiently in small firms (You 1995). Similarly, the optimal firm size in countries that are open to international trade may be larger than in countries that are less integrated internationally (see Chapter 5). Economic policy can also affect firm size. For example, simplified tax regimes for SMEs may provide an incentive not to grow, as firms may find it unprofitable to move to the standard tax regime (see Chapter 7 for a detailed discussion of this issue).

As discussed in Chapter 4, the largest fraction of small firms is composed of very small firms: those with fewer than five or ten employees. These firms constitute the "micro" firms in the context of the MSME sector (micro plus SME) and exhibit the lowest productivity.

SME Policies and Instruments

SME policies are targeted at firms below a certain size. Within this broad definition fall a wide range of policies. Almost all Latin American countries have a simplified tax regime (STR) or differential labor regulations for SMEs, programs to facilitate access to credit, and subsidies and services aimed at supporting SMEs. This chapter focuses on policies aimed at increasing firms' productivity, most often through the promotion of training, innovation, and quality certification. Although access to credit has been analyzed in Chapter 6, it will also be discussed here since it is a widely used instrument in SME policies.

The stated goal of most SME policies is to achieve higher rates of economic growth and reduce poverty (see Ayyagari, Beck, and Demirgüç-Kunt 2007). To meet these broad goals, SME policies have a variety of specific objectives including job creation, better entrepreneurship, higher productivity and/or competitiveness, greater access to credit, and lower barriers to entry.[2] When designing and implementing SME policies, policymakers often face restrictions and incentives that have little to do with market failures and are more related to political cycles, equality, and other political economy issues. This variety of objectives (often for the same program or policy) conspires against the coherence of SME interventions.

The main economic justification for SME programs is the existence of market failures that might specifically harm SMEs and limit their growth or productivity. For instance, in the financial market, banks often fail to assess the risk of lending to SMEs accurately and therefore reject some profitable projects, effectively reducing the supply of capital to smaller firms. In other cases, owners of small firms have incomplete information about the benefits of taking certain steps that might positively affect their firm's performance, such as offering training to their employees or obtaining external technical assistance. Sometimes, entrepreneurs do not take those actions because of scale problems; for example, this is the case when some goods and services are not available in the market in the small quantities that SMEs would optimally consume (these are the market failures due to indivisibilities and nonconvexities). In this context, the efficiency of SMEs may be constrained by the inability or unwillingness of crucial suppliers to scale down their services to meet the demand of smaller firms. Perhaps the most common example is the provision of small loans by credit institutions, but the concept could be applied to several services that demand an initial assessment of the customer's needs and characteristics, such as technical assistance and training. In these cases, the fixed costs of providing the services do not significantly decrease with the size of the clients, but the revenues shrink significantly, making the provision of services to smaller firms highly unprofitable. This argument has frequently been used to justify public policies that help SMEs coordinate and organize in order to present a joint demand for services. Networking and clustering policies, for instance, have often been justified for this reason, among others.[3]

In light of these arguments, public interventions may be justified to help SMEs either grow or improve their productivity. In both cases, policies have the potential to improve aggregate productivity, although the mechanisms by which productivity grows in the aggregate differ in each case. In the case of growth-facilitating policies, aggregate productivity increases because policies improve the use (allocation) of existing resources. When firms are constrained in their growth, providing them an extra unit of resources produces a very large return in terms of output that encourages labor and capital to be reallocated. In the case of policies that foster the productivity of individual firms, aggregate productivity increases because aided firms are made more productive.

Another broad set of justifications for SME policies relate to the (presumed or real) characteristics of SMEs that are deemed particularly desirable. First, it is argued that SMEs enhance competition and entrepreneurship and hence have external benefits on economy-wide efficiency, innovation, and aggregate productivity growth. This is the case only if SMEs are actually productive, highly efficient, and engage in innovation. Unfortunately, the incidence of

Table 9.1   Debate on SME Policies

Favorable view of SMEs	Skeptical view of SMEs
Market failures, such as asymmetric information, nonconvexities, and local externalities, particularly affect SMEs.	
SMEs enhance competition and entrepreneurship and hence boost economy-wide efficiency and innovation.	Large firms can exploit economies of scale and undertake large fixed costs associated with research and development (R&D).
SMEs are more labor-intensive than large firms.	SMEs are neither more labor-intensive nor better at job creation and do not provide better-quality jobs.
SMEs are more productive than large firms, but financial market and institutional failures impede their formation and growth.	Policies should strengthen the business environment overall and not focus only on size, as the optimal size varies by country and sector.
	Pro-SME policies are likely to fail precisely where they are needed (capture of benefits by elites that inhibit SME growth).

Source: Ayyagari, Beck, and Demirgüç-Kunt (2007); Levine (2005); and authors' analysis.

innovation tends to be much lower among small firms—meaning the benefits do not necessarily materialize. Second, SMEs are portrayed as labor-intensive; thus expanding the SME sector would boost employment more than expanding large firms. Yet some research finds that SMEs are neither more labor-intensive nor better at job creation than large firms, once their highest levels of job destruction are also taken into account.

There are other skeptical views of the efficacy of SME support policies (see Table 9.1).[4] Some authors, for example, argue that large firms benefit from economies of scale and create more stable and higher-quality jobs. Other authors question the validity of considering firm size as an exogenous determinant of economic growth. According to this view, pro-SME subsidies may actually distort firm size and potentially hurt economic efficiency. Another view stresses the importance of improving the business environment for firms of all sizes. Low entry and exit barriers, well-defined property rights, and effective contract enforcement create a business climate that is conducive to competition and private commercial transactions. While these factors may encourage SMEs, the focus of the business environment view is not on SMEs per se; it is on the environment facing all businesses. Finally, another skeptical view of SME policy argues that these policies are probably most needed in precisely those areas where they are less likely to succeed: if SMEs face institutional obstacles due to

Figure 9.1   Distribution of SME Programs by Country (percent)

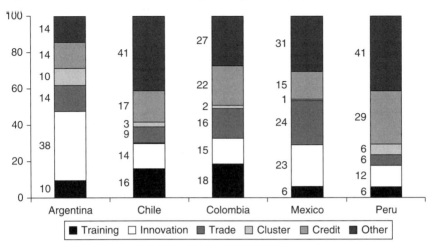

Source: Ibarrarán, Maffioli, and Stucchi (2009).

some sort of regulatory capture, it is very likely that SME programs will also be captured (Levine 2005).

Although there is no consensus in the debate, many governments in Latin America have introduced an increasingly complex set of SME policies. Figure 9.1 summarizes some SME policies applied in Latin America, aggregated in terms of the variable they aim to affect.[5]

SME policies come in various sizes and flavors. In terms of financial support, some programs provide credit at lower interest rates, on longer terms, or with less stringent requirements than the credit lines usually offered by the market. In some cases, these policies are implemented either directly through public development banks or indirectly through second-tier funding systems, whereby public financial institutions provide credit to SMEs through credit lines managed by commercial banks. Other financial programs provide guarantees aimed at facilitating access to credit. In this case, public financial institutions set up credit guarantee funds that complement collateral pledged by the SMEs. Other programs provide grants or fiscal incentives targeted at specific activities such as training, innovation, and exports. Many countries, for instance, offer matching grants or tax cuts to SMEs that purchase the services of accredited firms in order to provide training to their employees. To spur innovation, the widely diffused technology development funds (TDF) provide matching grants aimed at cofinancing SME projects that are aimed at developing process and product innovations. Export promotion programs provide packages of services and financial incentives to SMEs with export potential, including the cofinancing of specialized consultancies for foreign market analysis, quality control, and certifications. Finally, a new generation of public programs creates linkages between larger firms—in some cases, foreign firms—and small potential suppliers by cofinancing technical assistance aimed at adjusting the quality of SME production to the standards demanded by larger clients.

The Relationship between Firm Size and Productivity

SME policies can affect the aggregate level of productivity through two channels. First, they can directly influence the productivity of SMEs, and thus the productivity gap between SMEs and large firms. Second, if SMEs and large firms differ in productivity, SME policies can influence aggregate productivity by reallocating resources across SMEs and large firms.

The productivity in a sector or in the economy can be expressed as the sum of the productivity of large firms and the productivity gap between small and large firms, weighted by the share of small firms.[6]

$$P_t = P_{Large,t} + \omega_{SME,t} \left(P_{SME,t} - P_{Large,t} \right) \tag{1}$$

Therefore, the aggregate level of productivity (P_t) is determined both by the productivity of each size group ($P_{SME,t}$ and $P_{Large,t}$) and by the allocation of resources between the two size groups ($\omega_{SME,t}$). SME policies affect both mechanisms.

The impact on aggregate productivity induced by changes in the productivity of each size group is clear: aggregate productivity will be higher if there is an increase in the productivity of small or large firms. However, an increase in the share of the SME sector will increase aggregate productivity only if SME firms are more productive than large firms. Most existing evidence suggests that, on average, large firms have higher total factor productivity (TFP, a measure of productivity that takes into consideration the labor, capital, and materials that firms use to produce output). If SMEs are less productive than larger firms, policies that increase the proportion of firms in the SME sector—such as employment policies—without increasing their productivity may hamper aggregate productivity.

The lower productivity of smaller firms could also be due to the dynamic relationship between a firm's age and productivity (see, among others, Huergo and Jaumandreu 2004). New firms entering the market are usually relatively smaller in size and lower in productivity. However, new firms that survive the competitive selection tend to experience higher productivity growth than incumbent firms for several years.

Determinants of the Productivity Gap between SMEs and Large Firms

Is there any room for public policies to increase the productivity of SMEs? The best way to answer this crucial question would be to produce a significant number of studies on the impact of SME policies and their cost-effectiveness—which means their effectiveness compared to other policy options. Unfortunately, such a set of studies has not been developed, and the rare evaluations that address this issue rigorously do not provide enough critical mass to draw significant conclusions. Policymakers, scholars, and international agencies should drastically increase the resources devoted to impact evaluations of SME policies.

However, given the increasing availability of firm-level data, the magnitude of the productivity gap between SMEs and large firms can be measured.[7] This gap can also be decomposed into its major determinants, particularly the variables usually targeted by SME policies such as access to credit, innovation, training, and quality certification.[8] Once the determinants of the productivity gap have been identified and the relevance of the factors targeted by SME policies has been tested, the impact of expanding these policies on the productivity level can be simulated (see Box 9.1).

The evidence for the manufacturing sector in Latin America shows that SMEs tend to be less productive than large firms (see Chapter 4, confirmed in this analysis using the widely used measure of TFP).[9] Depending on the model specification, the gap ranges between 22 and 15 percent for small and medium firms, respectively. These computations do not include micro-enterprises and are based on the analysis of the World Bank's Enterprise Survey data for a large number of countries in Latin America and the Caribbean. Data presented in Chapter 4 suggest even larger differences among micro- and larger firms. In light of the framework previously discussed, this gap implies that policies that shift resources toward SME firms (without affecting firms' productivity) could lower aggregate productivity, because less productive firms would account for a larger share of economic activity.[10]

The data allows identifying which firms use credit, train their workers, innovate, or are certified. Controlling for such variables in a regression framework,[11] the analysis shows that a significant part of the productivity gap is actually explained by the factors usually targeted by SME policies. Among them, access to credit, training, and quality certification show a consistent and robust relationship with the productivity gap (see Table 9.2).

To assess the robustness of the results further, policy evaluation techniques assessed the potential effects of the policy variables on the productivity of SMEs and large firms (see Table 9.3). The results show not only a

---

Box 9.1　Firm Data

The empirical work in this chapter is based on firm-level data from the World Bank's Enterprise Surveys. The surveys are applied to a representative sample of firms in the nonagricultural economy and cover plants with more than five employees. The analysis is restricted to the manufacturing sector. The principal advantage of this dataset is that it provides homogeneous information for 16 countries in Latin America.

The datasets have two limitations. First, all the plants in the dataset belong to registered firms with more than five employees. This point is important because, in Latin American economies, micro- and informal firms provide a large proportion of total employment. The second limitation is that the surveys do not provide panel-data information. Given that most SME policies in the region target formal firms, the first limitation is not of major concern. The second limitation is more binding, however, since it limits the possibility of considering the dynamic effects of SME policy on firm survival and growth. The lack of panel data also restricts the type of productivity measure one can compute.

Enterprise Surveys allows the estimation of TFP at the plant level. It also provides information about the firm (ownership, other plants, organization); some characteristics of the plant (age, number of employees, sales); and a set of variables that are typically the target of SME policy, such as access to credit, training, and process innovation. The empirical analysis is drawn from Ibarrarán, Maffioli, and Stucchi (2009), and this study can be viewed for details on the construction of productivity measures, estimates, and simulations presented in this chapter.

---

consistent and robust relationship between access to credit, training, and quality certification and productivity, but also the greater relevance of the policy variables to SMEs than to larger firms (except for access to credit).[12] Overall, the results suggest that policies that promote these factors in SMEs have potentially positive effects on firms' productivity.

How Much Can SME Policies Increase Productivity?

Do these results imply that SME policies are justified? Even taking the results at face value, one should not jump to the conclusion that SME policies that are aimed at improving access to credit, training, innovation,

Table 9.2   Productivity Determinants (percent)

	Without policy variables	With policy variables	With policy variables and endogeneity control[c]
Productivity gap[a]			
Small firms	−22.1	−15.3	0
Medium-sized firms	−15.1	−11.3	0
Effect of variables that can be affected by SME policy[b]			
Access to credit	N.A.	6.1	18.1
Training	N.A.	5.5	23.4
International Organization for Standardization (ISO) certification	N.A.	13.1	22.1
Product innovation	N.A.	0	27.5

Source: Ibarrarán, Maffioli, Stucchi (2009).

Notes:

[a] Large firms were excluded. Thus, the coefficients measure the difference in productivity with respect to large firms.

[b] All the variables that can be affected by SME policy are dummy variables. Thus their coefficients measure the difference in productivity (in percentage) between firms with access to credit and firms without access to credit (the same for the rest of the variables).

[c] The equation was estimated using instrumental variables. All the variables that could be affected by SME policy were instrumented with the average of those variables at the country-industry, industry-size, and country-industry-size levels. The validity of the instruments was tested using the Sargan and Incremental Sargan tests. See Ibarrarán, Maffioli, and Stucchi (2009) for details.

N.A = Not applicable.

Table 9.3   Relationship between Policy Variables and Productivity (percent)

	Difference in productivity		
	All	SMEs	Large
Firms with training vs. firms without training but with similar characteristics[a]	7.1	10.5	7.2
Firms with access to credit vs. firms without access but with similar characteristics[a]	8.9	8.0	11.0
Firms with International Organization for Standardization (ISO) certification vs. firms without certification but with similar characteristics[a]	15.6	23.0	12.3
Firms with production innovation vs. firms without but with similar characteristics[a]	N.S	N.S	N.S

Source: Ibarrarán, Maffioli, and Stucchi (2009).

Note: (a) Propensity score matching was used to find firms with similar characteristics. For more details, see Ibarrarán, Maffioli, and Stucchi (2009).

N.S. = statistically not significant.

and quality certification would necessarily boost the overall productivity level. The analysis presented herein indicates that small firms that train their workers are more productive than small firms that do not, and that training accounts for part of the productivity differential with large firms. Yet it is not evident that SME policies actually induce beneficiary firms to engage in those activities that positively impact productivity. It may be, for instance, that firms that participate in a training program would have trained their workers anyway with their own resources. Also, the type of activities promoted with public policies is not necessarily the same type as those undertaken by firms on their own. For instance, the training provided by publicly supported SME programs may differ substantially from the training provided by the most productive firms.

Results also suggest that policies targeted to all firms, rather than only to small firms, may yield larger effects on productivity. Ibarrarán, Maffioli, and Stucchi (2009) compute the impact of SME policies on overall productivity, assuming that SME firms that are not engaged in training, external financing, or certification—but are very similar in their characteristics to firms that do so—engage in these activities as a result of the policy. The results of the simulation show that properly targeted SME policies might have a significant positive effect on aggregate productivity. In the sample adopted for the simulation, they would induce a 5.7 percent aggregate productivity increase (see Table 9.4). The overall effect on aggregate productivity would be due mostly to the "between-firms" term, which accounts for 65.5 percent of the aggregate productivity increase, while the "within-firm" term accounts for a 45.4 percent aggregate productivity increase. This implies that the effect on aggregate productivity is mainly due to the reallocation of resources toward those firms that were ex ante relatively more productive and that were able to expand their market share because of the policy.

What would happen if the same policies were applied (to the same number of firms) without any firm-size restriction? In this case, the simulation shows that the overall impact on aggregate productivity would be much higher than in the previous case, with a 10.5 percent overall impact on aggregate productivity. The decomposition of this effect is quite different than in the previous case. Most of the impact on productivity is due to the improved efficiency within firms, which accounts for 81.5 percent of the increase, rather than the reallocation of resources toward more productive ones. This is clearly due to the fact that policies not targeted at SMEs would affect the productivity of firms with larger initial market share.

The potential benefits of such policies should also be compared to their costs, which may outweigh the value of the additional output created with such policies. In that case, such policies could hardly be justified from

Table 9.4 Effect on the Aggregate Level of Productivity of Each Policy (percent)

	Impact on aggregate productivity	Percentage of impact explained by		
		Within-firms	Between-firms	Cross-firms
SME policy				
Credit	4.7	15.3	90.6	−6.0
Training	4.9	17.8	86.7	−4.4
Product innovation	5.0	20.4	84.9	−5.3
International Organization for Standardization (ISO) certification	4.5	0	99.9[a]	0
All	5.7	45.4	65.5	−10.9
Not targeted by size				
Credit	5.9	39.7	66.7	−6.4
Training	6.6	40.2	58.9	0.8
Product innovation	6.9	51.0	56.3	−7.3
ISO certification	4.5	0.8	99.1	0.1
All	10.5	81.5	26.2	−7.7

Source: Ibarrarán, Maffioli, and Stucchi (2009).

Note:

[a] In the case of the ISO certification targeted to SMEs, the results of the simulation show a complete dominance of the between effect over the within effect. This is due to the fact that very few SMEs in the dataset are adopting ISO certification and that the SMEs that do not adopt ISO, but have very similar characteristics to the adopters are also few and they are the most productive SMEs. As a consequence, when simulating the impact of a policy aimed at inducing these non-adopters to implement ISO certification, the between effect is very high because of the increase in share of the most productive SMEs. The within effect is almost irrelevant because of the very limited number and small size of the firms potentially affected by the simulated policy.

an economic standpoint, although they could still be appropriate from a social point of view.

The Track Record of SME Policies

As mentioned, rigorous impact evaluations would be extremely beneficial for a discussion of the effect of SME policies on aggregate productivity. Unfortunately, most SME policies in Latin America are not even properly monitored, and a rigorous analysis of their impact on fostering growth and productivity is missing.[13] Although large sums of resources are invested in SME policies, there is still very little information on their impact.[14]

A recent overview of SME policies in Peru, for example, shows that of the 18 most important programs, only one has a monitoring and evaluation component, although a rigorous evaluation has not been conducted (Díaz and Jaramillo 2009). The study also reports that SME policies in Peru are spread too thin: policies and programs work on a wide range of issues related to SMEs. These policies lack a diagnosis that would allow them to solve specific problems faced by SMEs. The coverage of SME policies is extremely low. This is probably inevitable, given the sheer number of small establishments. However, the lack of diagnosis leads to the absence of targeting or strategic criteria.

In Mexico, since 2000, Congress has required annual evaluations of all public projects managed by the federal government involving subsidies or transfers. A review of the most recent evaluations of SME projects shows that in most of them, monitoring and evaluation systems are not designed to gather information on results.[15] In 2007, the World Bank published a study on the evaluation of SME policies in Mexico and reported that only one program had impact evaluations that used comparison groups and looked at intermediate and ultimate objectives. The results of those impact evaluations suggest that SME programs influence intermediate outcomes, including training and technology adoption. The impact of these programs on final outcomes (improved performance, productivity, wages, and export orientation) remains elusive.[16] The conclusions of the study for Mexico are similar to those found for Chile by Goldberg and Palladini (2008), in that a comprehensive system to monitor and evaluate these programs is required.

In Colombia, the shortage of impact evaluations of programs that support SMEs is also apparent. One exception is an impact evaluation of the main program to support the development of SMEs in the country, Fondo Colombiano de Modernización y Desarrollo Tecnológico de las Micro, Pequeñas y Medianas Empresas (FOMIPYME), which showed mixed results. According to the evaluation (DNP-Sinergia 2008), the program had some positive impacts on employment and sales, but no impact on productivity. However, the same document notes that the lack of a baseline and serious data limitations are important caveats to interpreting the results of the evaluation as definitive. In terms of export promotion, Volpe and Carballo (2008) find that export promotion programs advance export diversification, but present no results on productivity.

In Argentina, evaluation work has been focused on innovation programs. Binelli and Maffioli (2007) evaluate the Programa de Modernización Tecnológica (PMT), which provided matching grants to firms for implementing innovative practices. Results show that the impact varies significantly. The more established firms, on average, use grants to displace innovation that they were already planning to undertake, whereas startup firms use the grants to finance innovation they otherwise would not have been able to undertake, generating an impact on innovation only on smaller firms. This evaluation also shows no clear effect of the program on firm's productivity.

Looking to developing countries outside Latin America, several models of financial incentives to firms in South Korea to promote training were implemented without success. However, when SMEs were given institutional and technical assistance, the results were reportedly positive, both in terms of the involvement and productivity of firms.[17] This experience also documents the need for an integrated SME policy, not only in terms of instruments (technical assistance, subsidies) but also in terms of working with clusters of SMEs in alignment with small-business organizations.

Conclusion

Have SME policies improved productivity in Latin America? Sadly, the enormous enthusiasm that governments and international agencies have shown toward financing SME policies and promoting the growth and development of the SME sector has not been accompanied by a similar eagerness to track the results and measure the impact of such policies. This worrisome reality is not limited to the productivity dimension: overall it is not clear if firms that have benefited from SME programs have, in fact, fared better or generated more employment than they would have had in the absence of such programs. Hence, it is largely unknown whether SME policies contribute to productivity growth, employment generation, and/or firm survival. At worst, SME policies may have reduced aggregate productivity by distorting the allocation of resources. This is particularly true if SME policies do not support the firms that have good ideas but are constrained in their growth, but rather, firms with very weak business models and little hope of improving their productivity enough to compensate for the cost of the intervention.

In many Latin American countries, returns to additional resources in small firms look, if anything, smaller than in larger firms—a factor that may be explained by tax and regulatory evasion that may contribute to making small firms larger than they should be. This again questions the wisdom of directing more resources to such firms unless they promote productivity gains—and formalization of the aided firms.

Therefore, it is crucial for programs to have clear objectives and state the channels by which they expect to improve outcomes. Proper monitoring and evaluation of the effects of SME programs on different performance dimensions is also key. Another critical issue for SME policies to be successful is proper targeting. While designing a specific targeting mechanism is beyond the scope of this chapter, some considerations can be noted. First, programs must have clear selection criteria that include past performance and specific objectives for the behavior and performance of the firm. If objectives are not being met, projects must set clear rules that halt support or reallocate firms to other types of programs.[18] This would prevent programs from supporting underperforming firms (relative to program objectives) for extended periods of time. Another risk is to support firms that would have performed well even in the absence of the program. To minimize this, programs must be designed with clear exit strategies for successful beneficiaries. If aimed at addressing market failures, policies should be temporary; once the firm is well on the road to realizing its potential, some of the market failures would be fixed or minimized.[19]

Another key issue is to make support to SMEs conditional on proper tax and regulatory compliance. However, for this to be effective, the business environment must be improved for all firms.

Can SME policies improve productivity in Latin America? In principle, yes, if they are properly targeted and foster training, innovation, certification, and access to credit: precisely those factors that seem to explain the productivity gap with larger firms. However, even setting aside the crucial issues of cost and implementation, expectations for these policies should be realistic. The potential of SME policies to boost productivity growth is limited and could be even lower than if the same policies were applied to all firms, not just SMEs. The drawback to the all-inclusive approach, however, is the greater risk of supporting firms that would have performed well without any public support.

Notes

1. In general, the upper limit of the number of employees used in the SME definition in Latin America is lower than in the European Union (EU) and the United States. The exceptions are the manufacturing sectors in Brazil, with a limit of 500, equal to that of the United States, and Mexico, with a limit of 250 employees, equal to that of the EU. According to the EU definition, a SME is a nonsubsidiary and independent firm that employs fewer than 250 employees and has an annual turnover of less than €50 million or an annual balance sheet of less than €43 million.

2. These are some of the most common objectives, and there is a clear confusion between instruments and objectives. This feature is common to developed and developing countries. For the former, Storey (1998) argues that "it appears to be a characteristic of governments in all developed countries to be, at best, opaque about the objectives of small business policy."

3. The emergence of highly competitive clusters and industrial districts—often composed of SMEs or combination of large firms and small providers has introduced new justifications for policies targeted at SMEs. In this case, the local concentration of SMEs specializing in a specific product line has been seen as a potentially efficient combination of production scale and flexibility; however, it requires important coordination efforts by the firms involved in rather complex production systems. In this case, specific policies have been advocated to support the process through which SMEs identify and finance joint activities aimed at improving the cluster's systemic efficiency and dealing with local externalities (for examples in Latin America, see Pietrobelli and Rabellotti 2004).

4. This discussion follows Ayyagari, Beck, and Demirgüç-Kunt (2007) and Levine (2005).

5. One important characteristic of the SME policy is that there are many programs. Since it is not possible to include them all in one figure, certain countries and policies were selected.

6. This equation comes from a decomposition of the aggregate level of productivity and is not an equilibrium condition.

7. There is the question of whether size determines productivity, or productivity determines size. Hsieh and Klenow (2007) propose a model in which firms with higher productivity grow to be larger. On the other hand, large firms may take advantage of economies of scale and scope and more easily cover some fixed costs, which if not accounted for will be measured as higher productivity. Small firms may also have greater flexibility to deal with changes in their environment. They may use cooperation to achieve economies of scale and scope similar to those of larger firms or they may simply focus on small and highly specialized markets.

8. In a simple framework, productivity is modeled as a function of size, a set of variables that are usually targeted by SME policies, a set of exogenous control variables, and a set of country-year and industry dummies. The analysis compares size effects whether policy variables are included or not. Given that these policy variables are most likely endogenous, an instrumental variable approach to deal with this problem was implemented (for more detail, see Ibarrarán, Maffioli, and Stucchi 2009).

9. Ibarrarán, Maffioli, and Stucchi (2009) compute productivity using the Solow residual method. The analysis was replicated with the Hsieh and Klenow (2007) methodology and the results were qualitatively similar. See their paper for additional details.

10. Notice, however, that if policies reduce market or policy failures, they may improve overall productivity even if they increase the fraction of small firms (Hsieh and Klenow 2007).

11. These policy variables represent firms' actions that are commonly targeted by SME policies. The underlying assumptions are that SME policies are able to promote these actions among firms that had not performed the actions

on their own, and that the actions adopted will have a similar impact. For example, if a firm has access to credit due to an SME program, it will benefit in a similar way to comparable firms that already have access to credit.

12. The inconsistent relationship between product innovation and productivity most likely reflects the fact that innovation takes time to produce an increase in productivity and its effect cannot be detected without panel data. For a discussion on this topic, see Hall and Maffioli (2008).

13. Although more pronounced in Latin America, the region is not alone its lack of systematic rigorous evaluations of SME policies. According to Storey (1998) and OECD (2005), few proper evaluations have been conducted in developed countries. Two examples of evaluations in developed countries are Roper and Hewitt-Dundas (2001) for Ireland and Motohashi (2001) for Japan. The former concludes that in Ireland, support to SMEs was successful in boosting employment but not productivity, while the latter concludes that in Japan, the new SME support model (that shifted from "lifting up the SME sector" toward more specific procompetition and innovation-inducing policies) had positive results; however, selection issues are still unresolved.

14. In Mexico, for example, more than 140 programs have identified working with SMEs as one of their objectives. Approximately US$3 billion has been spent on the largest 25 of these programs (see Soto 2009), about the same as the government spends on the conditional cash transfer program, *Oportunidades,* which reaches 5 million families.

15. See the 2007 process evaluations (Evaluación de Consistencia y Resultados) of the National Evaluation Council, CONEVAL.

16. See World Bank (2007). Also for Mexico, see OECD (2007a) and Storey (2008) for a review of the evaluation of SME support programs in Mexico.

17. See Lee (2006). However, the positive findings were measured in a pilot study and comprehensive evaluations are pending. This model, which includes training and technical assistance, was successfully implemented in Mexico (but was later abandoned) and has been tried in other countries, such as Panama.

18. This is parallel to the current trend in industrial policy of letting the losers *fail*: governments need to be ready to stop supporting those firms for which the program is not working.

19. Once a firm is able to establish credit, it could maintain it without government support. Or once it internalizes the benefits from training or innovation, it could continue those activities without receiving subsidies.

10

The Importance of Ideas: Innovation and Productivity in Latin America

The capacity of a society and its firms to generate and assimilate technological change is generally recognized as a key component of prosperity and growth. A long tradition of economic thinking that goes back at least to Schumpeter has identified a strong relationship between innovation and productivity growth. In developing growth theory, Solow (1956) attributed a vital role to technological change, and his vision of this issue remains a foundation of its understanding. Griliches (1986) formalized and specified the empirical content of these ideas by developing models aimed at measuring the impact of knowledge capital on productivity (Griliches proxied the research and development [R&D] stock for knowledge capital). Romer (1990) enriched the theory by modeling the determinants of knowledge creation, turning R&D into an endogenous variable in the understanding of growth instead of an external element. A considerable body of economic, sociological, and historic research has been accumulated in recent decades about the role of knowledge in economic development. This research is organized around the notion of innovation, understood as a concept that goes beyond R&D in the traditional sense—which implies that not all innovation has a technological origin (see Box 10.1).

The acquisition, adaptation, and creation of knowledge has become a major factor in economic development and is the common denominator in the successful development strategies followed by countries as diverse as Finland, Ireland, Singapore, South Korea, and Taiwan—and, more recently, China and India. Today's world economy is one in which innovation has become indispensable, even as the threshold for acquiring and disseminating knowledge is being lowered. This makes it possible, in

---

Box 10.1   Defining Innovation

The Frascati and Oslo Manuals of the Organization for Economic Co-operation and Development (OECD) are international references for the measurement of technology and innovation activities (OECD 2002; OECD and Eurostat 2005). The Oslo Manual, in particular, presents the guidelines to follow in analyzing and measuring innovation activities in firms. The innovation survey is widely used in most OECD countries. The Manual de Bogotá (RICYT et al. 2001), which is based on the Oslo Manual, is of particular importance for Latin American countries since it deepens the measurement of innovation, notably the areas of human resources, training, and organizational change. The most recent (third) edition of the Oslo Manual incorporates recommendations for the measurement of innovation in developing economies and adopts the essence of the message from The Bogotá Manual.

The latest edition of the Oslo Manual defines innovation as the implementation of a new or significantly improved product (good or service) or process, a new marketing method, or a new organizational method in business practices, workplace organization, or external relations. The first two types are traditionally more closely related with technological innovation. Firms are considered innovative if they have implemented an innovation during the period under review (usually two to three years).

Some surveys include additional questions on the degree of novelty of innovations. The Oslo Manual distinguishes three concepts: new to the firm, new to the market, and new to the world. Companies that innovate for local and international markets can be considered drivers of technological innovation. Many new ideas and knowledge originate from these firms. Information about the degree of novelty can be used to identify the developers and adopters of innovations, examine patterns of diffusion, and identify market leaders and followers (OECD 2009).

---

theory, to implement strategies built on faster catch up by adapting knowledge that has originated in advanced economies.

This chapter, written against the backdrop of persistent stagnation in productivity in Latin America, seeks to address the following questions: how and how much innovation takes place in the region and who are the innovators? What are the links between innovation, as it takes place in the region, and productivity? What can be done to encourage innovation? The initial hypothesis is that the current stagnation of productivity in Latin America can be traced, in part, to an innovation deficit. This hypothesis is underscored by the contrast with the very fast growth that has occurred in economies that not so long ago were poorer that those in Latin America—a growth process heavily leveraged by massive investments in innovation and technology.

Investment in Innovation and Research and Development in Latin American Firms

Innovation activities take different shapes, and go well beyond internal R&D, extending to expenditures on R&D external to the firm, capital goods that include embodied technology, hardware and software, licensing and purchasing of unembedded technology, technological training, engineering and consulting services, and industrial design, according to the Oslo Manual (OECD and Eurostat, 2005).

Despite this broad perspective of innovation, internal R&D efforts maintain a privileged role as part of the mechanism that leads to the creation and adaptation of new ideas and technological applications. R&D is commonly associated with the generation of new products and services capable of producing sustainable competitive advantages for firms. For a business that wants to engage in technology-based competition in a given market, having in-house technological infrastructure (Cohen and Levinthal 1989, 1990) provides several distinct advantages. Without such infrastructure, the use, identification, assimilation, adaptation, and exploitation of external know-how—embedded in the case of equipment or unembedded in the case of licenses or acquired patents—tend to be limited, and that diminishes the impact of innovation on productivity.

Table 10.1 focuses on a few select countries in Latin America and Europe and presents the main indicators of innovative effort in firms, the intensity of innovation, and information on human resources dedicated to innovative activities. As the first row shows, a high proportion of Latin American firms invest in innovation; the variation ranges from around 28 percent of firms in Uruguay to over 70 percent in Colombia.

However, Latin America exhibits some distinctive features regarding innovation. One is the low level of expenditure and intensity of effort on R&D. On average, firms' R&D intensity (as a percentage of sales) is less than 0.2 percent, far lower than the averages for Europe (1.6) and the OECD (1.9). The share of firms that invest in R&D exceeds 25 percent in Europe while in Colombia and Uruguay, the equivalent figure is about 6 percent.

A second distinctive feature of innovation in the region is the extent to which it centers on the purchase of capital goods and equipment. Expenditure on these items represents between 50 and 80 percent of total expenditure on innovation, while the corresponding share in OECD countries ranges from 10 to 30 percent.

Table 10.1 Inputs and Outputs of Innovation in the Manufacturing Industry, Selected Countries

	Argentina	Brazil	Colombia	Paraguay	Uruguay	France	Germany	Belgium
Innovation Investment								
Share of firms that invest in innovation activities (as a share of total companies)	61	65.7	77	63	27.8	n.d.	n.d.	n.d.
Innovation expenditure intensity (as a share of turnover)	0.9	2.8	0.8	n.d.[b]	2.2	3.6	5.2	4.3
Share of firms that invest in R&D (as a share of total companies)	25	20.7	6	11[b]	6.2	27.7	27.9	35.2
R&D investment intensity (as a share of turnover)	0.2	0.58	0.12	n.d.	0.12	2.7	2.9	2.1
Innovation Expenditures Allocation								
R&D (as a share of total innovation expenditures)	16	21.8	0.8	13	3.9	68.8	47.7	30.5
Capital equipment (as a share of total innovation expenditures)	54	49.7	66.4	66	81.2	9.7	23.8	33.8
Human Resources								
Human resources in innovation activities (as a percentage of total employment)	3.3	n.d.	3.01	1.41[b]	2.3	n.d.	n.d.	n.d.
R&D personnel (as a percentage of total employment)	1.96	1	1.9	1.01[b]	1.1	n.d.	n.d.	n.d.
Innovation Outputs (as a share of total companies)								
Firms that innovated (any type)	51	33.4[a]	25.3	59[a]	26.9	35[a]	66[a]	54[a]
Firms that introduced product innovation	39	19.5	n.d.	48[b]	14	23.3	52.2	39.1
Firms that introduced process innovation	37	26.9	n.d.	41[b]	20	27.4	40.8	42.4
Firms that introduced organizational innovation	30[d]	37.2	7.9	33[b]	12	35.5	56	39.9
Firms that applied for patents	n.d.	6.7	3.12[c]	14[b]	1.7	12	24	7.9

Source: OECD (2009) for France, Germany, and Belgium and refers to manufacturing industry. Argentina: INDEC (2006); Brazil: IBGE (2005); Colombia: Colciencias, DANE, DNP (2004–2006); Paraguay: CONACYT (2004–2006); and Uruguay: ANII (2004–2006).

Notes: Indicators refer to the manufacturing industry and shares of companies in the total panel of companies, except when otherwise indicated.
[a] Refers to companies that introduced product or process innovation (share of total firms in manufacturing industry).
[b] These indicators refer to the total sample (including agriculture, mining, manufacturing, and services).
[c] Patents are filings at any patent office during 1996–2004.
[d] Refers to commercial and organizational innovation.
n.d. = no data.

This combination of low R&D effort and high investment in technology embedded in machinery could signal problems. Even though acquiring technology by buying equipment and sophisticated machines can be an important step in catching up and advancing toward the technological frontier, the impact of embedded technology at the firm level can be very limited if internal capabilities in R&D are absent. Such an absence— notably the weakness of the human capital dedicated to innovation—can lead to a technological gain to the economy as a whole that is not sustainable, even after intensive periods of modernizing the manufacturing base in a given country (Hanson 2007).

R&D is highly concentrated in a small number of firms. In Argentina, for instance, one firm accounts for one-third of the entire manufacturing sector's expenditures in R&D, according to the 1998–2001 innovation survey.

Large firms have a higher propensity to invest in innovation. Economies of scale explain this tendency; large businesses find it easier to distribute the high fixed costs of innovation across a larger volume of sales and have better access to financial services, technology, consulting, and specialized human-capital markets. On the other hand, small and medium enterprises commit themselves to innovation efforts that are more than proportional to their size. Econometric analysis of the propensity to invest in innovation and innovation intensity yields results that are not inconsistent with the descriptive statistics presented so far, but suggest that there are additional determinants of investing in innovation, as shown in Table 10.2, which was elaborated employing a variation of the model developed by Crepon, Duguet, and Mairesse (1998), hereafter referred to as the CDM models.

The propensity of a firm to become involved in innovation activities, as well as its level of innovation effort, are positively associated with the presence of public financing for innovation, formal protection of intellectual property, technological cooperation with other firms (suppliers and clients), and laboratories and universities. Firms that give importance to the intellectual property protection of innovation efforts tend to make a stronger innovation effort (the analysis is very clear on this matter for Argentina, Chile, and Colombia).

Foreign Capital, Export Intensity, and Innovation

Innovation efforts in Latin American economies are related only weakly to the participation of foreign capital. There is no significant difference between firms with foreign capital and domestic businesses regarding the propensity to innovate or innovation intensity. Only in Colombia do firms with foreign capital report higher innovation expenditures per employee.

Table 10.2 Determinants of the Probability of Investing in Innovation and its Intensity

	Argentina		Chile		Colombia		Uruguay	
	1	2	1	2	1	2	1	2
Human capital (engineers and hard sciences employees in employment)	+		−	−	+			
Cooperation with other companies or institutes	+	+	+					
Market share		+		−		−		
Intellectual property protection (appropriability)		+		+	+	+		
Public sources of finance		+		+	+			
Foreign ownership		−			+	+	+	
Export intensity								
Sources of information for innovation								
Internal			+					
External (other companies and externalities)	+							
Scientific (universities, institutes of technology)	+		+			+		
Obstacles to innovate								
Cost-related	−		−					
Related to national systems of innovation	+							
Controls								
Industries	Yes	Yes	Yes	Yes	Yes	Yes	Yes	Yes
Company size (dummies)	+	+	+	+	+		+	
Periods	2 periods		4 periods (individual regressions)		3 periods available (last period used for regression)		3 periods (last period used for regression)	
Methods	Generalized Tobit		Generalized Tobit		Generalized Tobit		Generalized Tobit	

Source: Authors' compilation based on Arbeláez (2009); Arza and López (2009); Benavente and Bravo (2009); Cassoni and Ramada-Sarasola (2009).

Note: Model 1 refers to the probability of investing in innovation and Model 2 refers to the intensity of innovation expenditures (innovation expenditures relative to sales). The variables Sources of information for innovation and Obstacles to innovate are dummy variables that are equal to one if the company considers such source or factor with high or medium importance for innovation activities. The variables Intellectual property protection, Public sources of finance, and Cooperation with other companies or institutes are equal to one if the company was involved in such activity or had links with those actors in technological activities. The variable Foreign ownership is a dummy variable equal to one if the company has foreign ownership in capital. Only variables with statistical significance at 10 percent (or less) are reported.

The "+" and "−" symbols represent the sign of the coefficient obtained with the model. A "+" ("−") symbol indicates a positive (negative) relationship between the dependent variable and the independent variable.

It could well be that multinationals do not necessarily invest in innovation, given that their focus is on exploiting comparative advantages in terms of distribution costs or labor savings, for instance, and that they have a certain technological platform imported from their headquarters abroad.

The statistical models also show no connection between innovation propensity and export intensity. This relationship is not significant in Argentina, Chile, and Uruguay,[1] which suggests that export activity in Latin American businesses is not strongly linked to technology and innovation. This, in turn, could relate to the fact that the region's most important export items tend to be raw materials and low-tech products. A better understanding of this complex relationship, and the contrasting results for Latin America, would require taking a closer look at how and with what products economies participate in the international marketplace. Perhaps exporting certain types of products, or exporting to certain markets that are not particularly sophisticated, do not require considerable investment in technology.[2] A deeper understanding of this topic would require identifying the nature of the goods being exported (manufactured, mining, and agricultural products) and an assessment of their technological intensity, destination, and type of contracts involved. This is a necessary next step in research since the apparent disconnect between export activity and innovation in Latin America contrasts starkly with the experience in Asia where exports played a key role in learning and technology transfer processes undertaken through the interaction with global corporations (see, e.g., Gill and Karras 2007).

Sources of Financing

Access to financing sources external to the firm, including public subsidies, is correlated with investment in innovation activities in all countries for which information is available, in terms of both the propensity to become involved in innovation and the intensity of investment. These findings illustrate the importance of access to financing for innovators, who tend to engage in activities that have high fixed costs and considerable risk.

For those countries with available information, internal sources constitute the main source of financing for innovation, representing more than 70 percent of total financing (reinvestment represents 74 percent of total financing in Argentina and 76.5 percent in Uruguay), followed by commercial bank financing. As for public financing, 2 percent of Argentine firms and 2.5 percent of Uruguayan firms use public funding. The equivalent figure, according to the innovation survey, is 3.6 percent in Paraguay and 6 percent in Brazil: the highest in the region, but well below the benchmark of European countries.

Box 10.2   The Distinctive Contribution of Human Capital to Innovation and Productivity in Developing Countries

Since the seminal contribution of Nelson and Phelps (1966), it has been well established that a larger stock of human capital helps countries accelerate technological catch up. The propensity to innovate and the innovation intensity of an economy tend to be related to the quantity and quality of skills accumulated in the work force. Hanushek and Woessman (2009) have refined empirical models that point to a clear impact of cognitive skills on growth and have corroborated such a relationship for most Latin American countries.

Building on these and other precedents, López Boo (2009) analyzed the relationship between human capital, innovation, and productivity. She separated the effects of human capital on the two main channels through which such a relationship takes place: invention (radical innovations, or novelties for the worldwide market defined as those able to push forward the technological frontier) and adaptation (incremental innovation that moves products and processes closer to a preestablished technological frontier in the case of a particular firm or domestic market).

Using cross-country data for Latin America and other parts of the world, she finds that the connection between human capital and innovation in developing countries, and its corresponding impact on productivity, stem mainly from the contribution of skilled workers dedicated to adapting existing technologies: that is, from their contribution to moving closer to the technological frontier, rather than to expanding it. For this type of contribution to occur, the human resources must be located within firms or in close proximity to their operations. This is far from the case in Latin America.

The literature also points strongly to the need to invest not only in advanced scientific education but also in intermediate post-secondary technical degrees, such as those typical of community colleges or university technical colleges in the United States, Canada, and Europe. Aguion (2007) emphasizes precisely this point in his analysis of relationships between innovation and labor skills in the various states of the United States, as well as in several countries.

Human Capital

The CDM models tend to confirm what the economic literature has established regarding the importance of human capabilities in the decision to innovate and to spend on innovation (see Box 10.2). In Colombia, a stronger profile of technical competencies (counted as the proportion of engineers in total employment in firms) is associated positively with both innovation variables. In Argentina, the presence of professional technical skills is also associated with a higher innovation propensity. While evidence is limited, there are indications that firms invest in training associated with the purchase of technology embedded in machinery. Most of these results are difficult to benchmark to OECD figures, since these indicators are not regularly included in the innovation surveys used in those countries.

Linkages with the National Innovation System

Links between industry and other actors in national innovation systems[3] occur mostly as a result of the attempts by firms to gain access to information and know-how. Technology-led collaboration seems to be associated with higher investments in R&D and innovation in general. In Argentina, where it was possible to analyze information partitioned by type of cooperation, collaboration with scientific institutions and other businesses were all positively associated with the probability of a firm engaging in innovation initially.

Statistics based on innovation surveys demonstrate that Latin American firms most often establish technological cooperation agreements with clients and suppliers (the results are very strong for Argentina, Colombia, and Uruguay). Universities have a relatively minor importance, with the exception of Argentina, where this kind of collaboration is on par with that in European countries.

Obstacles to Investment in Innovation

Although the factors inhibiting innovation activity in Latin America are many and complex, the main obstacles, as reported by business people themselves, are constraints in securing financing for innovation, the inability of firms to wait for long periods before recovering investments, or realizing a positive return, the small size of the market, and the shortage of qualified personnel.

The lack of financing and access to credit is a major barrier for investment in innovation in Latin America. This might partly reflect problems in the functioning of the financial markets at large; Latin America has the highest cost of capital in the world. Moreover, since particularly risky investments, such as those associated with innovation, are difficult to finance everywhere, lack of financing points directly at Latin America's deficit in private financial intermediaries, such as venture capital or angel investors, as well as public financing directly aimed at encouraging private-sector innovation, particularly by small and medium businesses.

Problems linked to market structure and size suggest that the regional market is not integrated, meaning many businesses are confined to their domestic markets, which are often small by any measure. This would imply diseconomies of scale for innovation projects, many of which require relatively large investments upfront and longer time horizons to realize a profit.

The reported lack of skilled personnel seems to reflect deficits in the supply of technological services and capabilities as well as communication and coordination issues among the different components of national innovation systems, such as universities and commercial firms. Statistics regarding the availability of human capital for innovation confirm the report by firms of an overall deficit of qualified technical and professional personnel with relevant skills for innovation activities. This holds true even for the larger economies in the region (details can be found in Duryea, Navarro, and Verdisco 2008).

Innovation Outcomes and the Novelty of Innovations

The lower section of Table 10.1 contains information about the percentage of firms that introduced innovations because they decided to invest in innovation inputs. Between 25 and 59 percent of firms that invested in innovation obtained innovation outputs. In comparison, countries such as Canada, Germany, Sweden, and Switzerland regularly report rates of 60 percent or more.

According to the results of an econometric analysis, firms that invested in innovation inputs in Argentina, Colombia, and Uruguay[4] have a significantly higher probability of obtaining innovation outputs, a result that highlights the value of knowledge when applied to technological change in firms. In terms of sectors, those that report more innovation intensity also produce more innovation outputs. Firms with foreign capital, however, do not show a significant difference in terms of innovation outcomes when compared to purely domestic businesses—although Argentina seems to present an exception in this regard.

Turning to the type of innovation firms engage in, process innovation is more frequent than product innovation in most countries. This seems to be related to the pattern of acquiring knowledge embedded in capital goods, since embedded technology should directly impact production processes for the better.

Table 10.3   Novelty of Product Innovation in the Manufacturing Industry, Selected Countries

Percentages of firms that introduced product innovation	Argentina	Brazil	Colombia[a]	Paraguay[b]	Uruguay
New to the global market	25	0.19	6.3	8.13	1.8
New to the local (or domestic) market	49	3.24	9.4	40	7.3
New to the firm	24	16.22	10.7	48	6

Sources: Argentina: INDEC (2006); Brazil: IBGE (2005); Colombia: Colciencias, DANE, DNP (2004–2006); Paraguay: CONACYT (2004–2006); and Uruguay: ANII (2004–2006).

[a] Refers to all innovation outcomes (product, process, and others).
[b] Shares in the total sample (including agriculture, mining, manufacturing, and services).

Still another interesting way of looking at innovation outputs is to focus on the dominance of adaptation over invention. Table 10.3 reports the percentage of innovative firms in the manufacturing sector according to the degree of novelty of product innovation in some countries. In Latin America, technological innovation is highly concentrated in adaptive and incremental innovations, which are not aimed at reaching international markets. This explains the reported dominance of innovations "new to the domestic market" or "new to the firm."

Innovation and Productivity in Latin America: An Overall Picture

The preceding attempt to characterize innovation inputs and outputs in Latin American firms has served mainly to lay the foundation for a better understanding of the contribution of innovative activity to productivity growth in the region. This section attempts to capture the impact of innovation on labor productivity at the firm level.

Available evidence for Argentina, Chile, Colombia, and Uruguay resists simple generalizations, but Table 10.4 points fairly clearly to the positive impact of innovation on productivity. This is particularly true of product innovation. Chile, however, represents an exception in this regard. Although innovation has had a positive impact on sales in Chile, the impact on productivity did not manifest itself until two years after the initial introduction of innovation inputs. In the case of Colombia, innovation's impact on productivity seems to be confined to the case of incremental innovation (the new-to-firm type).

Table 10.4   Impact of Innovation on Productivity

	Argentina	Chile[a]	Colombia	Uruguay
Dependent variable: Labor productivity	Sales per employee	Sales per employee	Added value per employee	Production per employee
Process innovation	n. s.[b] (reduced sample) + (total sample)	− (only in 2001)		+
Product innovation	+			+
Product innovation new to the firm		+ (only in 1998)	+	
Product innovation new to the market (local/ global)				
Organizational innovation	−	− (in 1998) + (in 2001)		−
Capital per employee	+	+		+

Source: Authors' compilation based on Arbeláez (2009); Arza and López (2009); Benavente and Bravo (2009); Cassoni and Ramada-Sarasola (2009).

Note: All regressions have employed instrumental variables (using predicted values from innovation production models [2nd stage equation]). Only variables with statistical significance at 10 percent (or less) are reported.

[a] Dependent variable in $t+1$ (regressions by period: 1995, 1998, and 2001).
[b] Not significant in the reduced sample (for which information on capital per employee was available), and statistically significant in the total sample (excluding the variable capital per employee).

The "+" and "−" represent the sign of the coefficient obtained with the model.

In contrast, process innovation seems to have no significant effect on productivity. Uruguay is the only country reporting a positive and significant effect. For Chile, some delayed positive effects are noted at least two years after the introduction of innovation.

One reasonable hypothesis is that the learning process implicit in adopting new processes takes time in Latin American economies. This, in turn, could be construed as a disincentive for investment in R&D and innovation among the region's firms, which seem to put a premium on quick returns on investment.

Previous studies report similar results pointing at a neutral—or even negative—relationship between process innovation and productivity. Firms that implemented process innovations in Belgium, Brazil, Canada, France, Germany, New Zealand, and the United Kingdom exhibited lower productivity per worker in a recent report (OECD 2009). Two plausible explanations have been suggested. First, process innovation brings about changes in production processes and results in learning and adjustment costs that might temporarily reduce productivity. Second, firms seem better inclined to introduce process innovation in hard times when they are looking to compensate for a downturn by making production more efficient. In recessionary periods, however, gains from process innovation are potentially more important (opportunity costs are lower) and opposition to change tends to be weaker than usual. Some of this may be at work in Latin America.

As far as organizational innovation is concerned, there are negative effects in Colombia and Argentina. One possible explanation—built into the study that focused on Argentina (Arza and López 2009)—holds that this result may reflect inverse causality: less productive firms may be more inclined to introduce organizational innovation. Another possibility could be that organizational—and marketing—innovation imply short-term changes in the functioning of firms; thus, productivity declines in the short term.

Based on available analyses, the links between innovation and productivity in Latin American firms tend to mirror those of advanced economies. In those cases where variations can be detected, much of that difference can be explained by the constraints posed by limited data availability in Latin America. The most notorious limitation is the fact that all the analysis of Latin America remains based on cross-sectional data, as opposed to the far more desirable panel data.

Concerns about data notwithstanding, the analysis indicates several distinctive features of innovation in Latin American firms and differences in the way innovation and productivity interact in the region as opposed to advanced economies. The type of inputs is typically different; investment in R&D is lower in Latin America. The role of foreign investment does not seem to be the same. Innovations tend to be less radical and concentrated in nontechnology-based innovation. At the firm level, the time horizons seem to be longer for learning, for adjustments to lead to a visible effect on productivity, and to recover the investment in innovation. Human-capital and financing constraints seem to be larger obstacles for firms in Latin America.

These features suggest that Latin American firms are heavily involved in innovation, yet not necessarily in R&D; are moved by short-term concerns when making investing decisions—including investments in innovation; and invest in innovation mostly in the form of technology and know-how embedded in capital goods. This particular innovation strategy, as well as the dominance of new-to-firm and new-to-domestic-market innovation, clearly entails innovation activity based on adaptation of existing technology. Similarly, the preponderance of technology links with the supply chain rather than with universities, laboratories, or other technological institutions suggests that, for most firms, technological development is still at an early stage—if it is occurring at all. Apparently, most Latin American businesses operate far from the technological frontier—far enough away that incentives for innovation are not particularly strong since the payoff on innovation investment could be hard to realize and highly uncertain. Moreover, the absence of adequate infrastructure for research and knowledge transfer creates barriers to absorptive capacity, severely reducing the benefits of innovation based on adaptation and probably slowing down catch-up processes.

The balance of the discussion in this section suggests that even though innovation is fairly widespread among the region's firms, it seems to be failing to realize its potential as a major source of productivity growth. There are complex processes at play here, but some pieces of the problem stand out and are within the range of public policies for Latin American countries. A very important one is the low level of engagement with technology by most firms, even those that are innovative, which reveals a poor level of coordination between whatever R&D exists in a given country and productive activities. In other words, the main components of national innovation systems lack adequate articulation. This conclusion, in turn, invites a review of the current state of scientific and technological development in Latin American countries, so as to complement the firm-level perspective advanced thus far in this chapter with a macro perspective that provides information about the institutional and resource base—both human and financial—within which business innovation takes place.

R&D Activities in the Region

Almost every one of the relevant dimensions of the landscape of science and technology in Latin America differs greatly from the landscape of advanced economies. The difference in national investment on R&D is marked. While from 1995 to 2006, R&D expenditures as a share of GDP grew consistently in the advanced economies, they stagnated at a very low level in Latin America. On average, technological intensity in the region—measured not at the firm level, but in the national economy as a whole—is 0.6 percent, compared to 2.2 percent for OECD countries. In addition, investment in R&D is highly concentrated in the public sector, averaging 60 percent, compared to 36 percent for the OECD, regardless of whether the source of funding or the execution of expenditures is considered.

The differences regarding human capital are similarly great. While OECD countries average seven researchers per thousand in the population, Latin America does not reach even one per thousand. More importantly, the private sector employs relatively few researchers, in contrast with OECD

Figure 10.1   R&D Expenditure as a Percentage of GDP, 1995 and 2006

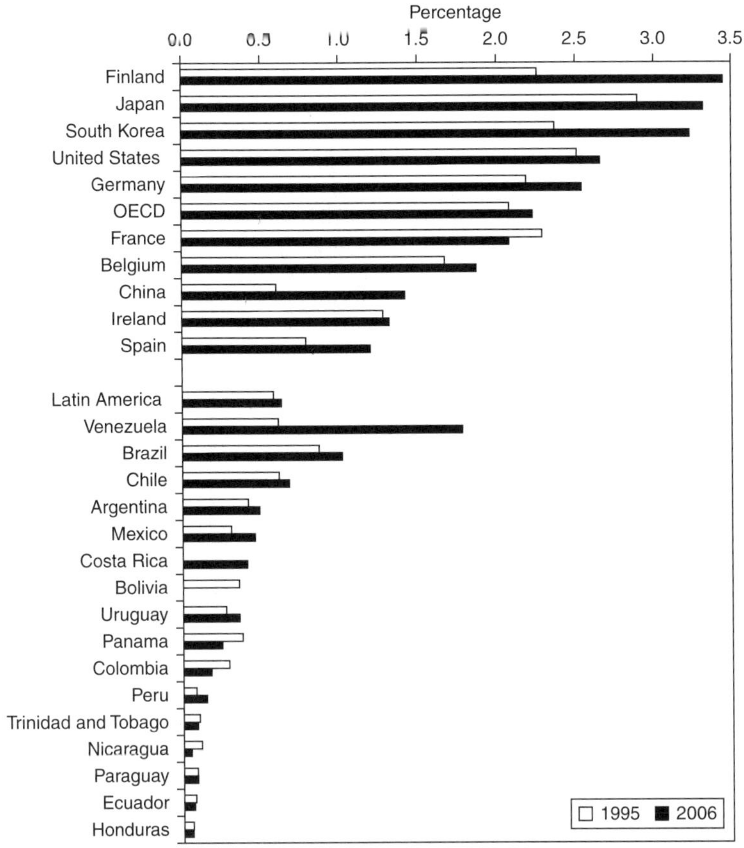

Sources: RICYT (2009) and OECD (2008).

businesses, which hire 64 percent of researchers in their economies (Figure 10.3). This fact echoes the previous finding that firms in Latin America invest sparsely in R&D development.

Figures 10.1 to 10.3 highlight not only the large differences between Latin America and OECD countries, but also the heterogeneity of the Latin American region itself, which makes some generalizations difficult. A closer look at the data indicates that Brazil—and to some extent Argentina, Chile, and Mexico—has evolved a technological profile closer to advanced economies, or at least to the less technologically intensive among them, such as Spain. Similarly, while the trend in several countries is to depend even more heavily on natural resources—corresponding, almost certainly, to being less technologically intensive—a few countries, such as Costa Rica and, arguably, Colombia, report a stronger participation of technology-intensive sectors in output and exports. Even

Figure 10.2   Composition of R&D Expenditure by Source of Financing, 2006

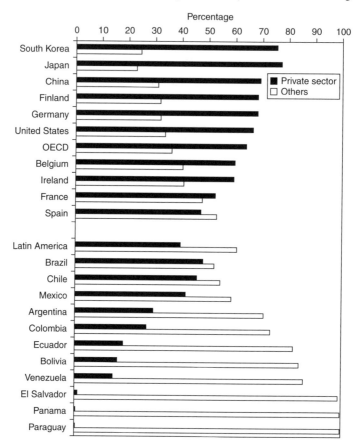

Sources: RICYT (2009) and OECD (2008).

Note: "Others" refers to government, higher education, and non-profit organizations.

for this group of countries, in which some build-up in technology has occurred over the past two decades, the relatively low investment in R&D and low share of researchers in the economy—especially in the private sector—remain serious concerns. An indirect indication of these problems is the relatively low level of foreign investment in R&D the region has received compared to other parts of the world.

The indicators are not particularly encouraging when shifting focus from inputs to the outcomes of innovation efforts either. Scientific performance continues to lag well behind developed countries: less than 50 publications per million population in Latin America, compared to over 300 in advanced economies (NSF 2008). Here again, the picture is more nuanced when considering the figures for Argentina, Brazil, and

Figure 10.3   Composition of Researchers by Sector of Employment, 2006

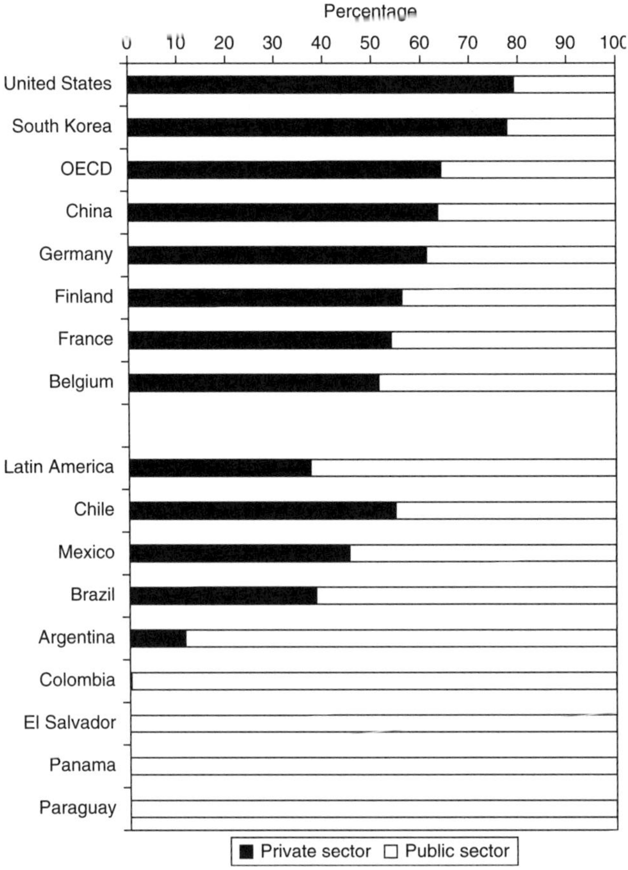

Sources: RICYT (2009) and OECD (2008).

Mexico, countries that have reached the top 50 in the world in terms of scientific publications. Moreover, the growth rate of publications from Latin America has tripled over the past decade and a half, outpacing other regions and consequently reducing the gap in this regard (OECD 2007b). These relatively positive trends contrast starkly with the relative scarcity of researchers in firms and prove that scientific and technological progress does not automatically solve the problem of developing effective national innovation systems. In other words, it is conceivable for a country to have an advanced scientific profile and still have few links between this considerable scientific knowledge and the economy.

Patents per capita continue to be relatively low. Patents per million population reached 150 for South Korea in 2005 (U.S. Patent Office), while they were less than one per million in Latin America. The low technological

Figure 10.4   High-Technology Exports as a Percentage of Exports in Manufacturing, 2000 and 2007

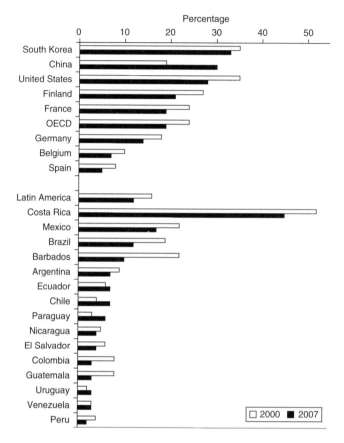

Source: World Bank (2009g).

intensity of Latin American economies is also evident in the relatively minor technological content of exports from all but a few countries in the region, as can be seen in Figure 10.4.

A Second Look at International Comparisons

Recent studies (see, most recently, Maloney and Rodríguez-Clare 2007) have suggested that international benchmarking exercises such as those presented above may distort the realities of innovation in Latin America. They argue that the comparison fails to adjust for the very different economic structures of developing and advanced economies. Thus, the argument goes, the optimal level of innovation in a given Latin American economy may be lower than the OECD average simply because of the low

technological intensity of the natural resources and other sectors characteristic of the region and would be similarly low anywhere they are present. Instead of an "Innovation shortfall," Latin America may be producing
a natural response to a particular economic structure. This is a highly
relevant argument that should be considered when comparing innovation
data across countries.

However, the empirical evidence suggests that even after correcting
for the industrial structure, the conclusion of low technological intensity
holds, confirming the existence of an innovation shortfall—and a large
one at that. Maloney and Rodríguez-Clare (2007) conclude that Chile is a
case in point. Benavente and Bravo (2009), comparing Chile and Australia
in the mining sector, and Chile and Finland in the paper-pulp sector, find
that R&D investments are considerably lower in Chile; this explains much
of the observed difference in productivity.[5]

Over the long term, the relationship of causality between technological effort and economic structure may very well be the opposite of what
it seems in the short term. A commitment to technological change and
more technology-intensive industries may very well steer economic
structure toward knowledge- and innovation-intensive activities, raising
productivity and living standards along the way.[6] There is little doubt
that the more prosperous a given economy is, the more it tends to invest
in R&D. Of course, a developing country has many urgent social needs
that compete with innovation policy for attention and resources. The
fact remains that the newly industrialized countries rapidly transformed
their economies into knowledge-based and highly competitive ones as
the consequence of intensive investments in technology and innovation
that quite often were far above what their income per capita level would
have predicted.

National Innovation Systems in Latin America Today

The stylized facts about the main dimensions of science, technology, and
innovation in Latin America indicate that the economies of the region
in the early twenty-first century tend not to be technology-intensive and
perform weakly in terms of innovation outputs. This is especially remarkable given the recent emergence of a global knowledge-based economy in
which the most dynamic sectors are precisely the most intensive in innovation and technology. A good share of the economic changes that have
brought about sustainable growth in productivity in advanced economies
and some emerging, mostly Asian, countries are closely related to successive technological revolutions. One in particular is the information and
communications technology (ICT) revolution (see Box 10.3). The region

Box 10.3 ICT in Latin America, or How to Arrive Late to a Technological Revolution

Latin America's access to new information and communication technologies has been late and partial, as illustrated by all available indicators, such as the number of personal computers, access to the Internet, and access to broadband. This lag is particularly important in relation to the effects of innovation on productivity. The integration of ICT into firms' operations, combined with the accelerated growth in ICT industries, is one of the main factors—if not the main factor—that explains recent productivity growth in the U.S. economy (Draca, Sadun, and Van Reenen 2006; Jorgenson, Ho, and Stiroh 2008). The productivity gap between the United States and Europe in the late 1990s and earlier in this decade seems to be highly correlated with a slower diffusion of ICT among European firms (Van Ark, O'Mahoney, and Timmer 2008). Similarly, there seems to be a close relationship between the diffusion of ICT and the reversal of low productivity in the U.S. service sector before 1990.

The experience of advanced economies suggests that the adoption of ICT takes time to affect productivity, since for improvements to occur, the presence of hardware embedded with the new technology is far from sufficient. A vital part of the realization of the potential of ICT has been complementary investment in organization capital, understood as the reorganization of workplaces and the accumulation of skills in employees and managers (Samaniego 2005). Considerable investment in ICT has failed to deliver returns in the absence of such complementary conditions (McKinsey 2003). In the case of developing countries, these complementary conditions tend to be weak (Edwards 2002).

Some exceptions among large firms that have followed good overall approaches to adopting ICT show that it is possible for Latin American countries to exploit the potential of ICT (Alves de Mendonça, Freitas, and de Souza 2008). But, in general, a lack of infrastructure and relatively high costs of adoption are producing an unproductive mix. The level of only one ICT adoption indicator is excellent in Latin America: the market penetration of cell phones. This is precisely a sector that has benefited from relatively lower costs for users, thanks in part to radical marketing innovations, such as the use of prepaid phone time. The end result is that Latin American economies have been largely deprived of one of the main engines of productivity growth in the rest of the world. This is particularly the case compared to certain Asian economies, which undertook selective but highly significant early investments in ICT, including support for the local ICT industry, with enormous positive payoffs.

arrived late, and then only partially, to this revolution, leaving open the question of whether it is prepared to benefit from upcoming techno-logical transformations based on nanotechnology, biotechnology, and materials science. A considerable build-up of technological capacity and innovation investment in the public and private sectors are required for Latin American economies to, at the very least, copy, adapt, and operate emerging technological applications, not to mention lead or make original contributions (RAND Corporation 2007; Pérez 2008).

The idiosyncratic features of business innovation in Latin America, the scientific and technological deficits characteristic of the region, and the lack of well-articulated national systems of innovation combine to present a for-midable challenge to public policy that is aimed at improving innovation.

Evolution and Challenges of Innovation Policy in Latin America

Innovation policy has hardly been at the core of development concerns in Latin America for the past fifty years. Even though the region has a long history with industrial policy, the traditional emphasis was on tariff pro-tection and subsidies to infant domestic industries. A group of insightful and prescient proponents advanced the idea of technological upgrade and the need to incorporate it into discussions about growth strategies, but policymakers rarely heeded their advice.[7]

Starting in the 1980s, and in line with the Washington Consensus, policy debate and policymaking itself became dominated by a framework based on policy neutrality, leaving the efficient allocation of resources among sec-tors to market forces and closing most of the room for any consideration of overall innovation strategy or selection of sectors. This is not to say that there was no innovation policy whatsoever; rather, it was peripheral to the mainstream of economic policy and growth strategies in Latin America.

The discussion that follows describes the evolution of science, technol-ogy, and innovation policy in an attempt to highlight the learning process underpinning the introduction of new instruments and decision makers' adoption of new priorities (called "approaches" or "generations" inter-changeably here).

The First Generation of Innovation Policies

Starting in the mid-twentieth century in most countries of South America and Mexico and continuing to the present, the dominant public policy in the sphere of science, technology, and innovation focused on expanding the human and physical resource base of these activities in each country. This approach focused largely on developing university institutions and research centers with the right infrastructure in scientific disciplines, as well as investing in advanced human-capital formation, mostly in natural sciences, math, and engineering. Much public support was channeled through university budgets, scholarship programs, and public research institutions.

The original versions of this approach offered few resources for competitive grant systems, innovation funds, or similar instruments; these would come later, in the context of the second generation of policy. This was in sync with the dominant understanding of worldwide innovation at the time, which viewed innovation as a linear process that started with basic scientific research, then moved to applied research and development, and finally focused on business processes and products.

Whatever scientific and specialized technological capabilities exist in the region can be traced to these initial efforts. In some countries, especially the larger ones, the scientific base has advanced to an internationally significant level—although in the region as a whole, the result is rather modest. In practice, this approach resulted in the growth of "curiosity-oriented research," the dominant role of scientific elites and very little input from the business sector to innovation policymaking.[8] To this date, innovation policy budgets reflect this original approach to a sometimes surprising degree, and the university-industry gap remains a key unresolved issue in the region.

A Second Generation of Policies

Around the mid-1980s, a new approach emerged that considered innovation a nonlinear process. According to this perspective, innovation is spurred not only by scientific discovery and basic research, but also by the search for solutions to practical problems in diverse industries. This systemic approach to innovation thus emphasizes the relationships among multiple public, private, and academic actors in the development of innovation. From these interrelationships arises the notion of national innovation systems.

Under the influence of this new approach, a whole set of new policy tools emerged, focused on filling the gap left by the former generation of policies in the key matter of business innovation. So-called innovation funds started to appear, conceived of as a response to market failures that hamper private investment in innovation, notably failures in the financial market.

While several countries in the region are just starting to use these policy tools, they have reached maturity in countries such as Argentina, Brazil, Chile, Mexico, and Uruguay, where they have proliferated as a family of instruments aimed at encouraging a wide range of innovative behavior among diverse groups of firms.

Thanks to this proliferation, a number of studies have appeared assessing the impact, costs, and benefits of innovation funds. A recent review of 13 program evaluations in six countries found that, in general, the economic results have been positive, as evidenced by the estimated rates of return and net present value. There is little evidence that justifies the main criticism of these funds (i.e., that they crowd out private investment). On the contrary, there is some evidence of a multiplier effect, meaning that public funds leverage private money for innovation—or, at the very least, accelerate private investments (López 2009). The use of these instruments remains confined to a very small share of businesses in each country, however, far from the level common in European economies.

In addition to innovation funds, some cross-cutting or horizontal policy instruments have been introduced, such as tax exemptions for business innovation expenditures, which often coexist with innovation funds in the same countries.[9]

Toward a Third Generation of Innovation Policy?

Starting in the mid-1990s, a new, third generation of policies rose in the region. This new approach aims at changing the emphasis of innovation policies in favor of a strategic perspective. The main concern has become coordination failures among the diverse actors of the innovation system. In this approach, innovation policy tends to position itself in the middle of the competitive strategy of a given country. It is concerned with business innovation and business-university relationships, but also with technological services, regulatory agencies, property rights regimes, and an expanded set of educational institutions beyond doctoral programs. It emphasizes the need to understand how these elements fit together and impact favorably on innovation. This approach is usually complemented by selectivity, whereby a few industries are targeted to receive special support and attention from innovation policy, since that policy envisions the creation of world-class economic niches as a result of the intensive use of knowledge and innovation.

This approach is in no way incompatible with the policy instruments of the two earlier approaches. It focuses rather on redirecting them to the chosen key sectors of the economy that have high potential for innovation.

A recent example of this policy evolution has been the launching of sector-specific innovation funds, a thrust made possible since the emphasis on sector-neutral economic policies began to recede in the late 1990s.[10] Programs organized around the notion of industrial clusters are also focusing on technology and innovation and are increasingly combined with efforts to strengthen regional and city-centered innovation systems. In addition, explicit instances of intersector coordination in innovation policy have been introduced, such as industry roundtables and dialogues on shared research agendas, as a deliberate attempt to improve coordination and encourage pooling of resources and sharing of priorities among the key actors of the innovation system (Avalos 2002).

Other traditional policy tools are undergoing a similar reorientation. Curiosity-oriented research is being replaced by research in the service of previously defined problems related to priority sectors. Scholarships are directed toward advanced degrees directly linked to those sectors, as well.[11]

The results of this type of policy are still not evident across the region. Some interesting precedents provide grounds for optimism. In a companion chapter in this book, Fernández-Arias describes how sector-specific policies have produced success stories in agricultural exports and mentions innovation and technology as key components of these successes. These efforts have placed particular importance on collaborative processes between public R&D institutions, producers, and technological transfer and extension services in Argentina and Brazil. A similar interaction among the public sector and private business, research, and national and local actors is also occurring in the production of radical innovations, such as the emerging agricultural machinery industry in Argentina (Lengyel 2009).

On the other hand, the trajectory of East Asian countries suggests that choosing priorities and engaging in strategic thinking can be important components of successful innovation policy. Whether to focus on developing brand-new high-technology sectors or turn around traditional, generally natural resource-based sectors through intensive technological upgrades is an issue several countries in Latin America are actively discussing. Given the risks of policy capture by vested interests in the domestic market and the uncertainties inherent in technological development and rapidly changing international markets, adopting a strategic and selective framework requires sustained attention to minimize such risks. In this regard, the idea of approaching innovation policymaking as a learning process is gaining ground in an effort to champion more flexibility (see the notion of self-discovery in Hausmann and Rodrik 2005).

Institutional Development and Policy Effectiveness

Each generation of innovation policy developed institutional vehicles in accordance with the most important policy objectives of each approach that constitute a singular contribution to building organizations, routines, and capabilities. Thus, the first approach relied mostly on universities and research centers, while policy was formulated from national councils for science and research (the traditional councils of science and technology—CONICITs—present in almost all countries). The second approach brought about agencies that were highly specialized in running innovation funds. The third approach has produced a surge of interest in "governance." The main goal is improving public-sector coordination and bringing innovation policy to the center of economic policymaking and development strategy. This is being tried through cabinet-level coordination and a variety of innovation and competitiveness councils around the region (akin to what the OECD has labeled the "whole government approach" to innovation). Information about these institutional developments and their affinity with certain policy instruments is presented in Table 10.5.

This table also provides an indication of the effectiveness of each policy instrument, as shown by the plus and minus signs. For many of the policy tools in the table, there is not enough information to validate their use. Notable exceptions include the innovation funds and scholarship programs. Beyond that, there is the pending task of improving program and policy evaluation in innovation policy. All in all, the arsenal of policy tools available to Latin American countries does not seem to be very different from the one available to OECD governments promoting innovation. The similarity, however, conceals some significant differences.

First, while advanced economies have a well-established institutional framework that is regularly financed and has considerable built-in management capabilities, such a framework is still in an early stage of development in most Latin America countries. A sudden economic or political crisis, or even the regular turnover of political appointees following an election, can leave innovation institutions weakened and scrambling to retain or recruit very scarce technical and managerial talent. Thus, there are frailties in innovation policy, which appear in different degrees across the region.

Second, Latin American countries must pay sustained attention and devote substantial resources to initiate and strengthen basic components of the national innovation system that developed economies can take for granted. A notable example is the difficulty that several countries in the

Table 10.5 Instruments, Institutions and Effectiveness of Innovation Policies in Latin America

	Human capital and investment in science	*Company innovation*	*Strategic selectivity*
Instruments and type of programs	Competitive funds for research projects in science and technology with low appropriability (+)	Company innovation funds, designed to adjust to different types of companies and different modes of innovation (+)	Sector innovation funds (+ −)
	Support for excellence centers, selected and specialized in technologies with universal application (ICTs, biotechnology, nanotechnology) (+ −)	Venture and seed capital, other financial instruments to support innovation (+ −)	Identification of priority areas or sectors (+ −)
	Scholarship programs for masters and doctorate abroad (+)	Tax and tariff exemptions (−)	Programs aiming to enhance production chains, technology poles, and business incubators (+ −)
	Reinforcing national postgraduates in science and engineering (+)	Technology extension services (+ −)	Instruments to reinforce regional innovation systems (+ −)
	Promotion programs for strengthening knowledge networks through repatriation of diaspora and attraction of global talent (+ −)		Dialogue mechanisms between actors of the national innovation systems
Institutional features	National Councils of Science and Technology specializing in human-capital issues	Agencies in charge of the management of funds for company innovation	National Councils of Science and Technology dedicated to coordination across sectors and the definition of the competitiveness strategy of the nation
	Agencies managing scholarship programs	Supervisory agencies for foreign investment	Creation of innovation tables
	Agencies managing competitive funds for research		In some cases, ministries of science, technology, and innovation

Source: Authors' compilation.

Note: (+): the evidence suggests positive results of these instruments; (−): the evidence suggests negative or limited results; (+ −): mixed evidence.

region have in securing adequate services and capacities in metrology, technical reviews of products, and quality certification.

Finally, Latin American countries are characterized by considerable social inequality and exclusion that are far more severe than anything that exists in advanced economies. In recognition of this fact, policymakers are paying increasing attention to the need to connect the innovation agenda to the social agenda, taking steps to ensure that innovation and techno-logical development tackle poverty, education, and public health issues.

The maturity and development of institutions and policies for inno-vation in the region varies widely. Table 10.6 shows which main policy instruments discussed in this chapter—organized according to the policy approach—each country in a group of thirteen can count on. In the case of human capital for innovation, all countries have at least a few instru-ments. By contrast, countries have fewer instruments devoted to strategic and selective policies, even in some countries with the most developed innovation policy institutions. Instruments closely linked to the second approach, organized around the promotion of business innovation, are at an intermediate stage of development and consolidation.

Conclusion

This chapter has gathered the available evidence on the current status of science, technology, and innovation in Latin American countries, and has attempted to analyze its connection to the productivity stagnation that plagues the region. In spite of recent progress, mostly concentrated in the larger economies, a serious deficit of investment in R&D and innovation exists in the region. This conclusion becomes apparent once indicators from Latin America are benchmarked with international standards, and holds even if adjustments are made for the particular productive structure of the countries included in the analysis. The size of this deficit varies by country, but not a single economy in the region—not even Brazil or Mexico—can be complacent about its current level of investment on this front.

Even more serious than this deficit, particularly from the perspective of productivity growth, is the widespread failure to link R&D capacity with firms. Even countries that have achieved substantial progress in research capacity have not necessarily advanced well in building constructive and strong relationships between research capacity and business activity.

Many firms in Latin America are innovative. At the same time, it is very clear that innovation travels through peculiar paths in the region, and these paths reveal a series of problems and constraints that hamper growth in productivity.

Table 10.6 Innovation Policy Instruments in Latin America, Selected Countries, 2008

Instrument/Country	Argentina	Brazil	Chile	Colombia	Costa Rica	Dominican Republic	El Salvador	Guatemala	Mexico	Panama	Paraguay	Peru	Uruguay
First approach													
Scientific research and technology funds	■	■	■	■		■		■	■	■	■	■	■
Support for creation of centers of excellence	■		■	■					■				■
Scholarships for graduates and postgraduates	■	■		■					■	■		■	■
Support programs for national postgraduates in science and technology	■			■					■	■	■		■
Wage incentives for research in science and technology	■	■							■	■			■
Strengthening linkages with national researchers working abroad	■		■						■	■			■
Second approach													
Funds for the promotion of innovation and competitiveness of companies	■	■		■	■		■		■		■	■	■

Venture capital, seed capital, and other financial instruments to support innovation													
R&D and innovation tax incentives													
Mechanisms for the promotion of technology and knowledge transfer to non-agricultural industry (technology extension, etc.)													

Third approach

Sector innovation funds													
Priority areas/sectors													
Promotion of technology clusters, technology and business incubators													
Other instruments to enhance regional innovation systems													
Dialogue mechanisms between actors of the national innovation systems (technology and innovation tables, etc.)													

Source: Authors' compilation based on RICYT (2009) database complemented with information from experts.

There has been no shortage of public policies and programs aimed at these problems. A variety of tools has been put in place by governments. There are well-designed and effective public programs for innovation in many countries, although institutional development across them varies considerably and the size of these interventions is suboptimal. This conclusion can be easily illustrated by comparing the proportion of firms that receive public support for innovation in Europe to Latin America. Depending on which country is considered, between 10 and 50 percent of businesses receive public subsidies for innovative activities in Europe, while even Brazil, the country with the largest program in the region, ranks below that minimum.

Moreover, the relative emphasis on some policy instruments may not have been the best given the particular characteristics of innovation in Latin America. Most firms in the region operate far from the technological frontier. They are small, for the most part. The largest share of their investment in innovation takes the form of acquisition of technology embedded in machinery. The skills profile of their workers tends to be relatively less advanced than that of businesses in advanced economies, where the machinery was originally manufactured. The main channel for innovation and technological progress in the region is the adaptation of imported knowledge, while the absorptive capacity needed to take full advantage of technology transfer is often lacking.

What would a policy adapted to these conditions look like? It would emphasize technological services to business, whether they originate in laboratories, universities, or engineering and consulting firms, as well as technological extension programs directly aimed at facilitating access to relevant knowledge for firms. These kinds of programs should be far more common and significant in the Latin American innovation policy mix to improve firms' absorptive capacity. Another much-needed emphasis would be on programs aimed at developing human capital for technology and innovation. There is special need to correct the bias in human resource policies in favor of advanced degrees, and focus instead on training intermediate professionals in technical fields. This type of human resource constitutes a key link in the innovation systems in advanced economies but is extremely weak in Latin America, given the seemingly low prestige and visibility of this type of education.

Finally, the deficit in strategic vision must be addressed. Both dominant approaches to science, technology, and innovation policy over the past few decades are well-established in most countries, and rapidly maturing in others. Those approaches, however, are limited in their ability to support the key role that R&D and innovation should play in development strategies.

While innovation policies have focused on developing instruments to encourage private-sector innovation and technological upgrade in industrial firms, as well as on improving scientific capacity, the general economic strategy of the larger economies in the region—or, perhaps, inertia—has moved the region's economies in precisely the opposite direction, pushing them away from technology and knowledge-intensive industries toward natural resource processing activities and food production (Katz 2006).

Some countries have learned from this experience and are moving toward adopting a strategic approach to innovation policy: one that is proactive in identifying sectors and niches as priorities for public support, as well as in placing innovation at the core of industrial policy. This type of approach emphasizes a system perspective of innovation and highlights coordination failures that block innovation activity and impede communication and integration among key actors and aspects of the national innovation system in order to promote access to financing for innovative firms, conditions that favor dynamic entrepreneurship, provisions for the efficient start-up and closing of business ventures, management of intellectual property rights, university-industry links, and technological infrastructure and services.

Ever since the industrial revolution, R&D and innovation have been two of the main engines of economic growth and better living standards. Over the past three decades, that traditional role has grown, given the global trend toward a knowledge-based economy. The most dynamic economic sectors in the global marketplace are those that are technology-intensive, and they depend on the capacity to generate, adapt, and utilize knowledge as the foundation of productivity growth.

All advanced economies, to different degrees but without exception, are transforming themselves into economies with these characteristics. The success stories among emerging economies that have been able to leap forward in terms of productivity and welfare—most of them in Asia—share the common denominator of business innovation and technological development at the heart of their competitive strategies (Dahlman and Utz 2005).

In this context, Latin American economies face numerous and diverse challenges in building effective growth strategies. This book squarely identifies the region's stagnation in productivity as a key issue that must be tackled. It would be surprising if Latin American countries manage to jumpstart productivity growth without focusing on science, technology, and innovation in ways consistent with the characteristics of their economies, firms, and institutions, and within the framework of the global movement toward knowledge-based economies.

Notes

1. A similar result is reported for Brazil in an OECD analysis (2009). In a study of Argentine and Brazilian firms, however, de Negri, de Negri, and Freitas (2007) find a positive relationship between innovative effort and exports.

2. This analysis does not take into account the possibility of knowledge spillovers produced as a result of the operation of multinationals in developing countries. Mongue-González and Hewitt (2009) find solid evidence of knowledge externalities in a case study of the highly innovative information and communication technologies (ICT) industry in Costa Rica, registering positive impacts on productivity growth.

3. A national innovation system is the set of distinct institutions that jointly and individually contributes to the development and diffusion of new technologies and provides the framework within which governments form and implement policies to influence the innovation process. As such it is a system of interconnected institutions to create, store and transfer the knowledge, skills and artifacts that define new technologies (Metcalfe 1995).

4. See Arbeláez (2009); Arza and López (2009); and Cassoni and Ramada-Sarasola (2009).

5. Blyde et al. (2007) applied the same framework to Brazil and found that 18 OECD countries included in the analysis would invest far more than Brazil on R&D if they had the same pattern of sector specialization as the Brazilian economy. Anlló and Suárez (2009), in comparing innovative behavior in a series of industries in Argentina, Brazil, France, Germany, and Spain, concluded that significant differences exist in the technological intensity of firms working within the same industry across countries.

6. Cimmoli et al. (2005) analyzed structural change in the economic structure of Latin America between 1970 and 2000, and compared it to Finland, South Korea, and the United States. They find that growth in Finland and South Korea is clearly associated with a change in economic structure in favor of knowledge-intensive sectors, which have a role in disseminating technology throughout the whole economy. In contrast, in Latin American, there was a reduction in the participation of high technology sectors in favor of natural resource–intensive sectors. The behavior of productivity in both groups of countries could not be more different. Productivity growth accelerated in Finland and South Korea and stagnated in Latin America.

7. For an excellent sample of the type and depth of analysis on technology policy in the 1960s and 1970s in the region, see Sagasti and Araoz (1975).

8. A few exceptions can be found in scattered uses of public procurement policies in the service of investments in technology, such as the development of Empresa Brasileira de Aeronáutica (EMBRAER) in Brazil.

9. A recent review of innovation policy in the OECD indicates that 16 of 25 countries utilize fiscal incentives as a policy instrument (Sheehan 2007). There is evidence that such fiscal incentives yield benefits for innovation, ranging from neutral to favorable (Hall and Van Reenen 1999), to the point

that they have come to dominate innovation policy in a few countries (e.g., Canada and the Netherlands). However, experts and analysts have criticized their use in developing countries, given their bias toward the largest firms—precisely the group that invests heavily in R&D anyway. For recent evidence, see Agapitova, Holm-Nielsen, and Vukmirovic (2002); Salazar (2007); and Mercer-Blackman (2008).

10. Brazil and Mexico were the first to introduce sector-specific innovation funds. See Ventura (2009) for a review.

11. Innovation policy in the area of human capital has also been evolving recently. More attention is being paid to the development of domestic graduate programs that will be able to accommodate the new cohorts of doctoral degree holders who are returning from abroad and consolidating domestic capabilities. More proactive steps are also being taken to manage talent flows across borders by designing specific policies directed at preventing brain drain and attracting the scientific diaspora of each nation.

Phantom or Phoenix? Industrial Policies in Latin America Today

What Are Industrial Policies?

This book focuses on productive development policies (PDPs) that improve the economy's aggregate productivity, be it directly through firms' productivity or by facilitating a more productive allocation of factors of production. As defined by Melo and Rodríguez-Clare (2006): "Productive development policies can be broadly defined as policies that aim to strengthen the productive structure of a particular national economy." This is evidently a very broad definition, including polices aimed at certain key markets or activities (such as research and development [R&D], exports, human-capital formation) in large sectors of the economy (manufacturing, agriculture) and in specific sectors (textiles, automobile industry, software production, etc.). Previous chapters reviewed a number of PDPs aimed at addressing failures in certain markets or economic activities; these are called "horizontal" PDPs, because they cut across economic sectors and clusters. This chapter covers "vertical" PDPs and is therefore concerned with policies directed to specific sectors and clusters. For short, vertical PDPs are termed industrial policies because they are PDPs specific to certain "industries," which are taken to mean sectors or clusters of economic activity. Note that industrial policies refer to any set of related private producers, not just manufacturing.

Well-inspired industrial policies focus on the thorny development issue of how to enable or activate latent comparative advantages in certain "industries." These economic transformations involve the concerted action of many independent agents for which markets may fail to provide the required individual incentives for each agent to perform its part, thus frustrating economic development. It falls to industrial policy to identify the sector or cluster of economic activities that merit selective policy, or to identify how to "create winners" or "pick winners" as advocates and critics, respectively, would prefer to put it. Government may, in the best case, have the right incentives to administer these policies, but also fail for lack of the information and entrepreneurial inclination of private agents. Coordination between the two spheres would ideally spawn a productive combination, but in practice may easily decompose into rent-seeking private agents and captured public agents. Depending on the relative confidence put on markets and governments to deal with these issues, industrial policy may be viewed as a medicine or a poison to productivity.

Industrial policy was essentially ignored in the 1990s by the so-called Washington Consensus, which was focused on stabilization and basic macroeconomic reform. Industrial policy was strongly disfavored in most countries in the region as a misguided and unworkable effort to bypass markets and "pick winners" by bureaucratic means. However, while this hands-off paradigm persists to a considerable extent, industrial policy is now coming back into vogue; developing countries are more assertively providing public inputs—infrastructure, phytosanitary, and other forms of regulation; research into new materials, processes, or genetic modifications; certain types of intellectual property protection; taxes; or other financial incentives—each customized and bundled to suit the needs of particular domains of economic activity, but not others. This industrial policy push is emerging from the interplay between countries in search of development solutions and new theoretical reflection. No doubt that the new "open economy" industrial policies have little to do with the import-substitution strategies of the past. However, the notion of a development strategy that targets specific sectors of economic activity and contemplates appropriate institutional arrangements to implement it lives on.

Policy interventions under the industrial policy umbrella can either take the form of a public input complementary to the market (e.g., infrastructure) or use of the power of the state to affect market incentives and in this way, through market action, alter the resulting outcome (e.g., subsidy or regulation). The choice of policies depends in part on the flexibility and resourcefulness of existing markets to arrive at the desired outcome under appropriate incentives and either type of policy intervention may be applicable to both vertical and horizontal PDPs. However, prima facie, a horizontal subsidy to compensate for an alleged social pricing failure in a given market appears more plausibly justified than a sector specific subsidy, which may be a telltale sign of rent-seeking, especially if it is permanent.

A useful way to organize the information above is to consider the following 2X2 matrix, which combines the Horizontal/Vertical dimension

Figure 11.1   Dimensions of Productive Developmental Policies

	Horizontal (H)	Vertical (V)
Public Input (P)	Business climate Educated labor force Basic infrastructure Exchange rate policy	Rural roads for certain areas Cold storage logistics Food safety controls
Market Intervention (M)	Research and Development (R&D) subsidies Training programs Tax exemptions for capital goods High uniform tariffs	Sector-specific import quotas Sector-specific production subsidies

Source: IDB (2009a).

of PDPs with the Public/Market channel of intervention. Thus, interventions on the left are general or horizontal in nature, while those on the right generate benefits for specific sectors or clusters of the economy. The Public/Market channel of intervention is represented on the vertical axis. PDP interventions on the top of the matrix represent direct provision of a complementary input by the state, while PDPs based on market intervention are placed at the bottom.

The combination of these two dimensions gives rise to four quadrants; Figure 11.1 includes a few examples of PDPs in each of them as an illustration. Some of the policy interventions included, however, are not necessarily well-justified. The previous chapters were confined to the Horizontal quadrants: (a) the Horizontal-Public (HP) quadrant, the core of traditional macroeconomic studies on competitiveness and the preferred domain of policies inspired by the Washington Consensus; and (b) the Horizontal-Market (HM) quadrant, which includes more intrusive policies aimed at rectifying specific markets (but not confined to specific economic sectors). This chapter on industrial policies deals with the Vertical quadrants: the Vertical-Public (VP) quadrant, perhaps the most common arena of industrial policy, and the Vertical-Market (VM) quadrant.

Vertical policies entail choosing among sectors and clusters. Public inputs are highly specific to certain sectors or clusters. For example, rural roads may be critical for agriculture in certain regions but unimportant for the rest of the economy or cold storage logistics may be a key input for fruits and vegetables but not for textiles. Even general purpose infrastructure, such as a port, contains sector specificity; for example, should it cater to grains or to containers? The quadrant of vertical-market interventions is possibly the most controversial one because it lends itself to rent-seeking behavior on the part of firms and favoritism, or outright corruption. However, it certainly cannot be ruled out as a preferred mode of intervention. The public sector may be ill-prepared to provide or arrange for the provision of inputs and may need to resort to market interventions as a second best. Moreover, there may be room for "strategic bets" based on some technical rationale that may be best placed through subsidies to steer behavior with price rewards (on top of specific public inputs).[1]

The distinction between horizontal PDPs and vertical PDPs, or industrial policies, is fundamental because of their distinctive economic rationale and perhaps even more importantly, because of their distinctive institutional requirements, since industrial policies entail choosing among sectors and clusters.

Rationales for Industrial Policies

Most economists would agree that industrial policy has the potential to solve specific bottlenecks in a focused way and may facilitate structural transformation, the core of economic development, in ways in which the market may fail. But there is also a general recognition that it is difficult to identify sectors/clusters for worthwhile interventions and that, partly for this reason, industrial policy is prone to capture by lobbies looking for rents or demanding the extension of what they may perceive as unjustified favorable treatment of other sectors/clusters. In other words, industrial policy is an area where government may easily fail. Horizontal PDPs, on the other hand, appear less subject to political-economy domination and government failure. It is mainly for these reasons that economists generally prefer horizontal policies, provided that a market failure rationale to justify the intervention can be established. It is useful, however, to separate the theoretical justifications for industrial policies, akin to those argued for "horizontal" policies, from the more stringent institutional requirements for their successful implementation.

Industrial policies can be theoretically justified in a number of ways.[2] The most obvious case is that of the so-called Marshallian externalities, by which sector productivity increases with the size of the sector. Since increase in size takes time, another way of couching the same argument is that the true or "latent" productivity of a sector is revealed only by a fully mature industry. These externalities are typically exemplified with knowledge spillovers within the industry that cannot be internalized by individual firms, for example, because an increasingly productive labor force benefiting from "learning by doing" is free to move across firms. The very nature of the argument restricts industrial policy on this basis to tradable sectors, because the size of nontradable sectors would be essentially determined by the size of the domestic economy and therefore has limited scope for productivity-enhancing growth.

Do these intra-industry externalities merit industrial policy? Not necessarily. It is critical that the "latent" productivity be sufficiently large to give this industry a comparative advantage in the country. Otherwise, the country would be better off importing this good even if externalities exist and are captured through industrial policy. In fact, not only should the sector eventually be competitive, but the social gains from realizing its latent productivity should be large enough and come quickly enough to offset the cost of industrial policy. An "infant industry" worthy of protection should develop into a substantial item in the export portfolio of the country. If so, then there is a case for industrial policy. Firms in temporarily unproductive "infant" industries may need support until they reach a mature, high productivity state: lack of comparative advantage in a certain sector may hide a "dynamic" comparative advantage if it were to develop. Since the only concern is the fast growth of the sector, the simplest policy—a subsidy to its income to artificially increase investment profitability—would also be the right one. Industrial policies inducing sector growth would provide this support on a temporary basis, perhaps with an up-front temporary subsidy.

Positive externalities may also take the form of interindustry externalities. In the simplest case, complementary industries, such as shipbuilding and automobiles/trucks in Korea (see Amsden 1989), support each other in the "learning by doing" spirit. Economies of scope may spring from the development of shared inputs for a number of sectors, such as sectoral public goods or private nontradable inputs specific to certain industries (e.g., a certain profile of skilled labor). This is a natural way to rationalize the path of structural transformation along products that are frequently exported together (Hausmann and Klinger 2006).

More generally, the benefit of larger industry size or maturation may disseminate through backward and forward linkages with other sectors of the economy and lead to geographic agglomerations of clusters with enhanced productivity. If so, the case can be made that the growth of a "strategic" sector that by its very dynamism puts in motion this positive chain of events is worth fostering with industrial policy. In fact, as with intra-industry externalities, a profit subsidy would be appropriate policy. Since what determines the externalities to the rest of the cluster is not the sector's output per se but the sector's activity, in contrast to the case of intra-industry externalities, a "strategic" sector of this type need not have a latent comparative advantage to be worth the support of industrial policy. At the same time, it is important that industrial policy ensures that the production process of the "strategic" sector can, in fact, unleash the benefits to other industries. Policies requiring foreign firms to use local content could be justified on these grounds. In this case, industrial policy could conceivably be justified on a permanent basis.

Since these rationales for industrial policies are so linked to the goal of developing internationally competitive sectors, it is useful to look at the relationship between international trade and country performance in search of macroeconomic clues on the role of industrial policy. By and large, the evidence indicates that economic growth is positively correlated with openness (trade shares) but uncorrelated with import tariffs, which strongly suggests that industrial policy to support export sectors is likely to be preferable to import protection or regulating domestic content requirements.[3] Thus, while the theoretical justifications for industrial policy are varied, there is a prima facie case to focus on those that directly or indirectly support exporting sectors that are eventually able to compete with ease. In this regard, policies that discourage capital inflows leading to currency appreciation and stabilizing real exchange rates may be an important complement to industrial policies (Hausmann, Rodríguez-Clare, and Rodrik 2006). At the same time, a number of studies conclude that the growth effects of openness depend on the composition of exports, which suggests the need to focus industrial policy on how to discriminate among exporting sectors. Most studies suggest that nontraditional export sectors (e.g., manufacturing or human-capital intensive goods as opposed to raw materials, or developed-country exports) and, more generally, diversification, are growth precursors. A fortiori, industrial policy aimed at this kind of sector selection would be favored. In this sense, trade agreements that facilitate structural changes in export patterns are also industrial policy.

However, the above focus on policies to foster growth in particular sectors is too narrow a perspective from which to discern the right policies. Industrial policy deals with economic transformations that require the concerted action of multiple players, within and across sectors. The modern view of industrial policy assumes that productivity is hampered by impediments to beneficial collective action among private producers. In theory, firms would be willing to jointly provide the required input if they could coordinate; in practice, it may take industrial policy to induce or provide it. Higher productivity to the satisfaction of all parties involved in the industry (including the government) is possible only if they coordinate their decisions. In this approach, the right policy would address the specific impediment blocking a coordinated outcome. This contrasts sharply with the traditional industrial policy of subsidizing certain sectors to bump their profitability. Clearly, the paradigm of industrial policy is shifting from subsidizing target sectors to stimulate their growth to targeting coordination problems in certain sectors to expand their opportunities for collective development.

Coordination problems may appear under different guises. In the case of an industry in which firms face intra-industry externalities, the issue would be the incentives for firms to coordinate to jointly build a competitive "industry." The Marshallian externalities mentioned above refer to labor-force training at the industry level; but intra-industry externalities may result from any other industry-specific condition external to the firm, such as the cold storage logistics to support asparagus exports in Ecuador or food safety controls to support high-quality cattle meat exports in Uruguay, both of which are identified in the matrix as examples of public inputs. This is a coordination problem because the presence of these industry conditions determines whether the sector enjoys high or low productivity and, therefore, whether the production cost is justified.

In the case of interindustry externalities, the scope for gains from coordination is even larger. In this case, the issue would be the incentives for sectors or elements of clusters to coordinate their joint development. In theory, benefiting firms would be willing to subsidize the development of the "strategic" sector if they could coordinate; in practice it may take industrial policy to induce it. More generally, so far the emphasis has been on the idea of key "dynamic" production activities whose development would bring benefits to the rest of the cluster or interlinked sectors, but there is also a more symmetric case of a set of complementary sectors whose individual viability depends on the rest. The classic case is the hotel industry waiting for the development of transportation logistics and vice versa because investment would not be profitable for each sector by itself: unless there is coordination between the hotel and the transportation sectors, the tourism industry will not develop even if it were highly productive once players were coordinated. Here, a case can be made for industrial policies, perhaps as unobtrusive as helping coordinate decisions in the spirit of "indicative planning" or as direct as providing public inputs (e.g., an airport).

The shortfall of "self-discovery" in Hausmann and Rodrik (2003), by which firms explore profitable opportunities and sometimes discover activities in which the country has high productivity, can also be couched as a coordination problem: firms fail to share the costs of exploration. As a result, the market underexplores because other firms may copy success or otherwise benefit from it without incurring the cost of exploration and, therefore, returns to discovery are partly external to the firm. While some form of protection of success that impedes diffusion, akin to patent protection, would lead to more exploration, the most efficient policy would induce the sharing of exploration costs or directly provide that exploration without taxing the dissemination of productive discoveries. The exploration itself may require coordination outside the beneficiary sector: the viability of exporting asparagus in Peru would not have been explored without infrastructure such as cold storage and transportation chains.

It is difficult to analyze the various instances in which one policy or another would be called for, but it is clear that, overall, they are bound to become increasingly relevant as economies establish the basics for economic progress and embark on more complex modes of production. Correspondingly, as the policy goal shifts from developing an output (say, an infant industry output) to providing specific missing inputs in complex economic systems (say, inadequate quality regulations for food exports or unavailability of the right labor skills for a specific activity), the policy focus correspondingly moves from identifying immature sectors with potential comparative advantages to addressing the shortcomings of nontradable inputs blocking the emergence of these advantages. In fact, after trade and financial liberalization, required tradable inputs may be easily secured through markets, and encouraged by market intervention if appropriate. But nontradable inputs, such as public goods or the skills of the labor pool, need to be produced and may therefore be policy intensive, especially in terms of public inputs. Furthermore, nontradable sectors such as some of the large and growing service sectors are substantial parts of the economy subject to similar coordination failures in need of similar industrial policies. Modern industrial policy emphasizes coordination impediments to the development of a productive open economy, both in its tradable and nontradable sectors.

An Overview of Industrial Policies in Latin America

Industrial policies are no strangers to Latin America. They had their heyday in the 1960s and 1970s, when industrial policy was an integral part of the policy apparatus of most countries, large and small. Policymakers were convinced that the market was too slow to produce the structural transformations that their economies required in order to grow at a rapid pace. The basic orientation of industrial policy was import substitution, so it is not surprising that the main policy instrument to promote new industries was tariff protection and nontariff import barriers (at the same time, countries evinced a strong distrust of foreign direct investment, FDI). While there may have been an argument for selective protection in countries with large domestic markets (e.g., Brazil, Argentina, Mexico)—on the basis of learning-by-doing cost reductions, Marshallian intra-industry externalities, or interindustry externalities—these arguments were much weaker in countries with small markets that could not provide the needed scale as an incubator for infant industries.

At the same time, many countries used the state to invest in what policymakers considered to be strategic industries, and state enterprises became an important actor in the economy in industries such as iron and steel, petroleum extraction and refining, public utilities, telecommunications, and many others. The view that the market would not generate investment in sectors that required large amounts of capital to be efficient became widespread. Finally, most countries set up development banks to promote industrialization through cheap credit to preferred sectors and to support private investments in those sectors. Industrial policy came to be associated with the manufacturing industry.

The debt crisis of the early 1980s swept away most of the policy apparatus that supported industrial policy, although it was poor macroeconomic policy that was mostly to blame. Although the so-called Washington Consensus of the 1990s was specifically concerned with macroeconomic stability rather than industrial policy, its liberalizing animus was applied in such a way as to further erode the standing of industrial policy in the region. Surviving industrial policies were mainly those created decades ago, sometimes as early as the 1950s, whose services had come to be regarded as integral to the economic life of particular sectors, not an intrusive and suspect government intervention to be eliminated. Many of the most effective of these long-standing industrial policies decentralized at least some decision making to local units that answered to local stakeholders, typically rural, as well as national authorities.[4] It is unsurprising, therefore, that the contribution of industrial policy to new exports from Latin America is manifest most consistently in the collaboration between research and extension services and their rural clients.

Arguably, this cleansing process indiscriminately dismantled the good and the bad. Nevertheless, while import-substitution policies are largely gone, many of the industrial policies survived in one guise or another, even in countries that embraced market-oriented policies with the greatest conviction (e.g., Chile). Moreover, new industrial policies were introduced at the same time (see Melo and Rodríguez-Clare 2006). Often they were introduced in response to perceived market failures and some resulted in efficiency gains, even if some of the interested parties were motivated by the capture of some rents. For example, coordination failures at the level of sectors or clusters may explain the introduction of a host of programs under the umbrella of competitiveness strategies in the mid 1990s (Rodríguez-Clare 2005; Rodrik 2004, 2007).

Interest in industrial policy is again on the rise, as economies have performed below expectations and governments have come to realize that good macroeconomic policies are insufficient to spur economic growth. Nonetheless, the new, open-economy approach to industrial policy is quite different from its import-substitution version.[5] The basic characteristics of industrial policy in the region in recent years are as follows:

- The emphasis is on competitiveness or export productivity (i.e., on creating or improving comparative advantage), rather than on import substitution.
- The emphasis on manufacturing is largely gone. Policymakers have become much more respectful of comparative advantage, actual and potential. Much of the new emphasis goes into moving up the technological ladder in industries that have proven themselves successful (agriculture, food products, and mining).
- Interventions emphasize technology development and acquisition.
- Much of industrial policy revolves around attracting FDI into specific sectors and the actions required from the state to ensure success in this effort.
- The provision of public inputs and the role of the state as coordinator are being increasingly recognized.
- The resources deployed, and the ambition of policymakers, are considerably more modest.
- Although the new policies lend themselves much less to rent-seeking, such activities have not completely disappeared, as suggested by the persistence of unjustified interindustry tax and tariff dispersion in several countries. This may be considered the dark, and socially harmful, aspect of industrial policy, even in its new garb.

Argentina, Brazil, and Uruguay have been successful in using public institutions to engage in technology improvements in agriculture, which are then transferred to the private sector. In Argentina, industrial policies seem to have been circumscribed to government-sponsored R&D in agriculture, but with the active participation of the beneficiaries. The development of two varieties of genetically-improved rice, which developed in close cooperation with private users, is one of the great successes of Argentina's Instituto Nacional de Tecnología Agroalimentaria (INTA). INTA does research that is useful for private producers, with whom it works together on specific technological innovations and then sells back to them for a royalty (Sánchez, Butler, and Rozemberg 2009). In a sense, INTA's role is to take into account the large economies of scale in research and the knowledge externalities that successful R&D generates. INTA has also been occasionally active in solving coordination problems in the agricultural field. In some sectors considered sensitive, in particular, automobiles, the old-style industrial policy emphasizing protection through various means has survived. As noted in Box 11.1, the Brazilian public agricultural research body, Empresa Brasileira de Pesquisa Agropecuária (EMBRAPA), was responsible for the development of soybean seeds well adapted to the low-fertility Brazilian savannahs. These innovations were later disseminated to private producers through Empresa de Assistência Técnica e Extensão Rural (EMATER), the government's agricultural extension agency.

Mexico has been particularly circumspect in the industrial policy field, although its development agency, Nacional Financiera (NAFIN), is strong and has an important presence in the financial sector. It is particularly important as a source of finance for small and medium enterprises (SMEs). Nonetheless, the government has launched programs aimed at the development of an internationally competitive software industry through tax incentives and grants to train personnel and purchase equipment. In addition, it has encouraged the relatively developed automotive industry to move upmarket into the provision of parts for the aerospace industry. Tax exemptions, training grants, and sponsorship of educational facilities have been the main policy instruments used in this effort (see Báez et al. 2009).

Public financing for developing new industries and strengthening existing ones has become a focus of industrial policies in several countries of the region (e.g., Banco Nacional de Desenvolvimento Econômico e Social [BNDES] in Brazil, Corporación de Fomento de la Producción [CORFO] in Chile, and NAFIN in Mexico). Over the years, the rationale had shifted from directed credit during the heyday of import substitution to correcting an important and increasingly recognized market failure: the lack of long-term credit for new initiatives in countries with very incomplete financial markets. Since the 1980s, the emphasis in most countries has been on making credit available horizontally, without choosing sectors, often on a second-tier banking model (i.e., allocating public financial resources through private banks).

Recently, a more focused approach has been emerging. What is perhaps most interesting is that, albeit tentatively, these institutions with a long history and a strong track record of success are beginning to pursue vertical policies rather than simply correcting a market failure in capital markets without concern for what sectors are involved. For example, in Chile, CORFO's support for innovation has gone from a first-come-first-served basis to providing support for projects coming from firms in

---

Box 11.1   Soybeans in the Savannahs: Developing a Leading Export Crop in Brazil[a]

Brazil is the world's second largest soybean producer, and the largest exporter, with soy exports representing 10 percent of total Brazilian exports in 2005. In the previous ten years, soybean exports had doubled. To achieve this result, cultivation of the legume was significantly expanded beyond its traditional, limited planting area in the temperate climate and rich soils of Rio Grande do Sul to the more abundant but much less hospitable savannahs or *cerrado* to the North; simultaneously, productivity was dramatically improved, with soy yields rising by 65 percent in 15 years (compared to just 6.5 percent in the past 10 years in the United States, the world's largest soybean producer). Solving the many coordination problems among producers of the inputs required for both expanding the planting area and increasing productivity have been facilitated by, and perhaps depended on, intensive collaboration between private growers and the Empresa Brasileira de Pesquisa Agropecuária (EMBRAPA), the Brazilian Agriculture Research Agency. Today, EMBRAPA is a vast entity that finances 37 research centers and employs 8,600 employees, of whom 2,220 are researchers, half with Ph.Ds. But, importantly, soybean cultivation in Brazil was successful thanks to its early exposure to export markets and to a constellation of domestic interests that protected growers from price controls, which deterred investment in a related crop—wheat.

EMBRAPA and soy production grew up together. The agency was created in 1973 as part of a drive to increase domestic food production in order to meet the needs of a rapidly growing urban population and provide export earnings. An initial task was creating technical capacity in all the disciplines relevant to the advanced agriculture of the day: between 1974 and 1978 some 1,500 researchers enrolled in post-graduate programs abroad under EMBRAPA's aegis. A central goal was to discover

---

clusters identified for development in the country's competitiveness and innovation program. In Brazil, BNDES is making available R\$210 billion (over 2008–2010) to firms in specific sectors identified by the Política Industrial, Tecnológica e de Comércio Exterior (PITCE, the government's productive development policy). These sectors include some that are already well established in the country but need to become more competitive (bio-diesel, footwear) and others that are emerging as important (capital goods, information technology, nanotechnology). Financing

(*continued*)

how to bring commercial agriculture to the savannahs despite their low fertility soils and irregular rainfall. Soybean was considered a strategic crop in this effort given burgeoning international demand for soy as a protein substitute for fish meal and the extensive experience of cultivating soy in the temperate south of Brazil. The challenges were clear: creating new soybean varieties adapted to low latitudes and developing methods of tilling, fertilizing, and conserving the soil to increase its fertility.

In 1980, EMBRAPA–SOJA created the first of a line of soybean varieties successively better adapted to Brazilian savannah soil. This and other results were widely diffused to farmers, large and small, through EMATER, the main public agricultural extension company. EMATER trained its agents to help farmers make effective use of what it termed "technological packages": bundles of complementary technologies found to be suited to particular agricultural producing areas. By the time EMATER was closed in 1991 in connection with a wave of deregulation, smaller farmers could rely on producer cooperatives to access innovative technology, or turn to state rural extension services, while larger planters could employ their own personnel to maintain direct contact with EMBRAPA and keep abreast of its developments. Of course, the government's role in the development of soybean production and exportation was not limited to technology development and diffusion: an important complement to the services provided by EMBRAPA was the creation of special credit lines that, until the wave of liberalization, subsidized investment in new soy technologies. Later, the Moderfronta program was developed to help finance investment in agricultural equipment, and it played a fundamental role in modernizing the Brazilian agricultural implement fleet, to the great benefit of productivity.

[a] Extracted from Monteiro et al. (2008).

covers a number of items, including trade financing on favorable terms for purchases of capital equipment made in Brazil.

Costa Rica and Chile provide interesting examples of policies aimed at encouraging industrial diversification through FDI. The Costa Rican Investment Promotion Agency (CINDE), a private institution with strong connections to the Costa Rican government, has chosen three sectors (medical instruments, advanced manufacturing, and modern services using information and communication technologies) to promote and sell services that are required by foreign firms in these sectors with a view to attracting them to the country. CINDE acts as a promoter of Costa Rica and as a coordinator, solving investors' needs ranging from legal advice to obtaining the training required by their workers. CINDE was instrumental in bringing an Intel chip assembly plant, Proctor and Gamble's back office operations for Latin America, Baxter Laboratories (a major supplier of medical implements), and a Hewlett Packard service center to Costa Rica.[6]

Since 2000, Chile has been operating the Program for Attracting Investment in High Technology to attract FDI in information and communication technology (ICT) and biotechnology with one-time grants tied to employment or installation costs. The CORFO administers this program and also provides services to solve coordination problems for newcomers, such as technical and English language training of the workforce. For instance, it has made agreements with Chilean universities to adapt their engineering curricula to the needs of the firms it is attracting and set up a directory of interested workers who have passed the test of English for international communication (TOEIC). Policies have become increasingly proactive, but are still fairly restrained, employing instruments that were used previously without a sector orientation (e.g., partially subsidizing innovation, providing access to credit, solving technological problems, etc). CORFO coordinates most of these activities and also provides longer-term finance and technical assistance to SMEs (Agosin, Grau, and Larraín 2009). So far, it has been successful in attracting business process outsourcing (BPO) firms, software producers, and departments of multinationals providing ICT services to Latin American subsidiaries (Agosin and Price 2009).

Most countries in Central America and the Caribbean, as well as some countries in South America, such as Peru, have used the legal figure of the export processing zone (EPZ) to attract FDI for export. Firms established in the EPZ are exempt from import duties on inputs and taxes on profits. While EPZs are not aimed at particular sectors, in practice they have attracted assemblers of clothing for the U.S. market. With the emergence of China as the main source of clothing imports into the United States, these zones are facing a severe reconversion problem. Some countries have been able to develop their industries from clothing assemblers to what is called the "whole package" by attracting firms that produce cloth (El Salvador is a good example). Others have moved, in response to market pressures and deliberate public policies, to other types of goods (medical equipment in Costa Rica and the Dominican Republic).

A number of countries have set up national competitiveness councils, with the participation of policymakers and representatives of the private sector, whose objective is to identify and help resolve problems to enhance competitiveness. These councils have been established in countries such as Colombia, the Dominican Republic, and Guatemala. The idea is to elicit information from the private sector and address problems by providing public inputs, although market interventions in the form of tax breaks and various kinds of subsidies have not been absent. In Colombia, as in Chile, efforts have also been made to identify sectors in which the country has already evinced international competitiveness, could scale up if coordination problems are resolved, and are likely to be dynamic in the world economy.[7] It is too soon to evaluate the effectiveness of these efforts, but the modest amount of resources allocated to them does not bode well for what they can achieve. The orientation of these efforts, however, seems to be on the right track: they seek to solve the coordination problem by eliciting information from the private sector, with the agency acting as the key link between a sector with good prospects and a provider of key inputs to secure success. Several countries in Latin America have been promoting tourism by providing a variety of public inputs (construction of infrastructure, including airports and roads, establishing quality standards, and promoting the country abroad) and by offering tax breaks for hotels, tour operators, and other firms involved in the activity. These countries include highly successful tourism destinations (Barbados, Costa Rica, Jamaica, and the Dominican Republic) and other late entries into the industry, who have had more problems (El Salvador, Colombia, and Guatemala), owing largely to public-safety issues.[8]

Although they have declined significantly since the heyday of import substitution, big strategic bets have not been absent in the region. Much of Brazil's current heavy industry, such as steel, petrochemicals, and cellulose, originated this way. One of the most interesting cases is Embraer in Brazil (see Box 11.2). Initially, given the large static economies of scale of this industry, the provision of public capital was essential in an environment characterized by rudimentary capital markets. In Chile, as well, the salmon industry was launched by the semipublic Fundación Chile (see Box 11.3), which, in the early 1980s, imported the technology for producing cultivated salmon and set up a profitable firm that it later sold to private interests. These efforts involved solving the coordination problem of producing and exporting a new good and addressing the asymmetry of information between potential domestic producers and foreign users of a nonpatentable technology. Nonetheless, these examples are more exceptions than a description of the state of affairs. That relatively modest policy efforts can yield such successes confirms their potential for spurring growth. That they have been so few and far between attests to the reluctance of policymakers to use them.

Box 11.2   Aeronautics in Brazil[a]

Embraer *(Empresa Brasileira de Aeronáutica SA)*, a formerly state-owned firm, is today, after Boeing and Airbus, the world's third largest civil aircraft manufacturer. It has been one of the top two Brazilian exporters since 1999.

The drive to create a sophisticated, domestic aircraft industry that served civilian and military needs was a key part of the national ambitions of the Brazilian technical elite from at least the time of the Second World War. In 1969, Embraer was founded as a mixed economy company controlled by the federal government and reporting to the Ministry of Aeronautics, to manufacture variants of a prototype of an eight-seat turboprop plane, which came to be called the Bandeirante.

In conformity with the reigning import-substitution strategy, the initial focus was on the domestic market. The Brazilian aeronautic authorities' tight regulation of regional civilian aviation created a largely captive market for Embraer planes. Convergent considerations led to collaboration with the Brazilian air force on complementary projects. The focus on the domestic market was not, however, incompatible with cooperation with foreign component makers and attention to export possibilities. The costs of project development in the airframe industry are dauntingly high, even for advanced-country producers with deep pockets. Embraer quickly realized that a way to reduce these costs was to share them with the producers of engines and other key components in exchange for long-term purchase agreements or a share of eventual profits. In the medium and long term, the remaining investment costs could be more easily amortized by boosting production runs through exports (thus achieving economies of scale and reducing unit costs).

The result was that Embraer, even in the 1970s, pursued a strategy of buying rather than producing high-technology, high value-added components. The firm was thus free to concentrate instead on aircraft design, fuselage production, and final assembly. In entering these cooperation agreements, Embraer was careful, on the one hand, to avoid licensing arrangements that would have limited its ability to export planes, and, on the other, to ensure that its partners transfer to it not only relevant product-specific technical knowledge, but also organizational know-how relating to series production in the aircraft industry. Aside from cutting development costs and risks, this strategy assured Embraer that key components were available at competitive prices (because its suppliers benefited from worldwide economies of scale)

(continued on next page)

(*continued*)

and helped create a potent lobby against trade restrictions on its planes, as large foreign suppliers had much to gain if Embraer products could be sold in their country of origin.

But beginning in the mid-1980s, the Brazilian state owner began to intrude more directly into the company's decision making than it had before. Perhaps the firm's undeniable successes emboldened officials and politicians, allowing them to imagine, imprudently, that Embraer was indestructible if not invincible. Worse still, the government forced the company to enter what proved to be unprofitable collaborative projects. As world recession hit in the early 1990s, and the government—now embracing the market-reform program—cut various export finance and incentive schemes, sales plummeted (from 211 planes in 1989 to 81 in 1992) and losses exploded. By 1994, Embraer had been sold to a consortium of banks and pension funds in a complex transaction that allowed the private acquirers to pay with government debt securities and the Aeronautics Ministry to keep a golden share in the company after its privatization.

Given decades of successful innovation and production, and the relative brevity of the state's meddlesome interference, it is perhaps unsurprising that privatization, and the accompanying large capital infusion, quickly returned Embraer to its winning ways.

Embraer as a private company continues to benefit from a range of public supports, including credit guarantees for financing foreign sales and inducements to foreign suppliers to establish domestic production subsidiaries. Hence the question: is the production of airplanes in Brazil sustainable without government support? Clearly, Brazil would still be competitive if subsidies were discontinued everywhere in the world (in compliance with WTO rules). Furthermore, the firm's need for direct public support of export financing is decreasing as its own costs of capital decline, in part because of improvements in the Brazilian financial markets, and in part because of its access to international credit. All signs point in the same direction: Embraer, having built a platform that connected it both to leading producers of key components and sophisticated, international markets for its final products almost from the beginning, is likely to continue as a major producer of commercial aircraft.

[a] Extracted from Castelar Pinheiro and Bonelli (2008).

Box 11.3   Fundación Chile: Fishing for Success

The transfer and adaptation of technologies and know-how from other parts of the world to Chile has been a key objective of Fundación Chile (FCh) since its creation in 1975 (Agosin, Grau, and Larraín 2009). Set up by the Chilean State and IT&T in compensation for the nationalization of the IT&T's Chilean subsidiary, FCh is an ingenious combination of an instrument for making strategic bets on new and promising industries and a venture capitalist in a context where there is no such segment in the capital market. FCh carries out a number of activities, most of them involving innovation or self-discovery (in the sense of Hausmann and Rodrik 2003). One of its major activities has been to set up profitable companies in new sectors of the economy and then sell them off to the private sector (either national or international). In the late 1970s it adapted Norwegian technology for salmon cultivation to Chilean conditions. It set up a profitable firm (Salmones Antártica), which it later sold at a large profit to Nippon Suisan, a Japanese food multinational. There was considerable learning-by-looking in the industry, and now Chile exports over US$2 billion in cultivated salmon.[a] FCh also played a role in developing the blueberry export industry (see Agosin and Bravo-Ortega 2009).

[a] The industry is now experiencing some serious environmental problems as a result of the failure of individual firms to cooperate with each other in protecting their common phytosanitary capital.

How Well Do Industrial Policies Work in Practice?

A cursory review of the international evidence on how well industrial policies work in practice yields mixed results (see Harrison and Rodríguez-Clare [2009] for a complete account). However, industrial policy is not the only public policy to suffer from this lack of clarity; just about any public policy in a complex area (such as education, health, social insurance, infrastructure, stabilization) shares with industrial policy a clear rationale for policy intervention and mixed evidence of practical results.[9] As in these other cases, dispiriting evidence should prompt a discussion about how to conduct polic y in better ways, not whether to do it. Bad (or incomplete) industrial policy should be replaced by good industrial policy, rather than no policy at all.

It is important to separate the discussion of the effectiveness of industrial policy in helping a sector to grow and improve productivity from the debate over whether it is justified in terms of a valid rationale. The first is evidently easier to prove but, by itself, is an insufficient justification. In the context of intra-industry externalities, industrial policy supporting an exporting sector would be justified only when the productivity gains from sector growth are substantial and enough to assure international competitiveness and offset the cost of industrial policy. The evidence on import substitution in the region, when analyzed through this lens, is mixed with respect to the first point: some studies find that less import competition did favor sector growth, as expected, but not necessarily productivity growth; actually, a number of studies find that when protection was later removed there were sector productivity gains. Even in countries with larger markets, where some temporary protection to infant industries could be justified, the political economy of protectionism made it impossible to remove dysfunctional import barriers. Nevertheless, the experience with import protection was not generally inspired by the rationales outlined earlier, and therefore its shortcomings cannot rule it out as an appropriate tool of industrial policy under valid rationales of infant industry protection (see Chapter 5 on trade and productivity).

In the same way that the experience with import substitution in Latin America and the Caribbean need not invalidate infant industry protection, the East Asian success does not demonstrate that widespread infant industry protection and targeted export subsidies are the right development strategy (besides the fact that by now they are largely forbidden by the World Trade Organization [WTO]). It has been forcefully argued that industrial policy protecting capital-intensive sectors allowed East Asia to realize its latent comparative advantage in advanced manufacturing (Amsden 1989; Wade 1990). However, the situation is not as clear on closer examination. Industrial policy in East Asian countries was intense and the success of these countries is beyond doubt, but was that the basis of the success? Interestingly, growth of total factor productivity (TFP) at the sector level is negatively correlated with the industrial policy support received (see Noland and Pack 2003). This is not necessarily incompatible with the rationales put forth above (Rodrik 2007) but contradicts widespread views on the miracles of East Asian development.[10]

At the same time, there are clear cases of successful industrial policies with substantial development impact that may be a guide for its future. For example, studies of the United States, Japan and other developed countries show how industrial policy protecting infant industries helped establish important industries in these economies; steel rails in the United States and semiconductors in Japan are cases in point. The cases of developing countries analyzed in Sabel (2009)—Finland, Ireland, and Taiwan—buttress the point. The Irish case is especially ambitious in defining comparative advantage criteria for choosing sectors (information

Box 11.4   Ireland: A Magnet for FDI

In the 1950s, Ireland began building an export economy by attracting advanced multinational firms—those that could credibly offer to create stable, high-skilled jobs—and learning together with them to improve the economy (Ó Riain 2004). The chief means of attraction were fiscal and other financial incentives. From the late 1950s, foreign firms paid no taxes on profits earned from manufacturing exports and even today, despite revisions to adjust to European Union (EU) competition rules as they became applicable, the tax rate for corporations is one of the lowest in the world. The chief vehicle of learning from the experience—for selecting the most promising collaborators from among those attracted by the incentives, and working with them to ensure incremental improvement of local supply networks, infrastructure, education and the like—was the Irish Development Agency (IDA).

Founded in 1949, the IDA took on a central role in recruiting foreign investment in the early 1960s, and by the end of decade had become the central agency in formulating and implementing industrial policy. Since 1969 it has been a quasi-independent state agency, funded by and reporting to the Department of Enterprise, Trade and Employment (and a stable board of directors), but outside of the civil service structure and therefore able to control its own internal organization and career ladders. In the early postwar years, officials of the IDA saw themselves as working in the manner of the Tennessee Valley Authority, the most ambitious and for a time the most successful of the New Deal economic development projects, and on occasion associated themselves with Roosevelt's description of "a corporation clothed with the power of government, but possessed of the flexibility and initiative of private enterprise."

Beginning in the 1970s the IDA focused on attracting firms from rapidly growing, high-technology and capital-intensive industries; firms making large investments in sophisticated manufacturing facilities were unlikely to pick up and leave at the first recession, unlike the many apparel manufacturers who in the preceding decade came to Ireland, but left quickly. High-tech, knowledge-intensive jobs would provide a market for Ireland's trained workforce, but would also be a prod to improve training. In practice this meant concentration on health care—pharmaceuticals and medical instruments—as well as electronics—principally mini- and micro-computer manufacture—and later software. Initial successes increased the likelihood of later ones. By the late 1990s, nine of the top ten (and 16 of the top 20) pharmaceutical companies in the world had facilities in Ireland, as did the market leaders in information and communication technology, including Dell, Hewlett-Packard, IBM,

(continued on next page)

(continued)

Intel, and Microsoft, and the top ten independent software companies in the world. In some years in the 1990s, Ireland, with 1 percent of the EU population, was attracting 20 percent of FDI to the EU.

An episode in the IDA's campaign to attract an Intel plant in 1989 illustrates the enormous coordination necessary to achieve these results. There was at the time no large-scale producer of microchips in Ireland, so Intel sought assurance that it could hire the experienced engineers it would need. In response, the IDA commissioned a consulting group to locate expatriate Irish engineers with the relevant semiconductor experience. Three hundred were found, mainly in the United States, all with between three and seven years' experience in the production of volume semi-conductors, and 80 percent of them were willing to return if given an attractive opportunity.

The IDA's attention to the economy-wide implications of its collaboration with groups of firms was particularly clear in the way it tracked and reacted to indications of possible skill shortages. Thus, between 1977 and 1979, the agency negotiated agreements with electronics firms that, together, would create demand for some 600 electrical engineers per year, about four times the number Irish universities and regional colleges were then graduating. As it takes between two and five years to educate technicians and engineers, there was need for a short-term remedy and a plan for a long-term expansion of the education system. The short-term solution was conversion of science graduates to electronics qualifications via one-year courses; the longer-term solution was expansion of existing courses and addition of new ones. The rapid response of the Higher Education Authority reassured subsequent investors that Ireland could supply the skills needed and helped renew the university and technical training systems.

There were similar systematic effects on physical infrastructure. Ireland's electro-mechanical telephone network of the 1970s was unsuited to the data-transmission needs of the early electronic and software companies. Again the IDA coordinated reform with the relevant agencies, spearheading creation of a new telecommunications agency and investments in a modern digital telephone system.

Beginning in the mid-1980s, the institutions of industrial policy were reconfigured, with increasing and successful efforts to support domestic high-tech firms, particularly in software. But the IDA remains a cornerstone of Irish economic development, and a continuing demonstration that, used as an instrument for detailed reflections on "infrastructural" constraints to growth, FDI can help build the foundations for prosperity.

technology and communications, pharmaceuticals, as well as financial and a host of other business services) in which to place strategic bets and use FDI as a tool of industrial policy (see Box 11.4).

However, industrial policies are hard to get right. This is largely the experience with fiscal incentives to promote clusters, which, despite aiming at sectors with substantial externalities, have little to show in terms of productivity gains (Pack and Saggi 2006). The reason may be that domestic markets are too small or not sufficiently sophisticated or competitive to elicit a productivity response; or perhaps firms do not coordinate around a future cluster and prefer the safety of growing with backward technologies that do not yield externalities. Furthermore, even if industrial policy is effective and captures substantial intra-industry externalities, the country may ultimately lack the right latent comparative advantage. One example in the region is the Brazilian microcomputer industry in the 1980s studied in Luzio and Greenstein (1995): although sector productivity grew, it could not match the pace of the technological frontier and became an increasing economic drag. According to the study by Ribeiro, Prochnik and DeNegri (2009), the domestic content clause and R&D expenditure conditionalities in the Informatics Law have been detrimental to sector productivity growth after 1995. At the same time, Brazil's industrial policy did succeed in creating competitive steel and aeronautics sectors, which are now important export items (see Box 11.2).

A review of selected experiences with industrial policies in a cross-section of countries in the region is also mixed. There are many examples of expensive industrial policy programs (many times hidden behind tax exemptions, or tax expenditure) lacking a valid rationale and at the same time, in most countries, there are programs that are well-inspired and make a positive difference.[11] At the same time, it is important to note that in a number of countries there is an institutional base for industrial policy to build on.

The transition from nonexistence to competitive export is in a sense the highest payoff for industrial policies seeking economic transformation in the direction of comparative advantage. In this light, industrial policy has been critical in launching radically new export activities in the region. A review of cases of the "discovery" of new competitive activities in the IDB research project "The Emergence of New Successful Export Activities in LAC" (IDB 2008c),[12] with a focus on whether industrial policy played an important role in their realization, reveals that, in a number of cases, industrial policy was important in solving coordination problems that led to discovery, especially in rural-based production (see examples in Boxes 11.1 and 11.5).[13] However, the successful cases are generally small and have not developed into the kind of breakthroughs that would be needed for substantial development effectiveness.[14]

Box 11.5   Veterinary Vaccines in Uruguay:
Public R&D and the Birth of a Biotech Industry[1]

Uruguay's exports of animal vaccines—mainly bacterial vaccines for anthrax and clostridia, but also viral vaccines for rabies and eye diseases—grew at a cumulative annual rate of 9 percent between 1995 and 2006, about double the current rate of growth of the market worldwide. The emergence of this highly competitive, technologically demanding industry is the outgrowth of decades of intellectual exchange between public and university laboratories and private-sector R&D aimed at controlling foot-and-mouth disease (FMD), and—with the success of those efforts—the emergence in recent years of an increasingly intense and formalized system of public-private collaboration in new areas of biotech. In this case too, the success of industrial policy depended on exposing the products it helped develop, whether these were initially exported or not, to the validating test of international competition.

With its 10 million head of cattle and location in the Río de la Plata estuary, Uruguay is, and has been for more than a century, a substantial part of one of the largest stock-breeding areas in the world. With cattle comes—at least until very recently—FMD; and the origins of the country's biotech industry date to the establishment in the 1930s of state laboratories to develop vaccines against the virus. Starting in 1946, private firms were authorized to produce vaccines; new state laboratories specializing in the disease were created in the following decades. The upshot, given convergent developments in Argentina and Brazil, was to create a pool of public and private expertise in animal health in the La Plata basin that attracted substantial investment by leading multinational firms in the form of acquisition of national laboratories with biological expertise.

Subsidiaries of four multinational firms thus came to dominate the Uruguayan market for FMD vaccines. But they did so under a regime that both facilitated quality improvement and innovation and potentially sanctioned the failure to achieve it: in 1968, as part of a national campaign against FMD, a state institution—Dirección de Lucha Contra la Fiebre Aftosa (DILFA)—was created to monitor the quality of all vaccine production. The standards it applied were strict enough to eventually force 7 of 11 producers from the market. Only the multinational subsidiaries survived. But in the same year, and despite the general thrust of the import-substitution strategy in place at the time, the government effectively removed duties on imports used to prevent or treat cattle-related diseases. Domestically produced vaccines

(continued on next page)

(*continued*)

could thus only succeed in the Uruguayan market if they were in fact as effective as alternatives available on world markets, ensuring that local producers, regardless of the nationality of their owners, were under continuing pressure to meet international standards. To facilitate innovation, Laboratorios Rubino, a public laboratory, and the DILFA were charged with transferring their research results to private firms. There was, however, no incentive to export, as the domestic market was huge and stable, and returns on capital were high.

The situation changed dramatically in the mid-1990s, when Uruguay sought and secured from the International Organization for Animal Health the certification that its cattle were "free of FMD without vaccination"—an extremely valuable label in global meat markets. To obtain this status, the government had to discontinue vaccination and prohibit handling of the live virus. These measures ended production of FMD vaccine in the country and sped up the withdrawal of several transnationals to Argentina and Brazil. This withdrawal in turn cleared the way for the reassertion of domestic capital in the industry and the redirection of production to new vaccines for export markets, particularly in developing countries. The new exporters that have emerged benefit in international competition from the comparatively low salaries of skilled professionals in Uruguay and from the lower costs of animal testing. Crucially, they rely on partnerships with many local academic groups and institutes, including the Department of Biotechnology at the Instituto de Higiene (the School of Medicine of the public university), to draw on local knowledge to improve their production processes and to develop niche products for export markets: industrial policy in this sense is crucial to their export success. As a manager at Santa Elena put his firm's strategy:

> We specialize in analyzing what the region needs. When the stockbreeders and the vets face a problem, they have no access to the R&D leaders of large companies, so they go to the local laboratories, and the same happens in Argentina. The problems we face in the region have nothing to do with Europe or North America. We have a pastoral system, concentrated or extensive, but an outdoors system. The Europeans have a confinement system; their cattle practically do not eat grass and do not walk. So, diseases are totally different in the two systems. Our first task is to identify our problems . . . Then we identify the people at the university who can solve these problems, we support their R&D up to the point that they reach the development

(continued on next page)

(continued)

ot an antigen. That is when Santa Elena takes over to develop the product at the industrial level . . . Industrial R&D at the laboratory never stops. The biggest investment is made inside the laboratory, and each time we get better results with lower costs, with faster and safer processes.

(Interview, July 24, 2006).

The development in Argentina of an export-capable industry applying biotechnology to plant and animal health confirms the pervasiveness of the Uruguayan experience. In Argentina as in Uruguay, farmers and ranchers have collaborated for decades with public entities to improve crop conditions and stock breeding: the Instituto Nacional de Tecnología Agroalimentaria (INTA) is the producers' principal state interlocutor, but university departments are active collaborators as well. In Argentina, as in Uruguay, collaboration between public entities and private firms has become more intense and formalized in recent years, as suggested by the profusion of new instruments of cooperation, such as agreements of technical assistance. The pace of innovation has been, if anything, more rapid in Argentina than in Uruguay, with the development of a commercially important mutagenic variety of red-rust resistant rice as a signal achievement. The story of the successful development of animal vaccines in Uruguay is, in light of this neighborly corroboration, a story that can be replicated.

ª Extracted from Snoeck et al. (2006).

Striking a Balance between Hands-Off and Gloves-Off Industrial Policy: Public-Private Cooperation

The mixed evidence on industrial policies confirms the relevance of the theoretical justifications for industrial policies but at the same time points to the challenges to getting them right and the risk of wasteful, or distortive, counterproductive policies. Successful implementation of industrial policies requires the identification of promising sectors or clusters, or creating/picking "winners." This problem has a purely technical dimension, because development economics does not yield clear operational rules in this regard, and a political-economy dimension, because special private interests stand to benefit from the selection and would be interested in capturing rents even if they know there is no prospective productivity gain. Arguably, both aspects are substantial sources of industrial policy underperformance.

On the one hand, economists who are confident that the market usually finds ways around problems and are fearful of government failure, either because of ignorance or because it would divert the market's energy toward rent-seeking, conclude that the best is a hands-off approach to industrial policy. That means a minimalist policy stance that is predisposed to abstain from action. On the other hand, economists who conceive of economic development as a transformational process that requires a governmental development strategy to realize some of the necessary qualitative breaks with the past, conclude that industrial policies ought to take a leading role and be bold enough to make strategic bets outside the market's comfort zone. In this view, industrial policy is a gloves-off fight that may entail major price distortions to thrust the market in the right strategic direction. The right approach is likely in the middle: proactive but restrained.

Market failures give ample justification for interventions in the form of "open-economy industrial policy," and actual experiences show that it is possible to successfully carry them out, including those with ambitious objectives. It would be foolish to ignore this tool at a time when the region desperately needs productivity solutions. However, it is important to recognize the challenges to making industrial policy a demonstrably winning proposition: a chance of success does not offset a high likelihood of failure. The farther away policy ventures into unknown territory and the more it brings opportunities for capture and rent-seeking, the riskier it is. Most successful "development strategies" are in reality ex-post rationalizations of policy reactions taken under specific conditions that cannot be replicated; sweeping industrial policy derived from a grand development strategy vision runs the risk of all untested fundamentalisms. Given the uncertainties concerning the right policy prescription (economic science) and the difficulties of implementing it (political economy), policymakers ought to exercise restraint as a matter of prudence. The challenge is to strike a balance between these two extreme views of industrial policy to arrive at a proactive and restrained approach. A fruitful approach to address this challenge is to focus on the policy processes that lead to the determination of policies, rather than the direct analysis of the policies themselves.

Industrial Policy Reform: Challenges

As a purely technocratic problem, identifying promising sectors is challenging because it requires the assessment of social returns resulting from complex interactions of interlinked sectors while market signals only reflect private returns, let alone the potential of new sectors that the market has not even produced. Even an able and well-intentioned government would find it difficult to make the right calls because it would lack the required information. The situation on this front is worsening as markets become more complex and the technical possibilities multiply. For the same reasons that the vertically integrated firm is ceding space to global supply chains of goods and services, industrial policy must recognize that its basic objectives of determining which kind of activities to pursue, which markets to enter, and how to do it are constantly changing. The decentralization of product development—away from advanced country headquarters and toward the global "periphery"—implied by the combination of vertical disintegration and increasing codesign creates new opportunities for developing country firms that can meet the heightened requirements for collaboration, and new barriers to participation in world markets for those that can not. Increasingly, policy must not only take a stand on how to enhance productivity but also contribute to the search for new opportunities. Industrial policy as a device to emulate advanced economies is increasingly obsolete. Helping firms acquire flexibility for a world characterized by ever-changing competitiveness—the introduction of new products and the emergence of new technologies and processes—is an aspect of industrial policies that is often ignored, but much needed.

The open industrial policy strand that is emerging is grounded in both theory and evidence. However, to be successful it needs to fully recognize the complexity of the problem. It needs to take a bottom-up approach and focus on the provision of public inputs or market interventions that relax constraints on the exploration of possibilities and the pursuit of promising ones. In essence, the focus is on how to eliminate the impediments inhibiting the private sector from investing in promising prospects and bringing them to fruition, a process that would in turn provide a platform for new ventures. Many of the obstacles reside in dysfunctional nontradable production inputs. However, in the case of exportable products, connection to the world economy is a necessary condition for this search, because collaboration with key actors in the world economy affords indispensable access to the capacity to scan for new opportunities and threats to current practice.

The information requirements largely exceed the capacity of bureaucracies, even the best ones. Successful industrial policy requires institutions that are "embedded" in civil society and the economy—otherwise they will lack access to the fine-grained information needed to inform their decisions (the "high bandwidth development policymaking" in Hausmann [2008]). The idea would be to create or adapt public institutions that can, in collaboration with private actors, determine what needs to be provided and organize its provision.[15] This requires a coherent set of public agencies with high-level political support and accountability as well as active private organizations with incentives to provide information so that together they can come up with programs designed to boost productivity, rather than to pocket rents. There is no question that public inputs, including the enforcement of regulations whose compliance benefits private producers, are valuable to the private sector. The question is how to make the right ones more valuable than the wrong ones and in that way reduce the likelihood that the private sector "games" the government, legally or otherwise.

There are numerous examples of public-private alliances that have contributed successfully to efficient policies and development strategies. For example, Devlin and Moguillansky (2009) review the experience of Australia, the Czech Republic, Finland, Ireland, Korea, Malaysia, New Zealand, Singapore, Spain, and Sweden. Some of these experiences are among the most successful developers of the last 50 years, all of them superior to Latin American and Caribbean countries. While the articulation of the public-private structure varied significantly across countries, the most successful were the ones with more stable public-private alliances, which were able to come to fruitful understandings. The venture capital support system developed by Taiwan that was based on public-private cooperation is also a successful model to emulate. By backing a diverse and changing portfolio of undertakings, and combining hands-on monitoring and mentoring with market selection, public and private investors in Taiwan organized through venture capital a process of continuous economic restructuring that transformed the domestic economy, linking it to the most demanding, capable sectors in global markets (Sabel 2009).

There are public institutions in many countries in the region that provide a foundation for further construction. The challenge is how to enhance existing institutions in light of superior experiences elsewhere, rather than starting anew and trying to replicate them. This approach puts emphasis on the policy processes that lead to the determination of policies, rather than the policies themselves.

Industrial Policy Reform: A Balanced Proposal Based on Public-Private Cooperation

Public-private cooperation requires the business sector to be able to organize collective action (to represent it in specialized councils, roundtables, mixed venture capital funds, etc.) and present well-justified demands to the relevant public agencies, which entails strengthening its technical and lobbying capacity. Entities organized for rent-seeking purposes are evidently unfit for these purposes. But at the same time it is important to recognize that effective lobbying capacity is a desirable characteristic of these organizations because the process requires their input.[16] This institutional capacity building may actually require public help to crystallize, because without the rent-seeking element, the incentives for free riding may make it difficult for the private sector to coordinate for productivity goals whose private benefits are more diffuse. Ideally, a consultative process would develop a common strategic vision, which would provide a framework for private actors to generate productive proposals and for public entities to select them rationally.

Public-private cooperation also requires competent public agencies to address these complex tasks. Fortunately, the region boasts examples of strong, capable public and semipublic agencies such as BNDES in Brazil, CORFO in Chile, CINDE in Costa Rica or NAFIN in Mexico. However, it is common for industrial policy agencies to be organized horizontally, by "topic" (exports, training, innovation, etc.), headed by agencies with little coordination among themselves; what will also be needed is a public sector that is organized vertically, able to latch on to the economic structure and adapt to the topography of clusters in the economy. For success, public agencies must also be able to elicit substantial cooperation from the private sector. Devlin and Moguillansky (2009) show that, in their sample, after 1990 in all of the public-private alliances, the public counterparts would at least consult the private counterpart (Korea, Malaysia, and Singapore), consult and seek agreement (Australia, the Czech Republic, and New Zealand), or engage in open dialogue (Finland, Ireland, Spain, and Sweden). Agencies unable to commit to a culture of shared information and collaboration will be unfit for the new tasks.

The decentralization process that has gained momentum in Latin America in recent years requires an additional layer of agencies and instruments. In many of the countries with a tradition of federal government (such as Argentina, Brazil, and Mexico), state, province, and local governments participate in public-private dialogue and enterprise development, facing new challenges to best adapt existing structures and mechanisms to incorporate local economic development priorities. On the other hand, countries with a more centralist tradition that are gradually making progress in the decentralization process, such as Chile or Peru, face the problem of creating brand-new institutions (in many cases, public-private agencies) and new legal frameworks to support local economic development from the bottom up. Subnational PDP institutions have the advantage of being more knowledgeable and receptive to the needs of the final beneficiaries. The challenge is to design functional institutional mechanisms among layers as well as checks and balances to ensure that these agencies are not captured by local interest groups.

The organization that emerges from this analysis includes strong private sector organizations able to articulate positions at the sector/cluster level and two types of public sector agencies: (a) coordinating agencies that are able to link to the private sector organizations and think through policy from the point of view of the sector/cluster in an integral fashion, across markets or activities; and (b) knowledge agencies of the traditional thematic type, where special expertise resides and can be accessed by both private and public vertical organizations. Increasingly, the budget resources of industrial policy would be allocated to coordinating agencies (in part, to support their private counterparts, if need be), which would in turn pay for the services of the knowledge agencies in their areas of expertise or other outside think-tanks with the required knowledge. Likewise, the viewpoints of individual ministries would be integrated into a central body with appropriate political support entrusted with overall responsibility for industrial policy as a development tool (e.g., in Ireland and Singapore these are the responsibilities of the prime minister). All these private and public entities would cooperate in two distinct functions: (a) the traditional function of defining policies to enhance productivity in existing clusters, upgrading their capacity and leveraging their resources; and (b) the novel function of exploring new possibilities to expand the reach of the cluster in productive directions (the "search engine" of each cluster).

Given the private sector information advantage, it makes sense to invite sector and cluster organizations to submit technically justified proposals for government support (notwithstanding public-originated proposals in consultation with private counterparts). It is in the public interest to strengthen private organizations to help them produce good proposals. The guidelines for the evaluation of these proposals should ensure that rent-seeking incentives are kept under control in such a way that proposals reveal the project with the highest overall productivity impact. For example, guidelines ought to stress that proposals be specific about expected productivity gains for the economy as a whole and favor public inputs over direct subsidies to discourage rent-seeking. Guidelines would also favor proposals that include a cofinancing portion in recognition of the additional profits that the productivity gains would entail to the proposing organization as a way of aligning incentives.[17] To ensure that proposals made with the information advantage are kept honest, it is important to review the quality of the proposals ex-post to detect exaggerated projections of productivity gains in order to give preference to proponents with a track record of truthful proposals. In particular, the cofinancing portion could receive an ex-post partial rebate if the productivity gains projected in the proposal did not highball actual gains.

For the overall system, just as it is important to produce proposals under reasonable incentives and evaluate them with reasonable guidelines, so too is it crucial to weed out supported projects that fail to perform, whose ancillary conditions are not met or whose sunset clauses have been reached. For this, rigorous monitoring and evaluation of results must be an integral part of the system. For all the difficulties in promoting and selecting worthwhile proposals, or more generally "picking winners," a well-designed system should be able to "let losers go," as Dani Rodrik puts it. Sometimes, failing programs are not discontinued because their cost is hidden and can be better defended by special interests, as in tax exemptions instead of explicit subsidies; the transparent and explicit recognition of costly support is an important feature to ensure that failed experiments make room for new experiments. More generally, the transparency of the public agencies is fundamental to enhance accountability and, consequently, encourage firms to play by the rules and discourage rent-seeking.

Finally, it is important that the institutions underpinning the system be stable over time to lend credibility to cooperation for long-term planning; a political understanding may be needed to ensure that policies and institutions of industrial policy are adaptable but not subject to political turnaround. This characteristic of the policy process has been identified as a prerequisite for success (IDB 2005; Scartascini, Stein, and Tommasi 2009); consensus building immune to the political cycle is also a key characteristic of success in the specific study of development policies in Devlin and Moguillansky (2009). Public-private cooperation would help establish a process to generate a consensus of this kind (Stiglitz 1998).

Would this be the end of "picking winners" as extreme critics of the practice would like? Probably not. In its extreme modality, the proposed system may work fully from the bottom up: it would receive proposals from existing clusters facing concrete coordination problems and make practical determinations on the basis of the case presented. This approximates the case of Colombia where the authorities elicit information from producers on the problems they face in becoming more competitive in world markets through the constitution of a public-private national competitiveness council. Even then, however, while a focus on coordination problems in the context of evaluation guidelines of the kind described above would constrain the scope for "picking winners," in a sense it cannot be avoided. A system of public-private cooperation may promote some degree of good self-selection but the evaluation of proposals requires a public-sector judgment (and in fact some degree of autonomy) to counterbalance the private-sector perspective in order to preserve the integrity of the policies. Prioritization of proposals also requires "picking," if for no other reason than because less organized clusters may misrepresent better projects. Furthermore, it stands to reason that guidelines for evaluating proposals allow virtual clusters whose latent comparative advantages have not yet been revealed to be considered if a solid case is made. Policymakers are "doomed to choose" (Hausmann and Rodrik 2006).

The proposed system may also allow for some public initiative or leadership to interact with clusters that have already established their viability to proactively address some of their coordination problems and scale them up. In other words, the public agency may also be interested in intervening in a given cluster and make its own proposal in consultation with a cluster. This approximates the more proactive stance of the system in Costa Rica, for example.[18] This more proactive but cautious modality is consistent with the recommendation in Rodríguez-Clare (2005) that industrial policy center on clusters that are revealed winners in the sense of having a comparative advantage and take the form of "soft industrial policy" that directly increases productivity through public provision instead of "hard industrial policy" that distorts prices through taxes and subsidies. In terms of the typology of public interventions, this means restricting policies to public inputs (including grants) as opposed to market interventions. This assignment of the instruments of industrial policy matches the focus on coordination problems of already established clusters, for which price-distorting market interventions are not required to make them viable.

Interesting examples of how to address some of these issues have successfully emerged over the past five years in a number of countries, all of them through programs with similar structures and approaches that are known mostly as "Cluster Programs."[19] These programs focus on identifying groups of firms (in general, firms that are in the same sector in a given geographical location) that share common problems that hinder their growth. Once identified, a process is set in motion to bring together local businessmen representing the cluster, international sectoral experts, and government officials (from the program, along with local staff from the local government and local research institutions and business support agencies) to jointly identify the missing public or semipublic inputs and organize their provision. The Program tries to redirect the provision of public inputs already offered to the actual demands identified, and sometimes the Program itself has additional funding to provide missing inputs that no other source can provide. The exercise includes the leveraging of private resources that firms themselves are willing to contribute once key obstacles to cooperation are removed, thus promoting public-private sector cooperation at different levels.[20]

Even if industrial policy proposals center on clusters with established or demonstrable comparative advantage, it is critical that the system's "searching" arm fosters conditions for the birth or the revelation of sectors with promise. PDPs supporting the exploration of new economic opportunities for sectors or clusters are an integral part of industrial policy in which the identification of a worthwhile sector is one step removed. For example, policies fostering diversification could play this role: diversification would make it more likely that sectors in which countries have comparative advantage, perhaps latent, would be born. In the context of Hausmann and Rodrik's "self-discovery," incentives to diversify would increase the range of exploration and, therefore, the rate of discovery. Then, a policy yielding more exploration would be beneficial. Industrial policies aiming at diversification, or outright exploration, in fruitful directions are critical for the success of the system over time. This activity would also be best carried out through public-private cooperation. For example, advanced countries on the technological frontier have substantial high-tech industrial policy that relies more and more on public-private cooperation (Box 11.6 illustrates the case of high-tech industrial policy in the United States).

In this context, a critical part of self-discovery depends on new firms, which require some form of special financing to start up. In developed countries, this high-risk financing is provided by venture capital, or the so-called angel capital, which has been responsible for some of the major innovations in information technology (e.g., Apple, Google, Microsoft). However, financial markets do not fulfill this role in Latin America and the Caribbean, even in the most advanced countries, and industrial policy is also called upon to fill this gap. This is the role played by Fundación Chile, which has been responsible for the emergence of new and extremely successful sectors in Chile (e.g., salmon, blueberries). This financial niche of industrial policy opens up ample room for public-private cooperation.

The question remains, however, whether policymakers' would be well advised to place bets on certain industries or clusters that have not yet emerged as viable. Chile's system may be an example of a more proactive arrangement in which the technical analysis of the bureaucracy can go a long way in promoting the development of new clusters or asking for proposals in very specific directions that do not spring from the existing clusters themselves but from strategic thinking (e.g., farmed salmon). The Chilean policy in recent years combines support of proven sectors with the proactive identification of new sectors thought to possess latent comparative advantages (with potential in the world economy and aligned with the country's productive factor endowments). Nine clusters have been identified, including mining, a variety of food industries, software, ICTs (especially in their application to mining and food) and new sources of

---

Box 11.6   Successful High-Tech Industrial Policy in the United States: The Case of DARPA

Essentially all advanced countries have variants of industrial policies in the sense used here, although these tend to be classified in domestic politics, and in the accompanying academic discussion as policies to encourage technological development, enhance research and development, improve regional competitiveness or assure the capacity of the national industrial base to produce vital components of sophisticated battlefield equipment. Consider the example of the United States, a country whose general commitment to free-market policies and (in comparative terms) famously fragmented national state apparatus would seem to radically limit, if not preclude, such policies. Yet it is widely known in what has come to be called the U.S. high-technology community, and in the academic circles central to it, that in the post–World War II era, the United States has indeed pursued resolutely, and with substantial success, the equivalent of an industrial policy.[a] The chief instrument of that policy has been the (Defense) Advanced Projects Agency—(D)ARPA—of the Department of Defense. Founded in 1958 as ARPA ("Defense" was added to its name in 1972, removed in 1993, and added back in 1995), its role is to fund or co-fund projects just beyond the current horizon of scientific and technical possibility that have a substantial probability of success, and whose realization will make possible broad advances in military equipment and industrial products and processes. "Darpa hard" is a term of art that captures the desired degree of difficulty, potentiality, and feasibility.

In the 1960s and 1970s, DARPA projects made pioneering contributions to interactive computer graphics (Sketchpad) and the fundamental internet protocols (ARPANET). The Very High Speed Integrated Circuit Program (1980–1988) led to advances in digital signal processing on which Texas Instruments would draw to become the world leader in that technology for mobile telephony. The Strategic Computing

---

energy. Brazil's very recent Productive Development Policy in 2008 is an even more ambitious effort to support the consolidation of existing industries and the emergence of higher-technology world-class industries that policymakers believe can be developed in the country (such as information technologies, nanotechnologies, and biotechnologies).[21]

The farther away it is from existing clusters, the more likely it is that industrial policy must cross the divide between "soft" and "hard" industrial policy, distorting prices to induce the required change in the marketplace.

(continued)

Program (1983–1992) yielded breakthroughs in parallel computing on which the current generation of Intel's dual-core microprocessors are based. Sematech (1987–present) organizes an association of semiconductor manufacturers to investigate common technical problems in semiconductor production. The Advanced Lithography Program (1988–present) helps develop successive generations of the technology used for inscribing ever smaller transistors on chips. The High Performance Computing and Communications Initiative (1992–present) supports research on supercomputers and high-speed fiber-optic networks. Significantly, the drift of policy has been in the direction of more and more explicit emphasis on the commercial or economy-wide value of projects. ARPANET and Sketchpad were essentially military programs and their commercial spillovers an accidental by-product. But the Very High Speed Integrated Circuit Program and the Strategic Computing Program were intended to produce commercial benefits. In the High Performance Computing and Communications Initiative, commercial and military goals are seen as roughly equal in importance, and in Sematech and other, more recent DARPA programs military benefits are regarded as secondary or even negligible. This shift in emphasis from military to commercial benefits has gone hand in hand with increases in the funds invested by both the public and private sectors, more complex forms of public-private cooperation in project selection and monitoring, and increasing coordination among government agencies participating with DARPA and the private sector in these projects. Thus, with regard to the crucial high-technology sector, the United States not only has an important and conspicuously successful instrument of industrial policy, but has been extending and refining it.

[a] The following draws extensively on Fong (2000), which includes extensive references to the relevant literatures.

In this vein, the higher the potential reward, the higher the risk of failure. The balance between risk and return depends on the public sector's policymaking capacity and the functionality of private sector organizations. Perhaps even more important, it depends on the political-economy feasibility of sustaining such a demanding system of cooperation.

The risk of ambitious industrial policy is heightened in bolder proactive proposals for larger-scale interventions based on grand development strategies. One good example is the set of industrial policy recommendations that could emerge from the novel structural transformation paradigm proposed by Hausmann, Hwang, and Rodrik (2007), in which the sophistication of export goods, as measured by the income per capita of their exporting countries, is found to be a precursor of growth.[22] In related work, Hausmann and Klinger 2006 operationalize the notion of distance to promising exports and derive concrete directions for industrial policies to aim at exports that are both sophisticated and well positioned as stepping stones to further progress. This is an untested theory, but nevertheless shows that progress in development (and institutional) economics may keep alive "hard industrial policy" despite its mixed historical record.

Where does an economy draw the line and abstain from more radical industrial policy? The argument could be made that if development economics offers a guide to policy that policymakers are willing to use when selecting proposals, to mention its most innocuous use, then why not bring it to bear proactively to its fullest extent, in more radical ways? If knowledge is good enough to pick proposals, why isn't it good enough to pick winners in general? Because it may not be prudent to move too far from clusters with a demonstrable comparative advantage, where the "too far" depends on the capacities of a country's public and private organizations. Uncertainty about the accuracy of available knowledge and recognition of the perils of implementation of industrial policy should make policymakers pause and, while "thinking globally," prefer to "act locally." Proactive but restrained.

Notes

1. This quadrant could also include some policies that are horizontal in nature, and therefore not of interest in this chapter, which for practical reasons are implemented through specific sectors especially affected by the market distortion being addressed.
2. See the survey in Harrison and Rodríguez-Clare (2009) for more formal elaboration and references.
3. The exception is capital goods tariffs, which are associated with low growth.
4. Agricultural research and extension services, established in many countries after World War II to help cultivators open new territories to agriculture, mechanize farming, and improve seed or livestock selection in ways specific to their particular and various conditions, fulfilled these conditions.
5. The information for this section was derived from the country studies prepared for the IDB projects on "Industrial Policies in Latin America and the Caribbean" (IDB 2009a). Country studies included Argentina, Barbados, Chile, Colombia, Costa Rica, Guatemala, Jamaica, Mexico, Paraguay, Peru, Trinidad and Tobago, and Uruguay. Studies for Panama and El Salvador using the same methodology were also undertaken afterwards.

6. Interview with Sandro Zolezzi, Research Director, CINDE.

7. For Colombia, see Meléndez and Perry (2009); for the Dominican Republic, Guzmán et al. (2009); and for Guatemala, Cuevas, Lee, and Pineda (2009).

8. For Barbados, see Artana, Auguste, and Downes (2009a); for Costa Rica, Monge-González, Rivera, and Rosales-Tijerino (2009); for El Salvador, Agosin, Acevedo and Ulloa (2009); and for Jamaica, Artana, Auguste, and Downes (2009b).

9. This point has been stressed by Dani Rodrik ("Industrial policy: conceptual and empirical issues," presentation made to IDB, December 2008).

10. Furthermore, the protection of "sunset" industries destined to disappear raises doubts about industrial policy as the basis of the East Asian tigers and suggests that policies there may have been less the expression of a heterodox development strategy and more the result of mundane political economy forces. Trade policy entailed import tariffs and export subsidies that cancelled out each other in the aggregate, again suggesting political economy interference more than a clearly defined outward-oriented strategy.

11. See country studies in the IDB research project "Industrial Policy in Latin America and the Caribbean"; IDB, 2009a, available at: http://www.iadb.org/res/projects_detail.cfm?id_sec=8&id=3776.

12. The project was conducted by country teams from Argentina, Brazil, Chile, Colombia, Ecuador, Mexico, and Uruguay.

13. This concentration in rural activities reflects the structure of the industrial policy in place rather than the failure of industrial policy in other areas; these successes suggest that industrial policy has a large untapped potential in other areas.

14. Another discouraging piece of evidence is that, according to the analysis in Chapter 10, there is little evidence of a link between development of new products and productivity growth at the firm level.

15. However, capitalism may by itself generate private sector institutions that end up solving coordination problems. A vibrant system of venture capital and Silicon Valley (born under the influence of Stanford University) in the United States show that public institutions may not be needed. An alternative approach to solving the potential problems associated with public sector involvement is to analyze the factors that impede the birth of catalytic private sector institutions.

16. Paradoxically, the system may require some rents to work efficiently, a point stressed in Hausmann (2008).

17. If all the interested private parties were involved in the proposal, in theory cofinancing should be 100 percent; in this case, presumably, the private sector would be self-sufficient to fully coordinate and industrial policy would be irrelevant.

18. It parallels both in terms of actual cluster policies (e.g., temporary subsidies to coordinate hotel and other tourism services to enhance this cluster) and in the search for opportunities through CINDE.

19. Programs of this kind are currently found in almost every country in Latin America and the Caribbean, although the largest and more advanced are in Argentina, Brazil, Chile, and Uruguay.

20. In a typical program, there is very active cooperation at the level of each cluster, where a governance structure emerges with representatives from cluster firms and staff from local institutions. Then, at the level of the Cluster Program there is a public-private advisory board that oversees the strategic direction of the whole program, and finally, these Programs are frequently based on public development agencies that have private sector representatives in their governance structure, such as CORFO in Chile or Serviço Brasileiro de Apoio às Micro e Pequenas Empresas (SEBRAE) in Brazil.

21. It is too early to tell about its performance. However, these kinds of efforts have a long history in Brazil and have met with both success and failure.

22. They associate an income per capita level to each export good and find the associated income per capita to a country's export basket. They claim that "high-income," sophisticated exports would "pull" GDP per capita, and therefore industrial policy should aim at sophisticated exports that appear within reach.

12

The Politics of Productivity

Latin American countries have fared relatively poorly in terms of fostering productivity. Latin America's productivity has been falling compared to other benchmark countries such as the United States, and the countries of the region have not even performed well in absolute terms. Had they performed at the same level as the world's average country, countries like Argentina would be among the world's richest. Yet, most Latin American countries have fallen behind.

Previous chapters have described some of the policies that have contributed to this unfortunate path. Credit is scarce, macroeconomic volatility is high, infrastructure is lacking (and hence transportation costs are high), social expenditures and policies do not generate the right incentives in labor markets, and tax policies distort resources away from productive uses. These distortions reverberate in complementary problems such as low incentives for innovation.

Policymakers in the region are aware of many of these problems, and some attempts have been made to implement policies that would steer the economy in the right direction. However, increasing productivity is a complex endeavor that requires identifying the right policies, understanding the tradeoffs among competing objectives, having resources to implement the policies, satisfying or compensating those who would prefer other policies, and maintaining sustained efforts over several policy domains at the same time over long periods.

Despite timid attempts in some areas, the task of increasing productivity has not been a very high priority in many Latin American countries. This is partly due to the fact that some important political actors demand other policies. For some actors, certain suboptimal policies provide more direct benefits (for instance, a business sector may receive protection from competition or subsidies that hinder competition and growth by more productive firms). Other actors may have higher priorities than increasing productivity (for instance, poor people may demand social programs that may not provide the best incentives in the labor market). Against the backdrop of recurrent crises and social demands in the context of unstable democracies, country leaders have often sacrificed policy objectives with longer horizons to focus primarily on more immediate goals, such as increasing employment and helping small firms survive. Moreover, Latin American countries have relatively little freedom to pursue certain policies because budgets are highly rigid.

Even if increasing productivity were an objective, identifying the key barriers to productivity growth at the country level is a complex technical task that requires substantial capabilities. For starters, it is far from obvious how different policies in various domains will impact productivity. Moreover, in many cases it is difficult for policymakers to predict people's response to a policy. For example, designers of new taxes usually have a hard time figuring out the ways in which taxpayers may react to the taxes, which can thwart collection efforts. It is even more difficult to predict the impact certain social policies may have on labor market incentives, firm size, market structure—and eventually on growth and productivity. In addition, productivity gains usually take a long time to manifest themselves. Giving a tax break to a sector or providing a social program for a group yields an immediate benefit to the recipient. However, productivity-enhancing steps, such as investing in infrastructure, take time to complete and even more time to have an impact on the productive structure or on the degree of competition. This difference in terms of when benefits accrue makes it less politically feasible to focus on the longer run.

Even if a country makes increasing productivity a priority and has a good diagnostic of what it takes to foster productivity, difficult political challenges arise. It is necessary to work on various policy fronts, and decisions must be made and implemented that affect other policy objectives, the interests of powerful groups, or the short-term interests of political leaders themselves. Raising productivity might require unpopular measures that are at odds with other desirable policy objectives (such as raising tax revenues or assisting the poor), especially those with a higher short-term political payoff. It is difficult to sell politicians on the idea that popular initiatives such as focusing tax enforcement on large companies, providing social benefits to informal workers, and subsidizing small firms may be harmful to productivity and hence to the long-term welfare of most citizens.

Raising productivity takes a long time and a willingness to invest substantial economic and political resources. For instance, financial liberalization usually increases risks in the short term, while its potential benefits tend to accrue in the long term. "Letting some firms go," which is crucial for allocating resources in the most productive way, can hurt employment in the short term. Building an effective infrastructure network, foregoing expenditures in good times to reduce macroeconomic volatility, establishing good regulatory regimes and enforcing them across the board, and foregoing certain sources of revenues to avoid distorting incentives are all costly in the short term. Latin American countries tend to face grave short-term problems that often propel policy actions, in keeping with voter sentiment: these actions may turn out to be harmful for productivity and hence for long-term welfare.

This chapter attempts to understand why, by and large, the countries of Latin America have been unable to foster productivity. It reviews recent trends in Latin American polities, and offers observations from a political and institutional perspective consistent with the logic of the recommendations made in previous chapters. The chapter emphasizes the politics behind the policies, tempering idealized policy recommendations with a greater degree of realism, and suggests ways to build institutions that would facilitate the adoption of productivity-enhancing policies.

A Model of Policymaking

The most stylized models of political representation assume that every person's preferences are taken into account in the policymaking process, and that policies are the outcome of the institutional mechanisms that determine how each person is represented.[1] These models are made more complex by explicitly incorporating the fact that most people tend to have strong preferences about certain issues (according to their endowments and role in society) and thus might try to affect public policy in ways other than voting for their representatives.

Accordingly, how people's preferences enter into the policymaking process and how these demands convert into policies depends on several factors. First, it depends on the actor's relative clout and his ability to coordinate with people with similar interests. Does each firm, for example, try to influence policy by itself? Do firms coordinate with other firms in their sector? What type of resources do they have at their disposal?

Second, it depends on the level of aggregation of these interests and their ability to internalize the preferences of other members. Do groups coordinate across sectors? Do they coordinate across geographical areas? Do they bring a unique policy proposal and make compromises within the group, if necessary?

Third, it depends on the way these groups interact with policymakers. Does everybody have to sit at the same negotiation table? Does each group have access to different policymakers acting in different places? This is important because productivity outcomes will differ depending on whether policies are decided at a unique forum or if they are the product of multiple policies, each decided upon and implemented by different policymakers in different arenas.

Fourth, it depends on policymakers' ability to identify potential policy responses, provide venues for discussion, implement and maintain policies over time, and compensate those that oppose certain welfare-enhancing policies. These issues are explored below.

Economic and Social Actors and Their Policy Demands

Different people can demand different things from the political system.[2] Each actor's demands depend on his or her interests, which in turn derive from his or her endowments, position in the economy, and perceptions. For instance, the profitability of an industry is critical to the economic well-being of the sole owner of a specific asset crucial to that industry. Thus the owner would favor policies that increase industry-wide profitability (such as barriers to competition or subsidies to its inputs) and oppose policies that decrease industry-wide profitability (such as taxes on that good or corporate taxes in general). Unemployed workers with low skills benefit from social programs mostly in the short run. In the medium to long run, they would benefit from an improved macroeconomy that would increase employment opportunities, from training programs that increase skills, and from the removal of various inefficiencies, which would increase the demand for high productivity jobs for workers with such skills.

As these examples illustrate, the different policies that each actor may demand can be better or worse for productivity. Incumbent interests might lobby the government for policies that reduce competition in their output markets, which tends to reduce productivity, but they might also lobby for efficiency-enhancing policies in the markets for some of their inputs, such as credit, labor, telecommunications, or infrastructure.

Which of these potential demands are effectively advanced, and which actors carry more weight in the political process, will influence the policies implemented and their impact on productivity. Collective action issues are very important in determining who becomes organized and who is influential in policymaking. The more cohesively the actors are organized and the more interests they share, the more likely collective action barriers can be overcome. Other crucial determinants are the number of actors and the intensity of stakes at issue. Economic sectors that are fairly concentrated (and have few large producers), and economic interests that have more at stake from a policy, are much more likely to organize politically. For instance, owners of fairly specific assets whose value depends directly on policy decisions (such as regulated utilities with large sunk investments) are more likely candidates for political organization than those with large substitution opportunities. Some potential groups find it more difficult to organize than others and remain latent or inactive.[3]

Aggregating Policy Demands in Political Arenas

One important determinant of what types of policies are demanded is the level of aggregation and form of articulation of economic interests.[4] The types of demands pursued in the political arena will differ, for example, if business actors enter the arena individually (as firms), at the industry level (textile, metallurgic), at the sectoral level (industry, agriculture), or through economy-wide associations. In general, higher levels of association lead to more encompassing interests and demands more oriented toward improving the general business environment (such as strengthening the judicial system or providing more infrastructure or credit).

When a firm enters the political process directly, it is more likely to focus its political energy on a small number of issues (possibly one) of direct interest to that firm, such as receiving a subsidy. When a large number of firms from various sectors aggregate their interests in, say, a national business association, they first must decide internally what to demand from the public sector. That collective decision will force exchanges that are unlikely to lead the association to demand the same set of individual subsidies that firms would have demanded in isolation. In those exchanges, it is likely that externalities will be internalized, making it more likely that the association will avoid demanding policies that, while beneficial to one particular firm, distort the business sector at large.

Also, most firms tend to benefit from efficiency and productivity in markets for key inputs, such as credit, labor, and infrastructure, as well as from favorable general conditions, such as a stable macroeconomy and a well-functioning judicial system. Those potential benefits sometimes might not translate into effective political demands, since the potential beneficiaries tend to be numerous and diverse. If firms are organized for political participation at a fairly aggregate level, they are more likely to overcome such collective action barriers and be able to demand those efficiency-enhancing policies.

The level of aggregation in which different actors are organized and their interests are articulated depends on a number of factors. One is the structure of the economy. In some cases, a few large sectors can lead the collective action of the entire business sector (as used to be the case in Colombia with coffee growers).

Another is the organization of government and of official policymaking, which can affect the opportunities available to actors in the political arena. In some countries, policymaking is highly concentrated and decisions related to productivity are handled by a small, cohesive group of public officials. In that context, groups may benefit by organizing themselves in a similarly concentrated fashion. This used to be the case in Colombia, where most groups would accept the representation of a few organizations (particularly the coffee growers and the manufacturing associations). When decision making is more fragmented, either because more people have a say in policy matters or because decisions are made at a more decentralized level of government, groups may choose to influence policies in a more fragmented way (as may be the case in Colombia today) or to concentrate efforts on trying to affect policies at the local level (which seems to be the case in Brazil).

Political systems that are encompassing, in which political parties represent relevant actors well, and in which the legislative arena provides for the bargaining and enforcement of political agreements, may provide an aggregation of interests adequate to the task of promoting long-term policies, such as enhancing productivity. On the other hand, political systems that offer multiple entry points for economic interests to get benefits in different stages of the policy process may invite decentralized rent-maintenance or rent-seeking actions that are likely to damage productivity.

Stable modes of interaction between state and private actors could lead to better, long-sighted policy demands that are beneficial for productivity. Such modes are more likely to develop if both "partners" are institutionalized and can take long-term action in an environment of high trust. Countries that have a limited ability to pursue consistent policy objectives over time tend to lack stable interactions and generate little incentive for institutionalization (which seems to be the case in some countries like Argentina).

States vary in their capacity to accommodate conflicting demands. Some polities are able to weight different interests appropriately and to enforce the agreed-upon decisions in a consistent and effective manner over time. Other polities tend to engage in a balkanized struggle on various issues, in which different actors secure bits of benefits through different venues and at different stages of the policy process.[5] The tendency in many Latin American countries has been toward such balkanized struggles, with large business actors[6] obtaining privileged policies through their access to the executive or the bureaucracy, unionized workers maintaining distortive labor and welfare benefits through electoral and mobilization strategies, and displaced workers who have turned to the informal economy, obtaining targeted social programs and small-firm benefits using a mix of public sympathy and newly found mobilization strategies such as road blocks (see Box 12.1).

The Incentives of Politicians, State Capabilities, and Public Policies

Policies are decided in public arenas such as congress, subnational layers of government, the bureaucracy, and the judiciary. These arenas are populated by a number of state actors or professional politicians, including presidents, party leaders, legislators, governors, bureaucrats, and judges. The incentives of public officials, as well as a number of state capabilities necessary to perform certain essential functions,[7] are key determinants of which policies are politically and technically feasible and sustainable. They even condition which types of political demands private actors will pursue. (These actors will not demand policies that they believe are unlikely to materialize.)

Politicians and government officials should be interested in increasing the productivity of the economy since that will generate desirable long-term outcomes for society as a whole. Whether they actually pursue such policies as a priority depends on a number of factors that vary across countries and over time, such as the transparency of the policymaking and political process, the level and quality of information on public opinion,[8] their disposition to cater to special interests or the general interest, and their incentives to prioritize short-term political payoffs versus long-term welfare outcomes.

As noted, effectively pursuing productivity-enhancing policies requires substantial state capabilities. These include the ability to maintain stable policies over time in order for the private sector to invest and innovate according to credible commitments by the government; the capability to change policies when they are failing and adapt them to changing economic circumstances; and the capacity to coordinate policies across various domains, such as various economic and social policies, taking into consideration the cross effects.

Politicians' incentives and state capabilities depend on a number of features of political institutions and of the political system: for example, whether political party systems are institutionalized; whether they are programmatic or clientelistic; whether the policy space is national in orientation or fragmented into local bailiwicks; whether national legislatures

Box 12.1   Trying to Help but Getting It Wrong: The Political Economy of Social Protection in Latin America[a]

In most countries in Latin America, targeted social programs are implemented in a decentralized way, which provides local governments with great opportunities to use social resources as instruments of clientelism.[b] From the viewpoint of politicians, the shift from welfare states centered on the labor market to targeted programs has made local political arenas more attractive, leading to the increased fragmentation of public arenas.

The fragmentation of policymaking in various policy venues and the lack of integrated strategies induce peculiar dynamics. Different actors get their benefits through different venues on different policy domains. For instance, labor unions are the most vocal players in labor-market policies. Given their political clout, they are able to sustain regulations in the labor market that may cause rigidities and lower employment, particularly for certain groups such as the unskilled (IDB 2004). In contrast, those who may be affected negatively by labor regulations (such as the unemployed) tend to have a weaker presence in that political arena. As regulations become more distortive, it may become harder for displaced workers to return to the formal sector, making it more difficult for them to regain political clout in labor-policy discussions. As displaced workers end up working in the informal sector, they have fewer incentives to organize to change formal labor-market policies. They may, however, organize to gain benefits related to their new role in the economy as informal workers, such as noncontributory social programs and microcredit.

Ultimately, the economy may end up with a set of suboptimal policies. Those with strong positions in favor of labor regulations and power in the

(continued on next page)

have strong policymaking capabilities and legislators have long horizons; whether judiciaries are independent or subservient to the government of the day; and whether civil service systems are well-developed and professionalized or are dependent upon political strings held by the government in power.[9]

Environments characterized by low capabilities will usually not be conducive to demands that would raise productivity. Because making demands on the government is costly (at least in terms of the opportunity cost of demanding something else), private actors will demand only those

(continued)

labor market may achieve policies that favor their situation, while those who are hurt in the labor market and move toward self-employment and informality tend to ask for social and redistributive policies. Hence, instead of discussions being held about the right degree of labor regulation between those who benefit and those who lose, each group demands inefficient policies in different political arenas (IDB 2008b).

All these tendencies are reinforced by the difficulties that most polities have in facing the complex tradeoffs of reforming Latin American social protection systems: tradeoffs that are not popular with the public. Without much information and without credible reforms on various fronts at the same time, few people would support the idea of eliminating noncontributory social programs. Thus, a vicious cycle ensues. Each time there is a new emergency, additional programs are demanded. Many politicians find it easier to add a new program than push for an integral reform of the system. Even though some countries have been able to finance these programs—thanks to higher revenues from higher commodity prices—they could eventually face a problem of long-term sustainability, especially given the low productivity this practice engenders.

[a] This box draws in part on Saavedra and Tommasi (2007) and references there, as well as from Levy (2008).
[b] See Gruenberg and Pereyra Iraola (2009) and discussions on Argentina (Auyero, 2000; Brusco, Nazareno, and Stokes, 2004); Brazil (Gay, 1998); Colombia (Martz, 1996); Mexico (Díaz-Cayeros, Estévez, and Magaloni, 2006); and Venezuela (Penfold-Becerra, 2006).

policies with a high probability of being approved and implemented. Imagine an interest group deciding whether to join similar interests in press for the construction of a port or for the implementation of a consistent strategy of facilitating long-term foreign market access or whether to demand a policy that could deliver immediate benefits with little long-term effort, such as receiving a subsidy or a tax exemption. If the government does not have the credibility to bring to fruition such long-term, productivity-enhancing policies, interest groups may end up demanding policies that deliver quick and more certain benefits for them, even though they produce much worse results for productivity (see Box 12.2).

Box 12.2   How Policymaking Capabilities Affect the Demand for Policies: The Case of Credit

Firms need credit to invest and grow (see Chapter 6). Improving the conditions that allow credit to flow more vigorously may have a particularly high payoff in Latin America, especially in countries that are more dependent on credit, given their economic structure.

The availability of credit depends on many policies, including banking policies, creditors' rights, and macroeconomic management (IDB 2004); ultimately, it depends as much on the soundness of macroeconomic policy as on the regulations that deal with property rights. Therefore, increasing credit depends on the government being able to identify the various policies and their impact on productivity, implement those policies, sustain them over time, and adjust them appropriately. Credit policies also require the ability to manage tradeoffs over time, including those stemming from the short-term costs and long-term benefits of measures such as financial liberalization. The empirical analysis performed in the background work for this study indicates that countries with better policymaking capabilities are able to foster better credit policies (see Table 12.1).

Not only are government capabilities a relevant factor, but the strength of the preferences of the economic agents and their relative weight on policy issues matters, too. Thus, credit should be more easily available in those economies where there is more demand for

(continued on next page)

Policymaking, Policies, and Productivity in Various Latin American Countries

As noted in previous chapters, policies in various policy areas are an important factor in understanding productivity performance. Table 12.1 summarizes indicators of the quality and appropriateness of policies for 21 countries of the region in various policy areas identified as important for productivity. The countries have been ordered according to their ranking in the policymaking capabilities index. This index, which comes from Berkman et al. (2008), classifies countries' polities in terms of key policy features such as high stability, high adaptability, high coordination, and high public regardedness, features that enable countries to change policies when needed yet keep them constant when economic conditions do not warrant change, to coordinate policies across sectors and levels of government, and to avoid favoring particular groups.

(continued)

credit-related policies by relevant economic sectors. Those countries where the main business sectors are highly dependent on credit are the ones that would potentially gain the most from increased credit availability. In those countries, governments might reap great benefits from sponsoring those policies because of their long-term impact on aggregate welfare. Moreover, the large sectors that would benefit from the policies would also have an interest in lobbying the government to implement policies that would increase credit in the economy. Given that requesting these policies has a cost (lobbies, campaign contributions, and the like), interest groups would demand them only if there is a good chance that the government can fulfill its promises. Thus, both should occur together: capable governments and economic sectors interested in demanding higher credit.

The empirical evidence is consistent with this reasoning. Becerra, Cavallo, and Scartascini (2009) proxy for the potential demand for credit using an index that weights the share of each manufacturing sector according to its credit dependency ratio (from Rajan and Zingales 1998). The results, using a large sample of countries for over 40 years, show that this index is significant to explain credit availability only in those countries with high policymaking capabilities. That is, high demand for credit translates into higher actual credit only in those cases in which governments are able to provide it.

The table shows that countries with high capabilities tend to also score high in the quality of their public policies, as reported in the Global Competitiveness Report (World Economic Forum, various years) and compiled in Mecikovsky, Scartascini, and Tommasi (2009).

As argued in this chapter, better quality policies in these areas are associated with higher growth of total factor productivity (TFP). Figure 12.1 confirms that positive relationship for a large sample of world countries using an index that compiles the quality of the individual policy areas reported in Table 12.1.[10] Looking only at the Latin American cases, which are highlighted in gray, it is obvious that not only does the positive relationship hold, but also that countries in the region generally have worse policies and lower TFP growth than most of the other countries in the world.

As noted, the ability of a polity to deliver successful policies in these productivity-enhancing domains depends on a number of policymaking capabilities including stability, adaptability, and coordination. Figure 12.2

Table 12.1 Policymaking Capabilities and the Quality of Public Policies

Country	Policymaking capabilities index	Credit index	Neutrality of tax system	Neutrality of government subsidies	Ease of registering start-ups	Efforts to improve competitiveness	Formal sector	Infrastructure index
Chile	*Very High*	Very High	High	Very High	High	High	Very High	Very High
Brazil		High	Low	Very High	Medium	High	Low	High
Uruguay		Medium	Low	Medium	Medium	Medium	Medium	High
Mexico	*High*	Low	High	High	Low	Low	Low	High
Colombia		High	Low	High	Low	High	High	Medium
Costa Rica		Medium	High	Medium	Medium	High	Medium	Medium
Jamaica		Medium	Medium	Medium	High	High	Low	High
Trinidad and Tobago		Very High	Very High	High	Very High	High	High	High
El Salvador		Medium	Very High	High	High	High	Low	Very High
Peru		Medium	Medium	Very High	Low	Low	Low	Medium
Panama		Very High	Medium	Medium	High	Low	High	High
Argentina	*Medium*	Low	Low	Medium	Medium	Low	Medium	High
Bolivia	*Low*	Low	Medium	Medium	Low	Low	Low	Low
Honduras		Medium	Medium	Low	Low	Medium	Medium	Medium
Dominican Republic		Medium	Low	Medium	High	Low	Low	High
Ecuador		Low	Medium	Low	Low	Low	Medium	Medium
Nicaragua		Low	Low	Medium	Low	Medium	Medium	Low
Venezuela		Medium	Medium	Low	Low	Low	Medium	Medium
Haiti				Low	Low		Low	Low
Paraguay		Medium	Very High	Low	Medium	Low	Low	Low
Guatemala		Medium	High	Low	Medium	Medium	Low	Medium

Source: Authors' calculations with data from Mecikovsky, Scartascini, and Tommasi (2010) and Berkman et al. (2008).

Note: The categories "Very High," "High," "Medium," and "Low" correspond to the quartiles in the distribution computed for the sample of developing countries.

The policymaking capabilities index corresponds to the policy index in Berkman et al. (2008).

Figure 12.1   Quality of Public Policies and TFP Growth

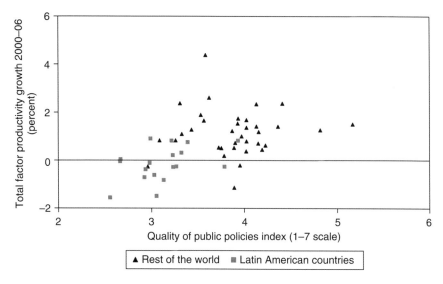

Source: Authors' calculations.

Note: TFP growth is based on data from Daude and Fernández-Arias (2010). Quality of public policies uses a scale based on a policy index from Mecikovsky, Scartascini, and Tommasi (2010).

Figure 12.2   Policymaking Capabilities and the Quality of Public Policies

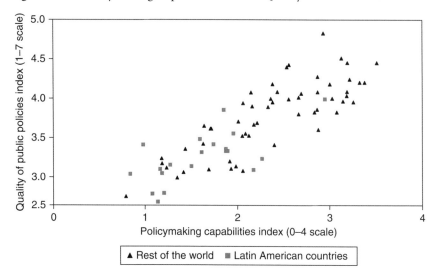

Source: Authors' calculations.

Note: Quality of public policies uses a scale based on a policy index from Mecikovsky, Scartascini, and Tommasi (2010). Policymaking capabilities uses a scale based on a policy index from Berkman et al. (2008).

plots the index of the qualities of the policies that are important for productivity against the index of policymaking capabilities, constructed for Latin American countries (in gray) in IDB (2005) and expanded for a wider cross-section of countries in Scartascini, Stein, and Tommasi (2009). The cross-country evidence in Figure 12.2 is consistent with the evidence for Latin American countries (in gray in the figure), which is reflected in more detail in Table 12.1, where countries are ordered by policymaking capabilities. Countries with higher capabilities tend to have better policies in almost every policy area.

As discussed earlier in this chapter and documented in IDB (2005) for Latin America and in Scartascini, Stein, and Tommasi (2009) for a wider sample of countries, these policy capabilities, in turn, are the outcome of the workings of political institutions such as congress, the party system, the bureaucracy, and the judiciary. These findings are confirmed in detailed case studies for a number of Latin American countries in Stein et al. (2008). The remainder of this section explores some differences in such institutions and in their policy capabilities within Latin America.[11]

Only a few countries in the region have been able to create the conditions in their public sector, and in its interaction with private and social actors, to develop stable and programmatic arrangements that are more likely to foster productivity. Chile is the one country that fits most of these requirements (and it is the country with the highest productivity growth in the last couple of decades). Some countries like Colombia used to have several of those conditions in place, but have been moving in the wrong direction (and so has productivity growth). Other countries such as Brazil have some of these elements in place, but not others (and it has a mix of successes and problems in line with its strengths and weaknesses). Still other countries such as Argentina seem to be missing most of those conditions, and with rare exceptions, have fared quite poorly recently. Other countries such as Bolivia have made some progress in institution building and in increasing productivity, but some of the weaknesses of their polities (such as the lack of inclusiveness) have backfired and put them on a track that bodes poorly for productivity.

Chile enjoys the highest value for almost every measure of policymaking capability (IDB 2005) including stability, adaptability, implementation, enforcement, and coordination.[12] Such effective policies are the outcome of the Chilean way of making policy with a fair degree of consensus, after debates and negotiations with adequate attention to technical input in well-institutionalized arenas. Political and policy exchanges are credible. Congress is an important arena both politically and technically;[13] political parties and coalitions are programmatic and institutionalized; its bureaucracy is quite capable by regional standards; and the judiciary is independent. Business participation in the policymaking process is well-institutionalized; business associations are quite capable and involved in policy discussion at a fairly high level of aggregation. That articulation and aggregation allow business actors to focus mainly on general demands beneficial for business in general, as opposed to pursuing particularistic benefits. In recent decades—particularly during the integration processes—close policy networks have evolved between public officials and business representatives, premised on mutual recognition of expertise in the public and private sector, and held together by close personal networks of loyalty and trust across the partisan and private-public divides (Bull 2008).

This ability of the Chilean polity to implement efficient political exchanges has been the foundation of a number of measures that have fostered high productivity levels. These include providing a stable macroeconomic environment; good credit policies; effective trade, regulation, and anti-trust policies; a relatively undistorted tax subsidy system; as well as other policies that have facilitated one of the lowest levels of informality in the region.[14]

Argentina, a country with structural similarities to its Southern Cone neighbor, has a weaker policymaking system, which negatively affects the quality of its policies (Table 12.1). The main factors leading to low-productivity growth in Argentina tend to relate to the instability and lack of credibility of its policy framework. Each new administration tends to replace the policies of its predecessor. These policy features, in turn, are a reflection of policymaking institutions and practices. A weak national congress, populated by transient legislators who tend to respond to the interests of provincial governors who are mostly interested in receiving fiscal financing from the center, together with a judiciary that has not evolved toward greater independence, leave the executive of the day with too much leeway to unilaterally push an agenda based more on short-term political considerations than on any long-term programmatic agreement.[15] The high volatility of the policymaking environment is mirrored in the short-term strategies of socioeconomic actors, such as business, unions, or social movements, all of which seek short-term benefits in a decentralized manner.

Colombia was a country characterized by a strong articulation of business actors (allied behind the coffee growers' federation) in the policymaking process, connected with the overall bipartisan political arrangement of the *Frente Nacional* era. This, together with the high quality of the economic bureaucracy, gave Colombia a rather compact outlook on economic policymaking, with achievements such as the best macroeconomic record in the region for decades, as well as various other consistent long-term productivity strategies. That political and economic model had various limitations, which over the last couple of decades have been addressed by a number of economic and political reforms. The economic reforms helped to diversify the economy (Olivera, Pachón, and Perry 2009) and the political reforms promoted inclusion in the political system. Yet those very same reforms had some (plausibly) unintended consequences of weakening the institutionality of economic policymaking, which casts some shadows on the ability of Colombia to increase productivity.

The end of the bipartisan agreement challenged the common practices between the private sector and the government. The economic conglomerates exercised ever greater power in their relationship with the president given their capacity and will to finance national political campaigns (Rettberg 2001, 2005). Because of these various political and economic changes, members of the private sector—who previously lobbied through business associations—decided to diversify their strategy to influence members of congress. Although pressure groups continue to collectively pressure the government on economic policy decisions, individual businesses now fund the campaigns of individual legislators. This way, specific businesses can intervene with help from their legislator to add exemptions or other favorable conditions to the policy mix.[16] This fragmentation of the policymaking process has led to a relative paralysis in broad productivity-enhancing reforms, as well as a proliferation of special particularistic policies.[17]

In Mexico, the main problems with productivity seem to stem from high prices and inefficient provision of services in some sectors, such as telecommunications, together with fairly distortive labor, social, and credit policies. Those productivity-reducing policies are the outcome of a policymaking process in which desirable reforms cannot be approved (due to the veto of affected interests in an increasingly fragmented legislature), and in which many big business players, privileged unions, and social actors obtain different benefits in various policy domains and institutional venues. Some big businesses secure privileges thanks to special access to legislators, and special treatment from the bureaucracy or an overburdened and poorly equipped judicial system. At the same time, some privileged unions resist badly needed labor and welfare reforms with a mix of legislative vetoes and direct action. Meanwhile, marginalized groups benefit from focused social programs, subsidies directed toward small firms, and the asymmetric enforcement of tax and labor laws. Public opinion does not object to these benefits because they seem to help the neediest and the long-term costs are not easily identifiable. At this time, there is no socioeconomic or political actor who truly understands the benefits of a productivity agenda enough to push for it.

Brazil's policymaking process enjoys some positive characteristics including the executive's good incentives for supporting policies with long-term benefits, its capacity to pursue its agenda through exchanges in congress, and the long standing professionalism of key areas of the public administration; these characteristics have led to a number of policies favorable to productivity, such as a stable macroeconomic environment, improved access to credit, and consistent trade policies. On the other hand, other aspects of the Brazilian political environment, and the rigidity imposed by constitutional spending mandates, may be impeding some policy reforms necessary to bolster productivity. Presidents in Brazil can design their policies with less opposition from adversaries and interest groups than in other Latin American countries. This independence helps keep finances under control and encourages some good macroeconomic policies. On the other hand, it may make it more difficult to ease some of the constraints on the economy that depend on decisions at lower levels of governments. For example, it may affect the ability to reform the tax system, forestall infrastructure projects, and make it easier for interest groups to have access to individual benefits at the state level.

In Bolivia, the economic reforms of the 1980s and 1990s had a positive impact on productivity, but they favored capital-intensive sectors, geographically concentrated in some regions of the country. Decentralization and other participatory political reforms favored the mobilization of grassroots movements of social sectors that felt excluded from the reform policies. In the end, two good things (productivity-enhancing economic reforms and political reforms to increase participation at the local level) have combined in a peculiar dynamic leading to a political backlash against those economic policies. The current situation is very uncertain. Even though inclusion has increased, it has so far occurred in a way that is leading to policies and a political situation that are very adverse for future economic development.

Improving the Odds for Productive Policies

As noted in previous chapters, productivity in Latin America is hindered by the lack of credit, macroeconomic volatility, high transport costs, distorted labor market incentives, fragmented social policy, discriminatory tax enforcement, and a dearth of adequate productive development policies. Identifying the key obstacles for productivity growth in a given country is easier than implementing a coherent set of policies to address them. Even recognizing productivity as a policy priority requires some nontrivial policymaking capabilities. The policy changes necessary to unlock productivity are sometimes difficult to sell to the public, as they entail short-term sacrifices and require substantial resources. Implementing such policies demands articulation in a number of different policy domains, as well as broad public-private cooperation.

Unfortunately, most Latin American polities lack precisely the capabilities required to implement such complex policy objectives. Not all countries face the same policy challenges, and not all countries share the same institutional configurations: ones that may facilitate or impede productivity enhancement. Thus, no universal policy or institutional recommendation can be made. Nonetheless, this chapter closes by identifying some political and institutional considerations to take into account to improve policy and enhance productivity.

Sharpen the focus on productivity in public discussions. While other policies and objectives, including the need to increase growth and improve competitiveness, are often discussed, productivity is usually not the focus of public and political debate. Just recognizing the role of productivity in generating other desirable outcomes may prove useful for improving policy discussion and policy demands, and may help channel resources toward studying and implementing pro-productivity policies.

Build sustainable consensus to orient policy for the long term. Crises have sometimes been used as a window of opportunity to sidestep difficulties and opposition and to overstate the benefits of reforms. While these strategies might help policy implementation in the short term, they do not help build cooperation and long-term credibility. Unless the reforms deliver at least as much as promised, they may generate a backlash against those and future reforms—as has happened in Latin America.[18]

Increase information about the allocation and long-term effects of various policies. The possibility of agreeing on a productivity agenda may depend on understanding the issue at hand, identifying the benefits and costs in the short and long term, and identifying the tradeoffs of different policies. For example, unless the long-term benefits are adequately understood, most people would find it hard to accept that "letting some firms go" can make sense as a policy objective.

Try to bring private actors into the productivity discussion in an encompassing manner. Individual business actors should be represented by fairly encompassing associations, so that they represent aggregate business interests and move beyond lobbying for sectoral or firm-specific benefits.

Strengthen private sector capabilities. If private sector associations were more capable, they might be able to help political actors design better policies and cope with conflicts within the group. Moreover, stronger and more capable associations might reduce dependence on the government to solve their problems as associations themselves become able to provide certain public goods, such as coordination of private activities.

Invest in those government capabilities that make the state more credible and more focused on the long-term consequences of current actions. Increasing the horizons of actors and encouraging cooperation has second-order effects and might create virtuous cycles. As actors become more interested in the long run, they have incentives to invest in their capabilities and in those of agencies and actors with whom they interact. For example, legislators who plan to stay in the legislature longer have greater incentives to invest in themselves and to invest in legislative institutions that would make their work easier and more efficient, such as advisory commissions. In addition, having stable and independent bodies may increase the credibility of promises. Institutions such as an independent judiciary are fundamental for this endeavor.

Turn to multilateral development banks and international aid agencies to add credibility to difficult policies. Credibility is one of the anchors of good policymaking and one of the main deficiencies in Latin America. Policies change regularly, political actors are highly unstable, and opportunities have been seized by those in power to grant benefits to particular factions. Solutions, such as the creation of funds and projects managed by independent agencies, could be developed domestically. But countries can also look to external organizations to add credibility to facilitate political transactions. For example, the multilateral development banks or similar organizations could take a role in compensating the losers of certain reforms or in sustaining the independence of some agencies or programs.

Keep in mind the possible consequences of policy reforms on the political game. Several policy and institutional reforms undertaken in Latin America, while beneficial in and of themselves, might have sown the seeds of undesirable political developments that, in turn, might be generating problems, including low productivity. For instance, the decentralization of the state and the clientelistic targeting of social programs (see Box 12.2) may have contributed to political fragmentation and to the weakening of centripetal institutional forces such as institutionalized party systems and aggregated modes of interest representation. This fragmentation is weakening the capacity of some Latin American polities to keep the big picture and the long term in mind, with negative impacts on productivity.

It is vital that governments and all the other actors involved in the political process in Latin America and the Caribbean keep this big picture and the long term in their sights as they discuss their policy agendas. Moreover, they must view political and economic reforms through not only the narrow lens of their individual interests but in light of their repercussions on productivity as well. The people of the region have paid dearly for the low productivity that has stunted the growth of their economies. It is time to highlight this issue in the policy debate. It is time to design policies aimed specifically at stimulating productivity. It is time to lay the foundations for sustainable growth and prosperity and usher in The Age of Productivity.

Notes

1. Basic economic models of policymaking are presented in excellent textbook treatments such as Persson and Tabellini (2000); Drazen (2000); and Mueller (2003).
2. The founding reference on economic and social actors and their policy demands is Olson (1965). Important recent treatments are provided in Grossman and Helpman (2001); Frieden (1991, 2000); and references there.
3. Moreover, various economic interests have alternative channels of attempting to influence collective decisions. In democracies, most people have the vote as an instrument of influence, but some actors have access to additional means of influence, such as money, swaying public opinion, or physical mobilization. Some privileged business actors have the sympathetic ear of key decision makers, including the president, through a number of exchange channels with various degrees of transparency. Certain segments of the population, such as unionized workers and some social movements, possess special mobilization capabilities that can be utilized to press for favorable policies.
4. On aggregation of interests and its determinants see Olson (1982) and Schneider (2004, 2010), as well as the chapters in Maxfield and Schneider (1997) and in Durand and Silva (1998) for business, and in Collier and Collier (1991) for labor.
5. Kahn and Jomo (2000) provide an account of policymaking in Asia that looks at the interrelationship among business, the bureaucracy, and politicians and presents a similar picture of contrasting systems with encompassing interest articulation and multiple entry points.
6. These large business actors include individual firms that dominate policy-dependent sectors, conglomerates (known as *grupos económicos*), and even individuals that own some of these firms or conglomerates.
7. A particularly good list of state capabilities has been drawn up by Weaver and Rockman (1993).
8. A number of factors condition the relationship between voters and politicians (and hence the relative weight of long-term, welfare-enhancing policies), that relate to the ability of voters to understand the effects of policies on outcomes of interest. As discussed in the 2009 edition of Development in the Americas,

Beyond Facts: Understanding Quality of Life (IDB 2008b), citizens often are not well informed about the welfare effects of policies. That is even more likely when such effects are indirect and involve rather complex general equilibrium effects, as is the case with several policies discussed in this chapter. This, then, adds additional importance to the capabilities and incentives of the political system, to put together and market politically acceptable policy packages that are beneficial in the long term.

9. IDB (2005) provides an analysis of the connections between the workings of political institutions and the characteristics of resulting policy capabilities for the case of Latin America. Stein et al. (2008) provides detailed case studies for a number of Latin American countries, confirming these results. Scartascini, Stein, and Tommasi (2009) explore those connections for a larger number of countries across the globe. Countries also differ in the degree to which they solve conflicts in institutionalized arenas. Scartascini and Tommasi (2009) and Trucco (2009) look at the multiarena mobilization strategies of different political actors and the use of alternative political techniques such as bribes and road blocks.

10. The index was constructed by calculating the simple averages using observations with no missing data. Neutrality of government subsidies was excluded because it contained too few observations. Each component was averaged over the years according to availability.

11. This section is based largely on a number of country case studies undertaken for this project. The studies are available at http://www.iadb.org/res/projects_detail.cfm?id=5611.

12. This is confirmed in qualitative studies of a number of specific policy areas. Tax reforms in Chile have been characterized as "reform by consensus" leading to one of the least distorted tax systems in Latin America (Bergman 2003). Public utility privatization and regulation has been characterized as "institutional consistency and stable results" in Chile, in contrast to "institutional weakness and volatile results" in Argentina (Bergara and Pereyra 2005). Similarly, with regard to international trade policy, Aggarwal, Espach, and Tulchin (2004) contrast Chile (and Mexico and Brazil) with Argentina, which is the only one of the four countries that "does not have a commercial strategy, since neither the state nor the private sector can resolve the dissidences among actors."

13. The Chilean congress has the longest tenure in Latin America, and personal expertise among legislators translates into institutional expertise (Montecinos 2003; Saiegh forthcoming).

14. Areas that need attention include modifying some aspects of the education system, as well as improving corporate governance legislation. Aninat et al. (2009) identify these unreformed areas as the outcome of the interests of some actors that are overrepresented at some margins of the (otherwise effective) political party system.

15. The actual state of policymaking oscillates between two phases, one of an overpowerful executive imposing his or her agenda by distributing fiscal largesse

to the provinces, and another of a declining executive with insufficient fiscal resources who is unable to impose any agenda on recalcitrant governors, who is just concerned with trying to become the next president.

16. "For individual legislators, these relationships with individual businesses represent a good bargain. Since their campaign funding mostly would be a function of their own individual effort, the willingness of the private sector became an important funding source. Consequently, the constant fragmentation of political competition made congressmen lobby the private sector" (Olivera, Pachón, and Perry, 2009).

17. The study on Colombia by Eslava and Meléndez (2009) presents an additional reason why policies with concentrated benefits are now relatively more important: the internal conflict prevalent in the country. Substantial amounts of aid in the form of subsidies and tax incentives have been targeted to economic activities in an attempt to keep the guerrillas at bay in particular regions, without much regard as to whether this aid is beneficial or detrimental to aggregate productivity. This is an extreme example of the point that other policy objectives can override productivity considerations.

18. In countries in which society has been brought to the brink of violence and breakdown because of fragmentation and polarization, the first order of business is to create consensus on some more basic objectives and modes of interaction; then productivity can enter into the picture in a sustainable way.

References

ACI (Airports Council International). 2004. *Airport Economics Survey, 2004.* Geneva, Switzerland: Airports Council International.

———. 2008. *Airport Economics Survey,* 2008. Geneva, Switzerland: Airports Council International.

Agapitova, N., L. Holm-Nielsen, and G. Vukmirovic. 2002. Science and Technology in Colombia: Status and Perspectives. LCSHD (Latin America and Caribbean Social and Human Development) Paper Series. Washington, DC: World Bank.

Aggarwal, V., R. Espach, and J. Tulchin. 2004. *The Strategic Dynamics of Latin American Trade.* Stanford, CA: Stanford University Press.

Aghion, P., G. Angeletos, A. Banerjee, and K. Manova. 2005. Volatility and Growth: Credit Constraints and Productivity-Enhancing Investment. NBER Working Paper 11349. Cambridge, MA: National Bureau of Economic Research.

Agnew, J., L. Szykman, S. Utkus, and J. Young. 2007. Literacy, Trust and 401(k) Savings Behavior. Working Paper 2007-10. Boston, MA: Center for Retirement Research, Boston College.

Agosin, M. R., C. Acevedo, and A. Ulloa. 2009. Política industrial en El Salvador. Unpublished document. Washington, DC: Research Department, Inter-American Development Bank.

Agosin, M. R., and C. Bravo-Ortega. 2009. The Emergence of Successful New Export Activities in Latin America: The Case of Chile. Research Network Working Paper #R-552. Washington, DC: Latin American Research Network, Inter-American Development Bank.

Agosin, M. R., and J. J. Price. 2009. La inversión extranjera: ¿Hacia una nueva política industrial? El Programa de Atracción de Inversiones de Alta Tecnología. Document prepared for CORFO, unpublished. Chile.

Agosin, M. R., N. Grau, and C. Larraín. 2009. Industrial Policy in Chile. Draft for the Project on Industrial Policies in Latin America and the Caribbean. Unpublished document. Washington, DC: Latin American Research Network, Inter-American Development Bank.

Aguion, P. 2007 Growth and the Financing and Governance of Higher Education. Keynote lecture for the 2007 Meeting of the German Economic Association. Unpublished document. Berlin, Germany.

Alejo, J., M. Alzúa, G. Cruces, L. Gasparini, A. Ham, S. Oliveiri, L. Ripani, and M. Viollaz. 2009. Labor Supply Responses to Cash Transfer Programs: Experimental and Non-experimental Evidence from Latin America. Unpublished document. Washington, DC: Inter-American Development Bank and CEDLAS Universidad Nacional de la Plata.

Alesina, A., S. Ardagna, R. Perotti, and F. Schiantarelli. 2002. Fiscal Policy, Profits, and Investment. *American Economic Review* 92(3): 571–89.

Almeida, R., and P. Carneiro. 2005. Enforcement of Regulation, Informal Labor and Firm Performance. IZA Discussion Paper 1759. Bonn, Germany: Institute for the Study of Labor.

Álvarez, R., and R. López. 2005. Exporting and Performance: Evidence from Chilean Plants. *Canadian Journal of Economics* 38(4): 1385–400.

Alves de Mendonça, M. A., F. Freitas, and J. M. de Souza. 2008. Information Technology and Productivity: Evidence for Brazilian Industry from Firm-level Data. *Information Technology for Development* 14(2): 136–53.

Amsden, A. H. 1989. *Asia's Next Giant: South Korea and Late Industrialization.* London: Oxford University Press.

Anderson, J., and E. van Wincoop. 2004. Trade Costs. *Journal of Economic Literature* 42(3): 691–751.

ANII (Agencia Nacional de Investigación e Innovación). 2004–2006. III Encuesta de Actividades de Innovación en la Industria Uruguaya. http://www.anii.org.uy/Imagenes/Encuesta_Innovacion_servicios_2004_2006.pdf (accessed July 2009).

Aninat, C., J. M. Benavente, I. Briones, N. Eyzaguirre, P. Navia, and J. Olivari. 2009. The Political Economy of Productivity. The Case of Chile. Unpublished document. Washington, DC: Research Department, Inter-American Development Bank.

Anlló, G., and D. Suárez. 2009. Innovación: Algo más que I+D. Evidencias Ibeoramericanas a partir de las encuestas de innovación: Construyendo las estrategias empresarias competitivas. Unpublished document. Buenos Aires: CEPAL-REDES.

ANTP (Associação Nacional de Transportes Públicos). 1999. Estudio de deseconomías del transporte urbano en Brasil: los impactos de la congestión. *Boletín de los Transportes Públicos de la América Latina.* Year 5, No. 30, São Paulo.

Arbeláez, M. A. 2009. Innovation, R&D Investment and Productivity in Latin American and Caribbean Firms: The Colombian Case. Unpublished document. Washington, DC: Latin American and Caribbean Research Network, Inter-American Development Bank.

Arbeláez, M. A., N. Leon, and O. Becerra. 2009a. Informality and Productivity in Colombia. Unpublished document. Washington, DC: Research Department, Inter-American Development Bank.

———. 2009b. Understanding Productivity Levels, Dispersion and Growth in the Hotel Sector. Unpublished document. Washington, DC: Research Department, Inter-American Development Bank.

Arellano, C. 2009. Productivity Levels, Dispersion and Growth in Ecuador. Washington, DC: Unpublished document. Washington, DC: Research Department, Inter-American Development Bank.

Arenas de Mesa, A., G. Bravo, J. Behrman, O. Mitchell, and P. Todd. 2006. The Chilean Pension Reform Turns 25: Lessons from the Social Protection Survey. Working Paper No. 12401. Cambridge, MA: National Bureau of Economic Research (NBER).

Arias, L. A. 2009. Regimenes tributarios simplificados para pequeños contribuyentes. Unpublished document. Washington, DC: Research Department, Inter-American Development Bank.

Arias, O., and M. Bustelo. 2007. Profiles and Dynamics of Informal Employment in Latin America. Unpublished document. Washington, DC: World Bank.

Arias, O., F. Landa, and P. Yáñez. 2007. Movilidad Laboral e Ingresos en el sector Formal e Informal en Bolivia. Working Paper. La Paz, Bolivia: Unidad de Análisis de Políticas Sociales y Económicas (UDAPE).

Arizala. F., E. A. Cavallo, and A. Galindo. 2009. Financial Development and TFP Growth: Cross Country and Industry Level Evidence. Working Paper 682. Washington, DC: Research Department, Inter-American Development Bank.

Artana, D., S. Auguste, and A. Downes. 2009a. Productive development policies in Barbados. Draft for the Project on Industrial Policies in Latin America and the Caribbean. Unpublished document. Washington, DC: Research Department, Inter-American Development Bank.

———. 2009b. Productive Development Policies in Jamaica. Draft for the Project on Industrial Policies in Latin America and the Caribbean. Unpublished document. Washington, DC: Research Department, Inter-American Development Bank.

Arza, V. 2008. ¿Cómo influye el contexto macroeconómico en el comportamiento de largo plazo de las empresas? Decisiones empresariales de inversión en I+D y en maquinaria en Argentina durante los años 1990s. *Desarrollo Económico* 47 (187): 459–84.

Arza, V., and A. López. 2009. Innovation and Productivity in the Argentine Manufacturing Sector. Unpublished document. Washington, DC: Latin American and Caribbean Research Network, Inter-American Development Bank.

Atal, J., M. Busso, and C. Cisneros. 2009. Productivity and Misallocation: The Case of El Salvador. Unpublished document. Washington, DC: Research Department, Inter-American Development Bank.

Atal, J., J. Behrman, J. Cuesta, L. Madrigal, H. Ñopo, and C. Pagés. 2009. Informalidad, Protección Social y Alfabetización Financiera en Perú. Unpublished document. Washington, DC: Inter-American Development Bank.

Auerbach, P., M. E. Genoni, and C. Pagés. 2007. Social Security Coverage and the Labor Market in Developing Countries. IZA Discussion Paper No 2979. Bonn, Germany: Institute for the study of Labor (IZA).

Auyero, J. 2000. *Poor People's Politics.* Durham, NC: Duke University Press.

Avalos, I. 2002. El Programa de Agendas de Investigación como intento de asociar a los tres sectores: Experiencias en Venezuela. Unpublished document. Washington, DC: Inter-America Development Bank.

Ayyagari, M., T. Beck, and A. Demirgüç-Kunt. 2007. Small and Medium Enterprises across the Globe. *Small Business Economics* 29:415–34.

Báez, V., M. C. Capelo, R. Centeno, and R. Estrada. 2009. Industrial Policy in Mexico. Draft for the Project on Industrial Policies in Latin America and the Caribbean. Unpublished document. Washington, DC: Research Department, Inter-American Development Bank.

Bagehot, W. 1873. *Lombard Street: A Description of the Money Market.*London, England: Henry S. King.

Baldwin, R. E. 2000. Regulatory Protectionism, Developing Nations, and a Two-Tier World Trade System. *Brooking Trade Forum* 2000:237–93.

Banerjee, A., and E. Duflo. 2005. Growth Theory through the Lens of Development Economics. In *Handbook of Economic Growth*, vol. 1A, ed. P. Aghion and P. Durlauf, chap. 7. Amsterdam: Elsevier.

Banerjee, A., and A. Newman. 1991. Risk Bearing and the Theory of Income Distribution. *Review of Economic Studies* 58 (2): 211–35.

Barlevy, G. 2003. Credit Market Frictions and the Allocation of Resources over the Business Cycle. *Journal of Monetary Economics* 50 (8, November): 1795–818.

Barr, A., and T. Packard. 2000. Revealed and Concealed Preferences in the Chilean Pension System: An Experimental Investigation. Discussion Paper 53. Department of Economics, Oxford University.

Barro, R. J., and J. Lee. 2000. International Data on Educational Attainment: Updates and Implications. CID Working Paper No. 42. Center for International Development at Harvard University.

Barros, R. 2008. Wealthier but not Much Healthier: Effects of a Health Insurance Program for the Poor in Mexico. Unpublished document, Stanford University.

Batista, C. J. 2008. *Trade Costs for Brazilian Exporting Goods: Two Case Studies.* Unpublished document. Washington, DC: Inter-American Development Bank.

Becerra, O., E. Cavallo, and C. Scartascini. 2009. The Politics of Financial Development. Unpublished document. Washington, DC: Research Department, Inter-American Development Bank.

Beck, T., R. Levine, and N. Loayza. 2000. Finance and the Sources of Growth, *Journal Financial Economics,* 58:261–300.

Benavente, J., and C. Bravo. 2009. Innovation, R&D Investment and Productivity in Latin American and Caribbean Firms: The Chilean Case. Unpublished document. Washington, DC: Latin American and Caribbean Research Network, Inter-American Development Bank.

Bencivenga, V., D. Smith, and R. Starr. 1995. Transactions Costs, Technological Choice, end Endogenous Growth. *Journal of Economic Theory* 67:52–177.

Bergara, M., and A. Pereyra. 2005. El Proceso de Diseño e Implementación de Políticas y las Reformas en los Servicios Públicos. Paper presented at the Workshop on State Reform, Public Policies, and Policymaking Processes, February 28–March 2. Washington, DC: Inter-American Development Bank.

Bergman, M. 2003. Tax Reform and Tax Compliance: The Divergence Paths of Chile and Argentina. *Journal of Latin American Studies* 35:593–624.

Bergoeing, R., P. Kehoe, T. Kehoe, and R. Soto. 2002. A Decade Lost and Found: Mexico and Chile in the 1980s. *Review of Economic Dynamics, Elsevier for the Society for Economic Dynamics* 5(1, January): 166–205.

Berkman, H., C. Scartascini, E. Stein, and M. Tommasi. 2008. Policies, State Capabilities, and Political Institutions: An International Dataset. Washington, DC: Inter-American Development Bank. http://www.iadb.org/RES/pub_List.cfm?id_sec=5&pub_topic_id= DBA&type=pub_type&pub_type_id=DBA&pub_type_id1=DBA&language=english.

Bernard, A., J. Eaton, B. Jensen, and S. Kortum. 2003. Plants and Productivity in International Trade. *American Economic Review* 93(4): 1268–90.

Bernard, A., B. Jensen, and P. Schott. 2006. Trade Costs, Firms and Productivity. *Journal of Monetary Economics* 53: 917–37.

Betancor, O., and R. Rendeiro. 1999. Regulating Privatized Infrastructures and Airport Services. World Bank Policy Research Working Paper 2180. Unpublished document. Washington, DC: World Bank.

Betcherman, G., and C. Pagés. 2007. Estimating the Impact of Labor Taxes on Employment and the Balances of Social Insurance Funds in Turkey. Synthesis Report. Washington, DC: World Bank.

Binelli, C., and A. Maffioli. 2007. A Microeconometric Analysis of Public Support to R&D in Argentina. *International Review of Applied Economics* 21(3): 339–59.

Birbuet, J. C., and C. G. Machicado. 2009. Understanding Productivity Levels, Dispersion and Growth in the Leather Shoe Industry: Effects of Size and Informality. Unpublished document. Washington, DC: Research Department, Inter-American Development Bank.

Blonigen, B., and W. Wilson. 2006. New Measures of Port Efficiency Using International Trade Data. NBER Working Paper 12052. Cambridge, MA: National Bureau of Economic Research.

BLS (U.S. Bureau of Labor Statistics). 2005. Business Employment Dynamics. http://www. bls.gov/bdm/; and http://www.bls.gov/news.release/pdf/cewfs.pdf (accessed April 2009).

Blyde J., and E. Fernández-Arias. 2005. Why Latin America is Falling Behind. In *Sources of Growth in Latin America. What Is Missing?,* ed. E. Fernández-Arias, R. Manuelli, and J. S. Blyde, chap 1, pp. 3–54. Washington, DC: Inter-American Development Bank.

Blyde J., C. Daude, and E. Fernández-Arias. 2009. Output Collapses and Productivity Destruction. RES Working Paper 666. Washington, DC: Research Department, Inter-American Development Bank.

Blyde, J., G. Iberti, and M. Mesquita Moreira. 2009. Integration, Resource Reallocation and Productivity: The Cases of Brazil and Chile. Unpublished document. Washington, DC: Inter-American Development Bank.

Blyde, J., A. C. Pinheiro, C. Daude, and E. Fernández-Arias. 2007. Competitiveness and Growth in Brazil, Unpublished document. Washington, DC: Inter-American Development Bank.

Bosch, M., and W. F. Maloney. 2007. Comparative Analysis of Labor Market Dynamics and Informality in Developing Countries. Unpublished document. Washington, DC: World Bank.

Bottia, M., L. Cardona, and C. Medina. 2008. Bondades y Limitaciones de la Focalización con Proxy Means Tests: El Caso del Sisben en Colombia. Borradores de Economía No 539. Colombia: Banco de la República de Colombia.

Bruhn, M. 2008. License to Sell: Business Start-up Reform in Mexico. Policy Research Working Paper 4538. Washington, DC: World Bank.

Brusco, V., M. Nazareno, and S. Stokes. 2004. Vote Buying in Argentina. *Latin American Research Review* 39(2): 66–88.

Buera, F., J. Kaboski, and Y. Shin. 2008. Finance and Development: A Tale of Two Sectors. Mimeo. University of California, Los Angeles.

Buera, F., and Y. Shin. 2008. Financial Frictions and the Persistence of History: A Quantitative Exploration. Mimeo. University of California, Los Angeles.

Bull, B. 2008. Policy Networks and Business Participation in Free Trade Negotiations in Chile. *Journal of Latin American Studies* 40:195–224.

Busso M., L. Madrigal, and C. Pagés. 2009a. Productivity and Resource Misallocation in Latin America. Unpublished document. Washington, DC: Research Department, Inter-American Development Bank.

———. 2009b. Reported Tax Evasion and Resource Misallocation in Chile. Unpublished document. Washington, DC: Research Department, Inter-American Development Bank.

Caballero, R., and M. Hammour. 1994. The Cleansing Effect of Recessions. *American Economic Review* 84(5, December): 1350–368.

CAF (Corporación Andina de Fomento). 2009. *Reporte de Economía y Desarrollo. Caminos Para el Futuro, Gestión de la Infraestructura en América Latina*. Caracas: Corporación Andina de Fomento.

Calvo, G. 2005. Volatility as an Innovation Deterrent: Adam Smith in Stormy Weather. Unpublished document.

Calvo, G., A. Izquierdo, and L. F. Mejía. 2008. Systemic Sudden Stops: The Relevance of Balance-Sheet Effects and Financial Integration. NBER Working Paper 14026. Cambridge, MA: National Bureau of Economic Research.

Calvo, G., A. Izquierdo, and R. Loo-Kung. 2006. Relative Price Volatility under Sudden Stops: The Relevance of Balance-Sheet Effects. *Journal of International Economics* 69(1, June): 231–54.

Calvo, G., A. Izquierdo, and E. Talvi. 2006. Phoenix Miracles in Emerging Markets: Recovering without Credit from Systemic Financial Crises. NBER Working Paper 12101. Cambridge, MA: National Bureau of Economic Research.

Calvo, G., and R. Loo-Kung. 2009. Should We Rush to Regulate Financial Institutions? Unpublished document.

Camacho, A., and E. Conover. 2008a. Manipulation of Social Program Eligibility: Detection, Explanations, and Consequences for Empirical Research. Mimeo, University of California, Berkeley.

———. 2008b. Effects of Colombia's Social Protection System on Worker's Choice between Formal and Informal Employment. Unpublished mimeo.

———. 2008c. Effects of Subsidized Health Insurance on Newborn Health in Colombia. Working Paper No. 14. Universidad de los Andes—Centro de Estudios Sobre Desarrollo Económico (CEDE).

———. 2009. Misallocation and Manufacturing TFP in Colombia. Unpublished document. Washington, DC: Research Department, Inter-American Development Bank.

Cárdenas, M., and R. Bernal. 2003. Determinants of Labor Demand in Colombia: 1976–1996. Working Paper No. 10077. Cambridge, MA: National Bureau of Economic Research (NBER).

Cárdenas, M., and C. Mejía. 2007. Informalidad en Colombia: Nueva Evidencia. *Cuadernos de Fedesarrollo,* No. 35. Fedesarrollo. Bogotá.

Carpio, S., and C. Pagés. 2009. Informality, Productivity and Resource Misallocation in Brazil. Mimeographed document. Washington, DC: Inter-American Development Bank.

Casacuberta, C., G. Fachola, and N. Gandelman. 2004. The Impact of Trade Liberalization on Employment, Capital, and Productivity Dynamics: Evidence from the Uruguayan Manufacturing Sector. Research Network Working Papers R-479. Washington, DC: Inter-American Development Bank.

Casacuberta, C., and N. Gandelman. 2009. Productivity, Exit and Crisis in Uruguayan Manufacturing and Service Sectors. Unpublished document. Washington, DC: Research Department, Inter-American Development Bank.

Casacuberta, C., and D. Zaclicever. 2009. The Causal Effect of Trade Protection on Productivity in Uruguay. Unpublished document. Washington, DC: Inter-American Development Bank.

Caselli, F. 2005. Accounting for Cross-Country Income Differences. In *Handbook of Economic Growth,* vol. 1, ed. P. Aghion and S. Durlauf, chap. 9, pp. 679–741. 1st ed. San Diego, CA: Elsevier.

Cassoni, A., and M. Ramada-Sarasola. 2009. To Innovate or Not to Innovate. Effects on Uruguayan Manufacturing Firms' Productivity. Unpublished document. Washington, DC: Latin American and Caribbean Research Network, Inter-American Development Bank.

Castelar Pinheiro, A., and R. Bonelli. 2008. New Export Activities in Brazil: Comparative Advantage, Policy or Self-Discovery? Research Network Working Paper R-551. Washington, DC: Inter-American Development Bank.

Catão, L., C. Pagés, and M. F. Rosales. 2009. Financial Dependence, Formal Credit and Informal Jobs: New Evidence from Brazilian Household Data. Unpublished document. Washington, DC: Research Department, Inter-American Development Bank.

Cavallo, E., A. Galindo, A. Izquierdo, and J. J. León. 2009. The Role of Ex-ante Relative Price Volatility in the Efficiency of Investment Allocation. Washington, DC: Research Department, Inter-American Development Bank.

CEDLAS (Centro de Estudio Laborales y Sociales) and World Bank. 2008. Socio-Economic Database for Latin America and the Caribbean (SEDLAC). http://www.depeco.econo.unlp.edu.ar/sedlac/eng/index.php.

———. 2009. Socio-Economic Database for Latin America and the Caribbean (SEDLAC). http://www.depeco.econo.unlp.edu.ar/sedlac/eng/index.php/ (accessed June 2009).

Cerra, V., and S. Saxena. 2008. Growth Dynamics: The Myth of Economic Recovery. *American Economic Review* 98(1, March): 439–57.

Cetrángolo, O, and J. Gómez-Sabaini. 2007. *La tributación directa en America Latina y los desafíos a la imposición sobre la renta.* Serie Macroeconomía del Desarrollo No. 60. Santiago, Chile: United Nations.

Chen, M., J. Wilson, and T. Otsuki. 2008. Standards and Export Decisions: Firm-level Evidence from Developing Countries. *Journal of International Trade & Economic Development* 17(4): 501–23.

Chong, A., and M. Gradstein. 2008. Institutional Quality and Government Effectiveness. Unpublished document. Washington, DC: Research Department, Inter-American Development Bank.

Chong, A., J. Guillen, and V. Rios. 2009. Taxes and Firm Size. Unpublished document. Washington, DC: Research Department, Inter-American Development Bank.

Chongvilaivan, A., and Y. Jinjarak. 2008. Cross-Country Tax Rates and Firm Size Distribution. Unpublished document. Singapore: Institute of Southeast Asian Studies (ISEAS).

Cimoli, M., G. Porcile, A. Primi, and S. Vergara. 2005. Cambio estructural, heterogeneidad productiva y tecnológica en America Latina. In *Structural Heterogeneity, Technological Asymmetries and Growth in Latin America,* ed. M. Cimoli, pp. 9–42. MPRA (Munich Personal Repec Archive) Paper No. 3832. Munich: MPRA/ECLAC.

Clark, X., D. Dollar, and A. Micco. 2004. Port Efficiency, Maritime Transport Costs, and Bilateral Trade. *Journal of Development Economics* 75:417–50.

Cohen, W., and D. Levinthal. 1989. Innovation and Learning: The Two Faces of R&D. *The Economic Journal* 99(397): 569–96.

———. 1990. Absorptive Capacity: A New Perspective on Learning and Innovation. *Administrative Science Quarterly* 35(1): 128–52.

Colciencias (Departamento Administrativo de Ciencia, Tecnología e Innovación) DANE (Departamento Administrativo Nacional de Estadística), DNP (Departamento Nacional de Planeación). 2004–2006. Encuesta Nacional de Innovación y Desarrollo Tecnológico. http://www.colciencias.gov.co/portalcol/index.jsp?ct5=301&ct=171&cargaHome=3&c odIdioma=es&ms=1 (accessed June 2009).

Collier, R. B., and D. Collier. 1991. *Shaping the Political Arena.* Princeton, NJ: Princeton University Press.

CONACYT (Consejo Nacional de Ciencia y Tecnología). 2004–2006. Encuesta de Innovación. http://www.siicyt.gob.mx/siicyt/docs/Estadisticas3/Informe2007/Innovacion.pdf (accessed June 2009).

CONEVAL (National Evaluation Council, Consejo Nacional de Evaluación de la Política Social). 2007. Evaluación de Consistencia y Resultados. www.coneval.gob.mx (accessed June 2009).

Coordinación del Gabinete de Política Social. 2005. Ficha de Caracterización Económica. Unpublished document. Dominican Republic.

Corbo, V. 2004. Policy Challenges of Population Aging and Pension Systems in Latin America. In *Global Demographic Change: Economic Impacts and Policy Challenges,* ed. G. H. Ellon, pp. 257–80. Kansas City, MS: Federal Reserve Bank of Kansas City.

Corbo, V., and K. Schmidt-Hebbel. 2003. Macroeconomic Effects of Pension Reform in Chile. In *Pension Reforms: Results and Challenges.* Santiago, Chile: International Federation of Pension Fund Administrators.

Córdoba, J. C., and M. Ripoll. 2008. Endogenous TFP and Cross-Country Income Differences. *Journal of Monetary Economics* 55(6) (September):1158–70.

Crepon, B., E. Duguet, and J. Mairesse. 1998. Research, Innovation and Productivity: An Econometric Analysis at the Firm Level. *Economics of Innovation and New Technology* 7(2): 115–58.

Cuesta, J., N. Millán, and M. Olivera. 2009. Shocks, Protección Social y Decisiones Laborales en Colombia. Unpublished document. Washington, DC: Inter-American Development Bank.

Cuevas, M., S. Lee, and B. Pineda. 2009. Industrial Policy in Guatemala. Draft for the Project on Industrial Policies in Latin America and the Caribbean. Unpublished document. Washington, DC: Research Department, Inter-American Development Bank.

Cummins, J. G., K. A. Hassett, and R. G. Hubbard. 1996. Tax Reforms and Investment: A Cross-Country Comparison. NBER Working Papers 5232. Cambridge, MA: National Bureau of Economic Research.

Dabla-Norris, E., M. Gradstein, and G. Inchauste. 2008. What Causes Firms to Hide Output? The Determinants of Informality. *Journal of Development Economics* 85:1–27.

Dahlman, C., and A. Utz. 2005. India and the Knowledge Economy: Leveraging Strengths and Opportunities. Washington, DC: The World Bank Institute.

DANE (Departamento Administrativo Nacional de Estadística). 2003. Ficha de Clasificación Socioeconómica: Sistema de Indentificación y Clasificación de Potenciales Beneficiarios para Programas Sociales (SISBEN). Unpublished.

———. 2005. Encuesta Continua de Hogares (ENH). Colombia. http://www.dane.gov. co.(accessed July 2009)

Daude, C., and E. Fernández-Arias. 2010. On the Role of Aggregate Productivity and Factor Accumulation in Economic Development in Latin America and the Caribbean. IDB Working Paper IDB-WP-131. Washington, DC: Inter-American Development Bank.

de Negri, J. A., F. de Negri, and F. Freitas. 2007. Does Technological Innovation Cause Exports in Brazil and Argentina? In *Technological Innovation in Brazilian and Argentine Firms,* ed. J. A. de Negri and L. M. Turchi, pp. 309–26. Brasilia: Institute for Applied Economic Research (IPEA).

De Soto, H. 2000. The Mystery of Capital: Why Capitalism Triumphs in the West and Fails Everywhere Else. New York: Basic Books.

de Vries, Gaaitzen. 2009. Productivity in a Distorted Market: The Case of Brazil's Retail Sector. Research Memorandum GD-112. Groningen: Groningen Growth and Development Centre. University of Groningen.

Demir, F. 2009a. Macroeconomic Uncertainty and Private Investment in Argentina, Mexico and Turkey. *Applied Economics Letters* 16(6): 567–71.

———. 2009b. Private Investment, Portfolio Choice and Financialization of Real Sectors in Emerging Markets. *Journal of Development Economics* 88(2): 314–24.

Devlin, R., and G. Moguillansky. 2009. Alianzas público-privadas como estrategias nacionales de desarrollo a largo plazo. Separata 97. Revista CEPAL.

DFID (United Kingdom Department for International Development). 2005. Agriculture, Growth and Poverty Reduction. DFID Working Paper on Agriculture and Natural Resources. London: Department for International Development.

DGEEC (Dirección General de Estadísiticas, Encuestas y Censos). 2006. Encuesta Permanente de Hogares (EPH). http://www.dgeec.gov.py/ (accessed April 2009).

Díaz, J. J., and M. Jaramillo. 2009. Políticas de fomento de las micro, pequeñas y medianas empresas en el Perú. Mimeo. Grupo de Análisis para el Desarrollo (GRADE). Lima.

Díaz-Cayeros, A., F. Estévez, and B. Magaloni. 2006. Vote-buying, Poverty, and Democracy: The Politics of Social Programs in Mexico, 1989–2006. Unpublished document. Palo Alto, CA: Department of Political Science, Stanford University.

DIGESTYC (Dirección General de Estadísticas y Censos). 2005. Encuesta de Hogares de Propósitos Múltiples (EHPM). El Salvador. http://www.digestyc.gob.sv/ (accessed July 2007).

Djankov, S., T. Ganser, C. McLiesh, R. Ramalho, and A. Shleifer. 2009. The Effect of Corporate Taxes on Investment and Entrepreneurship. Working Paper. Unpublished document. Cambridge, MA: National Bureau of Economic Research.

DNP (Departamento Nacional de Planeación)-Sinergia. 2008. Evaluación de Impacto del Fondo Colombiano de Modernizacio n y Desarrollo Tecnológico de las Micro, Pequeñas y Medianas Empresas FOMIPYME. Serie Evaluación de Políticas Públicas No. 8. Bogotá, Colombia: DNP.

Draca M., R. Sadun, and J. Van Reenen. 2006. Productivity and ICT: A Review of the Evidence. CEP Discussion Papers dp0749. London: Centre for Economic Performance, London School of Economics.

Drazen, A. 2000. *Political Economy in Macroeconomics*. Princeton, NJ: Princeton University Press.

Drewry. 2002. *Global Container Terminals. Profit, Performance and Prospects*. London: Drewry Shipping Consultants.

Duarte, M., and D. Restuccia. Forthcoming. The Role of the Structural Transformation in Aggregate Productivity. *Quarterly Journal of Economics*.

Durand, F., and E. Silva. 1998. *Organized Business, Economic Change, and Democracy in Latin America*. Miami: North-South Center Press.

Duryea, S., J. C. Navarro, and A. Verdisco. 2008. Learning about Education Quality and Perceptions. In *Beyond facts: Understanding Quality of Life*. Washington, DC: Inter-American Development Bank.

Easterly, W., and R. Levine. 2001. It's Not Factor Accumulation: Stylized Facts and Growth Models. *World Bank Economic Review* 15(2): pp. 177–219.

ECLAC (United Nations Economic Commission for Latin America and the Caribbean). 2003. Traffic Congestion. The Problem and How to Deal with It. Cuadernos de la Cepal No. 87. Santiago: Economic Commission for Latin America and the Caribbean (ECLAC).

Edwards, S. 2002. Information Technology and Economic Growth in Developing Countries. *Challenge* 45(3): 19–43.

———. 2007. *An East Asian Renaissance. Ideas for Economic Growth*. Washington, DC: World Bank.

Erosa, A., T. Koreshkova, and D. Restuccia. 2007. How Important is Human Capital? A Quantitative Theory Assessment of World Income Inequality. Working Paper 280. Toronto: University of Toronto.

Eslava, M., A. Galindo, M. Hofstetter, and A. Izquierdo. 2009. The Impact of Credit Markets on Productivity Behavior in Colombia. Unpublished document. Washington, DC: Research Department, Inter-American Development Bank.

Eslava, M., J. Haltiwanger, A. Kugler, and M. Kugler. 2004. The Effect of Structural Reforms on Productivity and Profitability Enhancing Reallocation: Evidence from Colombia. *Journal of Development Economics* 75: 333–71.

———. 2009. Trade Reforms and Market Selection: Evidence from Manufacturing Plants in Colombia. Unpublished document. Washington, DC: Inter-American Development Bank.

Eslava, M., and M. Meléndez. 2009. Politics, Policies, and the Dynamics of Aggregate Productivity in Colombia. Unpublished document. Washington, DC: Research Department, Inter-American Development Bank.

Ethier, W. 1982. National and International Returns to Scale in the Modern Theory of International Trade. *American Economic Review* 72:950–59.

Fajnzylber, P., W. Maloney, and G. Montes Rojas. 2006. Does Formality Improve Micro-Firm Performance? Quasi-Experimental Evidence from the Brazilian SIMPLES Program. Unpublished document. Washington, DC: World Bank.

FAO (Food and Agricultural Organization). 2009 AGROSTAT. Rome: Food and Agriculture Organization http://fao/stat.fao.org/site/291/default.aspx (accessed August 2009).

Färe, R., S. Grosskopf, M. Norris, and Z. Zhang. 1994. Productivity Growth, Technical Progress and Efficiency Change in Industrialized Countries. *American Economic Review* 84: 66–83.

Farrell, D. 2006. *The Productivity Imperative: Wealth and Poverty in the Global Economy.* Cambridge, MA: Harvard University Press.

Fernandes, A. 2007. Trade Policy, Trade Volumes and Plant Level Productivity in Colombian Manufacturing Industries. *Journal of International Economics* 71(1): 52–71.

Fernández-Arias, E., and C. Daude. 2010. Aggregate Productivity in Latino America. In *The Age of Productivity: Transforming Economies from the Bottom Up.* Washington, DC: Inter-American Development Bank.

Fink, C., A. Mattoo, and I. C. Neagu. 2002. Trade in International Maritime Services: How Much Does Policy Matter? *The World Bank Economic Review* 16(1): 81–108.

Fong, Glenn. 2000. Breaking New Ground or Breaking the Rules: Strategic Reorientation in U.S. Industrial Policy. *International Security* 25(2, Fall): 152–86.

Foster L., J. Haltiwanger, and C. Krizan. 2001. Aggregate Productivity Growth. Lessons from Microeconomic Evidence. NBER chapters in *New Developments in Productivity Analysis,* pp. 303–72. Cambridge, MA: National Bureau of Economic Research.

Foster L., J. Haltiwanger, and C. Syverson. 2008. Reallocation, Firm Turnover, and Efficiency: Selection on Productivity or Profitability? *American Economic Review* 98(1): 394–425.

Frankel, J. 2008. The Estimated Effects of the Euro on Trade: Why Are They Below Historical Effects of Monetary Unions Among Smaller Countries? NBER Working Paper 14542. Cambridge, MA: National Bureau of Economic Research.

Frankel, J., and D. Romer. 1999. Does Trade Cause Growth? *American Economic Review* 89(3): 379–99.

Frieden, J. 1991. *Debt, Development and Democracy.* Princeton, NJ: Princeton University Press.

———. 2000. The Method of Analysis: Modern Political Economy. In *Modern Political Economy in Latin America: Theory and Policy,* ed. J. Frieden, M. Pastor, and M. Tomz, pp. 37–43. Boulder, CO: Westview Press.

Freund, C., and B. Bolaky. 2008. Trade, Regulations, and Income. *Journal of Development Economics* 87:309–21.

Galiani, S., and F. Weinschelbaum. 2007. Modeling Informality Formally: Households and Firms. Working Paper 47. Buenos Aires: Centro de Estudios Distribuivos, Laborales y Sociales (CEDLAS), Universidad Nacional de La Plata.

Galindo, A., A. Chong, J. Guillen, and C. Pombo. 2009. The Effect of Taxation on Investment and Productivity: A Cross-Country Comparison. Unpublished document. Washington, DC: Research Department, Inter-American Development Bank.

Galindo, A., A. Micco, and G. Ordóñez. 2002. Financial Liberalization: Does It Pay to Join the Party? *Economia* 3(2): 231–52.

Galindo, A., F. Schiantarelli, and A. Weiss. 2007. Does Financial Liberalization Improve the Allocation of Investment: Micro Evidence from Developing Countries. *Journal of Development Economics* 83:562–87.

Gasparini, L., F. Haimovich, and S. Oliveiri. 2007. Labor Informality Effects of a Poverty-Alleviation Program. Working Paper No. 53. Buenos Aires: Centro de Estudios Distributivos, Laborales y Sociales (CEDLAS), Universidad Nacional de la Plata.

Gaviria A., C. Medina, and C. Mejía. 2006. Evaluating the Impact of the Health Care Reform in Colombia: From Theory to Practice. Bogota, Colombia: Documento Centro de Estudios Sobre Desarrollo Económico (CEDE) 2006-06, Universidad de los Andes.

Gay, R. 1998. Rethinking Clientelism: Demands, Discourses and Practices in Contemporary Brazil. *European Review of Latin American and Caribbean Studies* 66:7–24.

Glick, R., and A. K. Rose. 2002. Does a Currency Union Affect Trade? The Time-Series Evidence. *European Economic Review* 46:1125–51.

Goldberg, L., and C. Kolstad. 1995. Foreign Direct Investment, Exchange Rate Variability and Demand Uncertainty. *International Economic Review* 36(4, November): 855–73.

Goldberg, M., and E. Palladini. 2008. Chile: A Strategy to Promote Innovative Small and Medium Enterprises. World Bank, Policy Research Working Paper No. 4518. Washington, DC: World Bank.

Gollin, D. 2002. Getting Income Shares Right. *Journal of Political Economy* 110 (2): 458–74.

González, D. 2006 Regímenes Especiales de Tributación para Pequeños Contribuyentes en América Latina. Unpublished document. Washington, DC: Division de Integracion y Programas Regionales, Inter-American Development Bank.

Graham, D. 2007. Variable Returns to Agglomeration and the Effect of Road Traffic Congestion. *Journal of Urban Economics* 62(1): 103–20.

Greenwald, B., M. Kohn, and J. Stiglitz. 1990. Financial Market Imperfections and Productivity Growth. *Journal of Economic Behavior & Organization* 13(3): 321–45.

Griliches, Zvi (1986). Productivity, R&D, and the Basic Research at the Firm Level in the 1970s. *American Economic Review* 76(1, March): 141–54.

Grossman, G., and E. Helpman. 1991. *Innovation and Growth in the Global Economy.* Cambridge, MA: MIT Press.

———. 2001. *Special Interest Politics.* Cambridge, MA: MIT Press.

Gruber, J. 1997. The Incidence of Payroll Taxation: Evidence from Chile. *Journal of Labor Economics* 15 (3, Part 2: Labor Market Flexibility in Developing Countries, July); S72–S101.

Gruenberg, C., and V. Pereyra Iraola. 2009. El clientelismo en la gestión de programas sociales contra la pobreza. Documento de Políticas Públicas/Análisis 60 CIPPEC. Buenos Aires.

Guzmán, R., M. R. Agosin, M. Lizardo, and R. Capellán. 2009. Cuatro décadas de políticas de desarrollo productivo en la República Dominicana. Draft for the Project on Industrial Policies in Latin America and the Caribbean. Unpublished document. Washington, DC: Research Department, Inter-American Development Bank.

Hall, R., and C. I. Jones. 1999. Why Do Some Countries Produce So Much More Output Per Worker Than Others? *Quarterly Journal of Economics* 114(1): 83–116.

Hall, B., and A. Maffioli. 2008. Evaluating the Impact of Technology Development Funds in Emerging Economies: Evidence from Latin America. *European Journal of Development Research* 20(2); 172–98.

Hall, B., and J. Van Reenen. 1999. How Effective are Fiscal Incentives for R&D? A New Review of the Evidence. NBER Working Paper 7098. Cambridge, MA: National Bureau of Economic Research.

Haltiwanger, J., A. Kugler, M. Kugler, A. Micco, and C. Pagés. 2004. Effects of Tariffs and Real Exchange Rates on Job Reallocation: Evidence from Latin America. *Journal of Policy Reform* 7(4, December): 191–208.

Hanson, M. 2007. *Economic Development, Education and Transnational Corporations.* New York: Routledge Press.

Hanushek, E., and L. Woessman. 2009. Schooling, Cognitive Skills and the Latin American Puzzle. NBER Working Paper 15066. Cambridge, MA: National Bureau of Economic Research.

Harris, J., and M. Todaro. 1970. Migration, Unemployment, and Development: A Two-Sector Analysis. *American Economic Review* 60(1): 126–42.

Harrison, A. E., and A. Rodríguez-Clare. 2009. Trade, Foreign Investment, and Industrial Policy. NBER Paper 15261. National Bureau of Economic Research.

Hausmann, R. 2008. The Other Hand: High Bandwidth Development Policy. Harvard Kennedy School Working Paper No. RWP08-060. Cambridge, MA: Harvard University.

Hausmann, R. and B. Klinger. 2006. Structural Transformation and the Patterns of Comparative Advantage in the Product Space. Center for International Development, WP No.128. Cambridge, MA: Harvard University.

Hausmann, R., J. Hwang, and D. Rodrik. 2007. What You Export Matters. *Journal of Economic Growth* 12:1–25.

Hausmann, R., A. Rodríguez-Clare, and D. Rodrik. 2006. Hacia una estrategia para el crecimiento económico de Uruguay. In *Una nueva era de crecimiento económico en Uruguay*, ed. E. Fernández-Arias and S. Sagari, pp. 127–65. Washington, DC: Inter-American Development Bank.

Hausmann, R., and D. Rodrik. 2003. Economic Development as Self-Discovery. *Journal of Development Economics* 72(December): 603–633.

———. 2005. Self-Discovery in a Development Strategy for El Salvador. *Economía, Journal of the Latin American and Caribbean Economic Association* 6(1): 43–101.

———. 2006. Doomed to Choose: Industrial Policy as Predicament. Paper presented at the Blue Sky Seminar, Center for International Development. Cambridge, MA: John F. Kennedy School of Government, Harvard University.

Heckman, J., and C. Pagés. 2004. Law and Employment Lessons from Latin America and the Caribbean. NBER Conference Report. Chicago: The University of Chicago Press.

Herrendorf, B., J. Schmitz, and A. Teixeira. 2007. How Important Was the 19th Century Transportation Revolution for U.S. Development? Paper presented at the 2006 Meetings of the Society of Economic Dynamics, New York.

Heston, A, R. Summers, and B. Aten. 2006. Penn World Table Version 6.2. Center for International Comparisons of Production, Income and Prices at the University of Pennsylvania.

Hoffman, J. 2000. Tendencias en el Transporte Marítimo Internacional y sus Implicaciones para América Latina y el Caribe. Unpublished document. Santiago, Chile.

Honohan, P. 2004. Financial Development, Growth and Poverty: How Close are the Links? World Bank Policy Research Working Paper 3203.Washington, DC: World Bank.

Hopenhayn, H., and A. Neumeyer. 2008. Productivity and Distortions. Unpublished document. Washington, DC: Research Department, Inter-American Development Bank.

Hsieh, C. 2002. What Explains the Industrial Revolution in East Asia? Evidence From the Factor Markets. *American Economic Review* 92(3): 502–26.

Hsieh, C., and P. Klenow. 2007. Misallocation and Manufacturing TFP in China and India. NBER Working Paper 13290. Cambridge, MA: National Bureau of Economic Research.

Hsieh, C., and P. Klenow. 2009. Resource Misallocation in Mexico. Unpublished mimeo. Washington, DC: Research Department, Inter-American Development Bank.

———. Forthcoming. Misallocation and Manufacturing TFP in China and India. *Quarterly Journal of Economics.*

Huergo, E., and J. Jaumandreu. 2004. Firms' Age, Process Innovation and Productivity Growth. *International Journal of Industrial Organization* 22:541–59.

Hufbauer, G., B. Kotschwar, and J. Wilson. 2002. Trade and Standards: A Look at Central America. *The World Economy* 25: 991–1018.

Hummels, D. 2001. Toward a Geography of Trade Costs. Unpublished document. Department of Agricultural Economics, Purdue University.

Hummels, D., V. Lugovskyy, and A. Skiba. 2009. The Trade Reducing Effects of Market Power in International Shipping. *Journal of Development Economics* 89(1): 84–97.

Ibarrarán, P., A. Maffioli, and R. Stucchi. 2009. SME Policy and Firm's Productivity in Latin America. IZA Discussion Paper Series No. 4486. Bonn, Germany: IZA.

IBGE (Instituto Brasileiro de Geografia e Estatística). IBGE (Instituto Brasileiro de Geografia e Estatística). 2003. Economía Informal Urbana 2003. http://www.ibge.gov.br/home/estatistica/economia/ecinf/2003/default.shtm (accessed July 2009).

———. 2005. Pesquisa de Inovação Tecnológica 2005. http://www.ibge.gov.br/home/estatistica/economia/industria/pintec/2005/default.shtm (accessed July 2009).

———. 2007. Pesquisa Nacional por Amostra de Domicílios (PNAD). Brazil. http://www.ibge.gov.br/english/estatistica/populacao/trabalhoerendimento/pnad2007/default.shtm (accessed July 2009).

IDB (Inter-American Development Bank). 2002. *Beyond Borders, Economic and Social Progress in Latin America.* Washington, DC: Inter-American Development Bank.

———. 2003. *Good Jobs Wanted: Labor Markets in Latin America.* Economic and Social Progress in Latin America: 2004 Report. Washington, DC: Inter-American Development Bank.

———. 2004. *Unlocking Credit.* Economic and Social Progress in Latin America: 2005 Report. Washington, DC: IDB. http://www.iadb.org/res/ipes/2005/index.cfm.

———. 2005. *The Politics of Policies.* Economic and Social Progress in Latin America: 2006 Report. Washington, DC: IDB and Harvard University Press. http://www.iadb.org/res/ipes/2006/index.cfm?language=english.

———. 2005. *Unlocking Credit: The Quest for Deep and Stable Bank Lending.* Economic and Social Progress in Latin America Report. Washington DC: Inter-American Development Bank.

———. 2007. *Outsiders? The Changing Patterns of Exclusion in Latin America and the Caribbean.* Washington, DC: Inter-American Development Bank and Harvard University Press.

———. 2008a. All That Glitters May Not be Gold: Assessing Latin America's Recent Macroeconomic Performance. IDB Research Department Report. Washington, DC: Inter-American Development Bank.

———. 2008b. *Beyond Facts: Understanding Quality of Life.* Development in the Americas: 2009 Report. Washington, DC: Inter-American Development Bank and Harvard University Press. http://www.iadb.org/res/pub_desc.cfm?pub_id=B-632.

——. 2008c. The Emergence of New Successful Export Activities in LAC. Research Network WPs and selected proposals. http://www.iadb.org/res/projects_detail.cfm?id_sec=8&id=89 (accessed March 2009).

———. 2009a. Industrial policy in Latin America and the Caribbean. Research Network WPs, nonedited drafts and selected proposals. http://www.iadb.org/res/projects_detail.cfm?id_sec=8&id=3776 (accessed July 2009).

———. 2009b. Policy Trade-offs for Unprecedented Times: Confronting the Global Crisis in Latin America and the Caribbean. IDB Research Department Report. Alejandro Izquierdo and Ernesto Talvi, coordinators. Washington, DC: Inter-American Development Bank.

ILO (International Labour Organization). 2009a. LABORSTA Internet Database. http://laborsta.ilo.org/ (accessed June 2009).

———. 2009b. NATLEX Internet Database. http://www.ilo.org/dyn/natlex/natlex_browse.home (accessed June 2009).

IMF (International Monetary Fund). 2009a. International Financial Statistics (IFS), http://www.imf.org/external/data.htm (accessed July 2009).

———. 2009b. World Economic Outlook (WEO) Database. http://www.imf.org/external/ns/cs.aspx?id=28 (accessed June 2009).

INDEC (Instituto Nacional de Estadística y Censos de la República Argentina). 2006. Encuesta Nacional a Empresas sobre Innovación, I+D y TICs 2002-04. http://www.indec.mecon.ar/nuevaweb/cuadros/16/enit_02-04.pdf (accessed June 2009).

INE (Instituto Nacional de Estadística). 2001. Encuesta Industrial Anual. Venezuela.

———. 2002. Encuesta Continua de Hogares (ECH) Bolivia. www.ine.gov.bo (accessed June 2009).

———. 2004. Encuesta de Hogares Por Muestreo (EHM), Segundo Semestre. Venezuela. http://www.ine.gov.ve/ (accessed June 2009).

———. 2006. Encuesta Nacional de Condiciones de Vida (ENCOVI). Guatemala. http://www.ine.gob.gt/ (accessed June 2009).

INEC (Instituto Nacional de Estadísticas y Censos). 2006. Encuesta de Hogares de Propósitos Múltiples (EHPM). Costa Rica. http://www.inec.go.cr/ (accessed June 2009).

———. 2007. Encuesta de Empleo, Desempleo y Subempleo (ENEMDU). Ecuador. http://www.inec.gov.ec/web/guest/descargas/basedatos/inv_socd/emp_sub_des (accessed June 2009).

INEGI (Instituto Nacional de Estadística y Geografía). 2002. Encuesta Nacional de Micronegocios. Mexico.

———. 2002. Encuesta Nacional sobre Ingresos y Gastos de los Hogares (ENIGH). Mexico. http://www.inegi.org.mx/inegi/default.aspx?s=est&c=10205 (accessed June 2009).

———. 2003. Encuesta Nacional de Ocupación y Empleo (ENOE). Mexico.

INIDE (Instituto Nacional de Información de Desarrollo). 2005. Encuesta Nacional de Hogares sobre Medición de Niveles de Vida (EMNV). Nicaragua. http://www.inide.gob.ni/ (accessed June 2009).

Izquierdo, A.,G. Llosa, and E. Talvi. 2009. Firm Financing in Times of Recovery from Systemic Sudden Stops. Mimeo. Washington, DC: Research Department, Inter-American Development Bank.

Izquierdo, A., R. Romero, and E. Talvi. 2008. Booms and Busts in Latin America: The Role of External Factors. Working Paper 631. Washington, DC: Research Department. Inter-American Development Bank.

Jaramillo, M. 2004. La Regulación del Mercado Laboral en Perú, Informe de Consultoría, Grupo de Análisis para el Desarrollo (GRADE). Lima, Peru.

Jeong, H., and R. Townsend. 2007. Sources of TFP Growth: Occupational Choice and Financial Deepening. *Economic Theory* 32(1, July): 179–221.

Jermanowski, M. 2007. Total Factor Productivity Differences: Appropriate Technology versus Efficiency. *European Economic Review* 51:2080–110.

Johannsen, J., L. Ripani, M. Robles, and L. Tejerina. 2009. Targeting the Poor in Latin America and the Caribbean: Concepts and Practice in Conditional Cash Transfer Programs. Unpublished document. Washington, DC: Inter-American Development Bank.

Jorgenson, D. W., M. S. Ho, and K. J. Stiroh. 2008. Growth of U.S. Industries and Investment in Information Technology and Higher Education. In *Measuring Capital in the New Economy*, ed. C. Corrado, J. Haltiwanger, and D. Sichel, pp. 403–77. Chicago: University of Chicago Press.

Juarez, L. 2007. The Effect of an Old-Age Demogrant on the Labor Supply and Time Use of the Elderly and Non-Elderly in Mexico. Discussion Paper 07-06. Instituto Tecnólogico Autónomo de México.

Kanbur, R. 2009. Conceptualizing Informality: Regulation and Enforcement. Working Paper 2009-11. Department of Applied Economics and Management, Cornell University.

Kaplan, D., E. Piedra, and E. Seira. 2007. Entry Regulation and Business Start-ups: Evidence from Mexico. Policy Research Working Paper 4322. Washington, DC: World Bank.

Katz, J. 2006. Structural Change and Economic Development: Cycles of Creation and Destruction of Production and Technological Capabilities in Latin America. Unpublished document. Santiago, Chile: ECLAC (Economic Commission for Latin America and the Caribbean).

Kaufmann, D., A. Kraay, and M. Mastruzzi. 2006. Governance Matters V: Aggregate and Individual Governance Indicators for 1996–2005. Policy Research Working Paper Series 4012. Washington, DC: World Bank.

Khan, M., and K. S. Jomo. 2000. *Rents, Rent-Seeking and Economic Development: Theory and Evidence in Asia.* Cambridge, UK: Cambridge University Press.

King, R., and R. Levine. 1993a. Finance, Entrepreneurship and Growth: Theory and Evidence. *Journal of Monetary Economics* 32:513–42.

———. 1993b. Finance and Growth: Schumpeter May Be Right. *Quarterly Journal of Economics* 108:717–37.

Klenow, P., and A. Rodriguez-Clare. 1997. The Neoclassical Revival in Growth Economics: Has It Gone Too Far? In *NBER Macroeconomics Annual 1997,* ed. B. Bernanke and J. Rotemberg, pp. 73–102. Cambridge, MA: MIT Press.

———. 2005. Externalities and Growth. In *Handbook of Economic Growth,* Vol. 1A, ed. P. Aghion and S. Durlauf, chap. 11, pp. 817–61. San Diego, CA: Elsevier

Krueger, A., A. Valdes, and M. Schiff, eds. 1991. *Political Economy of Agricultural Pricing Policy: Latin America.* Baltimore, MD: Johns Hopkins University Press.

Kugler, A., and M. Kugler. 2009. Labor Market Effects of Payroll Taxes in Developing Countries: Evidence from Colombia. *Economic Development and Cultural Change* 57:335–58.

La Porta, R., and A. Shleifer. 2008. The Unofficial Economy and Economic Development. Working Paper 14520. Cambridge, MA: National Bureau of Economic Research.

Lederman, D., and W. F. Maloney. 2008. In Search of the Missing Natural Resource Curse. *Economia, Journal of the Latin American and Caribbean Economic Association* 9(1, April): 1–53.

Lee, K. W. 2006. Effectiveness of Government's Occupational Skills Development Strategies for Small- and Medium-scale Enterprises: A Case Study of Korea. *International Journal of Educational Development* 26:278–94.

Lengyel, M. 2009. La co-producción de la innovación y su diseño institucional: Evidencia de la Industria Argentina. Unpublished document. Washington, DC: Latin American and Caribbean Research Network, Inter-American Development Bank.

Levine, R. 1997. Financial Development and Economic Growth: Views and Agenda. *Journal of Economic Literature* XXXV: 688–726.

———. 2004. Finance and Growth: Theory and Evidence. NBER Working Paper 10766. Cambridge, MA: National Bureau of Economic Research.

———. 2005. Should Governments and Aid Agencies Subsidize Small Firms? Brookings Blum Roundtable. *The Private Sector in the Fight Against Global Poverty. Session III: Does Size Matter? SMEs, Microfinance and Large Nationals.* August 4, 2005. Washington, DC: Brookings Institution.

Levine, R., N. Loayza, and T. Beck. 2000. Financial Intermediation and Growth: Causality and Causes. *Journal of Monetary Economics* 46:31–77.

Levine, R., and S. Zervos. 1998. Stock Market, Banks, and Economic Growth. *American Economic Review* 88:537–58.

Levy, S. 2006a. Productividad Crecimiento y Pobreza en Mexico: ¿Qué sigue después de Progresa Oportunidades? Unpublished document. Washington DC: World Bank.

———. 2006b. Social Policies, Productivity and Growth. Background Paper for the Regional Study, Beyond Survival: Protecting Households from Health Shocks in Latin America. Washington, DC: World Bank.

————. 2008. Good Intentions, Bad Outcomes. Social Policy, Informality and Economic Growth in Mexico. Washington, DC: Brookings Institution Press.

Lewis, W. A. 1954. Economic Development with Unlimited Supplies of Labor. *The Manchester School of Economics and Social Studies* 22(2, May): 139–91.

Lewis, William W. 2004. *The Power of Productivity: Wealth, Poverty and the Threat to Global Stability*. Chicago and London: The University of Chicago Press.

Lora, E. 2008. El futuro de los pactos fiscales en América Latina. RES Working Paper 650. Washington, DC: Research Department, Inter-American Development Bank.

Lora, E., and C. Pagés. 2000. Hacia un envejecimiento responsable: las reformas de los sistemas de pensiones en América Latina. *Cuadernos Económicos Información Comercial Española (ICE)* 65:283–324.

López, A. 2009. Las evaluaciones de programas públicos de apoyo al fomento y desarrollo de la tecnología y la innovación en el sector productivo en América Latina: Una revisión crítica. Innovation Note. Washington, DC: Inter-American Development Bank.

López Boo, F. 2009. Human Capital and Productivity. Unpublished document. Washington, DC: Inter-American Development Bank.

López-Córdova, E., and M. Mesquita Moreira. 2004. Regional Integration and Productivity: The Experiences of Brazil and Mexico. Intal-ITD Working Paper 14. Washington, DC: Inter-American Development Bank.

Ludena, C. E. 2009. Agricultural Productivity Growth in Latin America, 1961–2007. Mimeographed document. Washington, DC: Inter-American Development Bank.

Ludena, C. E., T. W. Hertel, K. Foster, P. V. Preckel, and A. Nin. 2007. Productivity Growth and Convergence in Crop, Ruminant and Non-Ruminant Production: Measurement and Forecasts. *Agricultural Economics* 37: 1–17.

Lusardi, A., and O. Mitchell. 2006. Financial Literacy and Planning: Implications for Retirement Wellbeing. Unpublished Working Paper. Dartmouth College and University of Pennsylvania.

Luzio, E., and S. Greenstein. 1995. Measuring the Performance of a Protected Infant Industry: The Case of Brazilian Microcomputers. *Review of Economics and Statistics* 77:622–33.

Machicado, C. G., and J. C. Birbuet. 2009. Understanding Productivity Levels, Dispersion and Growth in the Leather Shoe Industry: Effects of Size and Informality. Washington, DC: Unpublished document. Research Department, Inter-American Development Bank.

Maloney, W. 2004. Informality Revisited. *World Development* 32:1559–78.

Maloney, W., and A. Rodríguez-Clare. 2007. Innovation Shortfalls. *Review of Development Economics* 11(4, November): 665–84.

Madrigal, L., and C. Pagés. 2008. Is Informality a Good Measure of Quality? Unpublished document. Washington, DC: Research Department, Inter-American Development Bank.

Martin, J. 1978. X-Inefficiency, Managerial Effort and Protection. *Economica* 45:273–86.

Martin, W., and D. Mitra. 2001. Productivity Growth and Convergence in Agriculture and Manufacturing. *Economic Development and Cultural Change* 49(2): 403–23.

Martz, J. D. 1996. *The Politics of Clientelism: Democracy and the State in Colombia*. New Brunswick, NJ: Transaction Publishers.

Maxfield, S., and B. Schneider. eds. 1997. *Business and the State in Developing Countries*. Ithaca, NY: Cornell University Press.

MCDS (Ministerio de Coordinación de Desarrollo Social). 2006. Encuesta de Caracterización Socioeconómica. Unpublished document. Ecuador.

McKinsey and Company. 2003. Information Technology and Productivity. Recent Findings. Presentation at the American Economics Association Meeting. Unpublished.

————. 2009. Analysis of Informality and Tax Incentives in Mexico. Unpublished document. Document produced for the Inter-American Development Bank.

MDS (Ministério do Desenvolvimento Social e Combate à Fome). 2001. Cadastro Único para Programas Sociais. Unpublished document. Brazil.

Mecikovsky, A., C. Scartascini, and M. Tommasi. 2010. Politics, Policies, and Productivity: An International Dataset. Washington, DC: Inter-American Development Bank. http://www.iadb.org/research/pub_desc.cfm?pub_id=DBA-013&long=on.

Meléndez, M., and G. Perry. 2009. Industrial Policies in Colombia. Draft for the Project on Industrial Policies in Latin America and the Caribbean. Unpublished document. Washington, DC: Research Department, Inter-American Development Bank.

Melitz, M. J. 2003. The Impact of Trade on Intra-industry Reallocations and Aggregate Industry Productivity. *Econometrica* 71(6): 1695–725.

Melo, A., and A. Rodríguez-Clare. 2006. Productive Development Policies and Supporting Institutions in Latin America and The Caribbean. February. RES Working Paper No C-106. Washington, DC: Research Department, Inter-American Development Bank.

Mercer-Blackman, V. 2008. The Impact of Research and Development Tax Incentives on Colombia's Manufacturing Sector: What Difference Do They Make? IMF Working Paper WP/08/178. Washington, DC: International Monetary Fund.

Mesquita Moreira, M., C. Volpe, and J. Blyde. 2008. *Unclogging the Arteries: The Impact of Transport Costs on Latin American and Caribbean Trade, Special Report on Integration and Trade.* Washington, DC: Inter-American Development Bank.

Metcalfe, S. 1995. The Economic Foundations of Technology Policy: Equilibrium and Evolutionary Perspectives. In *Handbook of the Economics of Innovation and Technological Change,* ed. P. Stoneman, pp. 409–511. Oxford, UK, and Cambridge, MA: Blackwell Publishers.

Micco, A., and T. Serebrisky. 2006. Competition Regimes and Air Transport Costs: The Effects of Open Skies Agreements. *Journal of International Economics* 70(1): 25–51.

Micco, A., E. Stein, and G. Ordóñez. 2003. The Currency Union Effect on Trade: Early Evidence from EMU. *Economic Policy* 18 (October): 315–43.

MIDEPLAN (Ministerio de Planificación y Cooperación). 2006. Encuesta de Caracterización Socioeconomica Nacional (CASEN). Chile. http://www.mideplan.cl/casen/ (accessed June 2009).

————. 2007. Ficha de Protección Social. Unpublished document. Chile.

Mongue-Gonzalez, R., and J. Hewitt. 2009. Innovation, R&D, Investment and Productivity in the Costa Rican ICT Sector: A Case Study. Unpublished document. Washington, DC: Inter-American Development Bank.

Mongue-González, R., L. Rivera, and J. Rosales-Tijerino. 2009. Productive Development Policies in Costa Rica: Market Failures, Government Failures, and Outcomes. Draft for the Project on Industrial Policies in Latin America and the Caribbean. Unpublished document. Washington, DC: Research Department, Inter-American Development Bank.

Montecinos, V. 2003. Economic Policymaking and Parliamentary Accountability in Chile. Paper No. 11. Programme on Democracy, Governance and Human Rights, UNRISD. Geneva.

Monteiro, J., and J. Assunção. 2006. Outgoing the Shadows: Estimating the Impact of Bureaucracy Simplification and Tax Cuts on Formality and Investment. Rio de Janeiro, Brazil: Department of Economics, Pontifical Catholic University of Rio de Janeiro.

Monteiro, J., A. Da Rocha, A. Darze, B. Kury. 2008. The Emergence of New and Successful Export Activities in Brazil: Four Case Studies from the Manufacturing and the

Agricultural Sector. Research Network Working Paper R-550. Washington, DC: Inter-American Development Bank.

Motohashi, K. 2001. Use of Plant-level Micro-data for SME Innovation Policy Evaluation in Japan. Discussion Paper Series 01-E-006. Tokyo, Japan: Research Institute of Economy, Trade & Industry (RIETI).

MTEySS (Ministerio de Trabajo, Empleo y Seguridad Social). 2003. Ficha de Identificación y Selección de Familias Beneficiarias de Programas Sociales. Unpublished document. Argentina.

Mueller, D. 2003. *Public Choice III.* Cambridge, UK: Cambridge University Press.

Muendler, M-A. 2002. Trade, Technology and Productivity: A Study of Brazilian Manufacturers, 1986–1998. Unpublished document. Department of Economics, University of California, Berkley.

Nelson, R., and E. Phelps. 1966. Investment in Humans, Technological Diffusion, and Economic Growth. *American Economic Review: Papers and Proceedings* 51(2): 69–75.

Neumeyer, A., and H. Hopenhayn. 2004. *Explaining Argentina's Great Depression of 1975–1990.* RE1-04-007. Economic and Social Study Series. Washington, DC: Inter-American Development Bank.

Neumeyer, A., and G. Sandleris. 2009. Productivity and Resource Misallocation in the Argentine Manufacturing Sector, 1997–2002. Unpublished document. Washington, DC: Research Department, Inter-American Development Bank.

Noland, M., and H. Pack. 2003. *Industrial Policy in an Era of Globalization: Lessons from Asia.* Washington DC: Institute for International Economics.

Ñopo, H. 2008. Matching as a Tool to Decompose Wage Gaps. *The Review of Economics and Statistics* 90(2): 290–99.

NSF (National Science Foundation). 2008. *Science and Engineering Indicators.* Washington, DC: National Science Foundation.

Ó Riain S. 2004. State, Competition and Industrial Change in Ireland 1991–1999. *Economic and Social Review* 35(1): 27–54.

Ocampo, A. 1984. *Colombia y la Economia Mundial 1830–1910.* Bogota, Colombia: Siglo Veintiuno Editores.

OECD (Organisation for Economic Co-operation and Development). 2002. *Frascati Manual. Proposed Standard Practice for Surveys on Research and Experimental Development.* Paris: OECD.

———. 2005. SME and Entrepreneurship Outlook 2005. Paris: OECD.

———. 2007a. SMEs in Mexico: Issues and Policies. Paris: OECD.

———. 2007b. *Science, Technology and Industry Scoreboard.*

———. 2008. Main Science and Technology Indicators 2008/2. Paris: OECD.

———. 2009. *Innovation in Firms: A Microeconomic Perspective.* Paris: OECD.

OECD and Eurostat. 2005. Oslo Manual. *The Measurement of Scientific and Technological Activities. Guidelines for Collecting and Interpreting Innovation Data,* 3rd edition. Paris: OECD/Eurostat.

Olivera, M., M. Pachón, and G. Perry. 2009. The Political Economy of Fiscal Reform: The Case of Colombia, 1986–2006. Unpublished document. Washington, DC: Research Department, Inter-American Development Bank. Forthcoming (in Spanish) in *Consecuencias Imprevistas de la Constitución de 1991,* ed. E. Lora and C. Scartascini. Bogota: Alfaomega Editores.

Olson, M. 1965. *The Logic of Collective Action: Public Goods and the Theory of Groups.* Harvard Economic Studies. Cambridge, MA: Harvard University Press.

————. 1982. *The Rise and Decline of Nations: Economic Growth, Stagflation, and Social Rigidities*. New Haven, CT: Yale University Press.

Österholm, P., and J. Zettelmeyer. 2007. The Effect of External Conditions on Growth in Latin America. IMF Working Paper 07/176. Washington, DC: IMF.

Pack, H., and K. Saggi. 2006. Is There a Case for Industrial Policy? A Critical Survey. *The World Bank Research Observer* 21(2): 267–97.

Packard, T. 2002. Pooling, Saving and Prevention: Mitigating Old Age Poverty in Chile. Policy Research Working Paper 2849. Washington, DC: World Bank.

Pagés, C., G. Pierre, and S. Scarpetta, 2009. *Job Creation in Latin America and the Caribbean: Recent Trends and Policy Challenges*. Washington, DC: Palgrave Macmillan and the World Bank.

Pagés, C., and. M. Stampini. Forthcoming. No Education, No Good Jobs? Evidence on the Relationship between Education and Labor Market Segmentation. *Journal of Comparative Economics*.

Panopoulu, G., and C. Vélez. 2001. Subsidized Health Insurance, Proxy Means Testing and the Demand for Health Care among the Poor in Colombia. Colombia Poverty Report Volume II, chap. VI. Washington, DC: World Bank.

Pavcnik, N. 2002. Trade Liberalization, Exit, and Productivity Improvements: Evidence from Chilean Plants. *Review of Economic Studies* 69: 245–76.

Penfold-Becerra, M. 2006. Clientelism and Social Funds: Empirical Evidence from Chávez's "Misiones" Programs in Venezuela. Unpublished document. IESA, Caracas.

Pérez, Carlota. 2008. A Vision for Latin America: A Resource-based Strategy for Technological Dynamism and Social Inclusion. Unpublished paper prepared under contract with the ECLAC (Economic Commission for Latin America and the Caribbean) Program on Technology Policy and Development in Latin America. Santiago, Chile.

Perry, G., W. F. Maloney, O. Arias, P. Fajnzylber, A. D. Mason, and J. Saavedra-Chanduvi. 2007. *Informality Exit and Exclusion*. Washington, DC: World Bank.

Persson, T., and G. Tabellini. 2000. *Political Economics: Explaining Economic Policy*. Cambridge, MA: MIT Press.

Pietrobelli, C., and R. Rabellotti. 2004. Upgrading in Clusters and Value Chains in Latin America: The Role of Policies. Sustainable Development Department Working Papers MSM-124. Washington, DC: Inter-American Development Bank.

Pratap, S., and E. Quintin. 2002. Are Labor Markets Segmented in Argentina? A Semiparametric Approach. Discussion Paper 02-02. Centro de Investigación Económica, Instituto Tecnológico Autónomo de México, México D.F.

Psacharopoulos, G. 1994. Returns to Investment in Education: A Global Update. *World Development* 22(9, September): 1325–43.

Rajan, R. G., and L. Zingales. 1998. Financial Dependence and Growth. *The American Economic Review* 88(3, June): 559–86.

Rancière. R., A. Tornell, and F. Westermann. 2008. Systemic Rises and Growth. *The Quarterly Journal of Economics* 123(1):359–406.

RAND Corporation. 2007. *The Global Technology Revolution 2020: Bio-Nano-Materials-Information Trends, Drivers, and Social Implications*. Washington, DC: RAND.

Restuccia, D. 2008. The Latin American Development Problem. Working Paper 318. Toronto: Department of Economics, University of Toronto.

Restuccia, D., and R. Rogerson. Forthcoming. Policy Distortions and Aggregate Productivity with Heterogeneous Establishments. *Review of Economic Dynamics*.

Rettberg, A. 2001. The Political Preferences of Diversified Business Groups: Lessons from Colombia (1994–1998). *Business & Politics* 3(1): 47–63.

————. 2005. Business versus Business? Economic Groups and Business Associations in Colombia. *Latin American Politics and Society* 47(1): 31–54.

Revenga, A. 1997. Employment and Wage Effects of Trade Liberalization: The Case of Mexican Manufacturing. *Journal of Labor Economics* 107(1): 255–84.

Ribeiro, E., and J. De Negri. 2009. Estimating the Causal Effect of Access to Public Credit on Productivity: the Case of Brazil. Mimeo. Unpublished document. Instituto de Economia, Universidade Federal do Rio de Janeiro.

Ribeiro, E., V. Prochnik, and J. DeNegri. 2009. Productivity Growth in the Brazilian Informatics Industry. Unpublished document.

Ricover, A., and E. Negre. 2003. Estudio de Integración del Transporte Aéreo en Sudamérica. Unpublished document. Washington, DC: Inter-American Development Bank.

RICYT (Red de Indicadores de Ciencia y Tecnología). 2009. Base de datos de indicadores, 2009. http://www.ricyt.edu.ar (accessed July 2009).

RICYT (Red de Indicadores de Ciencia y Tecnologia), OEA (Organization of American States), CYTED (Programa Iberoamericano de Ciencia y Tecnología), COLCIENCIAS (Departamento Administrativo de Ciencia, Tecnología e Innovación), and OCYT (Observatorio Colombiano de Ciencia y Tecnología). 2001. *Manual de Bogota.. Normalización de Indicadores de Innovación Tecnológica en América Latina y el Caribe.* http://www.sugestec.unam.mx/sugestec/UserFiles/File/SugestecLecturas/Manual-Bogota.pdf (accessed May 2009).

Robles, M., 2009. Aggregate Effects of Imperfect Tax Enforcement. Discussion Paper 00845. Washington, DC: International Food Policy Research Institute.

Rodríguez-Clare, A. 2005. Coordination Failures, Clusters and Microeconomic Interventions. *Economía (Journal of LACEA)* 6(1, Fall): 1–29.

Rodrik, D. 2004. *Industrial Policy for the Twenty-First Century*. Cambridge, MA: Harvard University.

————. 2007. Industrial Development: Stylized Facts and Policies. In *Industrial Development for the 21st Century*, United Nations., New York: United Nations.

Rofman, R., and L. Lucchetti. 2006. Pension Systems in Latin America: Concepts and Measurements of Coverage. Social Protection Discussion Paper 0616. Washington, DC: World Bank.

Romer, P. 1990. Endogenous Technological Change. *Journal of Political Economy* 98(5): S71–S102.

Roper, S., and N. Hewitt-Dundas. 2001. Grant Assistance and Small Firm Development in Northern Ireland and the Republic of Ireland. *Scottish Journal of Political Economy* 48(1): 99–117.

Rose, A. K. 2000. One Money, One Market? The Effects of Common Currencies on International Trade. *Economic Policy* 15:7–46.

Saavedra, J., and M. Tommasi. 2007. Informality, the State and the Social Contract in Latin America: A Preliminary Exploration. *International Labour Review* 146(3–4): 279–309.

Sabel, C. 2009. What Industrial Policy is Becoming: Taiwan, Ireland and Finland as Guides to the Future of Industrial Policy. Unpublished document. Washington, DC: Inter-American Development Bank.

Sagasti, F., and A. Araoz. 1975. Science and Technology Policy Implementation in Less Developed Countries. Publication number IDRC-067e. Lima: IDRC (International Development Research Centre).

Saiegh, S. Forthcoming. Active Players or Rubber-Stamps? An Evaluation of the Policy-making Role of Latin American Legislatures. In *How Democracy Works: Political Institutions, Actors, and Arenas in Latin American Policymaking*, ed. C. Scartascini, E. Stein, and M. Tommasi. Washington, DC: IDB and Harvard University Press.

Salazar, J. C. 2007. Evaluación de algunos instrumentos de política de innovación y desarrollo tecnológico y de su impacto en el sector manufacturero. Unpublished document. Bogota: Colombia. Departamento Nacional de Planeación

Samaniego, R. M. (2005). Investment-Specific Technical Change and the Production of Ideas. *Computing in Economics and Finance 2005*, 291. Working Paper. Chestnut Hill, MA: Society for Computational EconomicsSánchez, G. 2009. Understanding Productivity Levels, Growth and Dispersion in Argentina: The Case of Supermarkets. Unpublished document. Washington, DC: Research Department, Inter-American Development Bank.

Sánchez, G., I. Butler, and R. Rozemberg. 2009. Productive Development Policies in Argentina. Draft for the Project on Industrial Policies in Latin America and the Caribbean. Unpublished document. Washington, DC: Research Department. Inter-American Development Bank.

Sánchez, R., and G. Wilmsmeier. 2009. Liner Shipping Networks and Market Concentration. Unpublished document. Santiago, Chile: Economic Commission for Latin America and the Caribbean (ECLAC).

Santamaría, M., F. García, and A. V. Mujica. 2009a. El mercado laboral y la reforma a la salud en Colombia: incentivos, preferencias y algunas paradojas. Fedesarrollo. Unpublished document. Bogotá, Colombia.

———. 2009b. Los costos no salariales y el mercado laboral: impacto de la reforma a la salud en Colombia. Fedesarrollo. Unpublished document. Bogotá, Colombia.

Santamaría, M., and S. Rozo. 2008. Informalidad empresarial en Colombia: alternatives para impulsar la productividad, el empleo y los ingresos. Cuadernos de Trabajo de Fedesarrollo, No. 40. Bogota, Colombia.

SAS (Secretaría de Acción Social). 2005. Ficha para selección de beneficiarios. Unpublished document. Paraguay.

Scartascini, C., E. Stein, E. and M. Tommasi. 2009. Political Institutions, Intertemporal Cooperation , and the Quality of Policies. RES Working Paper No. 676. Washington, DC: Research Department, Inter-American Development Bank.

Scartascini, C., E. Stein, and M. Tommasi. 2009. Political Institutions, Intertemporal Cooperation, and the Quality of Policies. Research Department Working Paper 676. Washington, DC: Inter-American Development Bank.

Scartascini, C., and M. Tommasi. 2009. The Making of Policy: Institutionalized or Not? Unpublished document. Washington, DC: Research Department, Inter-American Development Bank.

Schneider, B. R. 2004. Business in Colombia: Well Organized and Well Connected. In *Business, Politics, and the State in Twentieth-Century Latin America,* ed. B. R. Schneider, pp. 128–51. Cambridge, UK: Cambridge University Press.

———. Forthcoming. Business Politics and Policymaking in Contemporary Latin America. In *How Democracy Works. Political Institutions, Actors, and Arenas in Latin American Policymaking,* ed. C. Scartascini, E. Stein, and M. Tommasi. Washington, DC, and Cambridge, MA: IDB and Harvard University Press.

Schumpeter, J. 1983. *The Theory of Economic Development: An Inquiry into Profits, Capital, Credit, Interest and the Business Cycle.* New Brunswick, NJ: Transaction Publishers.

SEDESOL (Secretaría de Desarrollo Social). 1997. Encuesta de Características Socioeconómicas de los hogares. Unpublished document. Mexico.

Sheehan, J. 2007. Incentives and Support Systems to Foster Private Sector Innovation. Regional Policy Dialogue in Science, Technology and Innovation. Washington, DC: Inter-American Development Bank.

Snoeck M., C. Casacuberta, R. Domingo, H. Pastori, and L Pittaluga. 2006. The Emergence of New Successful Export Activities in Uruguay. Research Network Working Paper R-556. Washington, DC: Inter-American Development Bank.Stiglitz, J. 1998. Towards a New Paradigm for Development: Strategies, Policies and Processes. Prebisch Lectures at UNCTAD, Geneva.

Solow, R. M. 1956. A Contribution to the Theory of Economic Growth. *Quarterly Journal of Economics* 70(1): 65–94.

———. 1957. Technical Change and the Aggregate Production Function. *Rev Econ Stat* 39:312–20.

Soto, J. M. 2009. Evaluación de la Política de Competitividad y los programas de apoyo a las Pymes en México. Unpublished document. Washington, DC: Inter-American Development Bank.

Stein, E., M. Tommasi, P. T. Spiller, and C. Scartascini. 2008. *Policymaking in Latin America: How Politics Shapes Policies.* Washington, DC: Inter-American Development Bank.

Stern, N. 1989. The Economics of Development: A Survey. *The Economic Journal* 99(397): 597–685.

Storey, D. J. 1998. Six Steps to Heaven: Evaluating the Impact of Public Policies to Support Small Business in Developed Economies. Working Paper No. 59. Warwick, UK: Warwick Business School.

———. 2008. Entrepreneurship and SME Policy in Mexico. Unpublished document. Washington, DC: Inter-American Development Bank.

Syverson, C. 2004. Market Structure and Productivity: A Concrete Example. *Journal of Political Economy* 112(6): 1181–222.

———. 2008. Markets: Ready-Mixed Concrete. *Journal of Economic Perspectives* 22(1, Winter): 217–33.

Thomson, I. 2000. Algunos Conceptos Básicos Referentes a las Causas y Soluciones del Problema de la Congestión de Tránsito. Unpublished document. Santiago, Chile: Economic Commission for Latin America and the Caribbean (ECLAC).

Timmer, C. P. 2002. Agriculture and Economic Development. In *Handbook of Agricultural Economics* vol. 2, ed. Bruce Gardner and G. Rausser, pp. 1487–546. Amsterdam: North-Holland.

Timmer, Marcel P., and G. J. de Vries. 2007. A Cross-Country Database for Sectoral Employment and Productivity in Asia and Latin America, 1950–2005. Research Memorandum GD-98. Groningen: Groningen Growth and Development Centre, University of Groningen (August). http://www.ggdc.net/databases/10_sector.htm (accessed February 2009).

Trucco, L. 2009. Instituciones y Tecnologías Políticas Alternativas en los Procesos de Policymaking. Unpublished document. Universidad de San Andrés, Buenos Aires.

Trujillo, A., J. Portillo, and J. Vernon. 2004. The Impact of Subsidized Health Insurance for the Poor: Evaluating the Colombian Experience Using Propensity Score Matching. *International Journal of Health Care Finance and Economics* 5:211–39.

Tybout, J. 1991. Linking Trade and Productivity: New Research Directions. *World Bank Economic Review* 6:198–212.

United Nations Industrial Development Organization. 2008. Industrial Statistics Database (INDSTAT). http://www.unido.org/index.php?id=1000077 (accessed June 2008).

United States Social Security Administration. 2008. Social Security Programs throughout the World: The Americas 2007. Washington, DC: Social Security Administration, Office of Retirement and Disability Policy, Office of Research, Evaluation, and Statistics.

U.S. Census Bureau. Various years. U.S. Census Bureau Dataset. United States.

Van Ark, B., M. O'Mahoney, and M. P. Timmer. 2008. The Productivity Gap between Europe and the United States: Trends and Causes. *Journal of Economic Perspectives* 22(1): 25–44.

Vega, H. 2008. Transportation Costs of Fresh Flowers: A Comparison across Major Exporting Countries. Unpublished document. Washington, DC: Inter-American Development Bank.

Ventura, A. K. 2009. The Need for a New Mechanism to Fund Research and Development Activities. Presentation at the Conference on Science, Technology and Innovation Policies: Towards a New Social Contract for Science, Regional Latin America and Caribbean Forum. Mexico.

Volpe, C., and J. Carballo. 2008. Heterogeneous Activities and Heterogeneous Effects: The Impact of Export Promotion on Developing Countries' Firm Performance. Unpublished document. Washington, DC: Inter-American Development Bank.

Wade, R. 1990. *Governing the Market: Economic Theory and the Role of Government in East Asian Industrialization.* Princeton, NJ: Princeton University Press.

Weaver, R. K., and B. A. Rockman. 1993. *Do Institutions Matter? Government Capabilities in the United States and Abroad.* Washington, DC: Brookings Institution Press.

Wilson, J. 2008. Standards and Developing Country Exports: A Review of Selected Studies and Suggestions for Future Research. *Journal of International Agricultural Trade and Development* 4(1):35–45.

World Bank. 2006. Enterprise Survey. http://www.enterprisesurveys.org/ (accessed January 2007).

———. 2007. *Evaluating Mexico's Small and Medium Enterprise Programs.* Washington DC: World Bank.

———. 2008. World Development Indicators Online. http://web.worldbank.org/WBSITE/EXTERNAL/DATASTATISTICS/0,,contentMDK:20535285~menuPK:1192694~pagePK:64133150~piPK:64133175~theSitePK:239419,00.html (accessed September 2008).

———. 2009a. Logistics, Transport and Food Prices in LAC: Policy Guidance for Improving Efficiency and Reducing Costs. Unpublished document. Washington, DC: World Bank.

———. 2009b. Doing Business. http://www.doingbusiness.org/ (accessed July 2009).

———. 2009c. The World Business Environment Survey (WBES). http://info.worldbank.org/governance/wbes/ (accessed July 2009).

———. 2009d. World Development Indicators (WDI). http://go.worldbank.org/U0FSM7AQ40 (accessed July 2009).

———. 2009e. Doing Business. Measuring Business Regulations. Paying Taxes data. http://www.doingbusiness.org/exploretopics/payingtaxes/ (accessed May 2009).

———. 2009f. World Development Indicators Online. http://devdata.worldbank.org/wdi2006/contents/Table2_9.htm (accessed July 2009).

———. 2009g. World Development Indicators Online. http://ddp-ext.worldbank.org/ext/DDPQQ/member.do?method=getMembers&userid=1&queryId=135 (accessed April 2009).

———. Various years. World Bank Enterprise Surveys. https://www.enterprisesurveys.org/ (accessed June 2009).

World Economic Forum. Various years. Global Competitiveness Report—Executive Opinion Survey. http://www.weforum.org/.

WTO (World Trade Organization). 2005. *World Trade Report, 2005. Exploring the Links between Trade, Standards and the WTO.* Geneva, Switzerland: World Trade Organization.

————. 2006. Second Review of the Air Transport. Developments in the Air Transport Sector. Geneva, Switzerland: World Trade Organization.

Yañez-Pagans, M. 2008. Culture and Human Capital Investments: Evidence of an Unconditional Cash Transfer Program in Bolivia. IZA Discussion Paper No. 3678. Bonn, Germany: Institute for the Study of Labor (IZA).

You, J. 1995. Small Firms in Economic Theory. *Cambridge Journal of Economics* 19:441–62.

Index

accumulated factors of production, 4, 23–25, 34, 36–41. *See also* total factor productivity

aeronautics, 267, *272–73*, 278

Aggarwal, V., 315n12

Aghion, P., 149n4

Agnew, J., 205n6

agriculture, 5, 14, 45–63, *46–47*, *49–56*, *59*, *62*, 66–67, 139, 147, 246, 259, 263, 266–67, *268–69*, *274*, 292n4; extension agencies, 267

Aguion, P., *230*

air freight, 109, 115–17

airports, 8, 66–67, 111–12, 117–19, *117*, 121n18

Alejo, J., 194

Alesina, A., 179n9

Alfaro, L, 179n9

Aninat, C., 315n14

Anlló, G., 254n5

Arbeláez, M. A., 160, 167

Argentina, 1, *29*, *35*, *39*, 42n6, *46*, 51, *51–52*, 55, 56, 61, *62*, 64, *126*, *135*; firm size and productivity, *73*, 77, *78–79*, *85–86*, *90*; industrial policy, 264, 266–67, *279–81*, 285, 292n5, 293nn; innovation, *226*, 227, *228*, 229, 231–39, *233–34*, *237–40*, 245–46, *250–51*, 254nn; policymaking capabilities, 295, *306*, 308–9, 315n12; SME programs, *211*, 218–19; social policy, *186*, *188*, *191*, 193, 205n5, 206n9; taxes, 155, *156–57*, 167, *172*, 174–76, *175*, 180n13; trade and transport costs, *107*, 108, *109–10*

Arizala, F., 125, 127

ARPANET, *290–91*

Aten, B., *25*

automotive industry, 267

Banerjee, A., 142, 151n37

bankruptcy, 91, 94, 129, 145, 147

banks, 135, 144, 147, 178, 180n13, 211, 229, 267. *See also* credit and financing

Barbados, *110*, *240*, 271, 292n5, 293n8

Barro and Lee database, *25*

Barros, R., 206n9

Baxter Laboratories, 270

Becerra, O., 160, 167, *305*

Belize, *55*, *110*, *156–57*

Benavente, J., 241

Bergoeing, R., 129

Bernal, R., 201

bilateral trade agreements, 97, 115–17, 121n16

Binelli, C., 218

biotechnology, 243, 268, *279–81*, 290

Blyde, J., 42n13, 109–10, *112*, 121n14

BNDES (Brazil), 267–68, 285

Bogatá Manual, *224*

Bolivia, 1, *29*, *34*, *35*, *39*, 42n6, *46*, 50–51, *51–52*, 55, 56–57, 61, *62*; credit and, *126*, 128; firm size and productivity, *73*, 75, *75*, 77, *78–79*, *85–86*, *90*, *93*; innovation, *237–38*; policymaking capabilities, *306*, 308, 311; social policy, 185, *186*, *191*, 193–94, *196*, 197–98, *199–201*, 205n5; taxes, 156, *156–57*, 161, *161*, 167, 171, *172*; trade and transport costs, *107*, *110*, 135

Bravo, C., 241

Brazil, 1, 7, 14, *29*, 33, *34–35*, *39*, 42n6, *46*, *51–52*, *55*, 56–57, *62*; credit, *126*, 134, *135*, 151n40, 160; firm size and productivity, 73, 87; industrial policy, 264, 266–71, *268–69*, *272–73*, 278, *279–80*, 285, 290, 293nn, 294nn; Informatics Law, 278; innovation, *226*, 229, *233*, 234, 237–39, *237–40*, 245–46, 249–52, *250–51*, 254nn, 255n10; Ministry of Aeronautics, *272–73*; policymaking capabilities, 300, *306*, 308, 311; Productive Development Policy, 290; SME programs, 220n1; social policy, *186*, *188*, *191*, *196*, 198, *199–201*; taxes, *156–57*, 156–58, 160, *161*, 164–69, *166*, *172*, 175, 179n7; trade and transport costs, *100–101*, 101, 106, *107*, *109–10*, 114–16, *116–17*, 120n7, 121n18

Bruhn, M., 169

business actors and organizations, 17, 299–301, 309–10, 312, 314nn

business process outsourcing, 270

Busso, M., 94n1

Camacho, A., 200, 203, 206n9

capital. *See* human capital; physical capital